WORLDING CITIES

Studies in Urban and Social Change

Published

The Creative Capital of Cities: Interactive Knowledge of Creation and the Urbanization Economics of Innovation
Stefan Krätke

Worlding Cities: Asian Experiments and the Art of Being Global
Ananya Roy and Aihwa Ong (eds.)

Place, Exclusion, and Mortgage Markets
Manuel B. Aalbers

Working Bodies: Interactive Service Employment and Workplace Identities
Linda McDowell

Networked Disease: Emerging Infections in the Global City
S. Harris Ali and Roger Keil (eds.)

Eurostars and Eurocities: Free Movement and Mobility in an Integrating Europe
Adrian Favell

Urban China in Transition
John R. Logan (ed.)

Getting Into Local Power: The Politics of Ethnic Minorities in British and French Cities
Romain Garbaye

Cities of Europe
Yuri Kazepov (ed.)

Cities, War, and Terrorism
Stephen Graham (ed.)

Cities and Visitors: Regulating Tourists, Markets, and City Space
Lily M. Hoffman, Susan S. Fainstein, and Dennis R. Judd (eds.)

Understanding the City: Contemporary and Future Perspectives
John Eade and Christopher Mele (eds.)

The New Chinese City: Globalization and Market Reform
John R. Logan (ed.)

Cinema and the City: Film and Urban Societies in a Global Context
Mark Shiel and Tony Fitzmaurice (eds.)

The Social Control of Cities? A Comparative Perspective
Sophie Body-Gendrot

Globalizing Cities: A New Spatial Order?
Peter Marcuse and Ronald van Kempen (eds.)

Contemporary Urban Japan: A Sociology of Consumption
John Clammer

Capital Culture: Gender at Work in the City
Linda McDowell

*Out of print

Cities after Socialism: Urban and Regional Change and Conflict in Post-Socialist Societies
Gregory Andrusz, Michael Harloe and Ivan Szelenyi (eds.)

The People's Home? Social Rented Housing in Europe and America
Michael Harloe

Post-Fordism
Ash Amin (ed.)

The Resources of Poverty: Women and Survival in a Mexican City*
Mercedes Gonzalez de la Rocha

Free Markets and Food Riots
John Walton and David Seddon

Fragmented Societies*
Enzo Mingione

Urban Poverty and the Underclass: A Reader*
Enzo Mingione

Forthcoming

Locating Neoliberalism in East Asia: Neoliberalizing Spaces in Developmental States
Bae-Gyoon Park, Richard Child Hill and Asato Saito (eds.)

Subprime Cities: The Political Economy of Mortgage Markets
Manuel B. Aalbers (ed.)

Globalising European Urban Bourgeoisies?: Rooted Middle Classes and Partial Exit in Paris, Lyon, Madrid and Milan
Alberta Andreotti, Patrick Le Galès and Francisco Javier Moreno-Fuentes

Paradoxes Of Segregation: Urban Migration In Europe
Sonia Arbaci

From Shack to House to Fortress
Mariana Cavalcanti

Iron Curtains: Gates, Suburbs and Privatization of Space in the Post-socialist City
Sonia Hirt

Urban Social Movements and the State
Margit Mayer

Fighting Gentrification
Tom Slater

Confronting Suburbanization: Urban Decentralization in Post-Socialist Central and Eastern Europe
Kiril Stanilov and Ludek Sykora (eds.)

Social Capital Formation in Immigrant Neighborhoods
Min Zhou

WORLDING
CITIES

ASIAN EXPERIMENTS AND THE ART OF BEING GLOBAL

Edited by

Ananya Roy and Aihwa Ong

A John Wiley & Sons, Ltd., Publication

This edition first published 2011
© 2011 Blackwell Publishing Limited

Blackwell Publishing was acquired by John Wiley & Sons in February 2007.
Blackwell's publishing program has been merged with Wiley's global Scientific,
Technical, and Medical business to form Wiley-Blackwell.

Registered Office
John Wiley & Sons Ltd, The Atrium, Southern Gate, Chichester, West Sussex,
PO19 8SQ, United Kingdom

Editorial Offices
350 Main Street, Malden, MA 02148-5020, USA
9600 Garsington Road, Oxford, OX4 2DQ, UK
The Atrium, Southern Gate, Chichester, West Sussex, PO19 8SQ, UK

For details of our global editorial offices, for customer services, and for information about how
to apply for permission to reuse the copyright material in this book please see our website at
www.wiley.com/wiley-blackwell.

The right of Ananya Roy and Aihwa Ong to be identified as the authors of the editorial material in
this work has been asserted in accordance with the UK Copyright, Designs and Patents Act 1988.

Wiley also publishes its books in a variety of electronic formats. Some content that appears in
print may not be available in electronic books.

Designations used by companies to distinguish their products are often claimed as trademarks.
All brand names and product names used in this book are trade names, service marks, trademarks
or registered trademarks of their respective owners. The publisher is not associated with any
product or vendor mentioned in this book. This publication is designed to provide accurate and
authoritative information in regard to the subject matter covered. It is sold on the understanding
that the publisher is not engaged in rendering professional services. If professional advice or other
expert assistance is required, the services of a competent professional should be sought.

Library of Congress Cataloging-in-Publication Data

Worlding cities : Asian experiments and the art of being global / edited by Ananya Roy
and Aihwa Ong.
     p. cm. – (Studies in urban and social change)
   Includes bibliographical references and index.
   ISBN 978-1-4051-9277-4 (hardback) – ISBN 978-1-4051-9276-7 (paperback)
   1. Urbanization–Asia. 2. Globalization–Asia. I. Roy, Ananya. II. Ong, Aihwa.
   HT384.A78W67 2011
   307.76095–dc22
                                             2011006751

A catalogue record for this book is available from the British Library.

This book is published in the following electronic formats: ePDFs 9781444346770;
Wiley Online Library 9781444346800; ePub 9781444346787; eMobi 9781444346794

Set in 10.5/12pt Baskerville by SPi Publisher Services, Pondicherry, India

2 2011

Contents

List of Illustrations

Figures

Table

Notes on Contributors

Chua Beng Huat is currently Provost Professor and Head, Department of Sociology, and Cultural Studies in Asia Research Cluster Leader at the Asia Research Institute, National University of Singapore. He is founding co-executive editor of the journal *Inter-Asia Cultural Studies*. His most recent publications are *Life is Not Complete without Shopping* and edited *Elections as Popular Culture in Asia*. His previous books include *Public Housing and Political Legitimacy: stakeholding in Singapore* and *Communitarian Ideology and Democracy in Singapore*.

D. Asher Ghertner is a Lecturer in Human Geography in the Department of Geography and Environment at the London School of Economics. He recently completed his PhD in the Energy and Resources Group at the University of California, Berkeley, where he was trained in urban geography, political ecology, and development studies. His research explores urban informality and governance, aesthetic politics, and the epistemology of rule. He is currently revising his dissertation into a book, tentatively titled *Rule by Aesthetics*. Based on two years of ethnographic fieldwork and legal research in Delhi, the book will examine how slum demolitions are discursively justified and given meaning, legally enacted, and experienced by slum residents. His recent articles have appeared in *Economy and Society* and *Economic and Political Weekly*.

Michael Goldman is a McKnight Presidential Fellow and Professor of Sociology and Global Studies at the University of Minnesota, in Minneapolis, USA. His latest book, based on a decade-long ethnography of the World Bank, is entitled *Imperial Nature: the World Bank and struggles for social justice in the age of globalization* (Yale University Press, 2005; Orient Longman India, 2006; Kyoto University Press, 2008 [in Japanese]). He is currently working on a project funded by the American Institute for Indian Studies, "Bangalore: The Making of a World City," focusing on the transformations of government and citizenship taking place under liberalization.

Chad Haines is currently on the Religious Studies faculty and is a researcher with the Center for the Study of Religion and Conflict at Arizona State University. Previously, he was a faculty member in Anthropology at American University in Cairo and taught at Duke University and the University of North Carolina at Chapel Hill. He is the author of *Nation, Territory, and Globalization in Pakistan: a view from the margins* (Routledge, 2011), as well as numerous articles on northern Pakistan. He is currently working on a new manuscript, *Being Muslim, Being Global: Dubai, Islamabad, and Cairo.*

Lisa Hoffman was trained as a cultural anthropologist and is an Associate Professor in Urban Studies at University of Washington Tacoma. Her work has examined new techniques of governing, subject formation, and questions of neoliberalism in contemporary China. She has been particularly interested in the rise of professionalism and the links between "human capital" development and urban transformation, focusing on Dalian, a major port city in the northeast. Her recent book, titled *Patriotic Professionalism: talent in the global Chinese city*, examines the rise of a professional middle class in urban China as the country has moved from the planned system and adopted socialist market practices. The book argues that young college graduates who find jobs on their own rather than receive assignments from the state express and embody "patriotic professionalism." This social form combines individualized career planning and calculative choice with an ethic of state-strengthening and love for the nation, challenging more standard analyses of neoliberalism, urban change, and subjectivity. Her more recent work has examined governmental rationalities of environmental city-building in China and sustainability as a governmental problem. Other publications include "Autonomous choices and patriotic professionalism: on governmentality in late-socialist China," *Economy and Society* 2006, 34(4); and "Enterprising cities and citizens: the re-figuring of urban spaces and the making of post-Mao professionals," *Provincial China*, 2003, 8(1).

Glen Lowry is Associate Professor of Cultural & Critical Studies, Faculty of Community & Culture, at Emily Carr University of Art + Design. He is a specialist in contemporary culture and poetics, and has published articles on contemporary Canadian literature, photography, film, and television. His recent work looks at practice-based (creative-critical) collaborations between artists and academics in the context of global urbanization. A senior research in Emily Carr's Social and Interactive Media (SIM) Research Centre (funded by the Natural Sciences and Engineering Research Council of Canada) and Chair of Online Learning, Lowry's work is also engaged with building new media platforms capable of connecting scholars, artists, and audiences across cultural and geographic distances. Current projects include *Maraya*, a large-scale, international public art initiative focused on urban waterfront sites in

Vancouver and Dubai, and linking artist, writers, and academics in Canada and the UAE. With Ashok Mathur, he has recently completed a qualitative study of the Outcomes and Impacts of Canada's Social Sciences and Humanities Research/Creations in Fine Arts grants pilot program. Since 2002, Lowry has edited *West Coast Line*. In 2009, he published *Pacific Avenue*, a book of poems.

Shannon May is a PhD candidate in the Department of Anthropology at the University of California, Berkeley. She has conducted fieldwork throughout China and in sub-Saharan Africa. Her work engages anthropological problems of governance, development, citizenship, community, and political ecology as constituted in everyday practice. She is currently writing her dissertation on the convergence of ecological and market rationalities in a project to "modernize" rural China, titled *Practices of Ecological Citizenship: global dreams for a Chinese village*.

Eugene McCann is Associate Professor, Department of Geography, at Simon Fraser University. He is an urban geographer with interests in urban politics, policy-making, and the relationships between urbanization and globalization. His current research explores how cities act globally through inter-urban policy mobilities – the processes of teaching, learning, and transferring policy knowledge among cities. He is co-editor, with Kevin Ward, of *Mobile Urbanism: cities & policy-making in the global age*, published by the University of Minnesota Press in Spring 2011, and is working on a co-edited volume, *Cities & Social Change*, with Ronan Paddison, for SAGE Publications, and a co-authored text, *Urban Geography: a critical introduction*, with Andy Jonas and Mary Thomas, for Wiley-Blackwell. He serves on the editorial boards of the journals *Urban Geography* and *Geography Compass*, and has co-edited special editions of the *Journal of Urban Affairs* and the *International Journal of Urban and Regional Research*. His work has appeared in these and other top international journals, including *Antipode, Environment and Planning A, Geoforum, Professional Geographer, Social & Cultural Geography, Environment and Planning D: Society and Space*, and *Urban Studies*.

Aihwa Ong is Professor of Socio-Cultural Anthropology and Southeast Asian Studies at the University of California, Berkeley. Her research interests focus on global technologies, modes of governing, techno-scientific assemblages, and citizenship in particular Asian contexts of emergence. She is the author of the now classic *Spirits of Resistance and Capitalist Discipline: factory women in Malaysia* (1987); *Flexible Citizenship: the cultural logics of transnationality* (1999); *Buddha is Hiding: refugees, citizenship, the new America* (2003); and *Neoliberalism as Exception: mutations in citizenship and sovereignty* (2006). She also co-edited *Global Assemblages: technology, politics, and ethics as anthropological problems* (2005); and *Privatizing China: socialism from afar* (2008). Her latest collection is *Asian Biotech: ethics and communities of fate.* Ong's writings have been translated into German, Italian, Portuguese, French, and Chinese. Currently, Ong is the president-elect of the Society for East Asian Anthropology.

Ananya Roy is Professor of City and Regional Planning at the University of California, Berkeley. She also serves as Co-Director of the Global Metropolitan Studies Center. Roy is the author of *City Requiem, Calcutta: gender and the politics of poverty* (University of Minnesota Press, 2003) and co-editor of *Urban Informality: transnational perspectives from the Middle East, South Asia, and Latin America* (Lexington Books, 2004). Her most recent book is titled *Poverty Capital: microfinance and the making of development* (Routledge, 2010). Roy's essays have focused on urban modernity, liberal, and post-liberal paradigms of planning, questions of praxis in the time of empire, and new geographies of urban theory.

Gavin Shatkin is Associate Professor of Urban Planning in the Taubman College of Architecture and Urban Planning at the University of Ann Arbor. His research focuses on urban inequality, community organizing, and collective action around issues of shelter and infrastructure delivery in developing countries, and the impacts of globalization on cities in developing countries. His recent articles have appeared in *Environment and Planning A*, *Cities, Urban Studies*, and other leading urban studies and planning journals. His book *Collective Action and Urban Poverty Alleviation: community organizations and the struggle for shelter in Manila* was published by Ashgate Publishers in 2007.

Helen F. Siu is Professor of Anthropology at Yale University. Since the 1970s, she has conducted historical and ethnographic fieldwork in South China, examining socialist transformations and the reach of the state, the revival of market towns, rituals, marriage practices, community festivals, and the reworking of the rural–urban divide in the post-reform era. Since 1997, she has worked on the "sinking and shrinking" generation of Hong Kongers who use urban space and global charisma to engage with China. Her publications and co-edited volumes include *Mao's Harvest: voices of China's new generation* (Oxford University Press, 1983); *Furrows: peasants, intellectuals, and the state* (Stanford University Press, 1990); *Down to Earth: the territorial bond in South China* (Stanford University Press, 1995); *Agents and Victims in South China: accomplices in rural revolution* (Yale University Press, 1989); *Empire at the Margins: culture, ethnicity and frontier in early modern China* (University of California Press, 2006); *SARS: reception and interpretation in three Chinese Cities* (Routledge, 2007); and *Hong Kong Mobile: making a global population* (Hong Kong University Press,

2008). In 2001, she founded the Hong Kong Institute for the Humanities and Social Sciences. The Institute, hosted by the University of Hong Kong, promotes creative, interdisciplinary research that allows scholars in North America, Europe, China, and Hong Kong to connect. In the next five years, the Institute will focus on research training stressing inter-Asian connectivity in historical and contemporary terms.

Series Editors' Preface

The Wiley-Blackwell *Studies in Urban and Social Change* series is published in association with the *International Journal of Urban and Regional Research*. It aims to advance theoretical debates and empirical analyses stimulated by changes in the fortunes of cities and regions across the world. Among topics taken up in past volumes and welcomed for future submissions are:

- Connections between economic restructuring and urban change
- Urban divisions, difference, and diversity
- Convergence and divergence among regions of east and west, north, and south
- Urban and environmental movements
- International migration and capital flows
- Trends in urban political economy
- Patterns of urban-based consumption

The series is explicitly interdisciplinary; the editors judge books by their contribution to intellectual solutions rather than according to disciplinary origin. Proposals may be submitted to members of the series Editorial Committee, and further information about the series can be found at www.suscbookseries.com

Jenny Robinson
Neil Brenner
Matthew Gandy
Patrick Le Galès
Chris Pickvance
Ananya Roy

Preface and Acknowledgments

This book grew out of our particular interests in the field of global metropolitan studies. It has also emerged from our shared sense that dominant conceptual frameworks and methodologies in this field do not capture the diversity of urban dreams, projects, and practices that are constitutive of cities in emerging world regions. We therefore seek to articulate a new ethnographic turn in global metropolitan studies. For us, such an orientation hinges on the idea of "worlding." We see the worlding city as a milieu of intervention, a source of ambitious visions, and of speculative experiments that have different possibilities of success and failure. We hold that such experiments cannot be conceptually reduced to instantiations of universal logics of capitalism or postcolonialism. They must be understood as worlding practices, those that pursue world recognition in the midst of inter-city rivalry and globalized contingency. We therefore focus on the urban as a milieu that is in constant formation, one shaped by the multitudinous ongoing activities that by wedding dream and technique, form the art of being global. Inherently unstable, inevitably subject to intense contestation, and always incomplete, worlding is the art of being global.

But also at stake in this book is how cities are worlded in geographies of knowledge. By insisting upon a shift away from the concepts of world cities and world systems to that of worlding practices, we seek to intervene in the ways in which global metropolitan studies "worlds" Asia. Impossibly heterogeneous, the idea of Asia functions in this book as much more than a geo-political location. While massive urban problems prevail in the region, "Asia" is increasingly invoked as the testing ground for successful models of economic growth, rational planning, and ecological sustainability. Inter-Asian comparisons and contrasts have become common practices in many urban initiatives to attain "world-class" status. Thus, in this book, Asia is a geographic location, a space of urban innovations, as well as an emergent symbol for urban renovations that have global applicability. But also in this book we pay attention to the constant experimentation with social formations, to the politics of solidarity that seeks to reformulate the urban question and domesticate the dream of Asian futures.

The book is organized around the themes of modeling, inter-referencing practices, and new solidarities. In somewhat unusual fashion, we have chosen to divide our editorial essays into an introduction and conclusion. Aihwa Ong's opening essay introduces the book and its key concept of "worlding" as situated practice and experimentation. She makes the case for viewing the city as a problem-space for which a range of solutions are created out of disparate local and circulating elements. Ananya Roy's concluding essay returns to the theme of "worlding," but examines how cities of the global South have been "worlded" in the discourses and imaginaries of metropolitan studies. Building on Ong's critique of urban political economy and postcolonial analysis, Roy seeks to shift the terrain of the political away from the standard icons of global capital and subaltern agency to the "worlding city" as both a site of emergence and as a mass dream. Together, the two editorial essays highlight different theoretical approaches to the common question of the "worlding city." We hope that such theoretical multiplicity makes visible the productive nature of the concept of "worlding" and the significance of locating the study of "worlding cities" in the context of inter-Asian urbanism.

We owe considerable thanks to the scholars who have contributed essays to this edited volume. It is their work that has led us to the conceptual frameworks that anchor this book. Hailing from different fields and generations, they present new research on the social, political, material, and symbolic interconnections that are proliferating between different Asian metropolises. Their work has challenged us as editors to address methodological approaches to global metropolitan studies in an era of Asian emergence. It has led us to be attentive to diverse conceptual and research questions and to thereby provide an open-ended account of experiments and possibilities, rather than promote a single unifying framework.

This volume emerged from an interdisciplinary workshop we organized for the "Inter-Asian Connections" conference that was convened by the Social Science Research Council in February 2008. We had the opportunity to hold a two-day workshop, quite appropriately located at a site that features prominently in this book: Dubai. We thank the SSRC for both the initial inspiration for this endeavor and for its generous funding of our workshop. At the forum, Michael M. Fischer and Abdoumaliq Simone made astute comments that added to our lively exchange on contemporary metropolitan experiences in the Asian region.

We are pleased to be a part of Wiley-Blackwell's *Studies in Urban and Social Change* series. We are grateful to two editors-in-chief of the series, Neil Brenner and Jennifer Robinson, for their interest in our project. The various chapters of the book have benefited from extensive comments provided by

Jennifer Robinson and Timothy Bunnell. At Wiley-Blackwell, Jacqueline Scott helped us navigate publication and Geoffrey Palmer copy-edited the manuscript with great skill and grace. At UC Berkeley, editing assistance was provided by Jerry Zee.

The book is dedicated to our doctoral students in common who are invested in the interdisciplinary work of building a truly global metropolitan studies here at the University of California, Berkeley. In addition, Aihwa wishes to express her appreciation of scholars based in Asia who are first-hand witnesses to the tumultuous changes under way in cities of the emerging world. Ananya wishes to thank Nezar AlSayyad for immeasurable support and for his own work on cities that continues to be an inspiration for her.

Aihwa Ong and Ananya Roy
Berkeley

Introduction

Worlding Cities, or the Art of Being Global

Aihwa Ong

... the skyline rises in the East.
Rem Koolhaas

Cities rise and fall, but the vagaries of urban fate cannot be reduced to the workings of universal laws established by capitalism or colonial history. Caught in the vectors of particular histories, national aspirations, and flows of cultures, cities have always been the principal sites for launching world-conjuring projects. Today, urban dreams and schemes play with accelerating opportunities and accidents that circulate in ever-widening spirals across the planet. Emerging nations exercise their new power by assembling glass and steel towers to project particular visions of the world. Once again, as Rem Koolhaas (2004) notes, "the skyline rises in the East," as cities vie with one another, and regional aspirations are superseded by new horizons of the global.

In the 1970s, New York City was celebrated for its architectural constellation, which fostered a "delirious" culture of congestion. Koolhaas (1997) called New York "The City of the Captive Global," one that unites the modern with perpetual motion. But by the early twenty-first century, the financial meltdown in the fall of 2008 (called the Great Recession) dealt a reversal of fortune for New York, London, and Tokyo. As these mighty cities struggle to retain their lead as financial powerhouses, Singapore and Dubai are emerging as centers of global finance. Meanwhile, China's role as the banker of the world has made Shanghai and Hong Kong the shares-selling capitals of the world. While capitals of big economies remain crucial players, Asian economies have skyrocketed, and the Asian world has witnessed the stunning emergence of cities of international consequence. The 2010 Shanghai Expo

Worlding Cities: Asian Experiments and the Art of Being Global, First Edition.
Edited by Ananya Roy and Aihwa Ong.
© 2011 Blackwell Publishing Ltd. Published 2011 by Blackwell Publishing Ltd.

has been the most explicit demonstration yet of a can-do determination to experiment with cutting-edge innovations in urban architecture, industry, and design. Indeed, if nothing else, the 2008 economic recession vividly invalidates magisterial views of how cities, their functions, and publics will change according to some master law of European experience. Today, Asian cities are fertile sites, not for following an established pathway or master blueprint, but for a plethora of situated experiments that reinvent what urban norms can count as "global."

Aspiring cities in the so-called global South challenge disciplinary controls that map cities according to a global division of global capitalist and post-colonial regions. Hegemonic theories of globalization and postcoloniality have long inspired a conceptual terra firma of generalizable global spaces, including cities and their destinies. As is the case with early modern nations, cities in the emerging world today have come to embody nationalist ambitions of wealth, power, and recognition. Major cities in the developing world have become centers of enormous political investment, economic growth, and cultural vitality, and thus have become sites for instantiating their countries' claims to global significance.

A recognition of the changing skylines of the world not only directs our gaze to emerging metropolitan centers, but also points to the fallacies of some key assumptions in metropolitan studies. In the social sciences, two major approaches have been dominant in defining the parameters and perspectives for investigating contemporary cities and urban conditions: (a) the political economy of globalization; and (b) the postcolonial focus on subaltern agency. Both models bear a Marxist pedigree and are thus overdetermined in their privileging of capitalism as the only mechanism and class struggle as the only resolution to urban problems. The political economy approach constructs the great metropolis as a site of capital accumulation and as the battleground for remaking citizenship and civil society. The postcolonial perspective views cities outside the Euro-American region as settings animated solely by subaltern resistances to different modes of domination. While there are many excellent studies that illuminate aspects of urban change through the prism of global confrontations between capitalism and democracy, the larger lesson seems to be that two universal principles of globalization – capitalism and postcolonialism – are each associated with a unified set of economic effects or political outcomes for shaping global spaces. By positing a singular causality (global capitalism) or a special category of actors (postcolonial agents), such universal principles tend to view significantly different sites as instantiations of either a singular economic system or the same political form of globalization. By studying situated phenomena through a lens that understands them as singular moments in a unified and integrated global process, analysts lose sight of complex urban situations as particular engagements with the global. We should account for the complexity of these particular engagements rather than subject them to economistic or political reductionism.

Indeed, such conceptual blind spots also overlook the unexpected effects of historical shifts, events, and crises. As the 2008 economic crisis quickly revealed, the political economic focus on city functions cannot account for the sudden economic collapse of heretofore global cities, or for the rapid rise of major Asian cities of global significance. Meanwhile Beijing, and by proxy, China, have emerged as the pollution capital of the world. In other words, besides the volatility of global markets, emerging nations and planetary threats variously exert influences on the roles, rankings, and achievements of particular metropolises.

Conceptual architectures that leave little room for empirical heterogeneity and changeability are thus invested in a given global status quo. Claims about city ranking and power, whether by urban analysts and city champions, are political statements that are inseparable from the processes of urban development. It seems reasonable to expect metropolitan scholars to treat identifiable urban achievements, and the global metrics that apply to them, as contingent measures subject to potential challenges, whether in the realms of academic theorizing or the contexts of inter-city rivalries. Normative codes cannot account for the situated ways in which urban aspirations play out in emerging sites, or how the entry of these local forms into the global one actually transforms the whole question of what counts as a global city in some significant way.

The contributors in this volume tend to bypass overarching principles of globalization, and are all sensitive to the geopolitical shifts and spectacular rise of cities throughout Asia. The city is viewed not as an exclusive site of capitalism or postcolonial activism, but as a milieu that is in constant formation, drawing on disparate connections, and subject to the play of national and global forces. Authors pursue, in more or less intensity, an analytics of urban practices, tracking a variety of projects engaged in remaking a city's fortunes despite, or perhaps because of, an awareness of the uncertainty of urban claims on the future. We thus focus not on established criteria of city achievements, but on the ongoing art of being global. We pay attention to an array of often overlooked urban initiatives that compete for world recognition in the midst of inter-city rivalry and globalized contingency. While contributors in the book take different analytical angles, there are some shared elements that favor situated investigations of urban phenomena in highly dynamic circumstances, and without the predetermining of social outcomes.

First, there is emphasis on the city as a field of intervention for solving an array of problems associated with modern life and national interests. For instance, specific urban issues – city infrastructure, investments, sustainable standards, political life, or aesthetic value, among others – are variously problematized as a sphere of action is called into question, and a set of difficulties are transformed into problems to which diverse solutions are possible (Foucault 1984). Second, the metropolis tends to be viewed not as a fixed locality but as a particular nexus of situated and transnational ideas, institutions, actors, and practices that may be variously drawn together for solving particular problems. In the shift from an analytics of structure to an analytics of assemblage, analysts stay close to the practices that rearticulate and reassemble material, technical, and discursive elements in the process of remaking particular contexts (Collier and Ong 2005). It follows that modes of interventions, at different scales, promiscuously draw upon ideas and objects, and find allies in multiple sources that are recontextualized for resolving urban problems. Third, city ambitions are reimagined in relation to shifting "forms and norms" (Rabinow 1991) of being global. Different chapters note that a striking aspect of Asian urban transformations involves seemingly unavoidable practices of inter-city comparison, referencing, or modeling.

Such discursive and non-discursive activities are spatializing practices that drive the flow of distinctive urban codes that gives the region a buoyant sense of being on the cusp of an urban revolution. These urban interventions are viewed as worlding practices; that is, projects that attempt to establish or break established horizons of urban standards in and beyond a particular city. World-aspiring projects are experiments in that they put forth questions, initiatives, and procedures in the midst of uncertainty, without guarantees about successful outcomes (Jacob 1998). Contemporary experiments to remedy an urban situation that has been assessed as problematic – aging infrastructure, underinvestment, neglect of the urban poor, lack of international profile, and so on – draw on global forms that are recontextualized in the city matrix, and then dispersed to other places seeking solutions. In such globalizing circumstances, the neoliberal as a global form comes to articulate situated experimentations with an art of being global.

Many have viewed "the neoliberal" as a set of market conditions that scale back the state, but in a more careful formulation, Neil Brenner and Nik Theodore (2002) have argued that that there is great variability in geographies of "actually existing neoliberalism." But the neoliberal as a logic of optimization (Rose 1999) refers not to a space or a form of state, but a set of maximizing rationalities that articulates particular assemblages of governing. The neoliberal as a mobile technology can be taken up by a government or any other institution to recast problems as non-ideological and non-political issues that need technical solutions to maximize intended outcomes (Ong 2006). As a logic of entrepreneurialism, neoliberal reason has even infiltrated domains that have been and are ideologically cast, by observers and by practitioners, as resolutely anti-market, such as NGOs, workers' organizations, and aesthetic/cultural production. If we recognize urban movements as ongoing experiments to expand social power, we should not be surprised at the apparently paradoxical interdependence of calculative practices of political entrepreneurialism and the progressive language of "anti-neoliberalism." The proliferation of neoliberal techniques thus contributes to the blossoming of an urban terrain of unanticipated borrowings, appropriations, and alliances that cut across class, ideological, and national lines even as it depends on the continual meta-practical discursive resedimentation of these boundaries. Even what appear to be opposed ideological positions are constituted in relation to each other; they are mutually imbricated and also linked through a set of semi-shared norms. This would make the judgment of "right" or "wrong" quite detrimental to an analytical practice aimed at probing the singularity and complexity of the phenomena in question. By circumventing normative ideological judgments on the "right" or "wrong" side of power, we can analyze a range of urban initiatives, large and small, as they struggle to move forward and also experience setbacks in the techniques of urban transformation.

Situating our inquiries in a region previously known as the "third world," we pay attention to urban efforts that experiment with visions of the global alternative to those where cities in the West are taken as an unproblematized benchmark of an apparently unsituated urban ideal. The critical mass and vitality of urban projects in Asian centers, especially, are destabilizing established criteria of global urban modernity. The following chapters will highlight distinctive practices of urban modeling, inter-referencing, and the forming of new solidarities that collectively seem to raise an *inter*-Asian horizon of metropolitan and global aspirations. This would mean the constitution of a set of distinctive visions of the global that exist without essential reference to the West, which is made sometimes conspicuously absent in practices of inter-Asian self-reference that spell the effective and often emphatic formation of an ex-Western urban referential space. Current methodological thinking, however, has both overdetermined and limited a serious engagement with actually existing metropolitan complexities and ambitions.

Singular Logics in Urban Change

Urban geography has been dominated by theories of globalization that have centered on finding a universal law – social, political, economic, and so on – that characterizes the current epoch, either in a singular form of global capitalism or in the pronouncement of an epoch defined by a universal condition of postcoloniality. This reliance on frameworks that depend on global generalization has shaped metropolitan studies to such an extent that empirical heterogeneity, flux, and uncertainty tend to be subsumed under a minimal set of explanatory conditions.

One hegemonic approach views a diffuse and abstract capitalism as the master driver of globalization; as capitalist operations roam the world, they busily determine the ranking of big cities, subdivide urban space, and thus paradoxically both dismantle political authority and undermine the public sphere. Under the "globalization" rubric, cities are largely viewed as functioning nodes in an integrated planetary capitalism, giving rise to the impression that great cities are more functionally integral to the workings of global capitalism than to that of their homelands. Building on the world-systems model, Saskia Sassen's concept of "global cities" (2001 [1991]) – paradigmatically embodied in New York, London, and Tokyo – identifies the material processes, activities, and infrastructures that these provide for the implementation of economic globalization. At the city scale, capitalist mechanisms subdivide the great city into a hierarchy of zones and labor categories according to their economic value. Sassen's paradigm is refined by Stephen Graham and Simon Marvin (2001), who use the term "splintering urbanism" to characterize the shattering effects of transnational infrastructural networks on urban environments and political conditions. This account depends on the fractal replication of the segmenting effect of Sassen's economic globalization at ever-finer spatial scales; just as the model of capitalist world-system splits the planet into core and periphery regions, global cities and second-tier cities, so capitalist operations fragment urban landscapes into precincts of value and limited value, high-tech and low-tech, rich and poor – into differentiated urban spaces that as a disarticulated aggregate splinters the public good in the service of the "corporate good" (Graham and Marvin 2001: 33). Such analyses aim to provide a generalizable rendering of corporate machinations, the avatars of capitalism *cum* globalization, as they come to shape urban functions, landscapes, and fortunes in the interests of a global capitalist machinery.

The overall effect, however, is to put the variation in and particularity of urban development, as well as metropolitan life, everywhere at the mercy of a universal force called globalization. The assumption is that there is a single system of capitalist domination, and a set of unified effects of regular causal factors that can foment nearly identical problems and responses in different global sites. An extension of the generalizable laws of capitalism culminates in Mike Davis's characterization of mega-cities in the global South in his apocalyptic "planets of slums" (Davis 2006). By piling on extreme statistics of density, migrant flows, and garbage production, Davis argues that the lack of industrialization in the "third world" has spawned giant shantytowns, creating global conditions that may lead to a great upheaval of urban proletarians. In this conceptual cul-de-sac, big cities in Africa owe their rapid growth to high concentrations of working poor, and inevitable urban revolution seems a foregone conclusion. In short, these all-determining theories of globalization are fundamentally interested in the homogenizing effects of capitalism. This singular capitalist process-force is presumed to account for engineering urban status and fate throughout the world.

Such schematic perspectives fail to enrich our understanding of particular challenges and solutions on the ground. The planet-of-slums approach, for instance, does not mention that Ibadan (Nigeria) and Nairobi (Kenya) have urban facilities and well-educated residents. Furthermore, the rapid demographic growth of cities in the former "third world" is resulting in more than the explosion of shantytowns. We learn that over the last decade, the world's ten fastest-growing cities of more than a million people are found in greater Asian region. Four are located in China – Guangzhou, Chongqing, Nanjing, and Wuhan – and, together with Dubai, have become centers of turbocharged middle-class growth (*Wall Street Journal*, 2009). Thus, accelerated urban population growth may be attributed to the influx of dispossessed peasants and/or the rise of the middle classes – as, for example, in Mumbai (see Ananya Roy, Conclusion, this volume). Variations in class composition mean that one cannot attribute urban expansion to a single collectivity or homogenized demographic, such as slum-dwellers, nor can one characterize the great city as the paradigmatic site of a global revolutionary multitude (Hardt and Negri 2000). By the mid-century, over half of the population in Asia will be urbanized. Perhaps the one sure claim that can be made about the staggering weight of this phenomenon is the equally huge size of their carbon footprints, and the urgent need for all cities to reverse this planet of pollution (Shannon May, this volume).

Anthropologists and humanists working in cities have a more subtle analysis of class interrelationships and practices, but the binary oppositions of globalization frameworks are reproduced in ethnographic accounts of life in the city. The city as the universal or promised space of citizenship and universal human rights remains a resonant political economic theme. The study of cities outside the Euro-American setting tends to focus on the class-driven fragmentation and the uneven distribution of urban privileges and rights to citizens and migrants alike. Teresa Caldeira (2000) examines São Paulo as a "city of walls," providing a rich ethnographic account of how the rich increasingly barricade themselves against the poor. In another study, Caldeira and Holston (2005) note that migrants in Brazil stream into the cities to claim citizenship rights by staking out land and putting pressure on municipal governments to deliver urban facilities. In a similar vein, Arjun Appadurai (2002) identifies a form of "deep democracy" in demands by Mumbai slum-dwellers for basic infrastructural services. These are rich and valuable accounts of political struggles, but so much of what progressive theory has to say about non-Western cities gives the impression that class and politics of outright resistance are the only significant urban events and activities in the developing world.

Postcolonial theory is another hegemonic approach for studying cities and urban conditions outside the West. There is the implicit suggestion that outside the West, the Rest is inescapably postcolonial, sharing the same set of global effects of former colonialism. Postcolonial theory is also invested in the idea that regularity in causal factors can instantiate nearly identical responses in different emerging sites, such as cooptation of the elites, or resistance by the exploited and marginalized. Thus, as non-Western cities are brought into metropolitan studies, the tendency has been to approach a spectrum of contemporary phenomena in studies whose form and concerns are overdetermined by the legacies of colonial rule.

Many insist, with some justification, that urbanization across the developing world should be viewed through the lens of distinctive histories and "postcolonial" experiences. Postcolonial cities must be understood through different paths of modernization that have roots in colonial experiences and postcolonial national liberation and transformations. For instance, anti-colonial struggles were shadowed by what Benedict Anderson calls "the specter of comparison" (1998: 2), a kind of psychological vertigo induced in Asian leaders by the distance to be traveled in order to catch up with the development benchmarks and metropolitan ideals established by and in the West. For a short while, newly independent countries came to view modernist architecture as a universal utopian form, and sought to build new capitals as literalizations of models of rational government and democratic aspirations (Holston 1999).

When it comes to urban studies, the logic of postcolonial globalization can be divided into two orientations. One kind of postcolonial formulation emphasizes urban features and norms that register colonial experiences but have since transcended the colonial. Under the rubric of "postcolonial urbanism," the continuation of the colonial past into the present urban culture and order is emphasized. Some note the historically and regionally specific urban features that make Southeast Asian cities a "supplementary" category to Western global centers (Bishop, Philips, and Yeo 2003). There is also attention to the historical continuities of regional flows and particular cosmopolitanisms that collectively endow a special character to those "other global cities" outside advanced capitalist countries (Marayam 2009). The approaches of scholars based in Asian cities tend therefore to emphasize the distance traveled since their brief engagements with colonialism, and the ongoing process of 'catching up' to modern or even civilizational measures of metropolitan greatness.

A second approach, inspired by postcolonial scholars, focuses on giving primacy to the agency of subaltern groups – for instance, racial, ethnic, class, and gender populations – that have been subjugated by a variety of colonial, neocolonial, and capitalist forces. When it comes to studying urban transformations in India since colonialism, the emphasis has not been on studying how cities attempt to "catch up," as is the case in Southeast and East Asian Studies, but rather has focused on the political agency of a special category of postcolonial subjects. Postcolonial theory is thus as much about how contemporary urban situations have been shaped by colonial legacies of injustice as by contemporary problems of urban underdevelopment.

The generalizable claims of postcolonial theory have been applied to other former sites of European colonialism. AbdouMaliq Simone (2008) famously celebrates the aspirational politics of African migrants whose everyday agency shapes emergent conditions of everyday life in the face of daunting urban inequalities. Such studies have much to recommend themselves in challenging the urban diacritics of the global North by recuperating the distinctiveness of postcolonial urban history, character, and the authenticity of subaltern subjects who inhabit and produce the ever-shifting landscapes of urban experience. However, the conceptual binarism of postcolonial studies seems to privilege postcolonial subjectivity and agency as the primary driving force in vastly different global sites that have been greatly transformed, through heterogeneous processes, colonial encounters, and postcolonial histories, in infrastructure, politics, and culture. In her modification of the postcolonial approach, Gayatri Spivak (1999) employs a concept of "worlding" that rejects the recuperation of subaltern subjects, thus moving postcolonial analysis away from the emphasis on subaltern subjects, political society, and street politics. Nevertheless, universal capitalist and postcolonial variants of neo-Marxism rely on singular logics of global change, focusing on homogenizing effects of capitalism and colonialism that are presumed to account for uniform conditions in a huge swath of cities throughout the world.

As it has become clear, we take the vantage point of an Asian region that cannot be reduced to the uniform expectations, logics, and prescriptions of structural Marxism or postcolonial theory. Collectively, our chapters tend to be open-ended rather than delimited by rich–poor, metropolitan–postcolonial frameworks. Urban environments are animated by a variety of transnational and local institutions, actors and practices that cannot be neatly mapped out in advance as being on the side of power or on the side of resistance, as if positions could be so unproblematically delineated. Only by liberating the city as a conceptual container of capitalism and subaltern agency can different analytical approaches explore methods for explaining how an urban situation can be at once heterogeneously particular and yet irreducibly global (Ong and Collier 2005). Any hope we have to grasp the particularity and variability of the great urban transformation demands situated accounts of how urban environments are formed through specific combinations of the past and the future, the postcolonial and the metropolitan, the global and the situated, but is not dominated by any single mechanism or principle.

Milieus of Intervention

Ideally, urban studies should be open to the multiplicity of events, interrelationships, and factors that, in ways both chaotic and strategic, expected and unforeseen, are in play in the formation of particular urban environments. A view of the city as a site of experimentation allows us to integrate qualities of fluidity, interactivity, and interactivity that crystallize the possibilities within which we reimagine, remake, and reexperience urban conditions and the notion of the urban itself.

Foucault counsels us to consider the city as a milieu, or "a field of intervention" in which individuals, populations, and groups put into conjunction of elements and events that circulate beyond the site itself (Foucault 2007: 21). Spatializing practices, in the dual senses of the gathering and the dispersing of circulating ideas, forms, and techniques, are constitutive of emerging globalized spaces. Spatializing practices thus form the urban as a problem-space in which a cast of disparate actors – the state, capitalists, NGOs, foreign experts, and ordinary people – define what is problematic, uncertain, or in need of mediation, and then go about solving these now-identified problems such as urban planning, class politics, and human capital. The starting point of analysis is thus not how singular principles define a city environment, but rather the array of problem-solving and spatializing practices that are in play in shaping an urban field.

In developing countries, a major player in configuring the urban environment is the state. It seeks to rethink and remake the contemporary world rather than being simply passively "globalized" by it. "Sovereignty capitalizes a territory," Foucault declares (2007: 20), and states in emerging nations have been especially active in drawing resources, methods, and capabilities to their cities, as well as circulating urban and nationalist interests overseas. Entrepreneurial governments from East and Southeast Asia to the United Arab Emirates (UAE) are often initiators of mega-urban projects, drawing sovereign wealth funds for the makeovers of old cities such as Shanghai and Beijing, or building totally new citadels in a desert landscape, as in Dubai. Through the renovation of cities, new political maps are drawn.

Urban planning takes place in conditions of uncertainty, and impressive built forms do not necessarily withstand the risks of market variability. Dubai is an overnight hypercity that emerged out of the confluence of post-9/11 repatriation of capital and Arab elites to the Middle East, and the petrodollar boom that followed. But the Dubai bubble burst in the 2008–9 financial catastrophe, and the city required a general bailout from oil-rich Abu Dhabi to get on its feet again. While Dubai will survive as the capital of Islamic banking and as a Middle East transportation hub and pleasure dome, its metropolitan flair as a global business hub has been undermined by the shifting sands of volatile capital flows. The building frenzy in brash new cities has been informed by a neoliberal logic of unlimited possibilities and risk-taking embodied in Dubai's vertigo-inducing towers. The entrepreneurial quest to remake the city's fortunes drives the circulation of global knowledge, actors, and talents. These are variously assembled by city officials, planners, activists, and citizens as they seek to shape a new space of governmentality attuned to global competition (Ong 2007). Political leaders view their city as a globalized field of intervention, a national space of problem solving that relies on methods both irrepressibly global and resolutely situated.

Worlding Practices

"Worlding" is employed here not to signal adherence to a world-historical logic of "world making," as in a crude reading of Marx's conception stagist historical development (cf., Marx and Engels 1848), but rather to identify the projects and practices that instantiate some vision of the world in formation. A Marxist view of worlding from above and counter-worlding from below reflects cosmopolitan ideals of emerging world citizenship. Worlding and reworlding were articulated by Spivak (1999) in her postcolonial attempt to recuperate subaltern subjects through a rendering of the Heideggerian concept of "being in the world." Hardt and Negri (2000) provide another structural Marxist view of world transformation through generalized class conflicts. They claim that the "multitude," a globally disenfranchised working-class collectivity produced through the contemporary workings of capitalism, are milling in the world's cities to confront Empire. In a follow-up to Hardt and Negri, Rob Wilson (2004) proposes that a variety of counter-worlding tactics, including art, can challenge the universalizing ideology and materiality of planetary capitalism. He calls the aggregate of these tactics "worldings against Empire." Such Marxist conceptualizations of worlding thus define a unified logic (class wars), set of agents (subalterns, working-class subjects, multitudes), and target (global capitalism) of world transformation. The everyday struggles of these special categories of historical actors are construed as coalescing, sooner or later, into a single counter-worlding movement against capital's Empire.

We do not make our case by invoking such singular laws of inevitable worlding planetary scale. An anthropological focus on mid-range theorizing

(Collier and Ong 2005) dives below high abstraction to hover over actual human projects and goals unfolding in myriad circumstances of possibility and contingency. We stay close to heterogeneous practices of worlding that do not fall tidily into opposite sides of class, political, or cultural divides. Rather, a non-ideological formulation of worlding as situated everyday practices identifies ambitious practices that creatively imagine and shape alternative social visions and configurations – that is, "worlds" – than what already exists in a given context. Wording in this sense is linked to the idea of emergence, to the claims that global situations are always in formation. Worlding projects remap relationships of power at different scales and localities, but they seem to form a critical mass in urban centers, making cities both critical sites in which to inquire into worlding projects, as well as the ongoing result and target of specific worldings.

Gilles Deleuze and Felix Guattari (1987) have suggested that in a world of flows, social formations emerge from the "rhizomatic" connections that cross-cut vertical integrated hierarchies (328–9). In this sense, worlding exercises are those lateralizing microprocesses that remap power by opening up new channels or reconfigure new social universes. In an echo of Foucault's notion of milieu or social field (2007: 22–3), this notion of the production of emergent spaces from the flows of ideas, actions, and objects is a radical departure from a conventional view of the world as stabilized into binary orders. In a related argument, Bruno Latour (2005) notes that a social system is formed through "a provisional movement of new associations" that effects a continual change in its topography. Extrapolating from these theorists, worlding refers not to a single unified political process, but to diverse spatializing practices that mix and match different components that go into building an emergent system. If the city is a living, shifting network, then worlding practices are those activities that gather in some outside elements and dispatch others back into the world.

Indeed, the very act of reimagining or redesigning an urban milieu – whether in changing material infrastructure, political possibilities, or aesthetic styles – is by definition aspirational, experimental, and even speculative. Donna Haraway (2008) notes that scientific experiments open "up to speculative and so possible material, affective, practical reworlding" in concrete and detailed situations (92–3). There is a mix of speculative fiction and speculative fact in worlding exercises as practitioners aim to build something they believe is for the better. It seems important to register that such creative and contingent activities are at the core of urban innovation, and that tinkering with a spectrum of urban ideas and forms is an art of being global.

It is therefore not surprising to observe that there is no singular or fixed standard of urban globality; there are many forms of "the global" in play.

The very contested nature of what counts as global in a shifting inter-urban field of power requires urban analysis to capture the reflexive dimension in many urban initiatives that go beyond local improvements to participate, however implicitly, in a bigger game of winning some kind of world recognition. Today, residents of Asian cities large and small like to think of their hometown as having some degree of global significance, or having attained some level of "world-class" standing. Indeed, as we shall see in the chapters that follow, major urban projects are invariably caught up in an inter-city competition over the "global" stature of hometowns.

Furthermore, in this emerging region, the tendency is no longer simply to turn to Western prototypes, but rather to develop from homegrown solutions to Asian metropolitan challenges, distinctive urban profiles, political styles, and aesthetic forms. Urban initiatives of all kinds are thus experiments with metropolitan futures, and they draw on disparate styles, actors, and forms that circulate in and through Asian metropolitan centers. In sum, worlding practices are constitutive, spatializing, and signifying gestures that variously conjure up worlds beyond current conditions of urban living. They articulate disparate elements from near and far; and symbolically re-situate the city in the world. By eschewing singular concepts of worlding, single standards of urban ranking that take for granted the terms in and through which cities can be ranked, and unified ways of achieving an already given future, we open up academic inquiries into a diversity of urban activities engaged in the transformation of contemporary urban living. In urban Asia, we encounter an art of being global that is invariably caught up in a political game that is allusive, contrastive, comparative, and contested, with cities in the region, but also beyond.

Modeling, Inter-Referencing, New Solidarities

Drawing on new research presented in the chapters, we identify three styles of being global that, while not exclusive to Asia, seem to be distinctive practices associated with urban development in the region. Worldwide, aspirant cities vie with one another in to leave some mark on the world stage. Different attempts to burnish city images, shape skylines, or push through innovative urban agendas can be found in many domains and scales of renovation. Besides mega-projects supported by politicians, planners, and boosters, there are also a variety of political, cultural, and economic projects pursued by activists, migrants, and artists to improve the condition and standing of their hometowns *vis-à-vis* others that are experienced as being in *de facto* competition in the game of urban ranking. All too schematically, for the sake of argument and organization, shared urban forms and norms in Asian metropolitan transformation seem to fall into three distinctive styles – modeling, inter-referencing, and association – that will be subtitles for different sections of this book.

Modeling

In recent decades, the renovation of cities in the non-Western world has given rise to the circulation of urban models that have become established values understood as desirable and achievable throughout the developing world. A number of Asian cities have come to stand as replicable models of an urban futurity that does not find its ultimate reference in the West. Here, Singapore, Shanghai, and Hong Kong, instead of New York, London, or Paris have become centers to be invoked, envied, and emulated as exemplary sites of a new urban normativity. Through the years of the tiger economies, city-states such as Singapore and Hong Kong led the way in solving urban problems – public housing, downtown development, clean industries, upscale districts, cultural and tourist attractions – that transformed them into world-class cities. Furthermore, the cultivation of transnational links with corporations, banks, and cultural institutions made them the centers of global networks. While Hong Kong sees itself as "Asia's World City," Singapore presents itself as the knowledge hub of a far-flung "effervescent" business ecosystem (Ong 2005).

Specifically, the mix of state entrepreneurialism on the one hand, and the development of "sustainable" infrastructure on the other, has generated a range of urban innovation models that promote "successful" urban conditions and lifestyles. Urban innovations such as the "garden city," subsidized housing, industrial estates, upscale residential enclaves, and even water resource management developed in Asian cities have become packaged as "models" that can be detached from the originary city and exported to other aspiring cities. "The Singapore model," in actuality a set of normative and technical urban plans, has come to inspire city innovation projects across Asia and beyond.

Urban modeling can be conceptualized as a global technology that is disembedded from its hometown and adopted in other sites. As a condensed set of desirable and achievable urban forms, the "Singapore model" has been raised in the imagination of planners and developers, and materialized in built forms throughout Asia and the developing world. The modeling process sets a symbolic watermark of urban aspirations on the one hand, and provides achievable blueprints for urban renovations on the other. Modeling involves discursive and material activities that are inspired by particular models of urban achievements in other cities. Modeling refers to actual urban projects that have been dubbed "garden," "sustainable," "livable," or "world-class," that planners hope to reproduce elsewhere in a bid to rebrand their home cities.

The use of blueprints, plans, or built forms as a guide does not mean that modeling is a faithful copy of the original, but rather a practice that tries to capture some aspect, style, or essence of that original. The modeling trend thus raises the question of whether one city can truly replicate a particular "model" of say, industrial zones, or financial districts, or sustainable infrastructure. After all, an urban model exported by Singapore has to be inserted into a different set of material and political conditions elsewhere. Furthermore, in Asia, city-modeling has complex political implications that ripple beyond improved urban infrastructure and livability. The import of an urban model can include its associated disciplinary effects such as the introduction of new governing norms or the incorporation of unwilling or skeptical subjects into a new scheme. Urban modeling is thus not only a technology for building garden cities and knowledge hubs elsewhere; it can become a political tool for changing the built form and social spirit of another urban environment.

In Part I of this book, chapters explore how urban planning in the form of modeling technologies come to define standard-setting forms and norms for cities aspiring to move up on some global scale of urban achievement. In the opening chapter, "Singapore as Model," Chua Beng Huat makes a case for how the urban planning innovations of the city-state are packaged as a marketing brand to be exported overseas, as yet one more category of commodities produced by the developing world. Chua maintains that while the Singapore brand has become a global technology, it is a composite technical and symbolic cluster that can be invoked or emulated but cannot be really be reproduced. Frequently, the Singapore model in circulation functions as a set of abstract standards for "realizable utopian" projects for cities in emerging countries.

In her chapter, Lisa Hoffman traces the influence of the Singapore model in various efforts to remake Dalian, a northern Chinese city, into a center of "green urbanism." Urban modeling, Hoffman argues, can affect different spheres of metropolitan living and has social implications beyond the city itself. First, Singapore as a garden city is invoked to initiate a new green regime intended to change the governance of both Dalian and its residents. Using a discourse of sustainability, city planners reshape city parks along with city manners in order to promote a new ethics of urban life. Second, the "green urbanism" improvements enable officials to position Dalian itself as a model other Chinese cities by defining a new "green" standard for ranking cities throughout the nation. Urban modeling is thus deployed as a tool for remaking the urban environment and reshaping sociality, as well as for making "sustainability" a new criterion for ranking cities in general.

For less up-to-date centers in Asia, the Singapore model of corporate and residential planning seems a packaged deal for raising the city profile. Manila has long been on the sidelines as other Asian cities played a game of catch-up in changing their urban infrastructure and investment appeal. Gavin Shatkin describes the material and social aspects of "planning privatopolis" in Manila, a downtown project that is in part modeled as a "Little Singapore." The development emphasizes self-contained zones, with requisite elements of "urban efficiencies" that can attract new investments. The broader reference to Singapore lies in the hope that a refurbished downtown with the "appropriate" urban conditions can "nurture a desired type of citizen – globally oriented knowledge economy workers who can form a creative and managerial core for a process of economic transformation." What is being emulated goes beyond concrete, glass, and steel; urban modeling also involves the mimicry of the neoliberal packaging of international glamour, talent, and entrepreneurialism that promises to animate a moribund metropolis.

These chapters reveal that the Singapore brand articulates different elements and scales of urban innovation, from offering an achievable standard of urban makeover and promotion on the one hand, to shaping an urban culture of self-managing and self-enterprising subjects on the other. From Dalian to Manila and beyond, modeling practices tend to recast "sustainability" in neoliberal terms as city governments and developers variously deploy and link techniques of green urbanism and urban entrepreneurialism.

Shannon May's chapter on "ecological urbanization" examines a different kind of modeling, an eco-city prototype hatched in Silicon Valley and implemented in rural China. The brainchild of an international consortium in partnership with the Chinese government, the eco-city model is tested in Huangbaiyu Village, northern China, as a potential solution to China's massive environmental problems and a slew of problems that have been associated with rural development and urbanization. May points out that an urban design on paper to deal with runaway pollution in the emerging world does not work out as intended in the actual environment of peasant China. Because the eco-city model ignores social and economic conditions on the ground, the infrastructural change results in the (unintended?) dispossession and outmigration of local peasants.

At other scales, however, the eco-city may not be considered a "failure," as the project enhances American corporate access to government contracts, and the eco-city provides support for Beijing's claim to be a serious player in environmental urbanism. Modeling an eco-city in this case appears to be less about sustainability than about two different but convergent political goals; that is, bringing Chinese peasants under a mode of global environmental governance on the one hand, and allaying global fears about China's mammoth carbon footprint on the other. This chapter highlights the complex political and ethical elements surrounding the cultural translation of urban competition, a question to which I next turn.

Inter-referencing practices

In recent decades, a variety of actors have sought to transform their cities by measuring their urban innovations against those of more impressive centers in the emerging Asian region. An idiom of referencing other cities can perhaps be traced to the dawn of market reforms in China. In 1992, the late Premier Deng Xiaoping visited Shenzhen and called for the creation of "a few Hong Kongs" (*ji ge Xianggang*) along the coast. As "development fever" caught fire, industrial zones sprang up around Guangzhou, Shanghai, and Xiamen, and Hong Kong and Taiwanese managers helped to shape the infrastructural and capitalist transformation of these mainland cities. This urban process of learning from established Chinese centers sparked a phenomenon whereby "Shenzhen is Hong Kongized, "Guangzhou is Shenzhenized, and the whole country is Guangdongized" (Cartier 2001: 242). While this began as a Chinese discourse of learning from other cities, the language of urban transmission continues to reference cities in the Asian tiger economies, including Singapore. Allan Pred (1995) has observed that the articulation of discursive and non-discursive practices produces spaces of spectacle and, one may add, of emulation. Indeed, gestures of inter-referencing are spatializing practices in that by constantly comparing and contrasting cities, new kinds of inter-city relationships are formed. This largely China-generated idiom of emulatable cities has become a driver of real estate and business values, and thus a resonant theme in the Anglophone inter-Asian world of business, media, popular culture, urban planning, and scholarly research (see below).

While urban modeling is a concrete instantiation of acknowledging another city's achievements, inter-referencing refers more broadly to practices of citation, allusion, aspiration, comparison, and competition. The practice of citing a "more successful city" – itself an unstable category – seems to stir urban aspirations and sentiments of inter-city rivalry as well as standing as a legitimation for particular enterprises at home. In India, inter-referencing practices operate as a kind of elite dreaming, as when leaders in Mumbai wonder when it will become the next Shanghai (Prakash 2008). English-speaking politicians frequently invoke Singapore and Shanghai in order to sell their real estate programs, justify unpopular measures to clear slums, and otherwise thwart political resistance from local residents (see the chapters in this volume by Michael Goldman, Ananya Roy, and Asher Ghertner). In East Asia, Shanghai's rise as China's preeminent financial center has been said to provincialize Hong Kong, spurring city managers to emphasize Islamic banking in order to rival Dubai. The circular nature of inter-city citation fuels a spiral of comparison. Singapore planners try to transcend their own staid "clean and green" image by opening a casino zone that they claim is "not like Macao," but perhaps more like Las Vegas. Through a process of multiple referencing, urban actors are constantly juggling heterogeneous multiple cultural norms of what constitutes urban success and achievements in a world of circulating city symbols.

Inter-Asia inter-referencing practices are thus inseparable from and in fact constitutive of an emerging system for the judgment of urban value. Through the favorable mention, allusion, and even endorsement of another city, actors and institutions position their own projects in a language of explicit comparison and ranking, thus vicariously participating in the symbolic values of particular cities. The idiom of inter-referencing pits cities in relation to one another, by invoking desirable icons of "world class" amenities – upscale hotels, shopping malls, entertainment and conventions facilities, symphonies, opera houses, international enclaves, and airports – as symbols of desirable urban attributes. Not least, as booming centers of the expansion of a new middle class, Asian cities have begun to compete with one another to provide improved conditions of working and living. By tweaking urban desires and aspirations in emerging countries, citational practices put into circulation a symbolic language of globally significant urban style that has traveled beyond Asia.

While speculations in capital are obviously not limited to Asian cities, inter-city comparisons reinforce the link between economic speculation and urban aspiration. Speculative discourses draw together the building of impressive urban structures and the imagination of a city's global future. The constant allusion to other cities energizes efforts to assemble ideas, forms, and alliances in order to "catch up" with pace-setting cities that now exist outside the West. As inter-referencing practices drive speculations on a city's future residents and citizens are often caught up as well in a kind of disciplinary inter-city rivalry. By pointing to another city that is ahead, planners and developers can persuade people to accept potentially controversial projects in the name of the greater metropolitan good. "World-classness" is a slippery term that tweaks anxieties and primes speculations about the fortunes of one's own metropolis, but it can also stirs the skepticism and resistance among some sectors of the population.

The proliferation of urban comparison and contrast shapes the inter-city consciousness, affecting the reflexive self-knowledge of citizens, residents, and migrants as they locate and see themselves in and through particular cities. In a time of accelerating growth, residents are extremely aware the rising or falling fortunes of their own city or nation in relation to other places. In the 1990s, Kuala Lumpur boasts that it has the largest shopping mall in Asia, where residents and tourists can pretend they do not live in a tropical, regimented Muslim environment. Meanwhile, Hong Kong residents have sought to distinguish the city from other Asian shopping meccas by cherishing old buildings that embody its recent past as a preeminent harbor city. Across Asia, citizen, denizens, and dreamers evaluate different cityscapes, mingle in each other's cities and comparison shop for consumer goods, ideas and lifestyles (Chua 2000). By visiting, living, and working in a variety of urban spaces, city-dwellers develop a sense and knowledge of themselves as subjects of more or less successful urban geographies.

In Part II, the chapters explore how different modes of inter-city referencing directly affect the perceptions, ambitions, and projects of ordinary and elite urban subjects. Helen Siu explores the vulnerabilities of middle-class Hong Kongers who experience a sense of provincialization in the broader context of Shanghai's rise as China's economic capital. The relative decline of Hong Kong *vis-à-vis* Shanghai undermines Hong Kongers' sense of cultural significance in a shifting global environment. While the Hong Kong elite have long been famous for their cross-border commercial skills, current conditions of globalized business are proving to be harder to navigate. Siu observes an interesting contrast in that professionals from New Delhi, compared to middle-class Hong Kongers, seem more capable and flexible in making a living in foreign cities such as Dubai and Singapore. The Hong Kong middle class, increasingly bypassed by shifting global capital circuits, is turning its attention to restoration projects that reclaim their urban history as a mercantile center in Asia.

Until the recent debt crisis, Dubai had become a dream-city for millions of citizens in Asia, Africa, the Middle East, and beyond. With its sleek Arabo-modernist facade, Dubai projects a vision of metropolitan modernity for elite South Asian migrants seeking their fortunes overseas. In the next chapter, Chad Haines traces a new stream of middle-class professionals from New Delhi to Dubai, where there were more lucrative jobs than available in India. Haines calls their aspirational migration practices a form of neoliberal self-branding that depends on working in what is understood as a more globalized city. The association between working under the Brand Dubai and being branded as world-class professionals produces a cultural validation back home in New Delhi. But even before Dubai's recent financial woes, Haines found cracks behind the facade of glitz and glamour, as Indian white-collar workers discover limits and obstacles to an affordable lifestyle and to "global citizenship" in the city.

The next chapter identifies ambitious cities as sources of iconic urban forms and actors that circulate through the Asia Pacific. Glen Lowry and Eugene McCann follow the transfer of corporate designs between Hong Kong, Vancouver, and Dubai, and analyze how the discourse and building of business zones link the cities together in a system of urban-corporate inter-referentiality. As residents of Vancouver, however, the authors wish to look beyond the flow of corporate urban forms to discover other mobilities that instantiate other cultural forms identified with the city. They interpret Henry Tsang's installation art, planted in one of Vancouver's public spaces, as an aesthetic intervention that draws on indigenous and migrant cultures to disrupt the framing of the city as a site of seamless capitalist urbanity. The authors argue that this aesthetic interruption of inter-city corporate parallelism recovers a view of Vancouver as constituted by an alternative cartography of transpacific cultural flows ("in-the mix").

Addressing the complex nexus between inter-referencing and speculative practices, Aihwa Ong explores dual aspects of "hyperbuilding" – both as a speculative of overbuilding and as a particular type of spectacular monument in East Asian cities. A message of inter-referencing is the role of the state in funding or fostering mega-projects. The political exception engenders a variegated governmentality of urban space, creating conditions for a synergetic interaction between speculative activities and spectacular spaces. Building frenzy is a mode of worlding that leverages value from real estate to other sectors of capital accumulation, although hyperbuilding can also lead to an asset bubble. Ong next looks at Rem Koolhaas' paradigmatic "hyperbuilding," the CCTV Headquarters in Beijing, as a hyperspace of Chinese sovereignty. While the CCTV complex symbolizes China's media power in the global realm, it has also become a symbol of overbuilding in pornographic jokes about the urban overbuilding and the political shadow it casts on ordinary people. With the shift of the urban hyperspace to China, what are the broader implications for a popular view that radical architecture makes allusions to the modernist utopia?

New solidarities

The crisscrossing references and borrowings so dominant in East Asian settings are echoed in city politics in South Asia. Asian sites are not only crucial platforms for experimenting with architectural and social forms, but also the contexts of evolving political practices that straddle deep class divisions. In cities where the state presence is weak, advantageous private–public partnerships and cross-class appropriations are becoming validated in reconfiguring the new social. "The social" is an idea that bypasses conventional notions of state–society divisions to register an emerging "form of life" constituted within a limited space by political and moral authorities that inscribe an intelligibility for regulating conduct and forming ethical subjects (Rose 1999: 100–1). Experimentations draw together disparate logics, techniques, and practices to shape new regimes of urban governance. Stephen J. Collier (2009) has argued from Foucault's later lectures that governmentality identifies a kind of governing reasoning (govern-mentality) that can be analyzed as a dynamic process of combining different rationalities and techniques, whereas neoliberalism refers to the recombination of techniques associated with advanced liberalism with other elements. Collier cautions that we should not confuse situated clusters of neoliberal reason and techniques with "some mysterious neoliberal 'whole'" (96–100). Instead, we need an anthropological investigation of particular recombinations of the neoliberal with other elements in shaping emerging situations of power. For instance, it has been illuminating to consider how a neoliberal logic of "governing from a distance" (Rose 1999: 49–50) has been deployed in China's authoritarian context not to rollback the government, but as a rational calculation in order to optimize conditions for self-governing by the educated urban elites (Ong and Zhang 2008). The neoliberal is a new relationship between government and knowledge through which robust state interventions are cast as non-political technical solutions to a host of social problematizations. Neoliberal techniques in urban governance are, however, rather unevenly and differently deployed in South Asian situations.

Indian cities have been studied as hotbeds of the deep and simmering class struggles. Partha Chatterjee's (2006) identification of "the politics of the governed," and Arjun Appadurai's (2002) concept of "urban governmentality" differently register the proliferation of community-initiated activism and organizations in Indian cities. As broker politics flourish, subaltern groups gain power to negotiate with official agencies to improve urban services for the marginalized and neglected. It appears therefore that Indian urban politics are not limited to struggles against class oppressions and contestations centered on the state. What seems dramatically different than in other Asian contexts is that non-government organizations are more likely than government authorities to wield neoliberal rationalities in order to optimize desired outcomes.

In cities where the relative absence of effective government by default opens up a space for community activism, the challenge is to investigate how the neoliberal has been variously deployed to shape emerging sociality. New urban solidarities that tend to straddle class, city, and national divisions, and particular projects tend to depend on novel combinations of entrepreneurial and civic elements. For instance, Ananya Roy and Nezar AlSayyad (2004) have noted a new kind of "informal governance" in Middle Eastern and South Asian cities where cross-class entities have developed new norms and forms for governing people and the use of urban space. But while such initiatives may invoke democracy and human rights – say, on behalf of the welfare of the urban poor – these urban initiatives cannot be neatly understood as a victory for "neoliberal" rule or for civil society. Frequently, such strategic partnerships are linked to official interests and party machines (e.g., Hezbollah), and their interventions effect an informal extension of corporate interest or state power, shaping a mode of "civic governmentality" (Roy 2009). In other words, the symbiosis between neoliberal calculations and social activism engenders a complex urban scene of multiple motivations, coalitions and borrowings that both destabilize and form new configurations of urban society.

Under this section, chapters on South Asian urban politics highlight the frequent use of "world-class city" as a talisman to endorse varied kinds of partnerships, justify mega-projects, and denote the necessity of dislocating inconveniently sited poor residents, a common practice in many cities, but one with special resonance in South Asian initiatives to spark long-delayed urban renewal. In "Speculating on the Next World City," Michael Goldman analyses how a transnational policy network seeks to boost Bangalore, India's famous cybercity, to the next level of urban stratosphere. In the midst of official corruption and lack of political oversight, a transnational mode of "speculative governance" claims eminent domain to dispossesses rural populations of their means of livelihood. "World-city" is wielded to justify the conversion of surrounding peasant lands into sites for IT corridors and an international airport. Goldman concludes that in the race to catch up with Shanghai and Singapore, Bangalore has become a new speculative model that strips ordinary citizens of their human rights.

Next, Asher Ghertner examines the different uses of "world-class making" in efforts to reposition New Delhi as a cultural center. He argues that a form of aesthetic governmentality is at work whereby slums are considered a blight on the image of the capital, an assessment that justifies the clearance of slums even when it violates existing land-use and environmental codes. State-run slum surveys associate slum-dwellers lack of property-ownership with aesthetic impropriety, while presenting state-issued resettlement plots as a means to propertied and aesthetic citizenship. In challenging the new urban aesthetics, slum-dwellers creatively appropriate bourgeois norms of aesthetic valuation by producing poster art, a kind of street-level contribution to "world-class" claims of city elites. Ghertner argues that such strategic borrowings of elite ideals also embody a call for world-class services, employment, and rights that the state has yet to offer the urban poor, thereby undoing the tie between state-imposed "world-class aesthetic" and urban property-ownership.

Finally, Ananya Roy argues that the rise of India as an economic superpower in the "Asian century" is also a project of making "world-class cities." The increase in urban renewal projects, peri-urban development, and special economic zones are instantiations of a "homegrown neoliberalism," a kind of public–private intervention that actively references other Asian cities. For the emergent middle class, the new urban spaces represent a civic ideal of the good city, embodying the set of urban forms that is called "Global Indian." Unsurprisingly, goals to realize such "world-city aspirations" have required the violent exclusion, even criminalization, of the poor in the urban–rural peripheries. In Kolkata, the dislocations of rezoning have been blocked by a popular political opposition that mobilized the rural-to-urban poor. While this blockade may be read as a refusal of imposed urban projects, the abandoned factories, stalled condominium projects, and fleeing investors leave behind a blighted landscape that once again becomes the condition for renewed speculations and collaborations for achieving the Global Indian city.

By bringing together interdisciplinary perspectives, the chapters in this volume variously recast concepts and methods toward a genuinely globalized urban studies. Instead of viewing particular urban settings as merely specific instantiations of general capitalist mechanisms or postcolonial agency, the authors examine an array of initiatives – economic, political, and cultural – that variously engage urban challenges and visions of the world. Instead of universal forms of global economic or political integration, we discover how situated webs of interrelationships create highly differentiated contexts of urban transformation. Instead of seeing the city as a fixed space or node, we approach the metropolis as a milieu of experimentation where diverse actors and institutions invent and aspire to new ways of being global, and in doing so, recuperate the global not as the endpoint to an already given urban developmental process, but as a terrain of problematization. Instead of abstract hierarchies and typologies of cities and citizenship, we are open to the variety of ideas, idioms, methods, and solutions that political leaders, developers, citizens, workers, and slum-dwellers deploy in a global game of claiming the world's attention through the staging of showy architecture, cutting-edge industry, and homegrown urban aesthetics.

This art of being global ignores conventional borders of class, race, city, and country. There are promiscuous borrowings, shameless juxtapositions, and strategic enrollments of disparate ideas, actors, and practices from many sources circulating in the developing world, and beyond. We identify urban modeling, inter-referencing practices, and new solidarities as the flamboyant features of worlding cities in Asia. The ubiquity of urban modeling both in the planning imagination and in the built forms of emergent cities indexes the challenges of these cities not only to catch up with one another, but also to create new conceptions of achievable metropolitan standards for the developing world. The discourses that sustain this inter-referentiality shape an intense inter-city consciousness of contrast, comparison, and rivalry, as a well as an idiom that initiates and legitimizes the extravagant claims of mega urban makeovers. International ties and private–public partnerships are involved in building urban industries as well as shaping new modes of urban governance and sociality that are not deterred by preexisting social barriers. States and governments capitalize on the global circulation of ideas, objects, codes, and standards to engage in a spectrum of experiments that reinvent notions of urban modernity.

Urban exercises are practical and symbolic practices constituting the urban out of varied situated and global connections. They both depend on and contribute to emergent forms of spatialization that they seek to plot, transform, and achieve. Human action in the urban problem-space is of course subject to the vagaries of history, geography, and the play of the unexpected. The metropolis, we are reminded, is still a site of exception surrounded by vast hinterlands strewn with old administrative seats, ramshackle settlements of various kinds, and countless towns and villages retreating into invisibility. Skylines are rising in the East, projecting urban gestures of the moment that claim to characterize an emerging age. But it is in the midst of the precarious past and the unknown future that myriad human experiments draw on inter-city, inter-Asian, and global flows to shape fragile metropolitan futures.

References

Anderson, B. (1998) *The Specter of Comparisons: nationalism, Southeast Asia and the world.* London: Verso.

Appadurai, A. (2002) Deep democracy: urban governmentality and the horizon of politics. *Public Culture* 14(1), 21–47.

Bishop, R., Philips, J., and Yeo, W.W. (2003) Perpetuating cities: excepting globalization and the Southeast Asian supplement. In R. Bishop, J. Philips, and W.W. Yeo (eds.) *Postcolonial Urbanism: Southeast Asian cities and global processes.* London: Routledge, pp. 1–36.

Brenner, N. and Theodore, N. (2002) Cities and the geographies of "actually existing neoliberalism," in N. Brenner and N. Theodore, N. (eds.) *Spaces of Neoliberalism.* Oxford: Blackwell, pp. 2–32.

Caldeira, T. (2000) *City of Walls: crime, segregation and citizenship in São Paulo.* Berkeley, CA: University of California Press.

Caldeira, T. and Holston, J. (2005) State and urban space in Brazil: from modernist planning to democratic interventions. In A. Ong and S. Collier (eds.) *Global Assemblages: technology, politics, and ethics as anthropological problems.* Malden, MA: Blackwell, pp. 393–416.

Cartier, C. (2001) *Globalizing South China.* Oxford: Blackwell.

Chatterjee, P. (2006) *The Politics of the Governed.* New York: Columbia University Press.

Chua, B.H. (ed.) (2000) *Consumption in Asia: lifestyle and identity.* London: Routledge.

Collier, S.J. (2009) Topologies of power: Foucault's analysis of political government beyond "governmentality." *Theory, Culture and Society* 26(6), 100.

Collier, S.J. and Ong, A. (2005) Global assemblages, anthropological problems. In A. Ong and S. Collier (eds.) *Global Assemblages: technology, politics, and ethics as anthropological problems.* Malden, MA: Blackwell, pp. 3–21.

Davis, M. (2006) *Planet of Slums.* London: Verso.

Deleuze, G. and Guattari, F. (1987) *A Thousand Plateaus: capitalism and schizophrenia.* Minneapolis, MN: University of Minnesota Press.

Foucault, M. (1984) Polemics, politics, and problematization: an interview with Michel Foucault. In P. Rabinow (ed.) *The Foucault Reader.* New York: Pantheon Books, pp. 381–90.

Foucault, M. (2007) *Security, Territory, Population. Lectures at the College de France, 1977–1978,* ed. M. Senellart, trans. G. Burchell. New York: Palgrave Macmillan.

Graham, S. and Marvin, S. (2001) *Splintering Urbanism: networked infrastructures, technological mobilities, and the urban condition.* London: Routledge.

Haraway, D. (2008) *When Species Meet.* Minneapolis, MN: University of Minnesota Press, pp. 92–3.

Hardt, M. and Negri, A. (2000) *Empire.* Cambridge, MA: Harvard University Press.

Holston, J. (ed.) (1999) *Cities and Citizenship.* Durham, NC: Duke University Press.

Koolhaas, R. (1997) *Delirious New York: a retroactive manifesto.* New York: Monacelli.

Koolhaas, R. and OMA (2004) Beijing manifesto. *Wired* 08/2004, pp. 1, 122; http://www.wired.com/wired/archive/12.08/images/FF_120_beijing.pdf (accessed December 28, 2009).

Jacob, F. (1998) *Of Flies, Mice and Men: on the revolution in modern biology, by one of the scientists who helped make it,* trans. G. Wiess. Cambridge, MA: Harvard University Press, p. 9.

Latour, B. (2005) *Reassembling the Social: an introduction to actor–network theory.* Oxford: Oxford University Press.

Marayam, S. (2009) Introduction. In S. Marayam (ed.) *The Other Global City.* London: Routledge.

Marx, K. and Engels, F. (1848) The communist manifesto; http://www.marxists.org/archive/marx/works/1848/communist-manifesto/index.htm (accessed August 13, 2010).

Ong, A. (2005) Ecologies of expertise: assembling flows, managing citizenship. In A. Ong and S.J. Collier (eds.) *Global Assemblages: technology, politics, and ethics as anthropological problems.* Malden, MA: Blackwell, pp. 337–53.

Ong, A. (2006) *Neoliberalism as Exception: mutations in sovereignty and citizenship.* Durham, NC: Duke University Press.

Ong, A. (2007) Please stay: pied-a-terre subjects in the megacity. *Citizenship Studies* 11(1), 83–93.

Ong, A. and Collier, S.J. (eds.) (2005) *Global Assemblages: technology, politics, and ethics as anthropological problems.* Malden, MA: Blackwell.

Ong, A. and Zhang, L. (2008) Introduction: privatizing China: powers of the self, socialism from afar. In L. Zhang and A. Ong (eds.) *Privatizing China, Socialism from Afar.* Berkeley, CA: University of California Press, pp. 1–20.

Prakash, G. (2008) Mumbai: the modern city in ruins. In A. Huyssen (ed.) *Other Cities, Other Worlds.* Durham, NC: Duke University Press, pp. 181–206.

Pred, A. (1995) *Recognising European Modernities: a montage of the present.* London: Routledge.

Rabinow, P. (1991) *French Modern: norms and forms of the social environment.* Cambridge, MA: The MIT Press.

Rose, N. (1999) *Powers of Freedom: reframing political thought.* Cambridge, UK: Cambridge University Press.

Roy, A. (2009) Civic governmentality; the politics of inclusion in Beirut and Mumbai. *Antipode* 41(1), 159–79.

Roy, A. and Alsayyad, N. (eds.) (2004) *Urban Informality: transnational perspectives from the Middle East, Latin America, and South Asia.* Lanham, MD: Lexington Press.

Sassen, S. (2001 [1991]) *The Global City: New York, London, and Tokyo,* 2nd edn. Princeton, NJ: Princeton University Press.

Simone, A. (2008) The last shall be the first: African urbanites and the larger urban world. In A. Huyssen (ed.) *Other Cities, Other Worlds.* Durham, NC: Duke University Press, pp. 99–119.

Spivak, G.C. (1999) *A Critique of Postcolonial Reason*. Cambridge, MA: Harvard University Press.

Wall Street Journal (2009) World: quiet revolution. December 21, p. E6.

Wilson, R. (2004) Preface: worldings against empire – some tactics and challenges. In R. Wilson and D. Watson (eds.) *Worldings: world literature, field imaginaries, future practices – doing cultural studies during the era of globalization*, vol. 1. Santa Cruz, CA: New Pacific Press.

Part I
Modeling

1

Singapore as Model: Planning Innovations, Knowledge Experts

Chua Beng Huat

Introduction

In the short 50 years as an independent city-state-nation, after separation from Malaysia in 1965, Singapore has transformed itself from a declining trading post in the twilight of the British Empire to a First World economy. It would be too easy to dismiss this economic success due to its size; an entirely urban economy without the drag of a rural hinterland of poverty. However, smallness has its disadvantages. Completely devoid of all natural resources, including land and population, it is dependent on the global market for everything – capital, labor, materials, and food – to develop its domestic economy. Opening up to the world is therefore not a choice, but a necessity. Turning this necessity into an opportunity, Singapore is ever alert and receptive to the opportunities that are thrown up by the global economy, from its very founding in the early nineteenth century as a trading post to the contemporary phase of global capitalism. Economically, the world has always been the horizon of relevance for Singapore.

Singapore's economic success is also often dismissed as on account of its authoritarian political regime. The People's Action Party (PAP), under the first Prime Minister Lee Kuan Yew, had ruthlessly suppressed dissent and opposition in the decade and a half in its ascendancy to absolute political power. By the early 1970s, the Party had eliminated all effective political opposition and has since governed as a single-party dominant state without any effective opposition in Parliament. Over the years, it has also modified electoral rules and procedures which practically insure the Party's return to power in the five-yearly general elections (Chua 2007). Empirically, such absolute authoritarian regimes have a general tendency to lead to corruption

Worlding Cities: Asian Experiments and the Art of Being Global, First Edition.
Edited by Ananya Roy and Aihwa Ong.
© 2011 Blackwell Publishing Ltd. Published 2011 by Blackwell Publishing Ltd.

and economic disasters in much of the Third World. Against this general tendency, Singapore's economic success is all the more remarkable.[1] Undoubtedly, the absence of political opposition shields the government and the civil service from public pressures. However, instead of allowing this insulation to encourage corruption, the government has been able to mold the civil service and other statutory bodies into agencies of development, to capitalize on the stability provided by the unchanging regime to set and implement long-term plans without intermittent disruptions caused by changes in government, factors that have been fundamental to Singapore's economic success.

Global City

The history of Singapore's rapid industrialization began even before it became an independent nation. Firmly believing that an independent city-state economy would not be viable, the first-generation PAP leaders were counting on the Malaysian common market for the viability of its nascent industrialization in the early 1960s. Political separation from Malaysia, in 1965, disrupted this trajectory. Apropos the cliché that, in Chinese ideograms, "crisis is also an opportunity" (危机), the potentially dire economic consequences did in fact open up new perspectives and opportunities. First, the negative economic consequences were quickly transformed discursively into the rhetoric of struggle for "survival." To survive, Singapore needs an armed force of citizen-conscripts, racial harmony must prevail, and political differences and dissensions must be kept to the minimum and under control. But above all, economic growth must be promoted at all costs, including investments in human resource and infrastructure developments, creating a business- and tax-friendly environment to encourage foreign capital investment and establishing state enterprises where private capital fears to tread. "Survival" has thus provided the discursive and governance space for an interventionist or activist state that closely regulates Singaporean everyday life as part of the necessary condition for its highly entrepreneurial pursuit of national economic development, in step with the changing shape of global capitalism.[2] Since then, "to survive as a nation" in every sense of the word has become the national ideology, naturalizing the historical into both a motivational and a disciplinary framework for Singapore as a nation and individual Singaporeans.

Second, the loss of the desired Malaysian market led to a spatial and geographic reorientation: the entire "world" became imaginable as Singapore's "market." This imagination was felicitously made realizable through an export-oriented industrialization made available at that time by the new international division of labor. It is now a common refrain among ordinary Singaporeans that "the world is our hinterland." As an independent city-state or an island-nation among a world of nations, "the world" was brought into the visual horizon of its political leadership, causing the then Minister of Foreign Affairs to declare Singapore a "global city" (Rajaratnam 1972), two decades before the concept circulated in freely in urban discourse.

Success as Identity

After five decades of independence, by all conventional measures Singapore has been economically successful beyond anyone's imagination, including even its first generation of political leaders, who were arguably the engineers of this success. Across the entire population, everyday material life has improved massively and the educational attainment level has increased, while abject poverty and homelessness are uncommon. Amidst this, Singaporeans are also well aware of the many shortcomings of the long-governing, single-party dominant PAP government. The commonplace suggestion that they are "apathetic" to its undemocratic or anti-democratic ways is but a caricature of a people who are well informed about the excesses of the government.[3] However, along with the improvements in material life, they share the idea of being part of a "successful" nation, whose history is recent enough for everyone to feel a sense of achievement. Iconic achievements such as being rated the "best" airline and airport and the busiest port in the world, secondary school students being placed well in international mathematics or physics Olympiads or robotic competitions, and international awards for urban planning and public housing development all add up, finally, to a sense of arrival at a First World economy.

"Success" has entered the process of "self-scripting" of Singapore as a nation and of individual Singaporeans; the script is an open frame, with success as the key feature. At the national level, "success" as the defining feature of Singapore has already been in play since mid-1980s, scripted into the titles of two influential books. The first was a semiofficial history of Singapore from 1959 to 1984, entitled *Singapore: struggle for success* (Drysdale 1984). The second was an edited tome of more than 1,000 pages, entitled *Management of Success: the moulding of modern Singapore* (Sandhu and Wheatley 1989), assessing comprehensively the different aspects of Singapore's political, social, economic, and cultural developments. Reflective of the self-confidence that comes with the success, a sequel, *Management of Success: Singapore revisited*, was issued in 2010 (Chong 2010), to "critically" reassess the success story. This line of framing Singapore's development story, arguably, reaches its peak with Lee Kuan Yew's own memoirs, entitled *The Singapore Story: from Third World to First* (2000). Economic success has become the emblem of the nation.

Individual Singaporeans also frame their subject positions in terms of Singapore's success, apropos their social class positions. For example, in assessing their wage-earning position, working-class Singaporeans are comforted by the fact that within Southeast Asia, they are much better off than the rest. Middle-class professionals have been reluctant to take up regional postings because of the relatively "underdeveloped" conditions in these locations. In instances when they do seek employment abroad, they will actively market the fact that they are Singaporeans, carrying the label "Singapore" as a brand name that signifies success, with nationally inflected personal qualities of being hardworking, efficient, and effective; the Singapore brand undoubtedly improves their likelihood to be recruited. So too do Singaporean entrepreneurs who venture overseas carrying the Singapore "brand" with them, as a signifier of quality and reliability with financial integrity, meaning without corruption. "Success" as a source of pride has become part of the technologies of the Singaporean self and a constitutive element of the Singaporean identity.

Yet, "failure" haunts success. Fear of failure becomes a motivation for individuals to compete fiercely to maintain – better still to extend – their success. The same fear of failure keeps the government constantly in search of the next niche for development thrown up by shifts in global capitalism. Arguably, it needs to extend success for political legitimacy, as a common-place opinion is that economic success is the bargain that has been struck between the PAP government and the citizens of Singapore. Should the economy cease to grow or, worse, regress, PAP's legitimacy of absolute dominance in political power would be severely disrupted. This may explain the PAP government's addiction to growth, to limitless accumulation of wealth in national reserves which are invested globally for further accumulation.[4] Nevertheless, it is sufficiently confident of its path to success that the Singapore Civil Service College established, in 2003, a Civil Service College International (CSCI), as a consultancy with a mission "to share Singapore's experience in public reforms and good governance with governments around the world to promote good governance and generate goodwill and coopera-tion across international borders."[5]

This aspiration to share the Singapore experience may be said to have been derived from many instances in which Singaporean public policies and state entrepreneurial activities have been studied and copied by other governments. When Tony Blair was Prime Minister of the United Kingdom, he floated, as part of his "Third Way" reforms, the idea of considering Singapore's compulsory social security savings scheme, the Central Provident Fund (CPF), in lieu of a national pension, although the suggestion was subsequently dropped. In general, the CPF is a model of an individual private account pension savings system that the Bush government tried to introduce in the United States, to ameliorate the foreseeable pension fund crisis due to extended longevity. Singapore's electronic road pricing system that taxes vehicular entry into the city has also been studied by various global cities, including London, where a version of the system is in place, and New York, where a pricing system was proposed by the mayor but defeated. Admittedly, these false starts and failures in attempts to transplant and institute the urban traffic-control system and the CPF social security system into Western liberal democracies, a very different political and social environment from that of Singapore, show that lessons from Singapore cannot be readily copied. Nevertheless, given these and many other instances, one can suggest that the aspiration of the CSCI is not misplaced. As this chapter will demonstrate, the aspiration has been matched by the expressed desires and actual practices of many cities in Asia which evoke "Singapore as Model" for their own developments.

Singapore as Model

The case of Bangalore is illustrative. According to Bangalore's urban historian Janaki Nair, the then Chief Minister, Veerendra Patil, made "a strong plea for a fresh vertical orientation for the city after a visit to Singapore in 1970 ... since then, dreams of Singapore have dominated the vision of Bangalore's future" (Nair 2005: 124), the general argument being that, 'With imaginative planning and foresight, Bangalore can be developed as the Singapore of South India" (Nair 2005: 124). Nair suggests that Singapore "exerts a powerful hold on the imagination of town planner, CEO, politician, and citizen alike. The reasons are not hard to find. Singapore is an achievable ideal, a realizable utopia as the city-state shares the common legacy of colonial rule with Bangalore, is an Asian society with some common social features, and above all, has transformed its spatial and economic identity in less than 40 years" (2005: 124).

At a more expansive national level, political leaders no less than the late Deng Xiaoping, the man credited with the capitalist transformation of China, had instructed the massive Chinese state bureaucracy thus: "Singapore's social order is rather good. Its leaders exercise strict management. We should learn from their experiences, and we should do a better job than they do."[6] This general instruction has provided an ideological umbrella for practical appropriations of lessons from Singapore in economic, political, and urban planning, management and governance at different managerial and spatial levels, scales, and sites. These range from replicating the practices of "clean and green" in the city of Dalian, examined by Lisa Hoffman in this volume, to joint ventures between Chinese municipal enterprises and Singapore state-owned companies in developing comprehensive estates where the Singapore experience, knowledge, and practice of urban planning are directly applied, often with little modifications, as in the case of the Suchou Industrial Park[7] near Shanghai, in 1992, or the Sino-Tianjin Eco-City project, initiated in 2008, where Singapore's planning practices are being combined experimentally with new technologies of urban sustainability. The success of Suchou Industrial Park is such that, according to the current Singapore Prime Minister, Lee Hsien Loon, during his week-long tour of inland China in September 2010, in every city, "the local Chinese government leaders want an SIP-like park of their own" (Peh 2010). At the managerial level, municipal officers from China have been arriving in Singapore, since 1992, to attend a special program, dubbed "The Mayors' Class," to learn of Singapore's experiences and practices in city government, at the Centre for Public Administration, at the Nanyang Technological University,[8] and, finally, at the state level, there have been high-level exchanges between the PAP and the CCP in order to learn from each other (Goh 2009). The Chinese and Bangalore examples are illustrative of the fact that across Asia "Singapore as Model" for lessons of development has been deployed from the merely rhetorical to actual practices in planning and governance to the fantasized without any likelihood of realization – such as in the case of the recently independent but continuingly politically and economically unstable Timor Leste, at different scales in different locations.

Fragmenting Singapore into Discrete Lessons

Singapore's economic success is the result of a comprehensive package of inextricably linked ideological, political, and economic practices. There are a number of active ingredients. They include the Cold War historical context, which tolerated excesses of political repression in anti-communist authoritarian regimes around the world and thus enabled the PAP to emerge as a absolute power in a greatly modified "Westminster" parliamentary political system (Rodan 2005). The new international division of labor, that began in the early 1960s, provided the economic opportunities for Singapore, along with the other newly industrializing "Tiger" economies in East Asia, to industrialize rapidly by serving as a low labor cost production location for the global market (Rodan 1989), and, subsequently, to continually intensify capitalization of its industrial sector into ever-higher technology- and knowledge-based industries as opportunities and niches in the global economy became available, the most recent being biotechnology and pharmaceuticals. The long-governing authoritarian but financially incorrupt political leadership used its absolute power to fully own so-called natural monopolies and other major sectors of the domestic economy and, subsequently, to corporatize the successful state enterprises into publicly listed companies in which the government continues to hold the majority shares, under its sovereign wealth funds (Low 2002; Saw and Low, 2009: 12–16, 22–6). The government used its absolute power to enact draconian compulsory land acquisition legislation (Koh 1967) that "empowers" it to nationalize land at radically increased levels of discount compared with the prevailing land prices, so as to facilitate the production of affordable public housing at the national scale (Chua 1997) and the implementation of a comprehensively planned land, air, and sea transport infrastructure network – realized incrementally over decades, within the budgetary capacity of the public coffer (Chin and Fong 2006) – and in early 1990s, the information technology infrastructure (Neo and Soh 1993), which is still continuously being enhanced, to keep pace with technological developments. Finally, all these economy-driven developments, along with the expansion of education institutions at all levels, which is essential to culturally socialize the population into an productive workforce, are wrapped around an ideology of "vulnerability" and "survival" (Chan 1971), which generates an intense mass anxiety that acts as a "galvanizing" and motivating force to compete and succeed at both the individual level and as a people, a nation. According to George Yeo, Singapore's Minister of Foreign Affairs and current PAP ideologue, "Our success is the result of anxiety, and the anxiety is never fully assuaged by success."[9]

Taken as a whole, this constitutes an inextricably tied network of factors, each interacting with and contributing in complex manners to the history of Singapore's development; indeed, the multifarious ways in which these facts interact synchronously at any one time and diachronically across the past 50 years defy any linear description. Each of the factors developed historically and contingently, to cope with a given situation in which the new nation found itself, and continues to be modified to adjust to changing domestic and global economic and political conditions. The contingent character of Singapore's success is constantly highlighted in political rhetoric. For example, when asked about the "secret" of Singapore's success by students of the Skolkovo Moscow School of Management, Lee Kuan Yew had a single response: "Luck," followed by "personal drive" and "sincerity of purpose."[10] By this, he is referring to the common refrain that Singapore is a country that will not have a "second chance"; that if its leaders make a single serious mistake in policy decisions, the entire nation's economy could unravel quickly and precipitously. The contingency of success is ideologically used both to warn and to motivate Singaporeans not to take success for granted, as success gets incorporated into the Singaporean identity. Singapore and Singaporeans are to stay competitive permanently, as development is likened to an "unending marathon."

These historically contingent developments have been drawn together by the PAP to constitute a relatively coherent national history of its success.

However, this holistic history of Singapore's economic success is not useful to others precisely because of its uniqueness, a uniqueness that might be interesting but is largely irrelevant, because it is well nigh impossible to reproduce the exact historical conditions anywhere else. Therefore, "modeling" after Singapore cannot be a process of "cloning" Singapore elsewhere. It is inevitably a process of fragmentary borrowing, mimicking, replication, and other modes of emulation, in the form of "lessons" learned from Singapore's experiences and practices.

In modeling after Singapore, the entire Singapore story is disaggregated or disassembled into a set of analytically and heuristically unrelated discrete practices, and each can be independently abstracted as a formula for "best practice" that can be dispersed across space and time in Asia and beyond. Each of these unique practices can be extracted and reassembled, singularly or in different combinations, with or without modification, in completely new contexts. Correspondingly, with confidence fueled by the very fact that it is being studied and emulated, the Singapore government and its agencies are happy to oblige. They transform home-grown contingent efforts at nation-building into abstract, technical lessons of urban economic development that can be imparted transnationally, that can be exported as urban planning expertise and management know-how, either as goodwill in the form of international aid or as profit-driven commercial consultancies, to the emerging economies of Asia and elsewhere. Together, appropriation by others and exporting by Singapore constitute a dovetailing process that realizes Singapore as Model.

The new assemblages can range, in ascending degrees of comprehensiveness, from mechanically replicating Singapore by reproducing its monuments – such as the Merlion sculpture, an icon invented by the Singapore Tourist Board to make it easier for foreign tourists to remember Singapore and, at the extreme of absurdity, a replica of the statue of Stamford Raffles, the putative founder of Singapore as a free port, with his head replaced by a bust of Beethoven – in Citra Raya, a private housing estate in Surabaya, Indonesia (Idawati 2010), through the greening of Dalian city to the construction of the Suchou Industrial Park. At the ideational level, Singapore is evoked, in ascending order of abstraction and lack of realism, for political and ideological justification for comprehensive long-term planning and implementation of urban infrastructure in the case of Bangalore, where "unlike Singapore, [the field of power is] composed of a range of forces over which the state has but a tenuous hold (Nair 2005: 124; see also Michael Goldman, this volume) to the complete fantasy of development dreaming in the case of Timor Leste, in its current state of severe political and economic instability. In these latter instances, one could say that Singapore's success is more "referred," as conceptualized by Aihwa Ong in the introduction to this volume, for a sense of "possibility" by its admirers rather than "modeled."

In either mode of evoking "Singapore as Model," the application of bits and pieces of "lessons" from Singapore often generates unintended consequences, as analyzed in the rest of this chapter.

Industrialization and Migration

The Tiger economies, including Singapore, had entered export-oriented industrialization at a propitious time – in the 1960s – in which, to escape high labor costs at home, manufacturing enterprises from developed economies of the West and from Japan moved low-end manufacturing to low production cost, cheap labor locations abroad. Crucially, in Asia, at the time, three of the largest "reservoirs of labor" were not available for capitalist exploitation: the People's Republic of China (PRC) was a communist state in the throes of the Cultural Revolution; India had its own form of "socialism" of state enterprises and import substitution; and Indonesia was in the middle of the political instability of the post-1965 coup and massacre and, also, by the early 1970s, had come into oil wealth. Consequently, the Tiger economies had very little competition for foreign direct investments (FDI) for two decades. Had the three large labor pools come into competition for FDI then, the achievements of the Tiger economies would undoubtedly be much less impressive than they are today. Again, the contingency of development cannot be over-emphasized.

Specific to Singapore, keeping this historical context in view reduces the claim that economic success has been due entirely to the foresights and decisions of the first-generation PAP leaders, individually or as a team. As it was, from the early 1960s, foreign capital flowed in, transforming the trading economy into low-end industrial manufacturing, quickly mopping up unemployed Singaporeans; the unemployment rate declined steadily from 8.3% in 1966 to 3.9% in the mid-1970s (Krause, Koh, and Lee-Tsao 1987: 190). By the early 1970s, there was a labor shortage and female factory workers from the immediate neighbors, Malaysia and Thailand, filled the textile and consumer electronics factories. By early 1980s, it became obvious that with its small population, Singapore could not possibly compete, in the low-wage and low-skill economic sector, with developing Asian economies with a large surplus labor force. The government radically increased wages by more than 40 percent in the mid-1980s, forcing low-end, labor-intensive manufacturing industries to either move out or invest in higher technology to reduce labor input. After the 1997 Asian Financial Crisis, Singapore intensified the shift to "knowledge-based" industries, especially in the financial sector and in the biosciences and pharmaceuticals industries. By the end of the twentieth century, the major export sectors were highly capital-intensive, technologically advanced, and knowledge-based industries – petrochemicals, pharmaceuticals, electronics, transport and logistics, financial services, and water-management technologies – and, in 2010, Singapore emerged as the fourth financial center of the world, behind New York, London, and Hong Kong.[11]

At every step of these economic development strategies, the entrepreneurism of the Singapore state is unmistakable. In the 1960s, a large area of coastal swamp was drained to develop the first industrial zone, the Jurong Industrial Park. In the 1970s, the waterfront district, which has always been the commercial district, was reclaimed extensively to extend the banking and financial district; the area quickly came to be known as the Golden Shoe, because of its real-estate value (Chua 1989). In the early 1990s, a set of seven small islets to the south of the main island was amalgamated by reclamation at a cost of $4 billion, to constitute Jurong Island, to be completely dedicated to petrochemical industries; by 2003, it was producing $22 billion of products (*Economist* 2004). Finally, the water-body at the mouth of the Singapore River has been reshaped as a bay through reclamation, with the reclaimed land being developed into a mixed-use district of offices, high-end condominiums, and arts and entertainment establishments, containing the iconic Esplanade Theatre on the Bay and the Sands casino and resort, and the shores of the bay reserved as public recreational areas – as are all coastlines on the island, except where taken up by port facilities. The Singapore River, polluted by decades of human settlement and the cottage industries on both sides of its banks, was subjected to a 10-year clean-up program and recovered to a gleaming pristine condition (Hon 1990).

All these highly valuable land reclamation projects have been financed completely by the state, without any dependency on private capital that might impede progress. Parcels of land are leased, by open tender, to carefully selected industrial players, who are often directly invited by the government, often as partners with state-linked companies. The Economic Development Board (EDB) has been the appointed agency, from the very beginning, to market these land parcels to potential multinational investors. The success of the EDB is often written up in hyperbolic language. Its former Chairman, Philip Yeo, has assumed "mythological" status for not only developing Jurong Island but also, since his appointment in 2001 as Chairman of the Agency for Science and Research (A*), for being credited with single-handedly developing the biotechnology industries; between 2000 and 2005, biomedical manufacturing sector output quadrupled from S$6 billion to S$23 billion, accounting for 5 percent of GDP. For his public service, Philip Yeo was decorated, in 2006, with the Order of Nila Utama (First Class), a national recognition of the highest order.

In each phase of this economic development over the past five decades, an adequate labor supply has been a constant problem. As mentioned above, by the early 1970s, barely a decade after the industrialization program had begun, there was already a shortage of labor. Since then, it has become an endemic problem. Given the increasingly complex economy, Singapore is now in permanent competition with other developed economies for "talents." This has spawned an aggressive immigration program to attract high-end educated labor to Singapore, euphemized as "foreign talent."[12] Unlike the unskilled or semiskilled contract workers – domestic maids, office cleaners, waiters and waitresses, and construction, shipyard, and other heavy industrial workers – who must be repatriated by their employers when the contract ends, the "foreign talents" population can be divided into two groups. At the lower end are predominantly educated middle-class immigrants from elsewhere in Asia, currently mostly from Malaysia, India, and the PRC; they might use Singapore as a stepping stone to a third country in the West or stay and become naturalized citizens. At the high end is a "flow-through" population of the globally mobile top professionals, including research scientists, and very senior managers of multinational companies, including Singapore state enterprises. These globally mobile individuals add value to their respective local industries during their few years of sojourn, even if Singapore is unable to hold onto them permanently. For example, the short-term tenure of bioresearch scientists since 2000 has been absolutely necessary to get the biosciences industrial sector off the ground and running.

The immigration policy goes beyond simply importing ready-made talents. Education policy is also used to provide scholarships for all level of education, from secondary schools to PhD scholarships to high-potential students from all over Asia. At the secondary and undergraduate levels, the ASEAN scholarships bring in high-achieving students from the region, and provide them with free education in exchange for their staying on in Singapore for two years of employment before returning home; many of these students remain in Singapore after graduation, as employment opportunities at home are likely to be no longer commensurate with their academic qualifications. At the postgraduate level, potential PhD candidates are asked to take up citizenship as part of the scholarship, in order to study in the premiere universities of the world. The biosciences industrial sphere is being staffed significantly by such recruits. The A* scholarship has become the most coveted scholarship among local and foreign students.

The aggressiveness of the immigration program is reflected in the population figures; the Singapore population has grown by 1.5 million in a decade, reaching 5 million in the 2010 census, of which more than one third are foreigners. The ubiquity of both high-end and low-end foreign workers has given rise to public debates. Unskilled migrant workers who are able to work for low wages because all their routine maintenance costs are borne by the employers have depressed wages and share the employment opportunities of low-income Singaporeans; the ready availability of such workers is indicative of their abundance in Asia, which the government reads as a competitive threat – thus the government has resisted the institution of a minimum wage (Abdul Rahim 2010). With regard to the "foreign talent" spectrum, the middle class, especially new entrants to the workforce, sense that they are not being trained on the job for greater responsibility and higher wages because of the readiness and ease with which companies can import employees who can take up a position immediately.

These employment-related resentments and the heavy pressure that the increased population places on public transportation, public health facilities, schools, and housing prices have roused the generally politically inactive Singaporeans to be vocal about their unhappiness. The government has responded by radically reducing the intake of permanent residents in 2010, the year it began to prepare for the 2011 general election; the intake of permanent residents dropped to less than 5 percent, from a high of more than 15 percent the previous year. Nevertheless, this is merely a slowdown, and not a shutdown, of the immigration program. Convinced that 6.5 million people are needed for sustainable economic growth, the government is determined to maintain the immigrant intake until the target population size is reached. It is prepared to face the potential political cost in its unwavering belief that the unpopularity of its decisions has always been short-lived, because they prove to be the "right" decisions in delivering economic growth, and that the current immigration policy should be no exception.[13]

In Singapore, as in other nations, the industrial and immigration policies and their implementation are decisions taken at nation-state level, beyond the powers of municipal or even provincial governments and administrations. In these macro-decisions, in Singapore as a city-state, it is the "state" that needs to be emphasized rather than the "city." No city, as a small part of a larger province and of an even larger nation, has absolute control over its territorial boundaries and the flow of population into it, as a state does. No city is permitted to monopolize major business sectors, so as to build up a huge capital base as financial resources to develop independently its own, self-contained physical infrastructure. Nor would a city be permitted by the nation-state government to define its own population policies, which include controlling inflows and outflows of immigrants. In exercising complete control over such policies, the Singapore government is acting as a state; in this sense, we should address Singapore as an "island-nation," with a single-tier state government that is well insulated from the conflicting pressures of multiple levels of city, province, and state governments and administrations, to avoid conceptual confusion caused by the concept of the "city-state."

Given the absence of control, discourses and practices of modeling after Singapore by another city inevitably misrecognize the former's success as the achievements of a "city" rather than those of a "nation." Without the power-monopolizing capacity of the state to develop in a coordinated manner, modeling after Singapore by other cities seems, unavoidably, to take the form of a generalized "referencing" to Singapore's success story, while in practice only taking away fragments of the integrated developments of Singapore as an island-nation, to be "replicated" locally. This often produces untoward rather than intended desired consequences. For example, as Michael Goldman shows in this volume, the infrastructure development of Bangalore, whose mayors and urban planners are wont to cite Singapore as Model, is largely that of a single corridor strip between the city and Mysore. Furthermore, without the financial resources for even the development of this corridor, the state government only assisted in the destruction of existing settlements through enforced land acquisition, creating opportunities for private investors to speculate on transforming the acquired agricultural lands into real-estate properties for the rising middle class.

Another example is the city of Shenzhen, in Guangdong, southern China. By the late 1980s, export-oriented industrialization had become the model for other developing countries around the world; in particular, China quickly became the "factory for the world." Cities such as Shenzhen were readily able to follow Singapore's early strategy in developing low-cost, export-oriented industries, initially financed by foreign investment capital from the Chinese diasporas in Hong Kong and Taiwan and, subsequently, by foreign capital from beyond the ethnic connections (Ye 2010). However, after more than two decades of rapid development of low-wage manufacturing industries that supply global brands, in May 2010, workers in Shenzhen went on mass strikes to demand higher wages and better working conditions after a string of suicides among the young workers at the Taiwan-owned electronics factory, Foxconn. The success of the workers in securing a significant hike in their monthly wage encouraged similarly poorly paid industrial workers to down their tools, and walk out of the factories to demand higher wages.

Shenzhen, like many other cities elsewhere in Asia – for example, South Asian cities with low-wage textile manufacturing – is apparently unable to escape from the trap of low-wage industrialization and move up the technological ladder, as Singapore has done with relative ease. This is partly because Shenzhen draws its low-wage workers from the rural areas of the country, where the supply of rural–urban migrant workers seems inexhaustible, which enables employers to depress the wage level. Second, the migrant workers are citizens of the Chinese state, although they might not be in Shenzhen legally according to the citizen registration system, rendering it difficult for the municipal government to discipline them without the risk of intensifying social unrest. This is in diametrical contrast with Singapore, where a very significant proportion of the industrial workers are foreign migrant labor who can be augmented or repatriated according to the demands of the economy, without any domestic political repercussions. This is again a result of the absence of the power of the municipal government to control the flow of migrants into the city. The relative permanence of the low-end migrant workers, in the face of Shenzhen's booming economy and a rising middle class, is reflected in the incident recalled by Ananya Roy in her closing chapter in this volume. During a press conference between a group of urbanists who were in Shenzhen for an international conference and a group of local reporters, an urban geographer from Singapore, Brenda Yeoh, "asked the reporters what they saw as the symbol of Shenzhen. Their answer, put forward without hesitation: the migrant worker." While, as Roy observes, this answer might have been influenced by the fact that "a few days ago *Time* magazine had named 'The Chinese Worker', specifically Shenzhen's migrant workers, as one of 2009's 4 'runners-up' for People of the Year," it is nevertheless not without empirical reality.

From Garden City to City in a Garden

An immediate impression for a first-time visitor to Singapore is its "orderliness," "efficiency," "cleanliness," and "greenness" as a city. Physically, the orderly efficiency is a result of a rigorously implemented master plan that remains largely unchanged, with periodic updating and detailing in actual developments. In early 1970s, a British colonial master plan that divided the island into urban, suburban, and rural belts was discarded. With the advice of a UN planning team, the government adopted a plan which conceptualized the entire island as one single planning and functioning entity. Initially, a "ring" of residential housing estates was to be developed around the water-catchment area of three reservoirs in the center of the island. A large area to the west was designated as the Jurong Industrial Estate, and the Changi International Airport was constructed at the eastern end of the island (Chua 1997: 27–50). Housing estates, light industrial facilities, and all the other land uses would fill up the interstitial spaces over time. An integrated road and mass rapid transit network was to eventually link all the functional districts, integrating the entire island into one functional unit. In general, this broad outline of the planned island has been maintained.[14]

In this total physical transformation of the city according to a single master plan, the first Prime Minister, Lee Kuan Yew, has claimed the credit for being the instigator of the idea of Singapore as a "garden city," as an environment that is conducive to attracting foreign capital and workers; an "oasis" of respite for the multinational managers who must venture regularly into the chaotic environment in the region. The prescience of this idea is attested to by the choice of Singapore as a regional headquarters for multinational enterprises. Assisted greatly by the tropical climate, in which plants grow readily, the economic motive behind the greening of the city is translated into a drive to "beautify" the city, with the National Parks Board importing flowering plants that will flourish in the local climate, from anywhere in the world. Conservation of local plant species takes a back seat to the ornamental decoration of the island.

The greenness humanizes the city. Visually, at ground level, the canopies of leaves reduce the height of the city, veiling the monotony of the concrete high-rise public housing blocks in which 90 percent of the island's population resides, and the steel-and-glass jungle of the office buildings and shopping complexes, where air-conditioning enables long hours of work and leisure, respectively.[15] Greening thus softens the harshness of the high-rise city, an unavoidable consequence of land scarcity; the trees reduce the city to a human scale. The canopies of leaves also shelter the streets from the sun, allowing the pedestrianization of the sidewalks throughout the city, in the tropical heat. Greening thus contributes greatly to the visual and livable qualities of the city – qualities increasingly recognized by cities around the world. Inspired by such recognition and, perhaps, by the intensification of "green" politics globally, in early 2000 the Urban Redevelopment Authority re-designated Singapore as a City-in-a-Garden, apparently reversing the equation between nature and the human-made environment. Alas, "nature" has not been allowed to run rampant.[16] The change of slogan from "garden city" to "city in a garden" is no more than an empty gesture, with limited symbolic value.[17]

The systematic cultivation of a green environment integrated into a totalizing city-state plan has inspired cities in Asia and beyond to develop their own "garden city" plans. For example, Dalian, a northern Chinese city, has not only drawn on Singapore as a model to undertake "greening," but has also adopted similar strategies in cleaning up the environment and transforming the city. According to Lisa Hoffman (this volume), "The city's policies of cleaning up industrial pollution, moving industrial facilities from the city center, opening up the seashore for recreational uses, and increasing the per capita green space also have garnered the attention of multinational businesses." She argues that the ability of the mayor to transform the city has been crucially supported by the central government, which declared Dalian itself as a "Model City of State Environmental Protection," giving him the power and authority to execute a comprehensive plan – executive power equivalent to that of the state, as in Singapore.

The National Public Housing Program

On an equally ambitious scale as the greening of Singapore is the national public housing program. In 1961, the two-year-old PAP government established the Housing and Development Board (HDB), as improving housing conditions was a covenant between the new government and the newly enfranchised citizen-electorate. The HDB began with providing very basic, one-room rental flats. However, within three years the government had instituted a home-ownership program which enables residents to own a 99-year lease on their HDB flats. In 1968, Singaporeans were allowed to use their social security savings, known as the Central Provident Fund (CPF), to purchase public housing.[18] It works thus: an employee is compelled by law to save a portion of the monthly wage, with proportionate contributions from the employer, as his/her CPF; the employee buys a 99-year lease on a public housing flat, using his/her CPF for the initial down-payment and monthly mortgage; and the fund is then transferred by the CPF Board to the HDB, which holds the mortgage. The transaction cost is minimal because interest on the mortgage is set at half-a-percent higher than the interest that is paid to the CPF savings. The entire closed-circuit transaction does not involve any commercial financial institutions. By the late 1980s, 90 percent of Singaporeans and permanent residents were living in HDB flats. The remaining 10 percent has been excluded from public subsidized housing on account of their high monthly household incomes or their personal preference to live in exclusive private housing. In practice, home-ownership in Singapore is now universal except for the bottom 10 percent of the income strata, who live in small public rental flats of one or two rooms. The government continues to devise new subsidy schemes to try to transform this bottom 10 percent into homeowners, for both economic and ideological reasons.

As mentioned earlier, this "universal" provision of public housing has been made possible by the nationalization of land – with very draconian land acquisition laws, offering excessively low compensation for the land-lords – from the early 1960s to the early 1990s, when the government started to pay the prevailing market value for acquired land. Fully aware that this violated the common understanding of property rights, the HDB's official stance was, "The government saw no reason why these owners should enjoy the greatly enhanced land values over the years without any effort put in by them" (Wong and Yeh 1985: 41). It counseled the landown-ers to see this as their contribution to the welfare of society. One might say that public housing is Singapore's mode of land reform and redistribution.

Compulsory acquisition of land affects more than just landlords. It always involves destruction of existing settlements and the displacement of their inhabitants. In contrast to common scenarios of displaced people being left homeless by developers or government agencies, the displacement and reset-tlement process in Singapore has always been handled with care. A survey of the settlement to be resettled is made to establish the number of affected households, including their business and agricultural activities, if any. No new households will be registered for resettlement after the survey. Resettlement will not begin until the replacement public housing flats for the affected households are ready. The compensation will factor in the size of the dismantled house and every productive aspect of the dwelling; new factory premises will be rented to those with cottage industries, and shop-houses to retailers, and there will be cash compensation for animals and fruit trees owned by semirural village households. Large extended families that cannot fit into a single flat will be allocated as many flats as there are nuclear families within them. No one will be made homeless by the resettlement.

The national home-ownership program has consequences beyond the housing sphere. It contributes to transforming and disciplining the population into an industrial labor force, as the monthly mortgage payment with the CPF can be maintained only by employment that offers a regular income. Home-ownership has enabled Singaporean households to build up a valuable asset that can be sold to realize capital or rented out for a source of steady income; this is especially important for retirees, as there is no national pension for the aged. Such vested economic interests, or what the PAP called a "stake" in the country, renders Singaporeans politically conservative and in support of the status quo, the continuity of PAP rule being seen as a guarantee of the preservation of property investment (Chua 2000). Finally, home-ownership provides the PAP with a high degree of political legitimacy, which contributes to its popular vote base during general elections (Chua 1997). With universal state provision, property ownership has been "democratized," leading the PAP government to pronounce Singapore "a home-owning democracy."[19]

Housing Estate Planning and Allocation

As practically the monopoly supplier of housing to the nation, the HDB is able to develop comprehensively planned housing estates along both pragmatic and ideological lines. Each new town, optimally of 250,000 households, is planned to be self-sufficient in meeting the daily needs of the residents. A town center houses a transportation interchange for buses and mass rapid transit trains; and a shopping center, usually with a supermarket, a department store, and, often, a Cineplex as anchor tenants. All the necessities of everyday life are thus available in the town center. Primary and secondary schools are located within neighborhoods. Every ten to twelve blocks of flats shares a "neighborhood center" within a twenty minute walking distance, where a fresh produce market and a cooked-food center and lower-order goods and services, from convenience stores and hair saloons to medical clinics, can be found. The cooked-food center has become a convenient substitute for home-cooking, particularly for dual-income families without children. Land is allocated for places of worship for all the major religions. In short, there is no need for any resident to leave the new town except to work and, occasionally, for high-value goods shopping in the city.

Many social policies are built into the planning and allocation processes of the public housing program. The blocks of rental flats that house the lowest 10 percent income households are placed alongside blocks of sold flats, without singling out and thus stigmatizing the lower-income house-holds. The visibility of income inequalities and poverty is thus radically reduced. Pro-family social policies are built into the allocation process; for example, cash grants are given to married children who choose to live near their parents. Race relations too are managed throughout the allocation process. The quotas for different "racial" groups – *Huaren*,[20] Malays, and Indians – approximately proportional to their presence in the national population, are maintained at every block of flats to avoid racial territorial concentrations and the formation of enclaves, purportedly to reduce the potential of racial violence.[21] Finally, homelessness, a visual manifestation of poverty, is a very rare sight anywhere. Whenever an instance of homeless-ness is reported in the media, the HDB will readily rent a flat to the family before it becomes a symbol of its failure to maintain its duty to provide for all citizens. A combination of planning and social policy has thus produced physical if not social integration of family, race, and class. The overall image of a HDB new town is one of "inclusiveness," of multiracial integration and harmony.

This projected "inclusiveness" hides the real hardship among the poorest 10 percent of the population. The loneliness and ill health of the aged living alone, and the hunger of children with single low-income parents and in the families of the working poor, are only "visible" due to the fact that there are 1,800 voluntary welfare organizations catering to more than 100,000 families who are in need of some form of charity. They are poorly served by a very rich state, with a massive foreign reserve locked up in sovereign wealth funds, which relentlessly eschews redistributive social welfare because the government insists that redistributive welfare destroys the work ethic amongst its people. As income inequalities intensify in train with globalization (the Gini coefficient is currently around 0.52, the worst in Asia and only second to the United States in a global comparison), the position of the poor has become more desperate, forcing the government to institute some distribu-tive schemes, including income top-ups for the very low income earners, while continuing its resistance to any system of social insurance schemes, as it points to the financial and operational difficulties of these schemes in European societies, especially the ballooning healthcare costs and the insolvency of public pension systems. The visual homogeneity of the physical environment of public housing estates thus hides the exclusion of the socially and economically disadvantaged Singaporeans who are the "collateral failures" of rapid capitalist economic development.

It should be obvious that every aspect of Singapore's national public housing program is inextricably tied to the political considerations of the single-party dominant government/state, whose longevity in holding onto parliamentary power depends crucially on its ability to improve incrementally, but continually, the living conditions, including housing, of the electorate. Ironically, in this aspect, the less than democratic single-party state appears not only more efficient but also more responsible to the basic needs of the entire population than a liberal democratic state. In Singapore, therefore, public housing is in every aspect a political good, beyond simply physical shelter.

The highly visible self-sufficient, high-density housing estates are a signal achievement of the PAP government. Every important visiting foreign head of government, from the UK's Queen Elizabeth to the late Deng Xiaoping of China, will be given a briefing about the planning process, a tour of one of the new towns, and an outing to some of the households. And the Singapore system never fails to impress. The political returns of a universal housing program are not lost on the visiting political leaders, who are all too conscious of their failures to provide universal housing for their respective populations. However, while the desire to "replicate" such a national program in their own countries is understandable, such a comprehensive national housing program has yet to be replicated anywhere in the world. As Janaki Nair writes with reference to Bangalore, "Singapore, as an ideal of city development, has thus inspired dreams of large scale infrastructural projects, rather than the more innovative public housing schemes that mobilized public (provident) funds for construction on a heroic scale" (2005: 336).

Exporting Urban Planning Expertise

However, the inability to mount a comparable national public housing program has not prevented the urban planning and implementation of high-rise housing estates from being carried out in Asian cities with rising middle classes and aspirations to be like "modern Singapore." Convinced that the Singapore urban planning guidelines and parameters "work," self-assured Singaporean government-owned and private architectural and planning consultancies have been marketing their expertise in environmental and infrastructure planning, and implementation of urban industrial parks and residential estates, to the world. In contrast to the traffic gridlocks, pollution, and generally unkempt environment of cities in developing, and even developed, nations, the orderliness, cleanliness, and efficiency of traffic movements may seem to Singaporeans and others prima facie evidence of Singapore's planning success. This self-confidence has been further reinforced by the energy efficiency of compact residential developments in view of the global depletion of fossil fuels and the deteriorating physical environment due to carbon pollution. So convinced of this compact mode of development is Singapore that its theme for the 2010 Venice architectural biennale was "*1000 Singapores*," imagining the entire world population of 6.5 billion living and working in 1,000 Singapore-size islands, as a solution to global sustainability. In the hands of the consultancies, the context and effects of the comprehensive planning of Singapore as one political, economic, and social unit are cast aside. The contextually and contingently determined urban and housing planning principles and guidelines are abstracted into formulas that can be applied transnationally everywhere, including Asia.

Two of the government-owned planning consultancy firms are notable. Surbana[22] is a subsidiary of the Housing and Development Board, the public housing authority, and Jurong International is an outgrowth of the Jurong Town Corporation, the company that was responsible for the implementation of Singapore's industrial estates. The metamorphosis of the functional state agencies into international infrastructure planning and engineering consultancies is obviously a result of confidence and knowledge gained in their success at home. Jurong International specializes in the development of industrial parks; as of 2008, it had a "project presence spanning 139 cities across 37 countries [almost exclusively in Asia, Middle East and Africa], amassing more than 1000 projects worldwide and counting."[23] Surbana has projects in the following countries: the People's Republic of China (PRC), India, Vietnam, Indonesia, Malaysia, Philippines, Qatar, the United Arab Emirates (UAE), and South Africa. It provides the entire range of urban physical development services: master planning, concept planning, infrastructural planning, architectural designs, mechanical and electrical engineering, and civil and structural engineering consultancies. The size of the projects ranges from reconceptualizing entire city districts, as in Doha, Qatar, to residential estates, and to single institutional buildings. This list of projects testifies to the recognition of Singapore's expertise by other governments and international private corporations. In addition to consultancies, Singapore's government-linked corporations (GLCs) have been invited to develop jointly industrial parks in different parts of Asia; such as in the Batam and Bintang Islands, Indonesia, Bangalore, and Vietnam, and the above-mentioned Souchou Industrial Park and Tianjin Eco-City in China. In all these projects, from master plans to industrial park developments, Singapore's planning guidelines are obviously followed; anyone who is familiar with Singapore's industrial parks and public housing estates will instantly see their replication in the Souchou Industrial Park.

Significantly, something happens in this transfer of knowledge and practice of urban planning from Singapore to other locations. In many instances, the Singapore model is evoked by private developers to rope in the government to alienate large tracts of land, including using its power to displace existing settlements, with the promise of developing Singapore-style comprehensive developments. The private developers subsequently turn the land into speculative property developments; Michael Goldman (this volume) provides vivid examples of what he calls "speculative urbanism" at the hands of the Indian-grown multinational technology companies in Bangalore. In other instances, the acquisition of land runs into severe resistance which completely blocks the way to development. Gavin Shatkin (this volume) documents the example of the failed attempt by the West Bengal communist state government to clear local settlements of urban poor and villagers, near Kolkata, to make way, ostensibly, for an automobile factory, but with enough land in reserve for subsequent real-estate development.

Where the Singapore residential planning model has been relatively successfully adopted, as in the high-rise housing estates developed by Singaporean or local developers in China and Vietnam, or the above-mentioned specific case of Citra Raya in Surabaya, Indonesia, a socially and politically consequential irony arises: "democratization" of home-ownership through public housing in Singapore is transformed into the privileging of real-estate investment for the wealthy elsewhere. The visual "homogenization" of the everyday lives of all citizens/residents, through the physical integration of family, class, and race in housing blocks, is transformed into the visual accentuation of segregation, and exclusion of the privileged class into the planned and gated estates. Without a politically motivated national housing program that universalizes housing provision and redistributes and equalizes services for all citizens, the application of lessons from Singapore results in the construction of upper-income privileged enclaves. In its transnational travel, the housing estate planning processes that contribute to national inclusiveness and integration in Singapore are transformed, ideologically and materially, into processes of privileging the wealthy and exclusion of the rest in rapidly developing economies and societies. Ironically, an instance that recalls the humble beginnings of Singapore's national public housing program of small rental flats – one that befits its then developing economic conditions – is registered halfway around the world from Asia, in Cingapura, a slum redevelopment project in São Paulo, Brazil, documented by Ananya Roy in her closing chapter.

Conclusion

In a short span of about 50 years, Singapore has transformed itself economically into a First World economy. This is the result of very conscious public policies that keep both local and global horizons in view. It is the result of a very active interventionist state that has implemented long-term urban development plans and a national public housing program at the center of social policies. It is the result, also, of an economically entrepreneurial state that adopts new growth industries as quickly as it discards those that have served their usefulness, and have become a drag on the twin economic necessities of moving up the technological ladder and in intensifying capital. The interventionist and entrepreneurial state is embedded in a hegemonic single-party dominant polity which, insulated from popular political pressures, is able to implement long-term development plans while remaining agile in order to make appropriate changes when necessary. The aim, since political independence in 1965, has been to be a global city, to move from the Third World to the First. In this, the perception of others matches Singaporean self-perception and self-projection: "Singapore, a successful nation."

Given its success, Singapore has been deemed worthy by many as a "model." However, the ideological consensus generated by a common apprehension toward collective "survival" as an island-nation that sustains an competent, efficient, financially non-corrupt, less-than-democratic, party-state is the open secret of Singapore's success – one that is not replicable. "Singapore as Model" cannot be and is not a desire for mimicry, for cloning. No doubt, as demonstrated above, a singular fragment – or a combination of several fragments – of the Singapore development journey and practices can be studied and assembled and inserted into new contexts, even if the results are, for various reasons, seldom without some slippage from the imagined or desired. More important, Singapore as Model is one of aspiration to a possibility, a possibility to be successful, just as Singapore has been successful. It is one of, "if Singapore can do it, so should we be able." This, indeed, seems to be the attitude of China, which shares some common political and cultural attributes with Singapore. According to George Yeo, Singapore's current Minister of Foreign Affairs, "from time to time, researchers and social scientists in China, they study Singapore and say, 'Oh well, if it can work here, maybe it can work there ... their interest in the Singapore experiment is episodic. From time to time when it confronts issues and it scours the world for solutions, it looks at what Singapore does. Sometimes it likes what it sees, sometimes it does not like what it sees. And then it draws and abstracts the relevant lessons. This of course puts Singapore in a rather interesting position *vis-à-vis* China."[24] One can imagine that the Minister says this with some satisfaction, because the largest nation in Asia, a rising global power, is studying the smallest one in Asia, and one that was thought, by most, unlikely to succeed.

Notes

1 Details of every maneuver and strategy, both political and economic, of the PAP government are readily available in the by now very extensive literature on Singapore. A list of selective references could include Chan (1971), Devan Nair (1976), Drysdale

(1984), Rodan (1989), Sandhu and Wheatley (1989), Chua (1995), Tremewan (1994), and Mauzy and Milne (2002).

2 The ideology of survival is more fully developed in Chan (1971).

3 For discussions of both the excesses of the government and citizens' consciousness of them, see Yao (2007).

4 Significantly, in contrast to past practices of his father, who insisted on locking up all the profits from global investments in the sovereign wealth funds, the present Prime Minister, Lee Hsien Loong, has amended the constitution to have half of the annual profits, including capital gains, transferred into the annual operating budget of the government of the day.

5 For more information about the CSCI, visit the Public Service Division, Singapore web site (www.psd.gov.sg/).

6 See http://www.nytimes.com/1992/08/09/weekinreview/the-world-china-sees-singapore-as-a-model-for-progress.html

7 For a detailed analysis of this industrial park, see Pereira (2003).

8 According to the Centre's website, "To date [December 2009], the two programmes have benefited 765 senior and middle-ranking Chinese officials from diverse provinces and cities across China, enhancing their effectiveness as public administrators, and enabling them to apply best practices to bring about positive transformation in China. These two programmes start with improving the participants' skills and leadership ability in management, while incorporating into the curriculum the successful experiences that Singapore has in public and economic administration."

9 George Yeo, cited in Kraar and Lee Kuan Yew (2010).

10 See the *Straits Times*, September 20, 2010.

11 See the *Straits Times*, October 21, 2010.

12 For discussion on the expansion of biosciences research and enterprises in Singapore and its effects on the politics of citizenship, see Ong (2005). There was a brief discussion in Ong's essay on Johns Hopkins University's place in biosciences in Singapore. Since 2007, the provision of biosciences training has ceased due to contractual disagreements between the university and the leading Singapore government granting agency, the Agency for Scientific and Technology and Research (A*STAR). See http/www.singstats.gov.sg/stats/themes/people/popindicators.pdf (accessed October 14, 2008).

13 This relatively open immigration policy is in radical contrast with elsewhere in Asia, which remains largely resistant to immigration because, first, underdeveloped Asian countries have a large surplus of underemployed domestic labor and, second, in developed countries such as South Korea and Japan, with a relatively homogenous society, racism and nationalism prevent them opening up to new immigrants, despite below-replacement birth rates and a rapidly ageing population.

14 See the 2001 Concept Plan, Urban Redevelopment Authority, Singapore.

15 When asked what the most important invention of the twentieth century is, Lee Kuan Yew answered that it is air-conditioning, because without that Singapore would be left in tropical stupor rather than achieving its current economic success; see George (2000).

16 Interestingly, when the producers of the Singaporean film *Return to Pontianak* – Pontianak being both the name of a town in Indonesia and of a female Malay ghost – were looking for a location with a lush tropical green forest as the setting for

the home of the ghost, they had to go to Johor, the southernmost province of neighboring Malaysia (Harvey 2008).

17 So far, the only visible act is the ongoing construction of a "temperate" botanic garden, to be housed in an air-conditioned greenhouse by the bay in the city center. Perhaps, is this a postcolonial fantasy of reversing the British practice of developing tropical plants in cold Britain?

18 Space does not allow detailed discussion on the CPF scheme. Suffice it to say that for most HDB households, the deduction from the wages plus the employer's compulsory contribution monthly for the social security savings exceeds the monthly mortgage payment needed on the flat; hence, ownership comes with no reduction in the monthly disposable income which would affect consumption in daily life. For details on the CPF, see Low and Aw (1997). What is also important is that the CPF is a source of capital for the government GIC; see Asher and Nandy (2008).

19 As the monopoly supplier of housing, the government is constantly monitoring the prices of public housing properties and regularly intervenes to either stimulate the market or dampen the market as the domestic economic conditions dictate.

20 "Race" rather than the less stigmatizing "ethnicity" is used here because it is the local practice. The term *Huaren* is used to designate ethnic Chinese in Singapore, so as not to confuse the national identity of PRC with the ethnic–cultural identity of Chinese Singaporeans.

21 There has not been a single instance of ethnic violence in the past 40 years, but this has not stopped the government from constantly harping on about the potential for such violence in a multiracial society such as Singapore. The desire for racial harmony has become a repressive rhetoric that obstructs open discussions of historical and structural racial inequalities; see Chua (2007).

22 Given the tendency of Singaporeans to create acronyms out of abbreviations, 'Surbana" is likely to be the acronym of "Singapore Urban Agency."

23 See http://www.jurong.com/presence.html (accessed October 20, 2008).

24 See http://beyondsg.typepad.com/beyondsg/2010/07/speech-by-minister-george-yeo-chinas-reemergence-on-the-global-stage-at-the-futurechina-global-forum.html

References

Abdul Rahim, F. (2010) Wages: workfare's the long-term answer. *The Straits Times*, September 22.

Asher, M.G. and Nandy, A. (2008) A plutonomy's response to ageing, inequality and poverty: the case of Singapore. *International Social Security Review* 61(1), 41–60.

Chan Heng Chee (1971) *Singapore: the politics of survival, 1965–1967*. Singapore: Oxford University Press.

Chin, H.C. and Fong, K.W. (2006) Issues in transportation planning – the Singapore experience. In S. Basbas (ed.) *Advances in City Transport: case studies*. Boston, MA: WIT Press, pp. 127–58.

Chong, T. (ed.) (2010) *Management of Success: Singapore revisited*. Singapore: Institute of Southeast Asian Studies.

Chua Beng Huat (1989) *The Golden Shoe: building Singapore's financial district*. Singapore: Urban Redevelopment Authority.

Chua Beng Huat (1997) *Political Legitimacy and Housing: stakeholding in Singapore.* London: Routledge.

Chua Beng Huat (2000) Public housing residents as clients of the state. *Housing Studies* 15(1), 45–60.

Chua Beng Huat (2007) Political culturalism: representation and the People's Action Party of Singapore. *Democratization* 14(5), 911–27.

Drysdale, J. (1984) *Singapore: the struggle for success.* Singapore: Times Editions.

Economist, UK (2004) Singapore's man with a plan. August 12; http://www.singapore-sindow.org/sw04/040812e2.htm (accessed December 9, 2010).

Goh Chin Lian (2009) Young PAP "school" takes a leaf from Communist youth. *Straits Times,* March 4.

Harvey, S.S. (2008) Mapping spectral tropicality in *The Maid* (2005) and *Return to Pontianak* (2001). *Singapore Journal of Tropical Geography* 29, 24–33.

Hon, J. (1990) *Tidal Fortunes: a story of change, the Singapore River and Kallang Basin.* Singapore: Landmark Books.

Idawati, D.E. (2010), Imagining Surabaya's new image: to be another Singapore? Paper presented at the Workshop on "Global Urban Frontiers: Asian Cities in Theory, Practice and Imagination," September 8–9, Asia Research Institute, National University of Singapore.

Koh, T.T.B. (1967) The law of compulsory land acquisition in Singapore. *Malayan Law Journal* 35, 9–22.

Kraar, L. and Lee Kuan Yew (2010) A blunt talk with Singapore's Lee Kuan Yew; http://money.cnn.com/magazines/fortune/fortune_archive/1997/08/04/229722/index.htm (accessed September 16, 2010).

Krause, L.B., Koh Ai Tee, and Lee (Tsao) Yuan (1987) *The Singapore Economy Reconsidered.* Singapore: Institute of Southeast Asian Studies.

Lee Kuan Yew (2000) *From Third World to First: the Singapore story 1960–2000.* Singapore: Times Editions.

Low, L. (2002) Singapore Inc. for competitiveness and global economy: promises and reality. Research Paper Series 22, Faculty of Business Administration, National University of Singapore, Singapore.

Low, L. and Aw, T.C. (1997) *Housing a Healthy, Educated and Wealthy Nation through the CPF.* Singapore: Institute of Policy Studies and Times Academic Press.

Mauzy, D.K. and Milne, R.S. (2002) *Singapore Politics under the People's Action Party.* London: Routledge.

Nair, J. (2005) *The Promise of Metropolis: Bangalore's twentieth century.* New Delhi: Oxford University Press.

Neo, Boon Siong and Soh, C. (1993) *IT 2000: Singapore's vision of an intelligent island.* Information Management Research Centre, School of Business and Accountancy, Nanyang Technological University, Singapore.

Ong, A. (2005) Ecologies of expertise: assembling flows, managing citizenship. In A. Ong and S.J. Collier (eds.) *Global Assemblages: technology, politics, and ethics as anthropological problems.* Malden, MA: Blackwell, pp. 337–54.

Peh Shing Huei (2010) Every city wants a "Suchou Park": PM. *Straits Times,* September 12.

Pereira, A.A. (2003), *State Collaboration and Development Strategies in China: the case of China–Singapore Suzhou Industrial Park, 1992–2002.* New York: RoutledgeCurzon.

Rajaratnam, S. (1972) *Singapore: the global city*. Ministry of Culture, Republic of Singapore.

Rodan, G. (1989) *The Political Economy of Singapore's Industrialization*. London: Macmillan.

Rodan, G. (2005) Westminster in Singapore: now you see it, now you don't. In H. Patapan, J. Wanna and P. Weller (eds.) *Westminster Legacies: democracy and responsible government in Asia and the Pacific*. Sydney: University of New South Wales Press.

Sandhu, K.S. and Wheatley, P. (1989) *Singapore: the management of success*. Singapore: Institute of Southeast Asian Studies.

Saw Swee Hock and Low, L. (2009) *Sovereign Wealth Funds*. Saw Centre for Financial Studies, National University of Singapore, Singapore.

Tremewan, C. (1994) *The Political Economy of Social Control in Singapore*. London: Macmillan.

Wong, A.K. and Yeh, S.H.K. (eds.) (1985) *Housing a Nation: 25 years of public housing in Singapore*. Singapore: Housing and Development Board.

Yao Souchou (2007) *Singapore: the state and the culture of excess*. London: Routledge.

Ye, Min (2010) Policy learning or diffusion: how China opened to foreign direct investment. *Journal of East Asian Studies* 9(3), 399–432.

2

Urban Modeling and Contemporary Technologies of City-Building in China: The Production of Regimes of Green Urbanisms

Lisa Hoffman

"Strive not to be the largest, but to be the best" (*bu qiu zui da, dan qiu zui jia*) was a guiding principle of urban development in Dalian, a major port city in northeast China, initiated under the leadership of Mayor Bo Xilai (1993–2000).[1] With this plan, the city government hoped to make Dalian a beautiful seaside city, friendly to investors and to the environment. By controlling the size of the city (currently approximately 6 million), Mayor Bo hoped to avoid the congestion and sustainability problems faced by mega-cities such as Beijing, Shanghai, and Shenzhen. A central part of the locally developed, but internationally connected, urbanization plan was to beautify and "green" the city, eventually making Dalian itself a leading model of environmental city-building and green urbanism in China, an identity also championed by subsequent mayors. Dalian had long been known for its heavy industry and pollution from oil refining, chemical production, and ship-building, making this environmental turn noteworthy. To become a "garden city" and an "environmentally friendly city," municipal officials looked to the experiences of other cities such as Singapore and Kitakyushu, Japan, referencing ideas of green urbanism developed elsewhere.

Through the example of Dalian and its garden city project, this chapter analyzes urban modeling as a governmental practice that shapes, disciplines, and produces particular kinds of spaces and subjects. The first half of the chapter addresses modeling as a mechanism of governing the urban in contemporary China, the models of urban development referenced by Dalian's plans, and the designation of Dalian as a national eco-city model

Worlding Cities: Asian Experiments and the Art of Being Global, First Edition.
Edited by Ananya Roy and Aihwa Ong.
© 2011 Blackwell Publishing Ltd. Published 2011 by Blackwell Publishing Ltd.

in China (see also Shannon May, this volume). The second half addresses modeling of a globalized "garden city" image and considers how diverse practices have converged to produce a new regime of green urbanism in Dalian. In particular, it considers how two technical and one ethical element in Dalian's green urbanism reference the Singaporean Prime Minister's "clean and green" governing, Kitakyushu's industrial clean-up methods – and aspects of Ebenezer Howard's 1898 Garden City vision.[2] Use of the term "garden city" in contemporary urban modeling practices suggests a reference of Howard's plan; and in the case of Singapore, a more direct and explicit link to Howard through colonial city plans (see Yuen 1996; Yeoh 2000).

Yet rather than identifying Howard's Garden City plan as the "origin" of these contemporary garden cities, and instead of presenting an evolutionary or chronological story about current garden city modeling, this chapter takes a genealogical approach that considers a more "complex course of descent" for these current urban practices (see Foucault 1984: 81). The complex inter-referencing of models across Asia may be related to "Western" urban theories, but they are not defined by them (Robinson 2002; Aihwa Ong, Introduction, this volume; Ananya Roy, Conclusion, this volume). The chapter argues that even without overt citation of Howard, consideration of how Howard's visions resonate with contemporary plans is analytically useful for understanding what may be at stake in the convergence of these elements – assemblages that produce more stabilized modes of governing and regimes of urbanism.[3] The regimes that emerge through modeling practices, I argue, not only construct new urban landscapes, but also, as former Dalian Mayor Xia Deren noted, may call for a new way of thinking (*xin silu*) about development, a new energy amongst the city's people (*quan shi renmin yao jiji xingdong qilai*), and greater participatory consciousness (*canyu yishi*) (Xia 2006). In other words, choosing which models to follow and reassembling practices from elsewhere into this regime not only impacts the physical construction of "green" cities, but also shapes the citizens who fill them. Moreover, this analysis of urban modeling suggests that "successful" visions of urban life may be circulated across non-Western spaces through practices of inter-referencing and the production of future models of "desirable" urban spaces and subjects.

Importantly, while incorporating a variety of practices and drawing on diverse forms of authority, the garden city modeling described here also is a state project. As such, it is rooted in national economic growth goals, interested in the cultivation of desirable citizen-subjects, and dependent upon state-sanctioned designations and regulatory mechanisms. In China, the goals of growth, long-term security, and state-strengthening have been integrated into the desire to be "green," framing the recent modeling practices. The state remains important in the legitimization and reinforcement of Dalian as a model city; in other words, even as the contemporary inter-referencing of urban models works through more localized decision-making and model-creation practices. Examining urban modeling and the production of new models thus also raises questions about late-socialist governmental forms in China.

Modeling as a Mode of Governing the Urban

A core argument in this chapter is that modeling is a mode of governing the urban in contemporary China that draws on disparate rationalities, sites of actions, and ways of knowing. Modeling has been used as a way to shape behavior in the Confucian tradition, and in Maoist political practices, but I also place contemporary modeling of green urbanism in relation to global urban planning practices. For instance, there is the "Vancouver model," found in the False Creek development, which has come to represent "good" urban density and sustainability that is modeled by planners in Dubai as well as Seattle (see Glen Lowry and Eugene McCann, this volume). In this sense, modeling is about place-making and place-marketing in the global competition for capital. At the same time, national projects of model creation in China mean that these place-making practices are connected to state goals. Urban governments across China have been encouraged to reach environmental targets by adopting measures and governmental rationalities proven elsewhere, such that the inter-referencing of cities itself has become an "embodiment of the implementation of urban sustainable development" (Zhao 2001: 4). Through exchanges with its sister city, Kitakyushu, Japan, for instance, Dalian has become a Model City of State Environmental Protection. At the same time, the municipal government has advertised and marketed Dalian to residents, investors, and visitors as garden-like, as "conserving natural resources" and as building an "environmentally friendly society" (Xia 2006).

Urban modeling requires both that a model exists – that is, that a place presents itself as a model – and that other places turn to this site as an example to follow. As Børge Bakken explains (2000), modeling involves emulation of the model, imitation and repetition of that model, and encouragement by the model to try something new, albeit in China an innovation that occurs in a deliberate and controlled manner. Modeling one's self or one's city after some exemplary citizen or site, as well as the necessary production and identification of models, may be identified in a variety of distinct moments. Historically in China, models were "presented to the people for emulation. These models were the sages and exemplary men of the past," who acted as guides for future actions (Bakken 2000: 60). Confucian traditions presented virtuous men as examples for how rulers should govern, how sons should be filial, and how individuals should behave; the emperor himself also aimed to rule as a model example for others; and people learned to paint scrolls and do calligraphy by imitating the exemplary work of masters.

Under Mao Zedong, model workers, such as Lei Feng, were identified by Party leaders as examples of socialist morality and ideologically and socially exemplary actions. Political campaigns and patriotic education textbooks extolled the virtues of the models, inciting and cajoling others to adopt their behavior, to be selfless, and to sacrifice for the nation. In recent times, the state has identified model researchers, teachers, and filial children (e.g., the good daughter-in-law), and has honored and promoted "model households" for emulation (see Anagnost 1992). In terms of places, Dazhai commune and Daqing, the oil city, were especially well-known national models of socialist modernization, hard work, self-reliance, and industrial productivity. Cities such as Wenzhou, Hong Kong, and Singapore have been showcased in the reform era as models of urban governance for their innovative spirit and attractiveness to global capital.[4] Significantly, even as political imperatives have cautioned officials "to avoid *copying* foreign models" (Hughes 2006: 67, emphasis added) as the country reforms its centrally planned system, sites within Asia – Hong Kong, Singapore, Kitakyushu – have become important sources of information, technical applications, and political approaches to the problem of environmentalism, greening, and sustainability.

While idealized models continued to be generated and promoted by the state in the reform era, modeling now also emphasizes the "attainability" of model examples,[5] the localized generation of models, and the more "voluntary" following of models than during the Maoist era. Municipalities such as Dalian have taken a more "active and direct role" (Skinner, Joseph, and Kuhn 2003: 5) in developing urban strategies, with the decentralization of decision-making and revenue-generation responsibilities from central to local authorities, what has been termed an entrepreneurialization of cities, and the "downloading" of responsibility.[6] The localization of urban planning decisions and financial responsibility coincided with governmental shifts away from the Maoist centralized socialist state system. A critical moment for this in Dalian was its designation in 1984 as a Coastal City,[7] the decision to allow Dalian to report directly to the central government on administrative and economic issues as a sub-provincial city (circumventing the provincial authorities), and the establishment of Dalian's Economic and Technical Development Zone (hereafter, the Zone). With these changes, Dalian experienced both greater autonomy from the central government and more pressure to devise and implement strategies to attract foreign investments. To attract capital, Dalian, like municipalities in similar situations, retooled its governance methods, including adopting new urban modeling practices and launching marketing campaigns aimed at de-emphasizing its industrial history and highlighting new images of the city. In these campaigns, city officials visited other sites and invited planners, politicians, technicians, and businesses to "teach" them, becoming part of a global "epistemic community" of urban developers (Olds 2001; see also Glen Lowry and Eugene McCann, this volume). Such methods reflect distinctions that are made between "master" plans and "strategic" urban plans as well, where "the aim of making a strategic plan is not to control development, but rather promote urban development" (Wu and Zhang 2007: 719).

While contemporary modeling practices are reminiscent of Confucian and Maoist traditions, they also rely on local governments generating models and striving to meet targets (environmental and economic) in more "voluntary" ways. In fact, Elizabeth Economy notes that China's national model city program is "[o]ne of China's flagship efforts to highlight the *capacity of local officials* to develop the economy *and* protect the environment simultaneously" (2006: 178, emphasis added), essentially institutionalizing the integration of entrepreneurialism and environmentalism in green urbanisms in China. Globally, greening projects have become attractive to "urban leaders seeking to move away from the dark and satanic image of the ... industrial city" (While, Jonas, and Gibbs 2004: 565) and toward a global and investor-friendly municipality.[8] In China, this is further illustrated in the Party formally incorporating sustainable development into the planning process in 1992 (Lo and Leung 1998), which was the same year as the UN environmental conference in Rio de Janeiro, and as Deng Xiaoping's famous tour (*nanxun*) of the Special Economic Zones in southern China. It was also in 1992 that the "socialist market economy" was formally adopted by the Communist Party. By working through "the principle of voluntary participation" (Zhao 2001: 4), urban modeling motivates local governments to reform their cities and meet economic targets.

It was in the context of localized revenue generation and decentralization of decision-making that Mayor Bo initiated his urbanization strategies and bold greening visions, working with sister-city Kitakyushu, Japan,[9] and emulating practices in Hong Kong and Singapore. As I have noted elsewhere (Hoffman 2006a), in the early 1990s, municipal officials in Dalian turned to Hong Kong as a worlding node of global capitalism and as a model of economic prosperity. City officials advertised Dalian to investors as the "Hong Kong of the North" (see Bo 1993; Liu, Ji, and Chang 1994; Yahuda 1994) and emphasized the city's diversified economy, service industries (e.g., finance and tourism), and gateway function to the resources of northeast China and even Siberia.[10] Yet as the 1997 return of Hong Kong to Chinese sovereignty grew closer, the political implications of modeling one's city after a British colony became more complicated. Hong Kong was critiqued as being too interested in profits and money, and not concerned enough with social and environmental issues, leading to emulation of other sites, such as Singapore.

Interviewees explained to me that Mayor Bo's "strive not to be the largest, but to be the best" policy referenced Singaporean Prime Minister Lee Kuan Yew's "clean and green" garden city model, which included a beautification component, strong social and population controls, as well as a successful way to stand out in the competition for investments. Singapore's beautification program has been emulated by cities across Asia, increasing its stature in the eyes of many. Within the city-state, the "Garden City Concept" is said to be "a powerful national symbol: it is one demonstration and visible manifestation of the quality of life and level of development the country has achieved" (Yuen 1996: 969; Savage and Kong n.d.; see also Chua Beng Huat, this volume).

Yet even as models, ways of knowing, forms of measurement, and "best practices" from sites outside of China have been incorporated into late-socialist governmentality, the state remains significant in the production of green cities. Recent Dalian Mayor Xia Deren pledged, for instance, to take up the national call for "raising consciousness of ecological safety" (*tigao shengtai anquan yishi*) and building an "environmentally friendly society" (*huanjing youhaoxing shehui*) (Xia 2006). The state's role also is apparent in the naming and classifying of certain places as "models" of "environmentalism" by state agencies. A recent white paper from the State Council Information Office, for instance, noted that the government has pursued "a campaign to build environmental-protection model cities" as part of a formal effort to protect the environment (SCIO 2005). In 1997, Dalian was one of six cities designated by the National Environmental Protection Agency as a "Model City of State Environmental Protection"[11] and by the Ministry of Construction as a Garden City (Murray and Cook 2002: 196). Dalian was also named an Environmental Model Zone Project to "spread" "Dalian's achievement" across China (KIEC 2007: 10). In conjunction with measurement practices and expertise promoted by transnational organizations such as the United Nations and the World Bank, what Michael Goldman terms an "eco-governmentality" wherein new regimes of rights and environmental truths are established (2001), new modes of governing through modeling emerged.

The designation of Dalian as "an environmental demonstration zone and environmental model city" grew out of the cooperation between Dalian and its sister city Kitakyushu, Japan. Kitakyushu's economy was based on heavy industry first developed in the 1950s, leading to serious pollution problems. A major environmental clean-up project turned Kitakyushu into what was termed "a miracle city that had accomplished environmental regeneration from heavy pollution" (KIEC 2007: 3). Kitakyushu wished to share its knowledge with other cities, such as Dalian, that had experienced greater industrial production and related environmental problems (Bai and Imura 2000; KIEC 2007). The first documented environmental exchange between the cities was in 1981, when environmental technicians went to Dalian through the Kitakyushu International Techno-Co-operative Association (KITA) (Shin 2007). With support from Japan's official development aid (ODA) and China's central government, this cooperation led to the Japan–China Environmental Development Model City Scheme, which included Dalian, Chongqing, and Guiyang, and to China's own National Environmental Model City program. A variety of technological and training exchanges were also established between Japan and China with the international Kitakyushu Initiatives Network for a Clean Environment and the Environmental Cooperation Network of Asian Cities, including Kitakyushu economic and cultural exchange offices in Dalian (see Economy 2006; Shin 2007; www.city.kitakyushu.jp; www.clair.or.jp/e/sien/jigyo/093.html).

In addition to these exchanges, designation as a model city occurred through central-level projects and detailed regulation and measurement of a city's "progress" by the state. China's model city program measures "basic conditions, social and economic development, environmental quality, environmental construction and environmental management" (Chang n.d. b: 3; see also Zhao 2001). Central to this is the data gathering by the State Environmental Protection Agency on twenty-nine indices through the Urban Environmental Quantitative Examination System (UEQES), "covering the areas of air, water, solid waste, noise, and afforestation [which] are evaluated and weighted to come up with an overall score for each city" (Sinkule and Ortolano 1995: 38; Rock 2002; see also Tilt 2010).[12] The UEQES ranking is published in the state environmental yearbook (Rock 2002: 1440), raising the stakes of public success or failure for local governments. Mayor Bo's environmental city-building practices led to Dalian winning "the cleanest" ranking for several years of the forty-six key cities measured[13] and a fifth-place 2005 ranking in the comprehensive national environmental competition (Xia 2006), reinforcing its model status, distinguishing Dalian from other cities, and leading to an increase in business and leisure investments as well as local real estate values (Li 2003; Xiao 2007). More recently, the State Environmental Protection Agency has named Dalian's Economic and Technical Development Zone a "National Eco-Industrial Park Demonstration Zone," making it "an example for other Chinese industrial zones to follow" (Geng, Zhu, Doberstein, and Fujita 2009). At the same time, however, administrators in the Zone also "voluntarily" implemented an "environmental management system" to help companies meet ISO 14000 series standards, which could "be a powerful economic tool to attract foreign investment … a cornerstone for Chinese industrial parks relying on foreign capital for growth" (Geng and Cote 2003: 787–8). Bryan Tilt argues that "local autonomy" related to – and responsibility for – environmental conditions "represents an application of the Reform and Opening logic to environmental issues as the central government continues to retreat from many of its heavy-handed oversight duties"

(2010: 111). These practices of green urbanism were developed locally and more autonomously than the generation of urban economic plans during the Maoist era, although certainly in concert with national projects of economic growth and prosperity.

Dalian's model city status also has been reinforced through the hierarchical ranking of cities and granting of awards by national governments and international organizations, methods that resonate with more typical world-cities (versus the art of worlding) assessments. The city has won numerous national and international honors – including the UN Habitat Scroll of Honor Award from the UN Human Settlements Programme in 1999 and UNEP's prestigious Global 500 Roll of Honor for Environmental Achievement in 2001 (first city in China; see Hoffman 2009) – suggesting that the city's reimaging campaigns to shed its polluted, industrial reputation have been successful. Geng and Cote note that "in a short period of 10 years, Dalian has accomplished what many developed countries have needed many decades to accomplish," supporting the city's accolades (2003: 788).[14]

Establishing places as models, whether through localized exchanges, by decree, or via international competitions and assessments, is an important tool of place-marketing and place-making for urban governments. As Dalian became a national model of environmental urbanism, the municipal govern-ment worked to spread this image, to take advantage of the positive press it generated about the city, and to transform this symbolic capital into long-term economic prosperity. Much is at stake, in other words, in *becoming* a model city, for it implies an increase in political and symbolic capital and is understood as leading to economic growth.

Emergent Regimes of Green Urbanism and Garden Cities

Dalian's official designation as a Garden City reflects both a national project of producing models and a global process of city modeling. In the following discussion, I highlight how modeling is a practice of assemblage that produces a new regime of green urbanism in Dalian. To understand modeling, I do not suggest locating the "origin" or "essence" of the garden city and green urbanism in contemporary Dalian but, rather, suggest explor-ing "the layering of often disparate, unrelated, and discontinuous practices" (Bray 2005: 1–2) that may come together in "fairly coherent sets of ways of going about doing things" (Dean 1999: 21). Thus, in this section I consider how practices outlined in Ebenezer Howard's 1898 remedy for the squalid living conditions and pollutions of early industrial living resonate with Kitakyushu's environmental clean-up experience, Singapore's "clean and green" garden city model, and Dalian's "greening" campaign. These are not explicit genealogical links to Howard; rather, this discussion highlights practices that reference and borrow from earlier models, appropriating pieces in different circumstances and perhaps even for cross-purposes.

In other words, use of the term "garden city" in Asia neither implies a wholesale adoption of Howard's 1898 model, nor does it suggest that elements that are appropriated retain the same meaning or significance that they had in Howard's vision. As F.J. Osborn notes in his 1945 Preface to Howard's *Garden Cities of To-Morrow*, the term "has been used persistently in a sense entirely different from, indeed opposed to, the author's definition" (1965 [1945]: 9), and followers have consistently drawn only selectively from Howard's vision (see Buder 1990; Ooi 2004). Peter Hall regards the ease with which the garden-city movement in particular "was exported from its homeland, but also how strangely it became transformed in the process" as "astonishing" (2002: 127). For example, many people devoted to Howard's Garden City ideal have ignored his proposal for collective land ownership and "gas and water socialism" (Fishman 1982: 49), instead adopting the aesthetic qualities, tree planting, and housing and density standards elements of his proposal.[15]

The aim of the following discussion, then, is not to idealize a timeless Howard vision, but rather to learn about contemporary inter-referencing practices, the modes of governing the urban that are adopted through modeling, and the related emergent green urbanisms. Like other regimes of practices, the modeling of garden cities has technical, political, and ethical components. In the remainder of this section I discuss two technical aspects – the prioritization of green space and the removal of industry from large city centers – and one ethical aspect – the production of cooperative and harmonious communities – of Ebenezer Howard's plan that we may also identify in places like Singapore and Dalian.[16] These aspects of garden cities are, as David Bray argues, "quite flexible and open to a range of reappropriations" (2005: 36) in settings historically and geographically distinct from their original explication and implementation. This analysis of the garden city thus allows us to bring these pieces together, and to consider how new models of green urbanism are generated in and across Asia.

Prioritization of green space

In the original Garden City proposal, Howard hoped to meld the town and the country and to mitigate the destruction of each by the Industrial Revolution. The countryside was losing people and vibrancy, and the cities were overcrowded and unhealthy. According to Lewis Mumford, Howard's "prime contribution was to outline the nature of a balanced community to show what steps were necessary, in an ill-organized and disoriented society, to bring it into existence" (1965 [1945]: 33). A central component of his proposal was green space, both as a permanent agricultural green belt

around the city and as parks within the city. In the center of "magnificent
boulevards," Howard explained, would be "a circular space containing
about five and a half acres, laid out as a beautiful and well-watered garden"
(Howard 1965 [1945]: 51–3). This technical aspect of city-building is seen
also in Singapore's and Dalian's plans.

The prioritization of green space as a technique of city-building emerged in
contemporary Singaporean plans as a "clean and green" city beautification
campaign. In the late 1960s, Lee Kuan Yew initiated the garden-city beautification policy as a way of improving the living conditions in a dense and quickly
urbanizing space; to distinguish Singapore from other places in Southeast Asia;
and to help the country move from "third world" to "first world" status.[17]
Similar to processes in China, it was a state-led project of national modernization that "embodied a vigorous developmentalist orientation" (Yuen 1996:
962), and at times, direct, authoritarian measures. This remaking of the city,
construction of new housing estates, and tree planting policies aimed "to
improve" the quality of life for the citizens and to improve the image of the
city with visitors. Some scholars (e.g., Yuen 1996) highlight the fact that
Singapore's "building" of "unnatural" green spaces is distinct from Howard's
goal of using agricultural green belts to separate settlements, but the Prime
Minister's program did result in many new parks, open spaces, tree-planting
experiences by Cabinet Ministers, and even new governmental committees
(e.g., the Garden City Action Committee) and departments (e.g., the Parks and
Recreation Department) to manage the increased green space.[18]

Mayor Bo's "greening project" in Dalian also intended to humanize the
city with plantings along major boulevards, investments in city parks and per
capita green space, and the construction of a large free-range wild animal
park and many public squares in the city. In the late 1990s, flowers appeared
on major roadways and the city promoted its extensive grass lawn in front of
the municipal building. The Zone, just north of the city, has also been called
"garden-like" and has adopted "urban landscaping" plans that aim for
"developing 10 public gardens per year and planting appropriate species"
(Geng and Cote 2003: 788, 791). As in Singapore, this technique of green
city-building was reflective of national economic goals, local entrepreneurial
city management practices, *and* concerns for the ecological and environmental well-being of the city. Incorporated into contemporary regimes of urbanism
in Asia, this technical aspect – also found in Howard's proposal – became a
hallmark of healthy living, urban civility, and even new tourist destinations.

The removal of industry

The second technical aspect of Howard's project that we may also identify
in Singapore, Kitakyshu, and Dalian is the movement of industry – "perhaps
under State encouragement and guidance" (Osborn 1965 [1945]: 25) – out

of the congested city center. While Singapore adopted the principle of movement away from the congested areas of the central city, it did so with the construction of satellite housing compounds and the transfer of people and commercial activities (see Yeoh 2000: 111–13; Ooi 2008).[19] Singapore's restricted space also made "the population-spatial area equation" central to planning decisions (Savage and Kong n.d.: 17). Moreover, the recent construction of satellite towns followed plans from the British colonial administration in Singapore (1819–1959) that built "new towns" and "green belts" based on Howard's vision (Yuen 1996; Yeoh 2000: 110).[20]

In Dalian, the transfer of industry away from what is now known as the "golden" real estate area in the central city was first noted as an urban policy in the 1982 reform era city plan (Li 2003: 41). The city plan in 1990 then "indicated that there would be no more large and middle-sized factories built in the central area," and the removal of factories from the city center began in earnest in 1995 under Bo Xilai (Li 2003: 43, 45), becoming "the main point for the government to implement 'the sustainable development strategy'" (Yu 2003; see also Chang n.d. a; NRSD 1997). Dalian's 1999 Plan and its 2003 supplement also were explicit about moving (and upgrading) polluting industries to the suburbs (Li 2003: 50; see also Murray and Cook 2002; Xiao 2007; Chang n.d. a). In 1995, 134 pollution-generating factories were identified for removal from the city center (Murray and Cook 2002: 68), and as of 2003, 130 had been relocated (Yu 2003).

Not only did this process reduce emissions in the city center; it also opened a significant amount of land for other uses. By 1999, for instance, after removal of ninety enterprises, 2.4 million square meters were turned to office, residential, and green space uses (Chang n.d. a: 5). Land values also increased significantly, as noted by Mayor Bo in an interview in 2000:

> It is well known that most of those enterprises are close to bankruptcy, the facilities and equipment are almost worthless, then how did those factories get enough money to remove themselves? The reason is the increased value of Dalian as a whole, so the value of the land where those factories located has also increased. Actually, the land value of 1999 is five times that of 1994.[21]

In addition, the removal of industry and the construction of industry-specific zones by planners were done precisely "to protect" populations from potential hazards (e.g., in the Zone; see Geng and Cote 2003). The city's policies of cleaning up industrial pollution, moving industrial facilities from the city center, opening up the seashore for recreational uses, and increasing the per capita green space also have garnered the attention of multinational businesses. Hitachi, Sony, Intel, and Dell have all made major investments in the city (Balfour 2005; *New York Times* 2007; Xiao 2007).

The removal of industry away from urban population concentrations and the downtown core reestablished urban planning principles and differentiated land valuations eschewed during the Maoist era. By mixing residential and industrial work spaces, the Maoist work unit (*danwei*) model helped to end capitalist valuations of property and to construct walking-scale communities. In contrast, the reform era plans, and specifically the policy to transfer industrial production to zones outside of the city center and away from *urban* residential populations and waterfront areas, reinstates the dominance of the downtown core area and commercial and tourist land uses (see also Zukin 1991). In addition, the transfer of industries also implied movement of pollution to areas "where peasants hold less political clout than their urban neighbors and have less-developed regulatory schemes for protecting the environment" (Murray and Cook 2002: 69), often resulting in the pollution of poorer regions (Economy 2006: 187). Although China passed the Environmental Impact Assessment Law in 2002, in his ethnography of rural industrialization, Bryan Tilt (2010) argues that the law and its enforcement are "still in [their] infancy," and explains in detail the health and food systems hazards experienced by residents in such areas.

Dalian's designation as a "Garden City" led to a transformation of the city's environment and production of new forms of value in the area. Mayor Bo's "greening project" did clean up a polluted river (although currently there are many critiques of how this was done), increase the per capita green space, and beautify the city, and Singapore's "clean and green" program established numerous parks and trees throughout the city-state. Yet, in both cases, the projects were implemented to support state economic growth policies, especially in "new growth points of the national economy" of tourism and real estate (Xiao 2007: 86), such that parks in Singapore were, for instance, "reinvested with new economic functions" (Yuen 1996: 967; Chatterjea 2006; Savage and Kong n.d.). Although it seems that *pro*-growth, *entrepreneurial* city management would contradict environmental and sustainable city-building, it has also been argued "that urban entrepreneurialism itself might depend on the active remaking of urban environments and ecologies" (While, Jonas, and Gibbs 2004: 550). Aidan While and his co-authors term this an "urban sustainability fix," which recognizes that cities may make progress on ecological issues, but that this spatial/social fix also "draws attention to the selective incorporation of ecological goals in the greening of urban governance" (2004: 551).[22] Similarly, US smart growth practices may be analyzed as both "green" *and* "pro-growth" (e.g., in terms of infill development), highlighting that such regimes of urbanism incorporate "variegated spatial rationalities" and "state territorialities" (Dierwechter 2008: 43–69). In China, these projects also relied on forced removals and non-participatory master planning, more authoritarian mechanisms of governing that worked in tandem with the production of more autonomous urban citizens.

Building communities, shaping subjectivity

As a mode of governing the city, modeling practices are not only about technical expertise and industrial policy transfer, for they also include a concern with people's behavior and self-government. The third element considered here is an ethical one, focused on community-building and subject-making. Population management and the fostering of particular kinds of subjects, whether responsible, entrepreneurial, or sustainable, are significant aspects of the inter-referencing of green city-building models in Asia. The search for new urban models, while being fueled by dramatic increases in urban population, national goals of long-term economic growth, new competition for global capital, and international concern for the environment, also is concerned with social engineering for the community and citizen-subject. This exhibits what Allan Pred called "the interplay of social and spatial structuring, the simultaneous making of histories and construction of human geographies" (1990: 35).

Ebenezer Howard was explicit, for instance, that "garden-city dwellers would perceive themselves as members of a cohesive community, bound together by shared moral and social values" (Buder 1990: 208). In Singapore, the greening of the city and construction of recreational spaces was understood "as an antidote to living in high-rise, high-density apartments" and as "a mechanism of community development" (Yuen 1996: 964). In describing his desire to build a "clean and green" Singapore that would be "an oasis in Southeast Asia," Lee Kuan Yew noted that it was easier to improve the physical infrastructure "than the rough and ready ways of the people" (Lee 2000: 173). The city-state employed "continuing social education and engineering of social behaviour and attitudes" to enhance environmental awareness and knowledge of the policies (Savage and Kong n.d.: 3). Government officials have been involved in tree planting, citizens have learned about littering and spitting, and businesses have been subject to educational campaigns and fines (Savage and Kong n.d.).

Dalian's greening experience also has been tied to the fostering of civilized (*wenming*) and quality (*suzhi*) citizens who have a sense of national obligation and social responsibility, as well as the skills desirable for the global knowledge economy. Through research on Beijing's Green Olympics and Shanghai's Green Expo, Jennifer Hubbert notes, for instance, that sustainability is associated with high levels of *suzhi* as well as "technological sophistication," so that being green is directly associated with being modern and civilized (2009). Likewise, many educational campaigns hope to simultaneously raise people's *suzhi* levels and increase environmental awareness by focusing on topics such as the hazards of industrial pollution, the benefits of gray water use, and even the public health and wellness implications of spitting.

In Dalian, stores now charge for plastic shopping bags, public washrooms have stickers encouraging people to conserve water, and communities have organized litter pick-up activities by volunteers. In the summer of 2010, I attended an elementary school event where children participated in a "toy exchange." For the exchange, the students brought old toys they no longer used either to exchange for something else or to sell for a nominal fee. The aim of the activity was to encourage the children to reuse items rather than purchase new ones, and thus to increase their environmental sensibility. This was followed by an activity in which the children presented used batteries and old cell phones they had collected, so that they could be disposed of properly. These kinds of practices aim to produce model citizen-subjects who educate themselves on the issues and who will "voluntarily" exchange items rather than purchase new ones, conserve resources, and protect the environment. As modes of self-governance, they exhibit individual and community responsibility. These practices also reflect "community-building" (*shequ jianshe*) processes that have gained prominence as modes of urban governance China. Presented in "model" forms as well (e.g., the Shenyang model), community-building practices offer "clearly articulated norms for the behaviour of both residents and cadres," with rules about taking care of gardens, avoiding clutter, and participating in family planning (Bray 2009: 99). Thus, like urban modeling of green urbanisms, community-building fosters "quality" citizens who will behave responsibly.

In 2006, then mayor Xia Deren noted explicitly that building an environmentally friendly society was an "urgent strategic task" in the city. It was a task that relied on individual efforts and broad participation by the people; it was also a "new state of social development" (*xinxing de shehui fazhan zhuangtai*). New environmental "thinking" was necessary at multiple levels to build this society, such as the local government's use of a "Green GDP" (*luse* GDP) and regulatory policies, but also the development of environmental education and information sharing, and people's participation in green consumption that could also support green industries (Xia 2006). Similar to the manner in which cities in China have been incited to choose correct models to follow in a more "voluntary" manner, urban subjects are increasingly governed through autonomously made, and yet responsible decisions. Yet voluntary and autonomous decisions "to live sustainably" by both cities and citizens are nevertheless wedded with projects of national economic growth and strength (Hoffman 2006b, 2010).

Conclusion

The search for models and better urbanisms is being fueled by exponential urban growth in many parts of Asia and the identification of current conditions as unhealthy, overcrowded, and unsustainable. Similarly, when

Howard and his compatriots (Le Corbusier and Frank Lloyd Wright)[23] presented their utopian visions, there was unprecedented urban population growth and increasing recognition that urbanization and industrialization generated severe social and economic crises.[24] Thus, we may understand the referencing of the garden city idea – in all its various substantive forms – and the modeling of cities more generally, as a modernist, progressive, and developmental mode of governing (see also Rabinow 1995; Holston 1989). These visions, like the well-cited Brundtland Report's (1987) definition of sustainable development – as "development that meets the needs of the present without compromising the ability of future generations to meet their own needs" – are future-oriented projects, concerned not only with technical aspects of governing, but also with questions of how to educate and persuade people to act sustainably for the long term. Thus examining the models and governmental programs shaping Dalian's practices allows us to ask not only how cities are governed, but also how subjects are formed.

While my discussion here has not been prescriptive in terms of "the best" planning agendas or environmentalisms, it does aim to lead to questions about the critical issues in these regimes of green urbanism and forms of governing. The garden city and greening practices transformed the demographics of downtown cores, relocated polluting industries to less "valuable" locations, and worked to educate and persuade citizens to be environmental on their own. Nevertheless, important questions remain about how people negotiate the regulation and discipline inherent in such urban modeling and green urbanisms – whether in the form of educational campaigns, punitive fines, or economic incentives. There certainly are numerous reports of environmentally based protests across the country.

This chapter has argued that "urban modeling" and the inter-referencing of those models within and across Asia are important aspects of urban governance. Moreover, it suggests that urban modeling in Asia may "reflect the experiences of a much wider range of cities" than commonly used terms of "global cities" or "mega-cities" do, potentially displacing the centrality of Western-generated models in urban studies (Robinson 2002: 532). The inter-referencing of expertise, technical interventions, economic growth, and subject formation in Dalian's garden city modeling thus may have greater explanatory relevance than previously recognized. The approach taken here allows us to identify cities and moments outside of the dominant, mainstream West and dominant planning theorizations as important sites where regimes of urban practices are generated, while also noting genealogical links. In addition, the extensiveness of Dalian's national and international environmental awards suggests that this urban experiment in green urbanism has the potential to stand as a "target" or "standard" to be emulated by cities outside of China. Even as these regional conversations are informed by global environmental discourses, the regime of practices described here also presents the possibility of becoming a more global model of green urbanism – whether intended as such or not.[25]

Acknowledgments

I would like to thank Aihwa Ong and Ananya Roy and the other participants in the Social Science Research Council Inter-Asian Connections Conference, Inter-Referencing Asia: Urban Experiments and the Art of Being Global Workshop, Dubai, 2008; panel and audience members at the AAA meetings in 2008, where I presented an earlier version; as well as Monica DeHart, Yonn Dierwechter, Susan Hoffman, and Jennifer Hubbert for engagement with me on these issues, and suggestions and comments on previous drafts. I also appreciate the comments from anonymous reviewers for this volume.

Notes

1 Lin Yongjin followed as mayor from 2000 to 2003, Xia Deren from 2003 to 2009, and Li Wancai from January 2010 to the present.
2 I use the term "garden city" in multiple ways in the following discussion. When it refers to an official designation or to Howard's proposal, I capitalize Garden City. When it refers to a specific plan in other cities – for example, to build a "garden city" – I put it in quotation marks. When it refers to a generalized approach to urban development, I use it in its generic form of garden city.
3 See also what Tania Murray Li describes as "*practices* of assemblage" which are "the on-going labour of bringing disparate elements together and forging connections between them" (2007: 263). On assemblages, see also Ong and Collier (2005) and Ong (2006).
4 On the Wenzhou model, see Parris (1993) and Zhang (2001).
5 Bakken argues that in contemporary times, "models are to be designed on the principle of recognition and attainability" (2000: 195).
6 On the entrepreneurialization of urban governance in China, see Hoffman (2006a, 2010), Wu (2003), and Wu and Zhang (2007). There is a rich literature on this phenomenon in Western cities; for a general discussion, see Harvey (1989). On the idea of "downloading" in China, see Skinner, Joseph, and Kuhn (2003).
7 The central government designated fourteen port cities as "Coastal Cities," including Dalian, Qinhuangdao, Tianjin, Yantai, Qingdao, Lianyungang, Nantong, Shanghai, Ningbo, Wenzhou, Fuzhou, Guangzhou, Zhanjiang, and Beihai. See also Phillipps and Yeh (1989) and Yeung and Hu (1992). Dalian also recently was awarded the designation of Dalian Changxing Island Seaport Industrial Area as both a state-level Economic and Technological Development Zone and a provincial-level Economic Experimental Reform Zone (2010).
8 This process has also been termed the "green neoliberal project" – a situation where "notions of market value and optimal resource allocation find common cause" (Goldman 2001: 501).
9 They became sister cities in 1979.

10 This policy built on the city's 1982 plan that "positioned Dalian as an industrial, port, and tourism city" (Li 2003: 41).

11 Dalian earned this designation in the first year of the Model City designation, along with Shenzhen, Weihai, Xiamen, Zhuhai, and Zhangjiagang, cities that "were deemed to have met the following criteria: capacity for sustainable development; socio-economic level; environmental quality; environmental management and public participation in environmental protection" (Murray and Cook 2002: 196; see also Zhao 2001). By 2007, sixty-six more cities had earned the Model City title, for a total of seventy-two (see http://english.mep.gov.cn/inventory/Model-cities/).

12 For a detailed description of how targets are bargained over, set, and met, see Rock (2002); see also Zhao (2001). In addition, it is important to note that the State Environmental Protection Agency was elevated to the ministerial level in 2008, becoming the Ministry of Environmental Protection (see Tilt 2010).

13 This was noted by the Vice Director of the Dalian Environmental Protection Administration at the China National Tourism Administration and World Tourism Organization joint project workshop, October 26, 2001 (in Li 2003: 45). Ningbo also has highlighted its rise from a ranking of thirty-fifth to that of fifth, and its own designation as an Environmental Model City (Chang n.d.).

14 Compare Dalian's record to that of Beijing, particularly in light of the controversies over air quality prior to the 2008 "Green Olympics" (ICSD n.d.; see also Hubbert 2010).

15 The official definition of a Garden City, adopted in 1919 by the Garden Cities and Town Planning Association and developed with Ebenezer Howard, is as follows: "A Garden City is a Town designed for healthy living and industry; of a size that makes possible a full measure of social life, but not larger; surrounded by a rural belt; the whole of the land being in public ownership or held in trust for the community" (in Osborn 1965 [1945]: 26). Jane Jacobs interprets the public ownership as "permanent control" that was meant "to prevent speculation or supposedly irrational changes in land use and also to do away with temptations to increase its density – in brief, to prevent it from ever becoming a city" (1993: 24).

16 These practices clearly are seen in the Soviet Union and the United States as well. My focus here is on the inter-referencing of models and emergent regimes in Asia.

17 Belinda Yuen (1996) identifies three phases in the development of the garden city program in Singapore: 1959–70, with a focus on employment and housing; 1970–80, with the city beautification program; and 1980 to the present, with a focus on the leisure and tourist industries.

18 Examples include budget increases for this work from 6 million Singapore dollars in 1973 to 63 million; and in 1975 a Parks and Trees Act was enacted to manage and protect the plantings and parks (Yuen 1996: 961).

19 An important aspect of the redistribution of people and land-use functions in Singapore was the construction of public and private housing developments in a "podium style." This style of tall buildings on top of retail businesses, markets, and other facilities reproduced the mixed-use spatial organization of the "original shophouse landscape" of traditional housing in Chinatown (Yeoh 2000: 114).

20 Belinda Yuen notes the importance of the 1958 Master Plan in incorporating these elements, developed in the 1944 Greater London Plan (1996: 959).

21 The interview was in the *People's Daily*, May 14, 2000, cited in Li (2003: 48). In that
    interview, he also said that ninety industrial enterprises had moved to suburban
    areas.
22 In a recent column in the *New York Times*, Thomas Friedman cites Dalian, its expo-
    nential growth, and its urbanization style (heavy energy use) as a reason why he
    remains a "climate skeptic" (2007). Thus we must recognize that while *green*, this
    regime of green urbanism is not necessarily "sustainable" – environmentally or
    socially (see also Goldman 2001).
23 Jane Jacobs identified both Howard and Le Corbusier as offering "garden" models
    that in her view were fundamentally anti-urban and over-planned. She termed Le
    Corbusier's "skyscrapers in the park" design the "Radiant Garden City" (1993: 32).
    I thank Yonn Dierwechter for reminding me of Jacobs's comments.
24 In the nineteenth century, London's population increased from 900,000 to 4.5
    million and New York's went from 60,000 to 3.4 million (Fishman 1982: 11).
25 A new "eco-city" in Chongming Island across from Shanghai, for example, aimed
    to "be a model for the world," according to Peter Head from the UK engineering
    firm hired to design this "demonstration" eco-city (Schifferes 2007).

References

Anagnost, A. (1992) Socialist ethics and the legal system. In J. Wasserstrom and E. Perry
    (eds.) *Popular Protest and Political Culture in Modern China: learning from 1989*. Boulder,
    CO: Westview Press.
Bai, X. and Imura, H. (2000) A comparative study of urban environment in East Asia:
    stage model of urban environmental evolution. *International Review for Environmental
    Strategies* 1(1), 135–58.
Bakken, B. (2000) *The Exemplary Society*. Oxford: Oxford University Press.
Balfour, F. (2005) China: golf, sushi – and cheap engineers. *Business Week*, March 28,
    2005, with Hiroko Tashiro; http://www.businessweek.com/magazine/con-
    tent/05_13/b3926068.htm (accessed January 18, 2008).
Bo, X. (1993) *Dalianshi shizhang Bo Xilai zai yantaohui shang de jianghua*, reprint of seminar
    speech by Dalian Mayor Bo Xilai, in Beijing, May 5, 1993.
Bray, D. (2005) *Social Space and Governance in Urban China: the* danwei *system from origins to
    reform*. Stanford, CA: Stanford University Press.
Bray, D. (2009) Building "community": new strategies of governance in urban China. In
    E. Jeffreys (ed.) *China's governmentalities: governing change, changing government*. New York:
    Routledge.
Brundtland, G.H. (1987) *Our Common Future: The World Commission on Environment and
    Development*. Oxford: Oxford University Press.
Buder, S. (1990) The future of the Garden City. In *Visionaries and Planners: the Garden City
    Movement and the modern community*. New York: Oxford University Press, pp. 199–216.
Chang, M. (n.d. a) *Kitakyushu Initiative for a clean environment: successful and transferable practices,
    Dalian (China): removal and modification of polluted enterprises*. Institute for Global
    Environmental Strategies; http://kitakyushu.iges.or.jp/successful_practices/by_
    country.html#China (accessed December 15, 2008).

Chang, M. (n.d. b) *Kitakyushu Initiative for a Clean Environment: successful and transferable practices, Ningbo (China): efficient application of integrated policies for the urban environment.* Institute for Global Environmental Strategies; http://www.iges.or.jp/kitakyushu/sp/over/Ningbo%20(Integrated%20Policies).doc (accessed January 9, 2008).

Chatterjea, K. (2006) Public use of urban forest, Its impact, and related conservation issues. In T.C. Wong, B.J. Shaw, and K.C. Goh (eds.) *Challenging Sustainability: urban development and change in Southeast Asia.* London: Marshall Cavendish Academic, pp. 53–79.

Dean, M. (1999) *Governmentality: power and rule in modern society.* London: SAGE Publications.

Dierwechter, Y. (2008) *Urban Growth Management and Its Discontents: promises, practices, and geopolitics in U.S. city-regions.* New York: Palgrave Macmillan.

Economy, E. (2006) Environmental governance: the emerging economic dimension. *Environmental Politics* 15(2), 171–89.

Fishman, R. (1982) *Urban Utopias in the Twentieth Century: Ebenezer Howard, Frank Lloyd Wright, Le Corbusier.* Cambridge, MA: The MIT Press.

Foucault, M. (1984) Nietzsche, genealogy, history. In P. Rabinow (ed.) *The Foucault Reader.* New York: Pantheon, pp. 76–100.

Friedman, T. (2007) Doha and Dalian. *New York Times,* September 19, 2007; http://www.nytimes.com/2007/09/19/opinion/19friedman.html?_r=1&oref=slogin (accessed January 18, 2008).

Geng, Y. and Cote, R. (2003) Environmental management systems at the industrial park level in China. *Environmental Management* 31(6), 784–94.

Geng, Y., Zhu, Q., Doberstein, B., and Fujita, T. (2009) Implementing China's circular economy concept at the regional level: a review of progress in Dalian, China. *Waste Management* 29(2), 996–1002.

Goldman, M. (2001) Constructing an environmental state: eco-governmentality and other transnational practices of a "green" World Bank. *Social Problems* 48(4), 499–523.

Hall, P. (2002) *Cities of Tomorrow,* 3rd edn. Malden, MA: Blackwell.

Harvey, D. (1989) From managerialism to entrepreneurialism: the transformation of urban politics in late capitalism. *Geografiska Annaler B* 71(1), 3–18.

Hoffman, L. (2006a) Urban transformation and professionalization: translocality and rationalities of enterprise in post-Mao China. In T. Oakes and L. Schein (eds.) *Translocal China: linkages, identities, and the reimagining of space.* London: Routledge, pp. 109–37.

Hoffman, L. (2006b) Autonomous choices and patriotic professionals: on governmentality in late-socialist China. *Economy and Society* 35(4), 550–70.

Hoffman, L. (2009) Governmental rationalities of environmental city-building in contemporary China. In E. Jeffreys (ed.) *China's Governmentalities.* London: Routledge, pp. 107–24.

Hoffman, L. (2010) *Patriotic Professionalism in Urban China: fostering talent.* Philadelphia, PA: Temple University Press.

Holston, J. (1989) *The Modernist City: an anthropological critique of Brasilia.* Chicago: University of Chicago Press.

Howard, E. (1965 [1945]) *Garden Cities of To-Morrow,* ed. F.J. Osborn. Cambridge, MA: The MIT Press.

Hubbert, J. (2009) Green and global: sustainability in the 2008 Beijing Olympics and the 2010 Shanghai World Expo. Paper presented at American Anthropological Association Annual Meetings, Philadelphia.

Hubbert, J. (2010) Spectacular productions: community and commodity in the Beijing Olympics. *City and Society* 22(1), 119–42.

Hughes, C.R. (2006) *Chinese Nationalism in the Global Era*. London: Routledge.

(ICSD) International Center for Sustainable Development (n.d.) Beijing 2008 Green Olympics Initiative; http://www.solarcities.org/beijingolympics.htm (accessed January 18, 2008).

Jacobs, J. (1993) *The Death and Life of Great American Cities*. New York: Modern Library.

KIEC (Kitakyushu's International Environmental Cooperation) (2007) *Eco, thereby Enhancing Global Partnership*. Office for International Environmental Cooperation Environment Bureau, Kitakyushu, Japan; http://www.city.kitakyushu.jp/file/26170200/gaikokugo/english.pdf (accessed November 5, 2008).

Lee, K.Y. (2000) *From Third World to First: the Singapore story: 1965–2000, Singapore and the Asian economic boom*. New York: HarperCollins.

Li, M. (2003) Urban regeneration through public space: a case study in squares in Dalian, China. Master of Arts thesis, Department of Geography, University of Waterloo.

Li, T.M. (2007) Practices of assemblage and community forest management. *Economy and Society* 36(2), 263–93.

Liu, Z., Ji, X., and Chang, B. (1994) *Dalian xiandai chenzhen tixi yu jiasu quyu chengshihuade zhanlue xuanze* (Dalian's strategic choices for city and town systematization and rapid urbanization). Dalian Urban Economy Working Group, Dalian, China.

Lo, C.W.H. and Leung, S.W. (1998) Environmental protection and popular environmental consciousness in China. In *China Review 1998*. Hong Kong: Chinese University Press, pp. 502–41.

Mumford, L. (1965 [1945]) Introduction: the Garden City idea and modern planning. In E. Howard, *Garden Cities of To-Morrow*, ed. F.J. Osborn. Cambridge, MA: The MIT Press, pp. 29–40.

Murray, G. and Cook, I.G. (2002) *Green China: seeking ecological alternatives*. London: RoutledgeCurzon.

New York Times (2007) World business briefing Asia: China: government approves plans for Intel plant. March 14; http://query.nytimes.com/gst/fullpage.html?res=9B0CE1D81131F937A25750C0A9619C8B63 (accessed January 18, 2008).

NRSD (National Report on Sustainable Development) (1997) Chapter 3: Actions and achievements in the major fields of sustainable development; www.acca21.org.cn/nrc3s3.html (accessed January 9, 2008).

Olds, K. (2001) *Globalization and Urban Change: capital, culture, and Pacific Rim mega-projects*. New York: Oxford University Press.

Ong, A. (2006) *Neoliberalism as Exception: mutations in citizenship and sovereignty*. Durham, NC: Duke University Press.

Ong, A. and Collier, S.J. (eds.) (2005) *Global Assemblages: technology, politics, and ethics as anthropological problems*. Malden, MA: Blackwell.

Ooi, G.L. (2004) *Future of Space: planning, space and the city*. Singapore: Eastern Universities Press/Marshall Cavendish International.

Ooi, G.L. (2008) Cities and sustainability: Southeast Asian and European perspectives. *Asia Europe Journal* 6, 193–204.

Osborn, F.J. (1965 [1945]) Preface. In E. Howard, *Garden Cities of To-Morrow*, ed. F.J. Osborn. Cambridge, MA: The MIT Press, pp. 9–28.

Parris, K. (1993) Local initiative and national reform: the Wenzhou Model of development. *The China Quarterly* 134, 242–63.

Phillipps, D.R. and Yeh, A.G.O. (1989) Special Economic Zones. In D.S.G. Goodman (ed.) *China's Regional Development*. London: Routledge, pp. 112–34.

Pred, A. (1990) In other wor(l)ds: fragmented and integrated observations on gendered languages, gendered spaces and local transformation. *Antipode* 22(1), 33–52.

Rabinow, P. (1995) *French Modern: norms and forms of the social environment*. Chicago: The University of Chicago Press.

Robinson, J. (2002) Global and world cities: a view from off the map. *International Journal of Urban and Regional Research* 26(3), 431–554.

Rock, M.T. (2002) Integrating environmental and economic policy making in China and Taiwan. *American Behavioral Scientist* 45(9), 1435–55.

Savage, V. and Kong, L. (n.d.) Urban constraints, political imperatives: environmental "design" in Singapore. Unpublished manuscript, Department of Geography, National University of Singapore.

Schifferes, S. (2007) China's eco-city faces growth challenge. *BBC News*, July 5; http://news.bbc.co.uk/2/hi/business/6756289.stm (accessed January 18, 2008).

SCIO (State Council Information Office) (2005) Environmental protection in China (1996–2005). State Council Information Office, Beijing; http://www.china.org.cn/archive/2006-06/05/content_1170355.htm (accessed August 10, 2010).

Shin, S. (2007) East Asian environmental co-operation: central pessimism, local optimism. *Pacific Affairs* 80(1), 9–26.

Sinkule, B.J. and Ortolano, L. (1995) *Implementing Environmental Policy in China*. Westport, CT: Praeger.

Skinner, M.W., Joseph, A.E., and Kuhn, R.G. (2003) Social and environmental regulation in rural China: bringing the changing role of local government into focus. *Geoforum* 34(2), 267–81.

Tilt, B. (2010) *The Struggle for Sustainability in Rural China: environmental values and civil society*. New York: Columbia University Press.

UNEP (United Nations Environment Programme) (2001) Press release: Dalian Municipal Government of China, one of 18 individuals and organizations to receive United Nations Environment Award. *UNEP News Center*, www.unep.org/Documents. Multilingual/Default.asp?DocumentID=201&ArticleID= (accessed May 18, 2005).

While, A., Jonas, A.E.G., and Gibbs, D. (2004) The environment and the entrepreneurial city: searching for the urban "sustainability fix" in Manchester and Leeds. *International Journal of Urban and Regional Research* 28(3), 549–69.

Wu, F. (2003) The (post-)socialist entrepreneurial city as a state project: Shanghai's reglobalization in question. *Urban Studies* 40(9), 1673–98.

Wu, F. and Zhang, J. (2007) Planning the competitive city-region: the emergence of strategic development plan in China. *Urban Affairs Review* 42(5), 714–40.

Xia, D. (2006) *Jianshe ziyuan jieyuexing huanjing youhaoxing chengshi* (Build a city that conserves natural resources and is environmentally friendly). Presentation by Mayor Xia Deren, June 5.

Xiao, G. (2007) Urban tourism: global–local relationships in Dalian, China. PhD thesis, Department of Geography, University of Waterloo, British Columbia.

Yahuda, M.B. (1994) North China and Russia. In D.S.G. Goodman and G. Segal (eds.) *China Deconstructs: politics, trade, and regionalism*. London: Routledge, pp. 253–70.

Yeoh, B.S.A. (2000) From colonial neglect to post-independence heritage: the housing landscape in the central area of Singapore. *City and Society* 12(1), 103–24.

Yeung, Y.M. and Hu, X.W. (eds.) (1992) *China's Coastal Cities: catalysts for modernization*. Honolulu: University of Hawaii Press.

Yu, D. (2003) Industrial relocation and transformation in Dalian. In *Proceedings of Kitakyushu Initiative Seminar on Industrial Relocation*. Ho Chi Minh, Vietnam.

Yuen, B. (1996) Creating the Garden City: the Singapore experience. *Urban Studies* 33(6), 955–70.

Zhang, L. (2001) *Strangers in the City: reconfigurations of space, power, and social networks within China's floating population*. Stanford, CA: Stanford University Press.

Zhao, H. (2001) Urban environmental management in China. Presentation at First Meeting of Kitakyushu Initiative Network, Kitakyushu, Japan, November 20–21; http://www.iges.or.jp/kitakyushu/mtgs/network/kin1/Presentations/Session%20IV/China.doc (accessed January 9, 2008).

Zukin, S. (1991) *Landscapes of Power: from Detroit to Disneyworld*. Berkeley, CA: University of California Press.

3

Planning Privatopolis: Representation and Contestation in the Development of Urban Integrated Mega-Projects

Gavin Shatkin

The past two decades have witnessed the emergence of a particular urban form throughout Asia, what I will refer to in this chapter as urban integrated mega-projects (UIMs). These are city or urban district-scale integrated development projects built on a for-profit basis, often by a single developer. While the specifics of these projects vary, they share a number of features in common. They are very large, spanning from a few dozen to thousands of hectares in area. Projects with projected populations of a half a million or more have been planned in Bangkok, Jakarta, Hanoi, Shanghai, Kolkata, and Mumbai, and dozens more projects with populations in the mere tens or hundreds of thousands have been proposed for many other large cities (Dick and Rimmer 1998; Marshall 2003). They are conceived of as self-contained urban entities, containing residential, commercial, office, and industrial space, in addition – in many cases – to schools, university campuses, hospitals, hotels, and convention centers. Finally, in a departure from past efforts at state-driven master planning and new town development, these projects are planned and built on a for-profit basis, often by a single developer or a consortium of investors, sometimes in partnership with government entities. As large-scale profit-oriented urban entities, these projects represent a vision for the transformation of the urban experience through the wholesale commodification of the urban fabric. In the context of Asia's rapid globalization, these projects are represented by governments and developers as a means of mobilizing corporate entrepreneurship and technology to create urban spaces that attract investment, create efficiencies, and enable residents to realize their potential as actors in a global economy.

Worlding Cities: Asian Experiments and the Art of Being Global, First Edition.
Edited by Ananya Roy and Aihwa Ong.
© 2011 Blackwell Publishing Ltd. Published 2011 by Blackwell Publishing Ltd.

This chapter views the proliferation of UIMs as indicative of a trend toward the *privatization of urban and regional planning*. By this phrase, I refer to the ascendance of private-sector actors from an historically fragmented and indirect role in shaping urban form to a central role in the core functions of urban planning – the visioning of urban futures, and the translation of these visions into the planning, development, and regulation of urban spaces and the network infrastructures that connect them on an urban and regional scale. This is not meant to imply that private-sector actors had not previously been involved in city building – indeed, in most Asian cities, private developers and individuals have historically built and owned most of the urban fabric. However, their planning and urban design efforts have generally previously been confined to the scale of a building, or at the most a block. What is new, I argue, is their function in the planning, design, and regulation of urban spaces at a much larger scale. This process of privatization has been driven by the (as yet tentative) shift in the role of states from imposing modernist visions for the transformation of cities, to a more entrepreneurial role in facilitating private-sector development as a means of capitalizing on the economic opportunities presented by globalization. Hence the development of UIMs is a critical manifestation of the transformations in statehood and citizenship under conditions of globalization that have been observed by a number of contemporary theorists (Holston and Appadurai 1999; Brenner 2004; Ong 2006).

Yet, as exercised through actual brick-and-mortar intervention, this transformation is far from complete, and in many instances has foundered upon a range of legal, political, and cultural obstacles. Outside of China (which is a notable exception), even the most successful projects have not attained their developers' ambitious objectives. The new town of Lippo Karawaci, for example, is one of the most successful UIMs in Southeast Asia, with a current population of around 40,000, yet it is far behind schedule on its initially projected population of a million by 2020 (Dick and Rimmer 1998; Lippo Karawaci 2009). Some projects have failed financially, most notably the massive Muang Thong Thani project. Located on the periphery of Bangkok, it was planned for more than 700,000 eventual residents, but large sections remained abandoned or severely underutilized more than a decade after the Asian Financial Crisis crippled Thailand's real-estate sector (Sheng and Kirinpanu 2000; Marshall 2003). And for every UIM that breaks ground, there are several more which have scarcely advanced beyond the concept stage, and in many cases likely never will. In India, massive new town projects in Mumbai, Kolkata, and Bangalore have foundered on issues surrounding land acquisition, legal controversies, difficulties in financing, and popular resistance. Very large initiatives in Vietnam, Thailand, and elsewhere have suffered a similar fate.

It is in this context of vaunted aspiration, contestation, and halting and uneven movement toward an urban transformation that this chapter will explore the Asian inter-referencing that is a central aspect of the UIM model. Privately built UIMs are perhaps the purest form of inter-referenced urbanism, as they represent the deliberate whole-cloth adoption of new models of urban design, planning, and governance based on an interpretation of how a global urbanism should look and function. Asian inter-referencing takes various forms in such projects: in their development either in whole or part through inter-Asian foreign direct investment (as when a Jakarta-based developer builds a UIM on the outskirts of Kolkata); in the explicit modeling of urban governance regimes on institutions and practices from elsewhere in Asia (as when a Singapore government-owned consulting firm employs models of urban design and land -use planning from Singapore in a project in China or India); and, more abstractly, when the example of "best practices" in global architecture and urban design from the region (notably the ubiquitous examples of Singapore and Shanghai) are selectively appropriated and interpreted as appropriately "Asian" models to be emulated through the development of UIMs. The underlying logic of such inter-referencing is that the common opportunities and challenges emergent with the globalization of urban economies necessitate the creation of urban spaces that nurture a desired type of citizen – globally oriented, knowledge economy workers, who can form a creative and managerial core for a process of economic transformation. Through inter-referencing, politicians, planners, architects, and developers seek to capture the essence of "successful" Asian global urbanism.

The chapter explicates the logic of Asian inter-referencing in UIMs, placing this discussion in the context of current debates about the changing nature of citizenship in urban Asia. It specifically makes three arguments. The first is that, inasmuch as they lead to displacement and disruption of existing economies and social relations, UIMs are often contested and subverted in the realm of politics and daily social practice. The degree to which such contestation and subversion succeeds in halting or significantly reshaping the projects depends in large part on the ability of social actors who oppose this agenda, or simply hope to bargain a better deal in its realization, to call on significant sources of political power. The second argument is that the plans of UIMs, and the representations that are generated to promote them, function in part as allegories – as idealized visions intended to illustrate a possible urban future. These utopian visions are used as a rhetorical strategy to garner support and discredit opponents of these developments by mustering the forces of social and political actors aligned with the project of creating a new global urbanity. The third argument is that the classic examples of "successful" global urbanism – most notably Shanghai and Singapore – are employed to represent a certain ideal characterized by a strong state, a global orientation, a master-planned urban environment, and a technocratic and market-oriented mode of planning. Hence inter-referencing is in part employed by developers and state actors to shape political and social discourse, and to present an argument for the dismantling of social and political obstacles to the achievement of their desired model of urban transformation.

The chapter will begin with a discussion of the context of UIM development and its relation to the changing role of the state in urban development in Asia. It will then discuss the factors that shape success in UIM development. Finally, the chapter will discuss two contrasting cases that reveal some of the variation in the actual outcomes of UIM plans in major Asian cities – these cases are Kolkata and Metro Manila.

The Historical Context of UIM Development

New town development is not new to Asia – the development of government-sponsored complexes incorporating residential, commercial, and other functions was a central element of planning in Singapore and Hong Kong from the 1960s onward. Industrial new towns and large-scale housing estates were also prevalent in India, China, and South Korea. What marks the contemporary projects under consideration in this study as different is their explicitly profit-oriented and commodified nature, and the powerful role of the corporate sector in their conceptualization, planning, development, and governance. Some precedents for such profit-oriented, city, or urban district scale interventions do exist in Asia. Corporate developers have played a key role in Japan's urban development through the development of commuter rail lines that are integrated with large commercial centers around terminals, and residential new towns on the periphery (Cervero 1998). Likewise, the Makati central business district, which dominates Metro Manila's global business functions, is wholly owned by Ayala Land, a private developer, which has master-planned it as an elite residential enclave and commercial and office center since the late 1940s (Batalla 1999). It has been since the late 1980s, however, that we have seen this model emerge as a predominant concept in urban development. In Jakarta, Dick and Rimmer (1998) list thirteen private-sector driven new towns initiated between 1987 and 1997, each over 750 hectares in size. In Vietnam, the massive (and yet to be realized) Hanoi North project was announced in 1996, while in Bangkok the lone UIM that has been realized, Muang Thong Thani, was conceived in 1992 (Marshall 2003). The UIM concept took root in India shortly after the liberalization of that country's economy in 1991, although none of the largest proposed projects has broken ground to date.

In each of these cases, global UIMs have in the past two decades emerged not only as a major form of real-estate development, but also as a predominant *state* strategy of urban development. Governments have aggressively pursued such projects by providing assistance in land acquisition (and in some cases the sale of state land), provision of links to urban infrastructure networks, regulatory relaxation, and, perhaps most importantly, rhetorical and political support for developer goals. Support has emerged among both national governments, which seek to create new spaces for economic growth in major urban regions that are increasingly seen as critical to national economic growth, and among local governments that view these projects as potential sources of revenue, and as a means of getting development goals accomplished with limited local government resources. Where the obstacles to a corporate role are daunting, or where national or local state actors aspire to move from entrepreneurial governance to the injection of a profit rationality into the very machinery of government, state entities have realized a more direct role in privatizing state land and maintaining an equity stake in commodified urban developments.[1] Hence the emergence of UIMs must be understood as a transformation of the role of the state in urban development.

The emergence of the global UIM model as a state strategy for urban transformation comes at an historical juncture marked by the confluence of a number of trends in state–society relations in the global era. Perhaps best understood among these is the entrepreneurial turn in urban governance, the reorientation of urban politics toward a focus on capturing investment and growth. Brenner (2004) has described this as a shift from "spatial Keynesianism," the post-World War II focus of national governments on employing urban and regional policy to achieve goals of inter- and intra-regional equity, to a focus on reconfiguring state institutions to foster competitiveness and growth in core urban regions. Mechanisms to achieve such a transformation have included the creation of new growth-driven urban redevelopment authorities that are insulated from public input and accountability, deregulation, the employment of new zoning strategies, and public–private partnerships in the provision of major new infrastructure and real-estate development. These strategies have been employed to create new economic areas (technopoles, cyberports, aerotropoli, enterprise zones), foster the development of business-oriented facilities (downtown revitalization), and create new amenities and tourism facilities (waterfront districts, theaters, new residential zones) (Jessop and Sum 2000; Fainstein 2001; Yeoh 2005; Ong 2006; Whitehead and More 2007). Within this context, for-profit UIMs represent a particularly ambitious model of reconfiguring relations between the state and the corporate sector to realize growth, an effort to enable capital to directly dictate spatial relationships between spaces of global command and control functions, high-technology production, residence and consumption of globalized elites, and the provision of amenities targeted toward these elites. Hence it is a partial response to the challenge identified by Harvey (2006: 101), who argues that, with globalization, major infrastructure projects represent a response to the need for disparate inter-dependent urban functions to "hang together in physical space in reasonably coordinate and mutually accessible ways" so that capital accumulation can occur.

A second trend shaping the UIM strategy is the continued population, spatial, and economic expansion of Asian cities – between 1950 and 2000, the population of Asian cities expanded from 232 million to 1.4 billion (UNCHS 2004). Particularly in the atmosphere of fiscal austerity that emerged in the 1970s, this growth has strained the housing, infrastructure, and service systems provided by governments. The consequent persistent growth of shadow economies – informal housing, extra-legal connections to water, electricity, and other services, the appropriation of streets and public spaces for economic activities – has fostered public debate in many cities over the terms of urban citizenship. As Benjamin (2008: 725) argues, the strident efforts of international institutions and governments to seek a technocratic fix to these issues has met with little success, and has done little to address the "deeply material public debate" that has accompanied the perception that the state had lost control of the city. This debate essentially focuses on whether their illegal occupation and use of urban space provides an adequate moral and legal basis for the exclusion of the poor from a range of citizenship rights, including the rights to personal security, to political representation, and to access to public space (Douglass 2005–6; Anjaria 2006; Shatkin 2008).

The failure of the state to control the city, as perceived in particular by middle- and upper-class urban residents, has fostered a variety of socio-political and cultural responses. It has been a motivating factor behind the wave of privatization of both infrastructure and city-building. It has also fostered a response at the grassroots level, as middle- and upper-class neighborhoods have witnessed increased associationalism, and in some cases vigilantism, in an effort to reassert control of the public realm (Baviskar 2003; Anjaria 2006). These debates and disputes have occasionally fostered direct and violent conflict – Baviskar (2003) provides one poignant illustration of this in her discussion of the murder of a young man by a mob that suspected him of defecating in a middle-class park in Delhi. In this respect, the project of a neoliberal rationality, described by Ong (2006: 5) as an effort to "recalculate social criteria of citizenship, to remoralize economic action, and to redefine spaces in relation to market-driven choices," is one that resonates deeply with a middle- and upper-class perceptions that the state, in losing the city, has lost its capacity to guide or control public behavior.

The final trend shaping the context of UIM development is the wave of democratization that swept through the region in the 1980s and 1990s. While this wave occurred unevenly, it has brought common elements to many countries in Asia – the spread of electoral democracy, the decentralization of authority to local governments, and the proliferation of NGOs and CBOs, many acting as advocacy groups for low-income people. The forces of political pluralization have provided the significant segment of the population that operates in the shadow economy access to political power, as what Chatterjee (2004) has referred to as "political society" – mobilizations of the urban poor seeking political influence – have bartered votes for recognition, protection, and access to services. This has resulted in a dramatic expansion of the legal gray zone of negotiation between the state and the urban poor through paralegal arrangements concerning land tenure, access to services, and the appropriation of public space. In India, where these gray zones dominate the urban landscape, Benjamin (2008) has characterized the resulting formation as "occupancy urbanism," which he views as constituting a powerful force to subvert efforts at urban transformation through master planning, and infrastructure and real-estate mega-projects. Hence campaigns for urban redevelopment represent an increasingly strenuous effort by state and civil society actors to overcome the logic of mass subversion of planning norms through the ground-level practice of electoral politics. The development of UIMs represents one particular response – the creation of elite urban spaces insulated from this disorder, and from the political pluralism that undermines efforts at master planning and urban cleansing. Specifically, their control by corporate actors and unaccountable government structures provides the political insulation needed to strictly implement zoning and building codes, and to effectively regulate public space.

It is in this context of maneuvering over the terms of urban political and social inclusion that an understanding of the rhetorical strategies of proponents of UIMs is analytically useful. In the contradictory environment presented by contemporary urban politics in the region, private-sector developed UIMs allow governments to present a model of urban redevelopment that potentially solves a sticky political riddle: How can governments identify a new model of urbanism that promises a path to economic growth and modernization within a global economic system, but that does so without evoking concerns about neocolonialism and dependency?

The question of what models of urban design and development to pursue post-independence has posed a significant dilemma for governments of the region. The 1950s and 1960s saw the rise of modernism as a model of urban design and architecture that resonated with state efforts to shape nation-states and create new subjectivities based on a set of ostensibly universal principles. Yet the adoption of models that had originated in the West was in many instances seen as politically and socially problematic, an act of last resort that must be rationalized or disguised. Chatterjee (2004), for example, argues that Nehru's choice of France's Le Corbusier for the design of the new city of Chandigarh was an "act of desperation" motivated by the perceived lack of Indian models of urbanism appropriate to the task of building a modern nation-state. Elsewhere, planners sought to legitimize their adoption of Western planning techniques by claiming indigenous precedents for models that were in fact borrowed from the West (Holston 1989; Lico 2003). In practice, as Holston (1989) has argued, state-driven modernist planning has often failed inasmuch as it has not taken adequate consideration of the social practices of the populations that inhabit urban spaces, setting the stage for the corruption of the schemes. Modernist models have often consequently lost their luster, and much of their political value, in the face of "occupancy urbanism." Hence, the failures, exclusions, and inequities that have characterized state-driven modernist projects have served to undermine claims of universal citizenship theoretically embodied in national governments.

The market orientation of privately built UIMs allows their governmental and corporate boosters to transcend debates about the propriety of the modernist models by presenting them as simply a response to market demand, as a new kind of space built for a new type of consumer, a global citizen. Advertising for these projects pays meticulous attention to the characteristics and perceived demands of their client groups – the "modern" and "world class" nature of the infrastructure, facilities, and spaces, and the elite nature of the clientele (King 2004). These depictions valorize and celebrate the inhabitants of these projects. In addition, the advertising emphasizes their role in connecting local economies to the global, focusing on the "international" quality of the spaces, amenities, and infrastructure. Implicitly, their market-oriented nature, and the arms-length role of government in their implementation, serves to mute critiques from civil and political society of state elitism or social engineering – they are (the argument goes) simply an entrepreneurial response to an emerging market for such spaces.

The ubiquitous Singapore and Shanghai models come in to play here as well, representing a refutation of criticisms of the globalization of urban economies and attendant redevelopment as a neocolonial imposition. In evoking these models, UIM proponents seek to legitimize their approach by making reference to a model of globalism that is rooted in a set of values (sometimes presented as a universal Asian set of values) that they argue is indigenous to their host societies. Two distinct sets of arguments are employed in the rhetoric surrounding these models. The first focuses on the institutional innovations around the governance of these projects, which combine a firm and paternalistic hand of government with market discipline. While this is a central argument in rationalizing UIMs, it is often made implicitly, as the assumption of new powers by the state and the adoption of new forms of state–corporate partnership are inferred to lead to a physical and economic transformation of the city. Hence large-scale land acquisition and displacements of communities is justified in the name of an effort to transform Bangalore into a new Singapore or Mumbai into Shanghai (Benjamin 2008). Indeed, Singapore has begun to capitalize on its reputation for non-corrupt, efficient governance by creating through its investment arm a township development consultancy, Surbana, that has embarked on a number of international projects, mostly in China and India (as Chua Beng Huat's chapter in this volume also notes). The second argument focuses on the physical form of the city itself. In Hanoi, for example, the planners of the massive Tu Liem project (which has yet to be built) modeled their project on Singapore, which the project designers interpreted as employing the iconic massing of buildings, efficient transportation networks, and state-of-the-art infrastructure to foster economic efficiency and create a globally recognized magnet for investment and growth (Marshall 2003).

The Singapore and Shanghai models also provide a template for a kind of politics and governance that creates possibilities for a wholesale urban transformation in the face of the increasing assertiveness of Chatterjee's "political society." Here, these models stand in for a paternalistic, pragmatic, technocratic, decisive, and powerful government that acts boldly, entrepreneurially, and decisively to achieve urban development objectives. Hence the oft-cited Vision Mumbai plan, written by the McKinsey consulting company on behalf of a consortium of local developers, corporations, and politicians, refers favorably to the record of accomplishments of Zhu Rongji – "one chop Zhu" – in cutting through red tape to realize the development of real-estate and infrastructure mega-projects and pave the way for massive economic growth (Bombay First/McKinsey & Company 2003). In Bangalore, the chief minister of the state of Karnataka drew on an interpretation of the "Singapore model" in pushing through a range of reforms. These included centralizing control over key development authorities, creating the corporate-driven Bangalore Agenda Task Force with a broad mandate to set an agenda for the city's development, and implementing e-governance as a mechanism for political accountability (Benjamin 2000). The Jawaharlal Nehru National Urban Renewal Mission (JNNURM), a major national urban development initiative, has subsequently encouraged the replication of these reforms in other Indian cities.

The discourses of the Singapore and Shanghai models represent mega-project development as a simple issue of political vision and will. In doing so, they disregard the exceptional circumstances that allowed massive urban transformations to move forward in these two cities. Specifically, as states with strong authoritarian (or at best semi-democratic) central governments that exercise an unusual degree of control over urban land (the Chinese state owns all urban land and the Singaporean government owns more than

80 percent of land in the city-state), neither has to contend to any significant degree with obstacles to land acquisition or alternative claims to land, or with political fallout from controversy generated by such projects (Haila 2000). To some degree, however, these realities are irrelevant – these narratives of paternalistic governance serve primarily to mobilize the elite constituents of UIMs, to provide a moral basis for their promotion by government, and to counter alternative claims to urban space.

This section has argued that the development of UIMs is rooted in a set of powerful political interests rooted in government, the corporate sector, and influential segments of society, and that governments and developers employ models of successful urbanism such as those of Singapore and Shanghai to legitimize urban change. Nevertheless, the halting and inconsistent progress of these projects also indicates that alternative claims to urban space are not entirely bereft of sources of power and influence, and that the state–corporate nexus that forwards this agenda is not entirely seamless and omnipotent in its exertions. The next section develops a framework for understanding why and how these visions succeed or fail.

When and Why Do UIMs Succeed or Fail?

The preceding discussion has attempted to reframe the discussion of UIMs by arguing that, far from being a coherent and inevitable project for the reformation of cities and citizenship, it is in fact a highly political and occasionally incoherent set of initiatives that has resulted in as many failures as successes. This line of argumentation leads to a distinctly different set of questions about the social, political, and cultural meaning of UIMs than has been pursued in past research. Most past studies have focused on the meaning and agencies of the development of a global urban culture, and have therefore focused their attention on the role of multinational developers and architecture and planning firms as the primary agents of the transmission of such a culture through the design of UIMs (see especially Olds 2001; Marshall 2003). It is notable that much of this research has looked at China, where, for reasons described in the previous section, multinational architecture and planning firms have had unusually free reign to use cities as a canvas upon which to explore themes of global urbanism. Yet China is an exceptional case, and there is a need to examine the tribulations of the UIM concept in other parts of Asia, where the grand schemes of architects and planners have fallen on rockier soil. This section will discuss some of the alternative sources of social power that complicate the ability of government and corporate actors to realize their designs, and that allow other actors to articulate and sometimes realize different urban outcomes in the face of UIM plans. It will focus on two specific factors: the terms of access to urban land, and political representation.

These two factors are, of course, closely interrelated – for as Benjamin's concept of occupancy urbanism and Chatterjee's formulation of a political society both imply, rights to urban land lie at the very heart of contemporary politics in many Asian countries. While the privatized UIM concept allows states to avoid some of the pitfalls associated with social engineering through more direct state intervention in the urban built environment, it nonetheless puts both state and corporate actors on a collision course with this nexus of land and politics inasmuch as such projects require the acquisition of large tracts of land, and usually the displacement of significant numbers of people/voters. The degree to which contestation over the terms of UIM development prevents their completion or significantly influences their form depends on a number of historical and contextual contingencies. Patterns of land-ownership are quite important, as the absence of concentrations of land in the hands of large landowners or state entities places a considerable onus on the state to facilitate acquisition of parcels of adequate size. The existence of legal mechanisms by which communities can resist eviction can provide communities with significant leverage, and the exercise of political influence by communities through the vote can provide them with means to shape the form of the projects or the process of their development. The reality of UIM development therefore reflects Jessop's (2002: 453) observation that the recent turn toward neoliberalism should not be seen as the assertion of a "singular, univocal, and internally coherent" set of discourses and practices, but rather as a contested set of transformations in which the neoliberal model "coexists with elements from other discourses, strategies, and organizational patterns." Specifically, social and political change associated with globalization should be viewed as emerging from the outcomes of specific contests for influence and power with "the relative balance of economic, political, and civic liberalism depend[ing] on the changing balance of forces within an institutionalized (but changeable) compromise" (Jessop 2002: 453).

That UIM development is subject to contestation and debate is reflected in the political strategies that state actors have employed to push these projects forward. These efforts have often focused on creating institutional and legal mechanisms to enable the consolidation of large parcels of land in the face of considerable obstacles. In India, the central government has attempted to overcome local political obstacles to urban redevelopment, and to UIM development in particular, through the JNNURM, which ties significant funding for urban redevelopment to what are intended to be a comprehensive set of state-level mandated reforms aimed at facilitating private-sector real-estate investment. These reforms include the repeal of Urban Land Ceiling Act, a 1976 law placing a ceiling on private landholdings that has been seen as an obstacle to the consolidation of land for urban redevelopment (Mahadevia 2006). Another modus through which large parcels of land are freed for development is the sale or leasing of government land. In the Philippines, the Bases Conversion Development Authority (BCDA) has been a major actor in the realization of large-scale real-estate and infrastructure projects through the sale of decommissioned military bases. As part of its mission to create "globally competitive and highly sustainable growth centers," the BCDA has played a key role in freeing land for private investment, most notably through the sale of Fort Bonifacio for a major UIM development (BCDA 2002: 2). A closely related strategy involves the redevelopment of large state-owned parcels of land through public–private partnership. In Bangkok, for example, the national government has actively encouraged state-owned enterprises and government ministries to develop public–private for-profit real-estate schemes on state land as a means of revenue generation. The reclamation of land through landfill and the filling in of waterways is yet another strategy for the creation of developable blocks of land – plans to develop global enclaves on landfill along Manila Bay and through the filling of Boeung Kak lake in Phnom Penh are but two examples of this strategy (Muijzenberg and van Naerssen 2005; Hughes 2008).

Each of the above examples represents a distinct response by states and private-sector actors to the particular constraints they face in consolidating land and overcoming opposition to development. Nevertheless, these strategies vary widely in their effectiveness, and their relative success or failure reflects both the historical realities of land-ownership and the tenacity of the political and social forces opposing redevelopment. The following brief discussion of the experience of UIMs in Metro Manila and Kolkata will provide two contrasting examples that illustrate how these differences in context lead to differences in both the politics of UIM development, and their actual impact on urban change.

Kolkata: The Quagmire of Political Society

Kolkata presents a case of a local state that is drawn to the tantalizing possibilities for growth through rapid integration into global markets, yet constrained by the forces of political society that are to a large degree of its own creation, and indeed form the bedrock of its political base. What has resulted thus far is a landscape of anticipation. Trunk roads extending from the city center are lined with fenced off spaces fronted by billboards proclaiming the imminent arrival of transformative global spaces, yet in reality the few projects that have progressed are relatively small and seem besieged by the teeming city around them.

In this regard, Kolkata is an extreme example of the fate that has generally befallen UIMs in India – most of the larger projects (Maha Mumbai and Kolkata's Dankuni Township being the most prominent examples) have stalled indefinitely despite government efforts to drive them to realization. The economic liberalization that was initiated in the early 1990s fostered a powerful wave of growth generated by information technology and business outsourcing industries, which in turn has generated demand for the creation of new urban spaces. The Indian government has responded by turning away from pre-liberalization efforts at urban master planning and new town development, which articulated Nehruvian ideals of a secularism, socialism, and modernism, to the aggressive espousal of a more entrepreneurial mode of governance. Legislation passed in 2005 allowed for 100 percent foreign equity stakes in township developments of 10 hectares or more, and stipulated the required characteristics of such projects; for example, that they be integrated, and contain a defined set of services such as hospital and school facilities (Sengupta 2007). Through the JNNURM and other initiatives, the national government has provided incentives to pursue the possibilities presented by this liberalization.

It is in Kolkata where the contradictions inherent in the shift from state-led planning with a focus on nation-building and social equity to privatized planning and entrepreneurial governance are felt most acutely. Politics in the state of West Bengal has been dominated for more than 30 years by the Communist Party of India-Marxist (CPI-M), which has maintained hegemony through an electoral base rooted largely in rural areas. Until recently, its urban platform focused on urban land reform, rent control, and the cultivation of political patronage among the urban poor. With liberalization, however, the CPI-M of West Bengal has made aggressive efforts to pursue global urban transformation through corporate-driven redevelopment. Roy (2003) argues that the CPI-M has historically deliberately created a context of legal ambiguity with regard to land-ownership in its past populist interventions in land markets, notably through relocation programs that did not provide resettled families clear title, and land-reform programs that rendered many existing landholdings technically illegal. With globalization and liberalization, the Party is now attempting to exploit that legal ambiguity in its efforts at land acquisition to realize privatized real-estate developments. Yet this ambiguity has proven a double-edged sword, as intensifying pressures for displacement have met with increased resistance from local farmers, and have highlighted the contradictions inherent in the efforts of a nominally Marxist political party to displace rural communities in order to develop commodified urban spaces. This contradiction has created political space for the emergence of alternative political voices, most notably in the person of Mamata Banerjee, leader of a breakaway faction of the Congress Party, who has risen to positions of considerable power through a series of populist protests over a number of issues, including the dispossession of villages and the urban poor. Particularly notable were protests held in 2006 and 2007 over the construction of an automobile factory on 400 hectares of land in Singur, some 30 kilometers from central Kolkata – the size of the land parcel involved led to some speculation that Tata had designs for a larger real-estate project beyond the factory itself. This project was eventually abandoned after protests by Banerjee and a number of other celebrities and prominent political figures.

The political fallout from the Singur project, as well as another project to develop a Special Economic Zone (SEZ) at Nandigram, have hexed other government efforts at UIM development. Most notable is the state government's centerpiece project, Dankuni Township, which at 2000 hectares and a projected population of 600,000 is one of the largest proposed privately built townships in India. One of the largest developers in India, DLF, was awarded the project in 2006, yet despite the state government's intention to begin land acquisition that year, at the time of this writing no land has been acquired. This is largely because of the awareness of both state officials and communities of the effectiveness of the community protests at Singur and Nandigram (*Telegraph* 2008).

In at least one other case, a UIM has made halting but steady progress toward realization, and the circumstances under which this has occurred are instructive. The Calcutta Riverside project was initiated when the property developer, Hiland Properties, entered into an agreement with Bata Footwear to redevelop the site of one of Bata's factories located on the banks of the Hooghly River, just outside Kolkata municipality, as an upscale integrated new town. The Bata factory occupies a lot of 125 hectares, although only 19 hectares of this is taken up by the factory itself, with the remaining 106 hectares consisting of a mix of worker housing and undeveloped land. In 2005, the San Francisco-based architecture and planning firm HOK delivered a master plan for the development, which was to include condominiums and villas, a nine-hole golf course, a retail mall, a convention center, a riverfront promenade, an information technology SEZ, and a school and hospital (HOK 2005). The project has broken ground, and it is slated to be built in three phases, with the first phase ready for occupation in late 2011. The eventual population of the area is projected at about 30,000.

Why has this project moved forward while others have stalled? There appear to be two major reasons. First, it does not involve the controversial conversion of agricultural land to urban uses, and it does not require the relocation of large numbers of existing residents off-site. Second, the relatively smooth progress toward implementation has arguably only been realized because Hiland and Bata have made significant concessions to the local population that appear to potentially subvert the conventionally exclusionary and commodified nature of many such developments. These include: the rehousing of all Bata employees (mostly factory workers) on-site free of cost; the on-site provision of market space for existing vendors occupying the site, in a facility located at a planned transportation hub; the inclusion of open space in the redevelopment plan that is explicitly intended to maintain community access for such important cultural functions as the Durga Puja; and the preservation of some existing public facilities such as schools and religious institutions (Riverbank Private Holdings Limited n.d.). Hence this exceptional case draws attention to the imperative in Kolkata that such projects avoid the political and social contradictions of the local context, and make significant concessions to local interests to a degree that may require a significant alteration of the character of the development.

Hence while the Singapore and Shanghai models are frequently evoked in the Indian context, the reality of UIM development in Kolkata reveals the limited efficacy of state actors in realizing the privatization of urban development. The CPI-M's willingness to stake its political future on its gambit to wrest control of land for large development projects is testament to the power of the incentives provided by the growth of the real-estate industry, but the gambit has largely failed. This failure reflects the Party's inability to control urban land in the context of: highly diffuse landholdings; a legacy of national and local legislation that has created a tangle of regulations, and programs that have clouded land title and created obstacles to the consolidation of land; and an electoral system in which the numeric dominance of the urban and rural poor insures that efforts to displace members of these groups in order to consolidate parcels for redevelopment will be punished at the ballot box. Indeed, the CPI-M suffered significant setbacks in 2008 municipal elections in West Bengal in the aftermath of the Singur and Nandigram controversies. While Kolkata may represent an extreme case, it nevertheless resonates with failed efforts to construct political coalitions around urban development elsewhere in India. Based on experience to date, while some projects have been pushed through by the use of sheer force, in other instances they have moved forward only after issues of displacement and access to urban space have at least been addressed in part through a process of negotiation with affected communities. Hence the tectonic collision between the forces of global change and those of political society has resulted in numerous tremors around specific efforts at urban transformation, but it is yet unclear how the urban landscape will be reshaped by these competing forces.

Metro Manila: "Booty Capitalism" and the Privatization of Planning

Metro Manila contrasts with the Kolkata case in the degree to which the city has seen significant progress in the development of UIMs – these projects have become a defining feature of Metro Manila's urban landscape. This trend has been facilitated by the relative weakness of both civil and political society in the context of a state which has been captured by elite economic actors (Shatkin 2008). The roots of this situation lie in the historical development of a plantation-based economy that developed during Spanish colonial rule, which resulted in the formation of an economically powerful landowning class (Sidel 1999). The American colonial regime, in place during the first half of the twentieth century, fostered the development of an electoral democracy, but did so in a way that deliberately maintained elite political control. Wealthy landowning families were able to use their resources to dominate electoral posts in local government and Parliament. The result is what has been referred to as a system of "booty capitalism," in which a "powerful business class extracts privilege from a largely incoherent bureaucracy" (Hutchcroft 1998: 20). In the aftermath of Marcos's efforts to achieve political hegemony, the country has witnessed a backlash from both this economic elite and civil society, against the vestiges of Marcos-era efforts to establish a strong, centralized regime. Metro-level bodies have consequently been stripped of all but the most basic sources of authority, and initiatives for democratization and decentralization have placed considerable urban planning and policy power in the hands of the seventeen cities and municipalities that make up Metro Manila. Simply stated, in the current governance structure, there exist few political institutions with significant power or legitimacy through which civil or political society can register concern over the direction of urban redevelopment.

In this context, UIMs have progressed through two channels. The first is through the acquisition by private corporations of large tracts of formerly hacienda land (Magno-Ballesteros 2000). This model in fact has deep roots, beginning with the development by the Ayala family in the aftermath of World War II of part of its Hacienda de Makati landholding as an alternative residential and business center on the outskirts of the City of Manila, which was heavily bombed during the war (Batalla 1999). This property eventually became the Makati Central Business District, which remains to this day the premier business, commercial, and elite residential area of Metro Manila. Ayala Land has subsequently acquired significant parcels from former agricultural and food-processing estates in, among other locations, southern Metro Manila (for the development of its 659 hectare Ayala Alabang UIM), and in the adjoining province of Laguna (the location of its newer projects at Laguna Technopark, Ayala Westgrove, and Ayala South).

The second channel is through the government sale of state land. A key actor in this regard has been the Bases Conversion Development Authority (BCDA), which is tasked with redeveloping former military bases in order to create growth centers (BCDA 2002). The BCDA was involved in the most significant project currently being implemented in Metro Manila, Bonifacio

Global City. In 1995, the Philippine government sold 214 hectares of Fort Bonifacio, a military facility adjacent to the Makati CBD, for more than $1 billion to a pan-Asian consortium of ethnic Chinese business families that included participants from Indonesia and Hong Kong as well as the Philippines (Muijzenberg and van Naerssen 2005). The property was subsequently bought out by Ayala Land Incorporated in the aftermath of the Asian Financial Crisis at a fraction of the original price, and is currently being developed as an extension of the Makati CBD. The project's master plan, also prepared by San Francisco-based HOK, calls for an elite residential, commercial, office, and high tech industrial park to accommodate 200,000 residents and a half a million daytime users (Liss-Katz 1998). Construction of Bonifacio Global City has moved forward steadily, and the development already contains several condominiums, shopping centers, and office buildings, and is emerging as a major urban node. There are several other major projects that involve the sale of public land, including Rockwell Center, a major mixed-use development built by Rockwell Land in 2009, on a site formerly occupied by a state-owned thermal power plant.

The political rhetoric and marketing around these initiatives has focused relentlessly on the achievement of a "global city" ideal embodied (either explicitly or implicitly) in the popular perception of Singapore in particular as the model for the realization of such an ideal. In reality, however, what has resulted is a much more fragmented urban landscape, characterized by the polarization of urban space between the congested spaces of the "public" city, and highly regulated, carefully designed spaces of elite consumerism and global business. This emerging reality has arguably only highlighted the tensions inherent in the persistent socioeconomic and political disparities that characterize Philippine society.

Conclusion

This chapter has argued that the inter-referencing of Asian models, rather than reflecting a naïve belief that cities can simply follow along the path beaten by other globalizing cities, instead reflects the shrewd employment of certain images and ideals to promote a very specific development agenda. UIMs represent an effort to realize a privatized model of urban planning in order to achieve state goals of the globalization of urban economies, as well as corporate goals of the large-scale commodification of urban land and the realization of unprecedented profit through real-estate investment. The referencing of Singapore, Shanghai, and other models provides design and governance templates that indicate the possibility of success, and therefore soften political and social opposition to these changes. The relevant question is therefore not whether this inter-referencing will "work" (e.g., lead to the replication of urban outcomes), but rather how the models that result respond to local opportunities and constraints, how effective they are in overcoming obstacles to urban redevelopment, and what implications the resulting models of urban governance and design have for social and political change.

The two cases reveal that states in highly divergent contexts face remarkably similar incentives to pursue such projects – the potential for realization of new sources of revenue from property taxes and the sale of public land, the creation of new spaces for economic growth, and the simple capacity to assert a semblance of control in the face of the atrophy of state capacity to regulate urban space. The variation in the impact of UIMs emerges, however, in histories, political cultures, and institutional dynamics of societies, which produce countervailing interests that states must balance with the pressures for growth. In Metro Manila, large developers and landed interests have long held considerable power, and this has continued as post-authoritarian political reform has placed planning authority at scales where they can continue to exercise influence through patronage and economic might. The result has been significant change to the built environment, resulting in the imposition of elite, profit-oriented spaces on the urban fabric even as the rest of the city, planned by the public sector, disintegrates physically and socially. In contrast, in India, the historical and institutional legacy reflects a generation of efforts to disempower urban government, weaken capital, and cater to the political interests of myriad groups, not least in the West Bengal case the rural and urban poor. In West Bengal, the result is that any efforts at master planning face daunting obstacles unless they are framed in a broader rhetoric of inclusion, poverty alleviation, and protection of the rights of the poor. The proponents of UIMs have sometimes attempted to impose such projects through force, and this strategy has had some success. However, thus far it appears that some degree of conciliation lends projects a greater chance of coming to fruition. As matters stand currently, the redevelopment agenda remains largely in question as the state and private developers muster their forces, solidify their claims, and make strategic concessions.

In both of the cases examined here, the change brought by UIMs is as yet tentative, and outcomes remain subject to the influence of policy and planning action and community-based mobilization. As such, the most fruitful research questions for consideration have to do with the terms under which debate about these projects takes place, and the contextual factors that shape the ability of different groups to shape outcomes. What strategies do state- and private-sector actors employ in moving projects forward? How do they respond to the resistance they face? What strategies do communities and other social actors employ in this engagement? What factors contribute to their ability or inability to form a collective response? Finally, under what circumstances do UIMs make progress, and how does engagement between the state, developers, and communities shape the final outcomes? This chapter has taken an initial step toward addressing these questions, but there is much more research to be done.

Note

1   See, for example, descriptions of state roles in UIM development in China (Marshall 2003) and Thailand (Douglass and Boonchuen 2006).

References

Anjaria, J. (2006) Street hawkers and public space in Mumbai. *Economic Political Weekly*, May 28, 2140–6.

Bases Conversion Development Authority (BCDA) (2002) *Taking the Next Step Forward: conversion through land and asset integration.* Metro Manila.

Batalla, E. (1999) Zaibatsu development in the Philippines: the Ayala model. *Southeast Asian Studies* 37, 1.

Baviskar, A. (2003) Between violence and desire: space, power and identity in the making of metropolitan Delhi. *International Social Science Journal* 175, 1.

Benjamin, S. (2000) Governance, economic settings and poverty in Bangalore. *Environment and Urbanization* 21(1), 35–56.

Benjamin, S. (2008) Occupancy urbanism: radicalizing politics and economy beyond policy and programs. *International Journal of Urban and Regional Research* 32(3), 719–29.

Brenner, N. (2004) *New State Spaces: urban governance and the rescaling of statehood.* Oxford: Oxford University Press.

Cervero, R. (1998) *The Transit Metropolis.* Washington, DC: Island Press.

Chatterjee, P. (2004) *The Politics of the Governed: popular politics in most of the world.* New York: Columbia University Press.

Dick, H. and Rimmer, P. (1998) Beyond the Third World city: the new urban geography of Southeast Asia. *Urban Studies* 35(12), 2303–21.

Douglass, M. (2005–6) Local city, capital city or world city?: civil society, the (post-) developmental state and the globalization of urban space in Pacific Asia. *Pacific Affairs* 78(4), 543–58.

Douglass, M. and Boonchuen, P. (2006) Bangkok: intentional world city. In M. Amen, K. Archer, and M. Bosman (eds.) *Relocating Global Cities: from the center to the margins.* Lanham, MD: Rowman and Littlefield, pp. 75–100.

Fainstein, S. (2001) *The City Builders: property development in New York and London, 1980–2000.* Lawrence, KS: University of Kansas Press.

Haila, A. (2000) Real estate in global cities: Singapore and Hong Kong as property states. *Urban Studies* 37(12), 2241–56.

Harvey, D. (2006) *Spaces of Global Capitalism: towards a theory of uneven geographical development.* London: Verso.

HOK (2005) *Batanagar Master Plan.* Kolkata: Riverbank Private Holdings Limited.

Holston, J. (1989) *The Modernist City: an anthropological critique of Brasília.* Chicago: The University of Chicago Press.

Holston, J. and Appadurai, A. (1999) Introduction. In J. Holston (ed.) *Cities and Citizenship.* Durham, NC: Duke University Press.

Hughes, C. (2008) Cambodia in 2007: development and dispossession. *Asian Survey* 48(1), 69–74.

Hutchcroft, P. (1998) *Booty Capitalism: the politics of banking in the Philippines.* Ithaca, NY: Cornell University Press.

Jessop, B. (2002) Liberalism, neoliberalism, and urban governance: a state theoretical perspective. *Antipode* 34(3), 452–72.

Jessop, B. and Sum, N. (2000) An entrepreneurial city in action: Hong Kong's emerging strategies in and for the (inter) urban. *Urban Studies* 37(12), 2287–313.

King, A. (2004) *Spaces of Global Cultures: architecture, urbanism, identity.* London: Routledge.

Lico, G. (2003) *Edifice Complex: power, myth and Marcos state architecture.* Quezon City: Ateneo de Manila University Press.

Lippo Karawaci (2009) Homes and townships; www.lippokarawaci.co.id/webform/housing_homes.aspx (accessed January 17, 2009).

Liss-Katz, S. (1998) Fort Bonifacio Global City: a new standard for urban design in Southeast Asia. In H. Dandekar (ed.) *City, Space and Globalization: an international perspective.* Ann Arbor, MI: College of Architecture of Urban Planning, University of Michigan.

Magno-Ballesteros, M. (2000) The urban land and real estate market in Metro Manila: a socio-economic analysis. Unpublished dissertation, University of Nijmegen.

Mahadevia, D. (2006) NURM and the poor in globalizing megacities. *Lok Samvad Newsletter,* October 1.

Marshall, R. (2003) *Emerging Urbanity: global urban projects in the Asia Pacific Rim.* London: Spon Press.

McKinsey & Company (2008) *Vision Mumbai: transforming Mumbai into a world class city;* http://www.bombayfirst.org/McKinseyReport.pdf (accessed June 24, 2008).

Muijzenberg, O. and van Naerssen, T. (2005) Metro Manila: designers or directors of urban development? In P. Nas (ed.) *Directors of Urban Change in Asia.* London: Routledge.

Olds, K. (2001) *Globalization and Urban Change: capital, culture and Pacific Rim mega-projects.* Oxford: Oxford University Press.

Ong, A. (2006) *Neoliberalism as Exception: mutations in citizenship and sovereignty.* Durham, NC: Duke University Press.

Riverbank Private Holdings Limited (n.d.) *Calcutta Riverside: continuing traditions of vibrant Calcutta.* PowerPoint presentation.

Roy, A. (2003) *City Requiem, Calcutta: gender and the politics of poverty.* Minneapolis, MN: University of Minnesota Press.

Sengupta, U. (2007) Housing reform in Kolkata: changes and challenges. *Housing Studies* 22(6), 965–79.

Shatkin, G. (2008) The city and the bottom line: urban megaprojects and the privatization of planning in Southeast Asia. *Environment and Planning A* 40(2), 383–401.

Sheng, Y. and Kirinpanu, S. (2000) Once only the sky was the limit: Bangkok's housing boom and the financial crisis in Thailand. *Housing Studies* 15(1), 11–27.

Sidel, J. (1999) *Capital, Coercion, and Crime: bossism in the Philippines*. Palo Alto, CA: Stanford University Press.

Telegraph, The (Kolkata) (2008) Dankuni delay has projects at risk, June 19.

UNCHS (United Nations Center for Human Settlements) (2004) *World Urbanization Prospects: the 2003 revision*. New York: United Nations.

Whitehead, J. and More, N. (2007) Revanchism in Mumbai? Political economy of rent gaps and urban restructuring in a global city. *Economic and Political Weekly*, June 23, 2428–36.

Yeoh, B. (2005) The global cultural city? Spatial imegineering and politics in the (multi) cultural marketplaces of Southeast Asia. *Urban Studies* 42(5–6), 945–58.

4

Ecological Urbanization: Calculating Value in an Age of Global Climate Change

Shannon May

On September 1, 2006, Zhao Qinghao and Yi Shiqin became the first residents of the Huangbaiyu China–US Sustainable Development Model Village. Four years earlier, a shared vision was formed between a consortium of Chinese national government leaders and US corporate representatives to "leapfrog past limitations and accelerate sustainable development" by building China's first sustainable community (CUCSD 2002). Where maize was once grown, in 2006 forty-two houses – 10 percent of the total planned model development – became the first harvest of the sustainable design expert William McDonough's plans for Huangbaiyu, a "sustainable rural village that the government hopes will serve as a prototype for improving the lives of 800 million rural Chinese" (*Harvard Business Review* 2006). Environmentalists and journalists across the globe have heralded the Huangbaiyu eco-city[1] project as critical in the fight to stem global climate change (BBC 2006; Friedman 2006; *Harvard Business Review* 2006; PBS 2006; Steffen 2006). Leading Chinese environmental commentator Elizabeth Economy has called the project "perhaps the most ambitious multinational effort to help redirect China on to a new development path" (Economy 2006: 182).

Yet, why does China need a new development path? Whose fears and ambitions led to a new city being built on maize fields? This essay is in part an investigation of the hybridization of international and national motivations to conjure a new world, to paraphrase Aihwa Ong's introduction to this volume, and how those disparate concerns came to work on soil and souls in a series of valleys in eastern Liaoning Province. I appreciate Ong's

Worlding Cities: Asian Experiments and the Art of Being Global, First Edition.
Edited by Ananya Roy and Aihwa Ong.
© 2011 Blackwell Publishing Ltd. Published 2011 by Blackwell Publishing Ltd.

revision of the oft-used suffix "-making" (as in world-making, city-making, self-making) to "-conjuring." Making implies a direct relationship, a process through which intention and action are closely coupled. To conjure a world, on the other hand, highlights that all may not be as it seems, and that perspective and focus, and perhaps misdirection – the keys to sleight-of-hand magic tricks – are at play in any attempt to create new worlds, new places, and new persons.

This essay is also about how claims to a universal knowledge of the good life are constituted – often with the handmaiden of science – and how easy, how logical, it can seem to take one's own life as an unalterable good, and others' lives as desperately in need of improvement – to be more like one's own. With science telling us that life as we know it may be threatened by global climate change, the twenty-first century will witness unprecedented changes in governance and subjectivity as persons become enmeshed in networks of power far beyond the scope of local, regional, or national geography.

But as the case of Huangbaiyu demonstrates, the dreams and plans from abroad – in this case from both the United States and China, because the dominant perspectives of urbanite, national leaders are geographically and ideologically foreign in Liaoning's valleys – do not ever encounter a blank slate, however much the drawing of development plans on blank pages may trick some into believing otherwise. Even as a singular, universal solution is sought, it is constituted through the amalgamation of the historically and subjectively situated fears and ambitions that animate the American leadership in the China–US Center for Sustainable Development and, similarly, the particular fears and ambitions of the various leaders on the Chinese side, themselves also particular to their own situatedness. Those desires and dreams then encounter the places and persons they seek to manipulate in the process of conjuring another world. Thus, my concerns are not only with the context and design of this internationally lauded exemplar of the supposedly necessary ecological urbanization of rural China, and the rural world in general, but also with the Huangbaiyu model as a physical manifestation of the desired relationship between persons, and between humanity and nature, that is emerging as an idealized form of governance in the twenty-first century – and the lives and livelihoods that this ideal disavows. To make an analogy after George Hegel, if philosophy is its time comprehended in thought, architecture is its time constructed in things. Attention to Huangbaiyu gives us a glimpse of how urbanization in China, Asia, and beyond in the twenty-first century may be ecologically justified, and how this juggernaut may make new subjects of rural residents through a process that would impoverish them even as it is celebrated by their own regional and national leaders, and international experts. At heart, this essay seeks to show the non-sense of that which is taken as common sense in our time.

Paying attention to the attempt to conjure a model eco-city in Huangbaiyu as an exemplar for a sustainable twenty-first century also shifts our perspective on urban theory. From the valleys of Huangbaiyu, we can analyze the urban in-formation: seeing how the urban is defined, by whom, for what purpose, and to what effect. What is easily taken for granted when we study existing cities is foregrounded in this case where the city is itself the intervention.

Touring the Exhibit, Living at Home:
Huangbaiyu Model Village

Five days after Zhao and Yi moved into the new development, a caravan of black Audi sedans drove past the 35-ton rock announcing the entrance to Huangbaiyu Model Village (Figure 4.1). As they entered the development, they passed a brass plaque naming it as a regional nominee to China's 100 Model Villages Project, and then parked in a line on the dirt boulevard leading to Zhao and Yi's new house. Provincial Party officials, scientists, and journalists on an official study tour emerged from their cars, and were taken on a tour of the site – a place its local developer, Dai Xiaolong, advertises as the "World's First Village."[2] In Huangbaiyu, global climate and energy problems would be solved through "cradle-to-cradle" principles,[3] "sustainable development," and "ecological" concepts manifested in the designs of the master plan being built there.

Zhao is flabbergasted each time government officials and visiting dignitaries arrive to inspect his house, and more than a bit confused by why they are all there. Afflicted with polio and married to a woman whose disabilities have led her neighbors to call her "the idiot," Zhao and Yi are not used to positive attention from others, let alone people whose great political and social worth is displayed in their cars, clothes, and cameras, as well as their unabashed practice of walking into Zhao's home uninvited, without notice, and without acknowledging him. He silently smiles as he limps out of the way of official after official, who never converse with him during their tour of his home in the model village, and who leave his wife to mop up their muddy footprints. He has tried to understand what in his house is so important – for he knew it was not himself, since no one spoke to or acknowledged him – by listening to the words used over and over by all the strangers who have come to see how he lives. But there are so many words with which he was unfamiliar, Zhao told me.

"Ecology," or 生态 (*shengtai*), is a term that has suddenly entered the language spoken around Zhao, but the meaning of the term remains elusive to him. Like the strong majority of women and most men I interviewed living in the valleys of Huangbaiyu's existing, "non-model" hamlets, Zhao and Yi

Figure 4.1 The entrance to the "sustainable development model village" in Huangbaiyu
Source: photograph by Shannon May, 2006.

stumbled at the term. When Dai and other visitors spoke of "ecology" while walking through their house, Zhao and Yi wondered why anyone was interested in their – or anyone else's – feelings about family planning policies. Trying to divine the meaning of this new term, Zhao had considered the common usages of the term's component characters: 生 (*sheng*), to give birth, to live; and 态 (*tai*), form, demeanor, or attitude. He had also thought about the only other time of which he knew when government leaders showed concern about the daily activities of a family's life inside their own house: when the family planning officials came on inspections. The visitors' talk of the use of a "cradle-to-cradle principle"[4] put forth by American William McDonough as the basis for the design of the model project just reinforced Zhao and Yi's thoughts that whenever Dai or other visitors hailed the coming of an "ecological age," that some new foreign-technology based, family planning policy was being implemented, and somehow these houses were part of it. Standing with his post-menopausal wife, this often caused Zhao to chortle.

Zhao does not laugh, however, when I tell him that this house and the master plan of which it is a part are designed as a model for how to improve the lives of 800 million other rural Chinese (*Harvard Business Review* 2006). A month after they moved into their new model house in the Huangbaiyu Model Village – a month after the first set of government officials had taken their photographs and left – I asked Zhao what he thought of sustainable development. Although he had heard "sustainable development" lauded by their national leaders on the nightly national news, what exactly that might have to do with the house he had just been moved into was beyond his imagination. He thought that sustainable development would *obviously* mean that at long last some development would come *his* way, that would sustain *his* life – providing him with a steady, reliable income to spend. "Sustainable development is *my* development," he said. "Then we'll be sustained instead of barely subsisting. That is what we [farmers] are waiting for."

This house in this "sustainable development model village"[5] had, on the contrary, brought greater insecurity into his future. In the "sustainable dream town" lauded as key to a global "future that is both bright and green" (Steffen 2006: 276), there was no room for his goatherd, or place to cure his maize. He was also now isolated from both his kin and neighbors with whom he had long-term reciprocal relationships in Zhao Family Village, the hamlet of Huangbaiyu in which he had been born and lived his entire life. Hearing that international experts and news media have heralded this model of development as one of the keys to stemming global climate change, he stared at me, dumbfounded. Zhao considered my statement while studiously rolling tobacco in his hands. "The business of leaders and commoners is different." This was not the first time I had heard human activity categorized in such a binomial way by people in these mountains. Personal and collective memory had cultivated an understanding of the world as comprised of those who have plans for their own lives, and those who have plans for others' lives.

In the pages that follow, I try to understand the "business" of leaders and commoners that is at stake in the model village being built in Huangbaiyu. Some of Zhao's confusion could be ascribed to the limits of his horizon. The towering mountains that frame the gullies in which he has farmed and shepherded over the 58 years of his life do not allow him to claim the global perspective that gave rise to the house in the model village in which he now lives. While the designers – architectural, governmental, and corporate – of the model village have never experienced Zhao's perspective, they take the ease of their mobility between geographies, languages, and scales as evidence that they have the wisdom to lead Zhao toward a better life. Unfortunately, mobility may belie understanding, as the assumptions of one context no longer abide in another. The shared intentions of a partnership may also be undermined by disparate motivations and historical contexts.

Through the lens of rural urbanization in China, I trace how the science of global warming is giving rise to a new calculus of value, one that is based on energy consumption and that pits the urbanization of the rural, less consumptive world, and in particular populous rural China, against the survival of life as now experienced in the already urbanized, consumption-based world. According to the International Panel on Climate Change, rapidly increasing energy consumption and its emissions of tons of carbon-dioxide equivalents over the next 100 years pose a dire threat to the current balance of the Earth's ecosystem (IPCC 2007). Yet, without increased consumption for the majority of China's population, both Chinese government officials and foreign analysts fear that economic inequality may lead to political instability. At the same time, the continued paving of China's farms to accommodate urban sprawl threatens food security. Eco-cities hold forth the promise of cutting the tie between urbanization, energy, and land consumption, enabling those who have heretofore been left behind by the Industrial Revolution to enjoy an increased quality of life without pushing the planet beyond an ecological tipping point. Yet, the promise of eco-cities from a global perspective, and even its success on such terms, can be perilous on another scale: on the scale of the lives and livelihoods of the families who bear the burden of living in these new, heralded spaces. Worlds and the lives they shape are not conjured out of thin air, but must be built upon the inheritance of what has already existed.

The Present Problem of a Future Uncertainty: Consumption

In a time when global warming has made already urbanized and developed regions wary of the spread of highly energy-consumptive lifestyles, China has become the location of the most widely lauded experimentation in ecological urbanization. As climate change models turn what were once envisioned as the industrial utopias of the twentieth century – the factories of mass production and convenience that would eliminate scarcity for all – into the polluting origins of planetary peril, eco-cities have become the new technology through which scarcity may be resolved for the betterment of the civilization.

While visions of eco-cities are being dreamed as extensions of urban metropolises, it is in their incarnation in the countryside that the lens of the eco-city is at its greatest focus. When eco-cities are built in the countryside as tools of ecological rural urbanization, it is not only a new hierarchy of value that comes into operation; there is also a new population upon which it operates. Proposed projects in Dongtan and Qingdao[6] seek to break technological and organizational ground to reduce current urban carbon footprints. But as expansions of existing metropolises in China, the residents of these newly urbanized areas will not be newly urbanized persons but, rather, are already well-off residents shifting residence. In a place that is in the process of being urbanized, what is urban cannot be taken for granted, but is rather physically established as criteria for living a good life. The city itself becomes the tool of intervention, and in this case posited as the salvation of not only the residents of these rural valleys, but for all of rural China; indeed, for all of rurality. Eco-cities built in China's countryside bring new bodies into a system of urban governance as an ingenious solution to rapid urbanization itself, and a balm to soothe the wounds of the people that industrial and capitalist revolutions have left behind.

When Deng Nan, then Vice-Minister of Science and Technology, and William McDonough met in 2002 as co-chairs of the China–US Center for Sustainable Development (CUCSD) to discuss how to bring American sustainable development expertise and technology to China, the conversation led to a radical hypothesis: Could building an eco-city – a sustainable community – in a Chinese village prove to be the model for urbanizing the rural population *in* the countryside while also reducing carbon-emitting energy use? Could the countryside be urbanized, and the benefits of urban life be brought to farmers? If so, China would lead the world in solving one of the most pressing political crises for every nation in the twenty-first century: defying historical precedent by inverting the relationship between increasing quality of life and fossil fuel usage. Within six months of the CUCSD's first joint board meeting, the site had been selected, and design discussions had begun: the valleys of Huangbaiyu would be the test sites for this grand hypothesis (see Table 4.1).

The juggernaut of energy and urbanization

The import of Huangbaiyu was clear to leaders in both the United States and China. While China's leadership is faced with the political need to provide the majority of its residents with the fruits of capital development – the goods, services, and opportunities that citizens of OECD countries have taken for granted for three to five generations – they must do so at a time when a carbon-fearing world is focusing on how China's growth may push the Earth beyond sustainable limits.

Without inverting the historical relationship between urbanization and energy use, both China's and the planet's future are considered bleak. In 2030, China is projected to have a population of 1.6 billion, 60 percent of which will be urban (Zhou and Lin 2005; Jie 2007). In the next 20 years, the potential transformation of the lives of 433 million newly urbanized people will radically alter China's physical geography and political topography. The per capita energy consumption of China's urban residents is 250 percent more than that of their rural counterparts (Xinhua 2004). If this new wave of urbanization follows in the wake of previous movements – and rural residents emulate the lifestyle of their urban counterparts as they enter the middle class – it is predicted that the concomitant chaotic rise of buildings and consumption may lead global climate change to regularly flood the streets from Calcutta to Shanghai, and Miami to New York, by 2050 (NASA 2006; Nicholls, Wong, Burkett, *et al.* 2007).

Table 4.1 The organizational structure of the China–US Center for Sustainable Development, and its implementation networks for the development of Huangbaiyu

	China Secretariat	US Secretariat
Leadership	Deng Nan, Chair, China Secretariat	William McDonough, Chair, US Secretariat
Execution and operation	Administrative Center for China's Agenda 21, Ministry of Science & Technology, Beijing, China (Host, China Secretariat) Board of Councillors = Ministry representatives	International Sustainable Development Foundation; Portland, Oregon (Host, US Secretariat) Board of Councillors = Fortune 500 companies
Huangbaiyu implementation partners	Tongji University, institutional advisor Benxi Sustainable Development Village Coordinating Committee, Government representative Benxi Municipality Nanfen District Sishanling Township	Dai Xiaolong, local developer, financial investor

Source: prepared by Shannon May, 2008.

Although it is the United States that carries the largest "natural debt" to the rest of the world for its cumulative carbon emissions since the start of the Industrial Revolution (Smith 1991), it is the rise of China and its rapid urbanization and increased per capita consumption that is portrayed as the greatest threat pushing humanity toward "mutually assured destruction."[7] In January 2008, American readers of *Mother Jones* confronted the New Year with a bristling question posed cartouche-like over the head of a Chinese boy with a Cheshire grin, standing at the foreground of obedient followers lining an interior courtyard of the Forbidden City: "The Last Empire: Can the world survive China's rush to emulate the American way of life?"

By continuing its current developmental model, China is portrayed as risking catastrophe at home, and causing it abroad. By forging a new developmental model – one that, according to President Hu Jintao, eschews economic growth at any cost in order to pursue "sustainable development with a scientific outlook" – China is looking (again) to leapfrog Western industrialized nations and become the worldwide leader of an emergent ecological age.[8] While there are many means of environmental protection, the eco-city is seen as the grail that will usher in a new developmental paradigm for human civilization.

Rather than addressing environmental degradation in a piecemeal fashion, identifying a source of pollution and seeking to scrub it or stop it, eco-cities are the embodiment of a way of envisioning the world in which there is no pollution. In the words that made Bill McDonough famous, it is a place where "waste equals food." In an eco-city, human habitat is designed with the recognition that the city, as the Earth, is a closed system. From this perspective, it is not only humans that have life cycles, but all things, from finished processed products, such as computers, to component elements, such as copper and carbon dioxide. When a thing ends its life cycle in a place in which it is treated as waste, it is polluting a closed system that will eventually become too full of detritus to support life. In this vision, by not recognizing the false premise of "waste" in a closed system, the economy of the Industrial Revolution and the cities it bore have replicated this cradle-to-grave mentality at the planetary scale. To shift to what McDonough and Michael Braungart have termed a "cradle-to-cradle" system, it is not enough to "fine-tun[e] the existing destructive framework" (2002: 90). In an eloquent reformulation of the 1987 Brundtland Commission definition of sustainable development, McDonough poses the present assignment to design civilization anew as the solution to the question, "How do we love the children of all species, for all time?"[9]

Before McDonough came to ask this question, he had come to see his world from a new perspective.

Global perspective on a planet in peril

While the American environmental movement began from a bird's eye view (Carson 1962), from which localized industrial processes and products were first seen to disrupt the harmonies of bodies both human and animal, it took the image AS17-148-22727, captured by NASA's Apollo 17 astronauts 28,000 miles above the surface of the Earth on December 7, 1972, to envision a single community of fate, no longer determined by kinship or citizenship. On Sunday, December 24, 1972, worldwide, men and women awoke to an early Christmas present delivered to their doors courtesy of NASA: the first image of the Earth without shadow and without horizon.[10] For the first time, the Earth was made visible to all in its fullness, and its finitude. On a handheld camera, the Apollo crew captured what would become the most widely distributed and recognized image in human history (de Blas 1999).

In that moment, and in the countless moments in which this image caught the imagination of persons across decades and continents, the omnipotent, omnipresent, and omniscient perspective humans had long imagined as the singular purview of the Divine became visible to the merely mortal. It was seeing this view that Al Gore (2006), McDonough (2005), and numerous other prominent environmental activists have stated as changing their understanding of their lives, their environment, and their mission on Earth.[11] From the perspective of space, humanity is deterritorialized – there are no national boundary lines. Humanity is not, itself, even visible. From the viewpoint in which an entire hemisphere of the Earth can be seen in one moment, there is no sign of humanity. It is "the life of the planet" that is witnessed (NASA 2005).

While these preserved moments of light from another time and place continue to enlighten us with knowledge previously unknown, they also blind us to the obliteration of human experience and difference that this perspective requires. Human beings are replaced by synecdochal representation with the Earth, and the planet. It is, after all, the "*planet* in peril" that has become a scientific and popular catchphrase of the early years of the twenty-first century. In the moment that the Earth comes to symbolize human existence, the lives of specific persons become invisible, and their moral worth is subsumed by a purported whole – the species, and the planet.

In 2005, the United Nations Environmental Program (UNEP) published *One Planet, Many People* to demonstrate over-exploitation of the environment through scientific measurement. Borrowing the title and approach of the 2006 UNEP atlas *Planet in Peril*, CNN aired its own much hyped mini-series on anthropogenic devastation of the Earth and its species. Bold type on a black screen sets the scene for tales of global eco-devastation to be told in the program's next four hours: "In the last 100 years, the world's population grew from 1.6 billion to 6.1 billion, a 400% increase. Our planet is in peril"

(2007). In January 2008, the rising dominance of the ideology of a precarious balance between the human species – and all that its individuals consume – and the natural systems of the Earth was attested by its parody on John Stewart's *The Daily Show*. The skit, "Our dead planet," begins, as did *Planet in Peril*, with the light of bold text floating on a black screen: "When will the ice caps melt? When will mankind become extinct? When will this planet in peril be perilized?"

My argument here is not with the data that indicates that industrial technologies have released more carbon dioxide into the Earth's atmosphere than its natural systems can process, contributing to observed rise in sea-level temperatures. Nor is my argument with the Fourth Assessment Report of the IPCC and its details of sea-level rise and species endangerment. My concern is with global warming as a way of knowing, and the politics to which it gives rise. Following Bruno Latour, I understand global warming as a hybrid – a complex intersection of social practices and natural processes captured by a single signifier (Latour 1993). The danger of these hybrids is that their basis in the materiality of the Earth elides the extent to which the complex assemblage it signifies is itself contingent, and constructed by human decisions. Contrary to popular convention, science is not the antithesis of politics, but its inadvertent collaboration, and sometimes its proof.[12] The carbon cycle may have definite pathways, but the paths of human engagement and reaction are infinite, until politics inscribes them.

The changed relationship between specific persons, the state, and the species due to the hybrid of global warming requires us to rethink how politics will be deployed in an ecological age. In his effort to understand the practices of governmentality that marked the threshold of modernity, Michel Foucault directed his attention to "the endeavor, begun in the eighteenth century, to rationalize the problems presented to governmental practice by the phenomena characteristic of a group of living human beings constituted as a population: health, sanitation, birthrate, longevity, race" (1997: 73). At the beginning of the twenty-first century, population is again being reinscribed, this time as a species. In the view of the Earth from 28,000 miles away that is guiding ever more political decisions, there are no political boundaries, no states. Carcinogenic benzene leaked into the Songhua River in China flows into Russia, and lung-debilitating air particles rising from smokestacks near Beijing come to rest on the peaks surrounding Lake Tahoe, California. To govern the lives of their own population, states must now govern the lives of the global population. This is the supraterritoriality that makes the present form of globalization distinct from international interactions in the past (Scholte 2007).

The dominant discourse of a "planet in peril" is representative of an orientation to space and social relations that takes the Earth as the site of human interaction, responsibility, and organization in its own right. The

Earth, rather than the household, city, or state, becomes the unit of analysis. This "globality," to follow Jan Aarte Scholte, "indicates that people may live together not only in local, provincial, national and regional realms, as well as built environments, but also in transplanetary spaces where the world is a single space" (2002: 14). The politics of such an ecological age often discursively erases the history of the Industrial Revolution and the unequal distribution of its fruits among states, and within domestic populations. With the viability of "spaceship Earth" in the balance, international treaties seek to prevent carbon emissions from surpassing levels set at a contemporary usage point. Measured as a global aggregate, this reinscribes global asymmetries of power and wealth. Measured as a state aggregate, this legitimizes existing patterns of exploitation and poverty. So far, however, the global consciousness that has arisen, authorizing the reorganization of value of both persons and places, has under the surface of its cosmopolitanism continued and extended us/them politics and capital relationships into places that no one thought mattered before – places like Huangbaiyu.

Rural Problems, Urban Solutions: Subsistence to Service

Concerns over per capita consumption have a different tone when asked within China. Deng Xiaoping's famous policy for development, "Let some people get rich first," is fomenting mass protests by those left behind by economic growth – growth that often dispossesses them of their land. There were 87,000 such mass protests in 2005, an increase of 50 percent since 2003 (PRC 2007). It is estimated that from 1995 to 2010, 55 million farmers will have lost their land, and means of livelihood, due to urbanization (PRC 2007).

There was a subordinate clause to Deng's famous slogan that while rarely said, has not been forgotten by those waiting for its words to become reality: "Let some get rich first but the nation should finally move to equal prosperity."[13] Since the time of Deng, rural residents have witnessed the income of their urban comrades outpace their own by more than 3:1 (*People's Daily* 2005) to as much as 6:1, when urban in-kind subsidies are included – the largest urban–rural income gap in the world (Dong, Song, and Zhang 2006). The "moderately prosperous society," or 小康社会 (*xiaokang shehui*), that Deng promised would arrive by 2000 never materialized for the approximately 60 percent of the Chinese population who remain rural.

Infrastructure as the structure of the urban–rural divide

In their investigation of rural urbanization in the mid-1990s, Lisa Hoffman and Liu Zhongquan found that government officials thought that bridging the divide between the rural and urban required what could be called citification of the countryside. Urban residents (in contradistinction to the rural) live in apartment buildings and villas; have improved access to water, sanitation, electricity, paved roads, and telephones; and live proximate to schools and entertainment centers, as well as having the needs of daily life attended to by retail stores, barbers, beauty salons, and hospitals (Hoffman and Liu 1997). While conceived through multiple axes, this definition of urbanity's nodal point is (still) consumption: the urbanite is not self-sufficient, but interdependent. He does not build his own house, but buys it. He does not grow his food, but buys his sustenance processed by many other hands.

Communal services – or public infrastructure – are the life-giving veins that form the city's circulatory system, supplying the necessities of biological life so that urban labor power is freed to circulate within the capital market.[14] This binding yet libratory tie of the person to a distributed public is the distinction of urbanity in China: urban residents receive their sustenance through the pipes and wires managed by government, and through this system are governed.[15] The urban–rural divide in China should therefore no longer be thought of as a divide only between types of economic activity (farmer versus worker), as the remains of historical geographic divisions (mapped demarcation of "urban" versus "rural"), or as the entailments of the household registration policy (farmer versus non-farmer, and allied benefits). To be urban is to be managed and measured through circuits of consumption. To be rural is to be responsible for the provision of one's own biological needs: shelter, heat, water, food.

It is through this distinction that the discourse of the modern and the backward, the urban and the rural, should be understood in China. This relationship, long-concealed in the Maoist focus on production as the distinction between populations, and obscured by the shadow of the household registration system into the reform era,[16] is made apparent by the National Bureau of Statistics' announcement in November 2006 that any area – regardless of nomenclature as a commune or village or the economic activity of its residents – would heretofore be deemed urban if its buildings were integrated with government-provided infrastructure.

National agendas, local lives, and the rationalization of space

With the promised day of arrival of "moderate prosperity" having come and gone, and rural residents made aware of the extent to which they have been left behind by the images of modern lives lived in Shanghai and Houston broadcast nightly into their homes, achieving the millenarian "moderately prosperous society" has again been made a national priority. Hu Jintao has promised that he will bring the "moderately prosperous society" by 2020, and that to do so "the three rural problems" – the knotted triplet of the countryside, agriculture, and farmers – must be unbound. In the eleventh five-year plan from 2006 to 2010, the first strategic task for the country is to "build a socialist new countryside." It is now time, Premier Wen Jiabao announced during the National People's Congress in March 2006, to reverse the developmental trend of the past fifty-some years by now "letting the cities feed the villages" (Wen 2006).

What is new in this latest wave of "socialist modernization" (PRC 2007) to build a "socialist new countryside"? In the 1950s, building a socialist countryside had meant cooperative land collectivization. For places like Huangbaiyu, being at the vanguard of building a socialist *new* countryside has meant cooperative land *consolidation*, and the reorganization of villages considered to be scattered, inefficient, and wasteful into a master planned town which rationalizes the use of space, enabling the construction of integrated infrastructure systems and a new land pattern to come into being. Both iterations of a socialist countryside share a determination to bring perceived piecemeal, inefficient uses of natural resources into a nationally rationalized master plan. While collectivization eventually led to the reorganization of the primary energy consumption of food into communal kitchens in order to eliminate domestic labor in favor of nationally oriented production, the drive for land consolidation is leading to the experimental reorganization of the energy consumption of heat and electricity into communally provided services. What is openly discussed as a project to create a model village of energy-conscious urbanization, is at once also a project to create a consumptive lifestyle, presumably supported by a reorganization of labor. With subsistence needs met by public infrastructure, the "surplus labor" – labor that does not contribute to nationally measurable economic growth – being wasted in the rural, agricultural population can be freed for wage labor.[17]

Ecological urbanization of the countryside through provision of environmentally conscious public infrastructure promises to solve "the three rural problems" that have been troubling China since its foundation. Consequently, the experiment in Huangbaiyu has received extensive local, provincial, and national support – in addition to the international accolades it has received for being "ecological." Urbanization requires the consolidation of scattered settlements. The rebuilding of settlements allows not only for an improvement in and standardization of building structures and the introduction of communal infrastructure, but also for a rationalized consolidation of piecemeal, so-called "backward" farming methods. Public infrastructure makes possible what was heretofore impossible: the measurement and regulation of rural energy use. It also brings rural residents who were once largely self-sufficient and productive of their own needs for subsistence into complex consumptive relationships in order to receive basic services. Instead of managing their own forest plots for fuel, building their own houses, and digging their own wells and toilets, residents are recast as homebuyers with monthly utility bills. Once the rural population is urbanized, its previously unknowable and unmonetized per capita consumption can be managed, regulated, and redirected to generate the greatest value for the state, and the planet.

Building a socialist new countryside may make it possible for the Chinese to have their cake and the world to eat it too. If building out a new quality of life in the countryside is done ecologically, the nationally dangerous deprivation of the rural population can be addressed while assuring a highly consumptive, but carbon-fearing world that an increase in Chinese per capita energy consumption will not contribute to the carbonization of the globe. Moreover, China's dependence on an export-driven economy may receive relief from the inclusion of millions of additional persons in consumption-based lifestyles.

Speaking in her role as Chinese co-chair of the China–US Center for Sustainable Development, Deng Nan, Deng Xiaoping's daughter and then Vice Minister of the Ministry of Science and Technology (MST), announced in 2005:

> We have realized that China as a populous country in the world needs to change its production and living styles if it wants to achieve harmonious co-existence between man and nature. ... we [cannot] do what we are doing now, achieve rapid economic growth by consuming huge amount of resources and energy. All these ways of doing are unsustainable. But we in China have to sustain such rapid economic growth because we need such growth to address employment issues and migration of rural population to cities. ... In another word, we need to establish a mode of development that is oriented to the circling economy.[18]

Ecologically driven rural urbanization offers an elegant solution to this need. With a single master plan, a community is built, energy usage and carbon emissions managed, and cultivated land increased. At the same time, farmers' income is projected to rise and regional GDP to grow, all without internal labor migration and the increase in carbon emissions that conventional urban expansion and consumption brings. In this plan hangs a leading hope for sustainable development in the twenty-first century: eco-cities in the countryside.

Making Wasteland Productive: The Reorganization and Redistribution of Value

In the narrative accompanying the master plan completed by William McDonough + Partners, the key principles of the Huangbaiyu design are outlined. Required use of cradle-to-cradle cycles and renewable energy sources lead the ecological requirements. Household centralization makes renewable energy distribution economical, as well as increasing the goals of "convenience and comfort" (McDonough 2004: 1). With the community "powered by the sun" and fuel coming from human or agricultural waste "positively affecting the community's carbon balance" (McDonough 2004: 1, 9), this eco-city will insure that growing rural consumption will not alter the global carbon calculus.

Throughout planning sessions for the Huangbaiyu project, centralization was highlighted as necessary to provide the infrastructure that would improve rural residents' quality of life to a point more closely approximating that of urban residents. Centralization makes an integrated running water and indoor sanitation system feasible, as well as providing the necessary density of population to support a biomass gasification plant that uses agricultural or human wastes to provide cooking and heating fuel to each residence. The local municipal government's Coordinating Committee for Huangbaiyu has regularly highlighted that a functioning biogas energy system would remove the necessity for each family to clear more than four metric tons of firewood per year from the surrounding forests.

Centralization as a prerequisite of public infrastructure has another, concomitant effect: consolidation of previously scattered plots of surrounding land. "In this new conception of the rural Chinese village," the intention from the start was also to "optimize the use of the valuable productive land" (McDonough 2004: 1). In describing the project to me, the Executive Director of the American secretariat of the CUCSD summarized its goals succinctly: "We're supporting Huangbaiyu, making a center, a vibrant economy, and an ecosystem in the countryside … [in] connection with national policy to gain farmland." In the midst of the early design process in 2003, a member of the Benxi municipal government requested that the master plan include settlement consolidation. By consolidating all residences into a central valley, the Master Plan allows for the clearing of housing structures from three presently populated valley areas and four ravines, with the goal of creating an additional 722 Chinese mu[19] of land available for cultivation. Adding this to an estimated 700 mu of land currently categorized by project documents as "wasteland," the total area available for cultivation would increase from 830 mu to 2,252 mu, an increase of 171 percent.[20]

In this context, the Huangbaiyu project has been announced as a potential example of how China's 600,000 villages should be reorganized and urbanized to make a "wasted" population productive, and generate additional land for the state, and thereby also income for farmers. With an additional 1,422 mu to be distributed across 400 households, each family could receive future earnings on an additional 3.55 mu. Yet, with land consolidation achieved through eco-city construction, rural consumption can increase, all while keeping those same farmers from adding to the nation's carbon emissions.

Through ecological urbanization, it is hoped that the knotted three rural problems may be cut loose from China's neck without transferring the noose to the world. The means of doing that, though, has been the business of leaders, to return to the words of Zhao Qinghao, rather than commoners. The focus of the solution was adjusted at the national and global scales rather than at the scale of the life of the farmers who are supposedly the first beneficiaries of its sustainable development.

Making waste into food

When architect and designer William McDonough took on the challenge of designing a sustainable housing development in this rural valley, he remembered his vow to build a better world from taking the perspective of all species on the Earth into account in his designs. He turned to the perspective of a bird to guide him to decide the overall design of the habitat, and followed the drainage of the watershed to indicate where the new sustainable development should be constructed in the valley.[21]

Following both the guidelines of established practices in the field of sustainable design and the suggestions of his Chinese counterparts, McDonough inadvertently designed an ecologically sound plan – from the perspectives of both birds and the green movement – that would devastate the local economy and bankrupt the households whose lives were to be improved. From an ecological view, McDonough and his counterparts in the design process did evaluate aesthetic, natural resource, and social values as the foundation upon which to proceed (McHarg 1971). From the perspective of lessening both the burden of the Earth in processing carbon and the burden of rural residents to labor untold hours to simply generate enough heat to stay alive, shifting the local fuel source from wood to agricultural waste seemed a brilliant solution. Carbon emissions would not be released into the world, but labor power would be. If the project was to simultaneously improve the quality of life of the local population as well as mitigate the peril of the planet, the mistake was having government officials and designers categorize what was "waste" and what was "food" in an economy in which they did not participate. Yet the implementation of the Huangbaiyu master plan, in destroying one world in order to create another, makes the values through which leaders tend to structure the world apparent – before they are obscured again by the banality of the everyday.

When I asked Zhao Qinghao if there was wasteland in the surrounding valleys, he looked at me quizzically. "Wasteland? No, no," he replied shaking his head. Then thinking that perhaps I had misspoke, he offered, "Do you mean to ask about extended land [the land claimed beyond what is officially leased by the hamlets to each household]?" In the minds of valley residents, all land was used to produce something, albeit for varied purposes. There was crop land and garden land; land for goats, cows, and mules; land for homes and land for graves; land for sitting and gathering; and land for walking paths and land for waterways. Half of the wasteland that municipal government officials and the CUCSD design team thought would be the source of the 171 percent increase in arable land – land that was slated to be converted for cropping – was in fact not wasteland, but primarily the garden lands and lands for animals that formed a critical foundation to household economy.[22] In order to increase the median household income by 16 percent through an increase of 3.55 mu, families' gardens would be severely limited and animal lands eliminated.

Yet units of garden and animal land are far more valuable to households than cropland, despite being considered a "waste" by new national and global priorities. Due to the constraints of both climate and capital, food is hard to come by if not grown by the household. The truck that plies the village roads from Nanfen District, the town over the mountains, sells produce at a higher rate than found in the cities, and does not reach these valleys most years between November and February. Without an extensive garden to prepare a winter store of pickled cabbage, root vegetables, and dried sliced vegetables, hunger leads to weakness, and weakness to disease in these frigid mountains. Moreover, profit from the annual maize crop provides the median household only 23 percent of their annual total net income, or RMB1,750 out of a total of RMB7,641. The sources of the additional 77 percent of annual household income vary by household to include various proportions of income from raising trout, goats, silkworms, and cattle; non-grain agriculture; and contract and day labor. Thirty percent of households in Huangbaiyu raise goats for cashmere. Of these households, the median profit from the sale of cashmere is RMB5,030 per year. The sustainable model village that Huangbaiyu is to become would lower these families' annual income by 49.5 percent. What is wasteland according to national and global priorities is the lifeblood of local livelihoods.

The soil near the streams within the watershed was also deemed inefficient, and current uses of the watershed polluting. McDonough and a US ecological advisor have concluded that the land near the various streams running through the valleys is of poor drainage, and inefficient for growing maize, although there was no experimental testing on the drainage and no crop yield studies were performed. Nor were the protein levels downstream of the 12 percent of households with aquaculture pools tested or a species mortality or morbidity analysis conducted before the farmers' use of the waterway for enterprise was categorized as polluting. The streams and adjacent lands were incorporated into the housing plan, and in the middle of the new eco-city development a lake was created as a community gathering point and scenic spot. What were working lands and waterways were to be converted

Figure 4.2 In the late fall, maize stalks are stacked in preparation to take back to the goats'
corrals as winter feed − the model sustainable development's biogas plant requires that this
feed be turned into biogas as part of the energy-saving program for ecological urbanization
Source: photograph by Shannon May, 2006.

from "wastelands" and a "polluted" watershed into an aesthetically pleasing
town center with a water feature.

Maize stalks and cobs were also (mis)taken for waste by the development
team, yet are the critical winter food supply for the cashmere goats (see
Figure 4.2). In Huangbaiyu, the maize stalk "waste" already "equal[ed]
food" (McDonough and Braungart 2002: 92−117) long before the CUCSD
arrived with its plans. The stalks were already being recycled, so to speak,
by the households whose income depends upon selling cashmere fiber each
spring: without the maize stalks, their herds would have no winter food, and
the family little income. Perhaps because there was no space in the master
plan allocated for livestock, this was never a concern of the development
agency and the local municipal Coordinating Committee formed to support
the project's development.

It was, however, a concern for Zhao Qinghao who, as the first resident of
the "sustainable development model village," was forced to sell his goatherd
at a bargain rate, and was told that bills would soon be coming for heating
and water usage.[23] With his own income drastically reduced, Zhao has no

idea how he will make a living in what many residents of Huangbaiyu's non-model hamlets call "workers' houses" in a still rural valley. After a month of begging and subsequent intervention by the project's Coordinating Committee, Zhao was hired by the local developer, Dai Xiaolong, as a night security guard for Dai's defunct cattle barn at a rate of RMB500 a month. His income is less than before, and he sees his wife – awake – but for an hour or two a day. What income will the other 399 households who are to move here rely upon? How will it be an improvement of their quality of life?

From farmers into workers, small capitalists into wage laborers

At the heart of the promise of eco-cities in the countryside is the provision of public infrastructure to liberate families from the burden of survival, freeing up their time for more productive pursuits. While the biogas plant taking agricultural "waste" devastates the families that require that fuel as feed for herds, it also takes precious cash from the limited purses of every household. Along with the benefits of centrally provided public service come the costs of regular cash payments. Central provision of energy and water may free up time for wage labor from subsistence labor, but this is only economically beneficial if, first, wage labor is available, and second, if the wage labor provides more cash than must be spent on subsistence goods and services, such as centrally provided water and energy.

While a biogas plant may free up hundreds of labor hours per year per household, there is no employment to be had in this valley in the dead of winter. For the small minority of men who do labor outside of the village, it is construction labor that employs them. This is only available seasonally, as construction labor is only available in May to September, when the weather is warm enough for cement to cure. Consequently, chopping down wood and burning fuel is the most economical use of one's time in the winter, as it saves the family the expense of paying for services (if they were available) with cash that is dear. With family forestlands reasonably managed over 8–10 year cycles for household use, each plot is a renewable resource for its own household.[24] Cash income is not.

In the case of the Huangbaiyu biogas plant, between 15 and 20 percent of the median household's annual income would now have to be paid to the utility, with not only no increase in cash available from new employment, but drastic reductions in annual income due to the loss of gardens, goats, and fish from the household economy. These added costs directly compete against families' ability to pay for a spouse's healthcare or a child's education, or save for a son's wedding. In Huangbaiyu, the implementation of a biogas plant would impoverish the local community while at the same time still meeting the goals of globally measured sustainability: lowered emissions of metric tons of carbon dioxide equivalents.

It was not only the cost of infrastructure services of this celebrated "new developmental path" that would increase the financial burden on the rural poor. Zhao Qinghao and the rest of the families of the valleys that were to be emptied to create the new, consolidated, model way of living for China's rural poor were expected to pay for the privilege of moving into the model houses. While the national and Liaoning provincial governments were willing to pay the developer subsidies for increases in cultivable land, they were not willing to invest in the construction of the master-planned community that they were encouraging. In fact, McDonough and the CUCSD had never intended for sustainable development in Huangbaiyu to be financed either by the Chinese government or by American philanthropy. "Neither is scalable, we will only do what can be done at scale," McDonough announced at the 2005 CUCSD Joint Board Meeting. To pull themselves up from what national and provincial officials have deemed "backward" and into "modernity," each family must also engage in a self-funded market transaction. As Xie Baoxing, member of the municipal Coordinating Committee, said to me, "We cross the river by feeling the stones. Modernization requires that farmers feel the stones of the market."

Without government investment in construction, a burden of RMB60,895 is left on each family. The median household in Huangbaiyu must work eight years to earn that sum, and at the national household savings rate of 16 percent (IMF 2005), would have had to *already* saved for almost 50 years at *current income levels* to pay the price of not contributing to an increase in China's carbon emissions.[25] The cost of the model houses and the unlikelihood of families having been able to save such a sum over the previous 25 years when it was even possible to earn cash income (albeit not at current income levels and a steady savings rate!) was not a priority concern for the leaders, whose concerns were tied to a global perspective of a planet that faces an unknown future state of peril. From this perspective, radical interventions in the present and future conditions of specific families seem necessary. Since such interventions are thought to benefit the ecosystem of the *planet*, it was presumed that they would *obviously* also benefit the families in the future whose lives were altered now.

The case of Huangbaiyu reveals that there is a familiar industrial logic embedded within current designs to stem the rising energy consumption of rural populations through settlement consolidation and provision of public infrastructure: turning subsistence producers into market consumers, and shaping household economies to produce nationally recognized economic growth. With the labor needed to simply survive made obsolete through public utilities, labor is freed for wage work. With ecological urbanization heralded as the solution to planetary crisis, we should realize that urbanization is not just a change of housing, but also the making of a working class.[26] The very same structures that would enable the model eco-city planned for the valleys of Huangbaiyu to provide what was thought of as an increase in quality of life without increasing the dangerous wastes of energy would also require that residents' relationship to the world around them change abruptly.

No longer builders of their own homes, they are to purchase them. No longer providers of their own heat and water, they are to purchase them. No longer having the land for growing their own food, they are to purchase it. No longer having the space needed for agribusiness, they are left to find wage work – in a place that has little. Huangbaiyu was rural by all accounts, after all, before the plan to make this valley a developmental a model for 600,000 villages across China began. The "three rural problems" of the countryside, agriculture, and farmers were knotted together precisely because in the countryside the only means of surviving was living off the land. If there were other forms of work available to the population, it is likely that families would have already chosen to live closer to each other on less land and with shared public services, just as many towns and cities have evolved before.

The work done by the logic of this lauded, ecological "prototype" is to make the lives of specific persons subordinate to the value of the protection of the species. This logic claims a biological necessity, but it is a political argument. Determining when a species-threatening catastrophe is being *risked in the future* by current actions, and whose livelihoods must be *sacrificed now* to avert a predicted catastrophe, are political questions. In order to change the mundane today, those who would be leaders must speak threateningly about how the world will end tomorrow (Douglas 1999). Unfortunately, the world that is being protected from the uncertainties of future change all too often preserves a political and economic geography of powerful hierarchies, discriminating regulations, and economic inequities – ecosystems of power whose protection is justified in the name of ecosystems of biology.

Conclusion

There is urgency in the pressure to urbanize Asia's populations, and in particular China's. This pressure is often described as an unquestionable reality that must be faced, and acted upon immediately, lest the planet cease to exist as we know it. The work of these doomsday predictions is to generate a climate of fear that enables a shift in what is deemed of value, and authorizes methods of social control to protect these new concerns (Douglas 1999). With leaders in China fearful of the frustrations of the majority of their population who have been left behind by industrial development, and leaders in the United States fearful of how increased consumption, comfort, and convenience for those same impoverished Chinese will put their own population's future ability to live as they do today at risk, these two projections of catastrophe have brought together transnational consortiums to imagine another future, an ecological future: eco-cities in the countryside.

While this experimental urbanization in Huangbaiyu has been lauded by both environmental researchers and the press as a critical new technological form to insure the health of the planet (BBC 2006; Economy 2006; Friedman 2006; *Harvard Business Review* 2006; PBS 2006; Steffen 2006), the case of Huangbaiyu makes clear how a new fear can generate authority to continue old patterns of power and domination. Unless attention is focused on what – and who – a new hierarchy of (carbon) value *de*-values, an ecological age may prove to be little different from the present industrial age, albeit following the values of ecology rather than simply economy. Yet the seemingly immutable laws of ecology often share the same foundational assumptions as classic economics: political-arguments-as-laws that have long protected the status quo – current practices and patterns of inequity – while purporting to be necessary for the health and wealth of both the nation, and humanity at large (Smith 1778; Malthus 1798).

The grand hypothesis of Huangbaiyu failed in its goal to create a better life for its residents while insuring that their increased energy use would not put the "planet in peril." This failure succeeded, however, in making an often-obscured assumption of ecological thought transparent: ecosystems presume an existing pattern and hierarchy of life, normalizing present conditions as the way things "should" be rather than simply what now "is." Both scientific and popular discourse frame the peril of the planet as coming from the future possibility of the world's "undeveloped" populations – the "commoners" – taking the liberties taken as the birthright of American and European populations to be equally their own. When individual lives and livelihoods are obscured through synechdochal representation by "the planet," what is beneficial for some people at the expense of others is argued to be for the necessity of all.

In the hopes and promises of both the Chinese officials and American participants in the plan to remake Huangbaiyu into a beacon of a "future that is both bright and green" (Steffen 2006: 276), real-estate development was confused with economic development. Cities were understood primarily as a place with a certain type of housing and infrastructure, rather than as a place of specific economic and social relationships, which housing then supports. While eco-cities in the countryside may seem like the solution to a planet in crisis from pollution, when designed from the purported perspective of a bird they exacerbate the ethical crisis of inequity that has plagued the Earth for centuries. With leaders across the globe calling for a "new development path" (Economy 2006: 182), and China singled out as the place from which planetary peril will arise, the myriad ways in which the model of sustainable development for Huangbaiyu would impoverish the local population for the benefit of the already powerful and wealthy should be remembered as a harbinger of things to come if "global solutions" continue to be sought for "global problems."

Acknowledgments

Primary research for this chapter was conducted through 18 months of fieldwork in 2005–6, for 14 months of which I lived in Dry River Bed Hamlet, Huangbaiyu Village. Extensive interviews were conducted with all leading officials of the China–US Center for Sustainable Development (CUCSD), as well as with dozens of additional local, municipal, and provincial government officials. I was also present during the CUCSD's 2005 and 2006 Board Meetings. I conducted a stratified, randomized 10 percent household survey amongst the Huangbaiyu population in August–October 2006. A member of the CUCSD's Board of Councilors, Intel Corporation, provided dissertation-funding support through the Peoples and Practices Research Group, as did the National Science Foundation Graduate Research Fellowship Program and the University of California at Berkeley Dean's Office.

Notes

1   Throughout this chapter, I refer to the Huangbaiyu master plan as an eco-*city* project, instead of an eco-*village* project. While government designation will continue to list Huangbaiyu as a village and its residents will remain farmers by household registration status, the work of the project is more than a master plan to mitigating climate change; it is a master plan for urbanization. As such, the correct conceptual marker is an eco-*city*.

2   The splash page for Dai Xiaolong's original Huangbaiyu web site features this phrase and the image of Huangbaiyu in relationship to the globe: http://www.benxi-window.com/web/hby/. The Chinese text (世界第一村-黄柏峪) is here poorly translated as "The world is the first village—ONE-HUANGBAIYU."

3   The phrase "cradle-to-cradle" throughout this chapter references the philosophy and practice as delineated by William McDonough and Michael Braungart in their 2002 book, *Cradle to Cradle: remaking the way we make things*.

4   In the translation of "cradle-to-cradle principle" in project planning meetings and in the title of McDonough and Braungart's book, "cradle" is translated directly as "摇篮" (*yaolan*).

5   I have placed the commonly used name of the Huangbaiyu project, the "sustainable development model village," in quotation marks not only to set off this phrase as a name, but also, following James Ferguson's practice (1990), to problematize its component terms: sustainable development, model, and village.

6   The Dongtan project is financed by the Shanghai Industrial Investment Corporation, the Hong Kong-based investment arm of the Shanghai Municipal government, with

design and engineering led by London-based, Arup. As of August 2010, it is indefi-
nitely delayed (May 2010a). The plans for "eco-blocks" in Qingdao are designed by
Harrison Fraker and his team at UC Berkeley, with funding from the Moore
Foundation; it is also engineered by Arup.

7   McDonough frequently uses the phrase "mutually assured destruction" to describe
    the "end-game" of industrial designs: catastrophic environmental pollution. The
    more people who consume industrially design products, the faster we destroy our
    species and the planet. I first heard him use this phrase during the May 19, 2005
    Joint Board Meeting of the CUCSD held in Beijing, China, when he postulated that
    there was now a new "cold war" being fought, with molecules embedded in
    consumer products instead of the threat of nuclear warheads. He also used this
    phrase in a similar context during his speech at TED in February 2005; see
    McDonough (2005: 17:15).

8   It is important not to forget that the ideological and technical competition between
    China and the countries in the West is not new, but is now just in another stage.
    China turned to communism not as a retreat from the world, but as its methodology
    of leapfrogging the West's capitalist methods in order to provide a better life for its
    people.

9   McDonough uses this sentence with little variation in the majority of both his texts
    and speeches from 2002 to 2010. For representative examples, see McDonough and
    Braungart (2002: 186) and McDonough (2005: 4:00).

10 NASA released AS17-148-22727 for publication and it was widely distributed in
    presses worldwide on December 24, 1972. For an example, see *New York Times*
    (1972).

11 See Cosgrove (2003) for a history of the globe and globality as an imaginative and
    poetic object.

12 For an in-depth treatment of one presentation of this argument, see Latour's
    Reassembling the Social (2007). Shapin and Shafer (1985) provide a fascinating history
    of Boyle's Law as handmaiden to the England's Glorious Revolution of 1688.

13 For a recent quotation of this statement in the context of China's development
    policy and outreach to the poor, see the summary of President Hu's official trip to
    rural Gansu at the start of the lunar year in 2007 (see PRC 2007).

14 See Amin and Thrift (2002), particularly Chapter 4, "The Machinistic City," and
    pp. 81–3, for a discussion of circulation through "mundane instruments of encoun-
    ter" as integral to the city.

15 For an analysis of the significance of communal infrastructure in the governance of
    pre-and post-socialist Russia, see Collier (2001).

16 For extensive historical information and political analysis of the household registra-
    tion system in China, see Solinger (1999) and Zhang (2001).

17 Official Benxi municipal and Nanfen district documents outlined the problem of
    "surplus labor" in the countryside under their jurisdiction, and the priority within
    the "socialist new countryside" campaign to engage these persons in "productive,"
    "non-subsistence labor."

18 Deng Nan gave these conclusions at the close of the morning session of the second
    day of the annual CUCSD Joint Board meetings held in Beijing, China on May 20,
    2005. She was summarizing the importance of the work that the CUCSD is carrying

out in China, and how the eleventh five-year plan (2006–10) will need to reflect the concerns of sustainable development, particularly in the countryside.

19 One Chinese mu equals approximately 1/15 of a hectare, or 666.67 square meters.

20 While official government records hold that there are only 830 mu under cultivation, these records have not been amended since the introduction of the Household Responsibility System in 1982. Since then, an additional 3,032 mu have been claimed by families from the surrounding forests, bringing the total land under cultivation to 3,862 mu. Consequently, the model development project in Huangbaiyu only will increase land under cultivation by 37 percent. This means that the financial increase to the crop farming households from projected crop sales are 79 percent less than the project claims. See May (2007b).

21 McDonough frequently invokes the perspective of "a migrating bird" when discussing how he designs in speeches and interviews. See Pedersen (2005) for his discussion of the importance of a bird's eye view while designing cities in China, including Huangbaiyu.

22 All data on land use and household income in this and subsequent paragraphs are derived from the stratified, randomized 10 percent household survey conducted amongst the Huangbaiyu population in August–October 2006.

23 When Zhao moved into the new model house, however, no communal infrastructure was functioning, not electricity, heating, nor water supplies. This situation has remained unchanged through 2009. The reasons for this are explored in May (2007a, 2009).

24 In this frigid, forested region, the lands allocated under the household responsibility system included cropland, garden land, and forest land.

25 The mortgage is an unheard-of financial instrument in rural China; in Huangbaiyu, many residents are regularly declined agricultural credit loans of less than RMB1,000, let alone loans for tens of thousands.

26 The relationship between the Huangbaiyu Master Plan and the politics of labor and consumption is explored in depth in May (2010b).

References

Amin, A. and Thrift, N. (2002) *Cities: reimagining the urban.* Cambridge, UK: Polity Press.

BBC (2006) Making cities work, part three: Huangbaiyu. Radio program, June 21; http://news.bbc.co.uk/2/hi/programmes/documentary_archive/5134234.stm (accessed February 8, 2011).

de Blas, A. (1999) World Environment Day: Spaceship Earth. Earthbeat [radio program], transcript of interview with Mike Gentry, Media Resource Center, NASA, Australian Broadcasting Corporation Radio, May 6; http://www.abc.net.au/rn/science/earth/stories/s28387.htm (accessed December 12, 2007).

Carson, R. (1962) *Silent Spring.* New York: Fawcett Crest.

CUCSD (China–US Center for Sustainable Development) (2002) Mission statement; http://www.chinauscenter.org/purpose/mission.asp (accessed May 18, 2005).

CNN (2007) Planet in Peril: Two Part Anderson Cooper 360 Special Report, October 23–24.

Collier, S. (2001) Post-socialist city: the government of society in neo-liberal times. Dissertation, Department of Anthropology, University of California at Berkeley.

Cosgrove, D. (2003) *Apollo's Eye: a cartographic genealogy of the Earth in the Western imagination.* Baltimore, MD: Johns Hopkins University Press.

Daily Show, The (2008) Our dead planet. Melting Cities, episode 13,004, January 10.

Dong, X., Song, S., and Zhang, X. (eds.) (2006) *China's Agricultural Development: challenges and prospects.* Aldershot, UK: Ashgate.

Douglas, M. (1999) Environments at risk. In *Implicit Meanings: selected essays in anthropology.* New York: Routledge.

Economy, E. (2006) Environmental governance: the emerging economic dimension. *Environmental Politics* 15(2), 171–89.

Ferguson, J. (1990) *The Anti-Politics Machine: "development," depoliticization and bureaucratic power in Lesotho.* New York: Cambridge University Press.

Friedman, T. (2006) Addicted to oil. Discovery Channel.

Gore, A. (2006) *An Inconvenient Truth: the planetary emergency of global warming and what we can do about it.* New York: Rodale Books.

Foucault, M. (1997) The birth of biopolitics. In P. Rabinow (ed.) *Ethics: subjectivity and truth. Essential works of Foucault, 1954–1983*, vol. 1, trans. R. Hurley *et al.* New York: The New York Press, pp. 73–9.

Harvard Business Review (2006) The HBR List: breakthrough ideas for 2006. February, Reprint R0602B, pp. 1–28.

Hoffman, L. and Liu, Z. (1997) Rural urbanization on the Liaodong Peninsula: a village, a town, and a Nongmin Cheng. In G.E. Guldin (ed.) *Farewell to Peasant China: rural urbanization and social change in the late twentieth century.* Armonk, NY: M.E. Sharpe, pp. 151–82.

Huangbaiyu, Benxi, China web site (中国本溪黄柏峪网站) splash page; http://www.benxi-window.com/web/hby/ (accessed February 8, 2011).

IMF (International Monetary Fund) (2005) Global imbalances: a saving and investment perspective. In *World Economic Outlook: building institutions.* Washington, DC; http://www.imf.org/external/pubs/ft/weo/2005/02/index.htm (accessed December 10, 2007).

IPCC (International Panel on Climate Change) (2007) Climate change 2007: synthesis report summary for policymakers; http://www.ipcc.ch/pdf/assessment-report/ar4/syr/ar4_syr_spm.pdf (accessed February 8, 2011).

Jie, C. (2007) Rapid urbanization in China: a real challenge to soil protection and food security. *CATENA* 69, 1–15.

Latour, B. (1993) *We Have Never Been Modern.* Cambridge, MA: Harvard University Press.

Latour, B. (2007) *Reassembling the Social: an introduction to actor-network-theory.* New York: Oxford University Press.

Malthus, T. (1798) *An Essay on the Principle of Population.* London.

McDonough, W. and Braungart, M. (2002) *Cradle to Cradle: remaking the way we make things.* New York: North Point Press.

May, S. (2007a) A Sino-US sustainability sham. *Far Eastern Economic Review*, April 2007, 57–60.

May, S. (2007b) How much arable land is there out there? Lessons from Huangbaiyu. Paper presented at Berkeley China Initiative conference, Panel VI: Sustaining development: Inhabiting urban and rural space, China's Environment: What do we know and how do we know it? Berkeley, CA, December 8; http://www.youtube.com/watch?v=3yIIR16fgV8, 1:01:30-1:22:19 (accessed February 8, 2011).

May, S. (梅嬉蝶) (2009) 逐利生态村 (zhuli shengtai cun), 新知客 (xinzhike) no. 6: 76.

May, S. (2010a) Dongtan, China. In N. Cohen (ed.) *Green Cities: An A-to-Z Guide*. SAGE Publications; http://www.sage-ereference.com/greencities/Article_n48.html (accessed November 9, 2010).

May, S. (2010b) Ecological modernism and the making of a new working class. In A. Parr and M. Zaretsky (eds.) *New Directions in Sustainable Design*. New York: Routledge, pp. 37–52.

McDonough, W. (2004) *Huangbaiyu: creating a cradle-to-cradle village*. Charlottesville, VA: William McDonough + Partners and McDonough Braungart Design Chemistry.

McDonough, W. (2005) William McDonough on cradle to cradle design, talk at Ted conference, Session: Earth. Monterey, CA, February 26; http://www.ted.com/talks/william_mcdonough_on_cradle_to_cradle_design.html (accessed February 8, 2011).

McHarg, I. (1971) *Design with Nature*. Garden City, NY: Doubleday/Natural History Press for The American Museum of Natural History.

Mother Jones (2008) The Last Empire: Can the world survive China's rush to emulate the American way of life? Cover page, January–February.

NASA/Earth's Observatory (2005) Blue planet: next generation; http://earthobservatory.nasa.gov/Newsroom/BlueMarble/BlueMarble.html (accessed December 22, 2007).

NASA/Goddard Space Flight Center (2006) NASA looks at sea level rise, hurricane risks to New York City. *ScienceDaily*, October 28; http://www.sciencedaily.com/releases/2006/10/061025180408.htm (accessed December 17, 2007).

New York Times (1972) The Earth [image], Sunday edn., December 24, p. 1.

Nicholls, R.J., Wong, P.P., Burkett, V.R., Codignotto, J.O., Hay, J.E., McLean, R.F., Ragoonaden, S., and Woodroffe, C.D. (2007) Coastal systems and low-lying areas. In M.L. Parry, O.F. Canziani, J.P. Palutikof, P.J. van der Linden, and C.E. Hanson (eds.) *Climate Change 2007: Impacts, Adaptation and Vulnerability. Contribution of Working Group II to the Fourth Assessment Report of the Intergovernmental Panel on Climate Change*. Cambridge, UK: Cambridge University Press, pp. 315–56.

Pedersen, M. (2005) The eternal optimist. *Metropolis*, February; http://www.metropolismag.com/story/20050124/eternal-optimist (accessed February 8, 2011).

People's Daily (2005) China's urban–rural income gap may reach the highest in history. December 5; http://english.peopledaily.com.cn/200512/05/eng20051205_225741.html (accessed December 17, 2007).

PBS (Public Broadcasting System) (2006) Deeper shades of green. In e²: Economies of Being Environmentally Conscious, narr. Brad Pitt, season 1, episode 5.

PRC (People's Republic of China, the Central People's Government) (2007) Chinese leaders reach out to poor on holiday eve. February 18; http://english.gov.cn/2007-02/18/content_530120.htm (accessed September 1, 2007).

Scholte, J.A. (2002) What is globalization? The definitional issue – again. CSGR Working Paper No. 109/2; http://www2.warwick.ac.uk/fac/soc/pais/staff/brassett/teaching/scholte-globalization.pdf (accessed February 8, 2011).

Scholte, J.A. (2007) What is "global" about globalization?" In D. Held and A. McGrew (eds.) *The Global Transformations Reader*. Malden, MA: Polity Press.

Smith, A. (1778) *The Wealth of Nations*. London.

Smith, K. (1991) Allocating responsibility for global warming: the Natural Debt index. *Ambio* 20(2), 95–6.

Solinger, D. (1999) *Contesting Citizenship in Urban China: peasant migrants, the state and the logic of the market*. Berkeley, CA: University of California Press.

Steffen, A. (ed.) (2006) *Worldchanging: a user's guide for the 21st century*. New York: Abrams.

UNEP (2005) *One Planet, Many People: atlas of our changing environment*. United Nations Environment Programme.

UNEP/GRID-Arendal (2006) *Planet in Peril: atlas to current threats to people and the environment*. United Nations Environment Programme.

Wen, J. (2006) Report of the Government, March 5.

Xinhua News Service (2004) China's energy shortage blamed on growing demand, inefficiency. June 13.

Zhang, L. (2001) *Strangers in the City: reconfigurations of space, power, and social networks within China's floating population*. Stanford, CA: Stanford University Press.

Zhou, Q. and Lin, Y. (2005) China's urbanization encounters "urban disease." *China News Service*, November 11; http://www.chinanews.cn/news/2005/2005-11-18/14441.html (accessed December 3, 2007).

Part II
Inter-Referencing

5

Retuning a Provincialized Middle Class in Asia's Urban Postmodern: The Case of Hong Kong

Helen F. Siu

Introduction

Historically, Hong Kong had global self-perception and a regional material presence as a trading node. It claimed to have transformed from a fishing village and colonial outpost in the nineteenth century to a brand-named Asian city and financial hub in the twentieth century. The age of mercantile capitalism allowed the city to share urban modeling strategies (in architecture, political and legal institutions, and cultural styles) with a network of colonial cities as far as the British Empire had stretched. It flaunted a character as an encompassing node for multicultural entrepreneurial talents.

The past few decades have seen Hong Kong standing at the convergence of several geo-political trends – postwar decolonization and industrialization, postindustrial global development, and a reemergent Asia. On the receiving end of massive inflows of capital and migrants from China after World War II, Hong Kong modeled and competed with other "small Asian dragons" to become the world's assembly line. From the late 1970s on, as manufacturing activities moved across the border to Guangdong, the city transformed itself once again as a gateway for the world to reach a China that was recovering from Maoist closure.

In the first decade of the twenty-first century, the city faces another set of challenges. A new round of self-fashioning has been on the horizon. Making Hong Kong "Asia's world city" is a banner on Cathay Pacific Airline as well as a development strategy for the post-1997 SAR government. In competition with emerging mega-cities in the region (Shanghai, Singapore, Mumbai,

Worlding Cities: Asian Experiments and the Art of Being Global, First Edition.
Edited by Ananya Roy and Aihwa Ong.
© 2011 Blackwell Publishing Ltd. Published 2011 by Blackwell Publishing Ltd.

Dubai), it tries to reposition itself in a fluid geo-political environment, the essence of which has been China's dramatic rise as world factory and Asia's major consumer. The age of the Asian postmodern is driven by dramatic developments in information technology and global finance, and cultural competition. Massive city reconstruction, institutional and political retuning, class positioning, and identity politics are the hardware and software of Hong Kong's urban renaissance today.

How have city populations in Asia contributed to these transformations in recent decades? As illustrated in other chapters in this volume, they have experienced unprecedented volatility in life and work due to intense flows of capital, technology, migrant workers, cultural resources, and fundamental changes in political sovereignty. A rising, predominantly expatriate, middle class in Dubai banks on the city's future, and that in Mumbai lives for the present, Bollywood style (Chad Haines, this volume). However, a provincialized middle class in Hong Kong seems painfully aware of its having overdrawn past advantages. The emergence of China as a global power provides Hong Kong with opportunities, but exacerbates its vulnerabilities. Circulation of its population is key for future survival or aggrandizement. But in the postwar decades, Hong Kong's diverse migrant population has become grounded, homogenized, and inward looking. With limited political vision, institutional resources, and cultural flexibility, the city and its residents might not have the compass to navigate an intensely competitive China and a connected Asia that are quite beyond their imagination. What are the future "worlding" prospects for a city if its citizens lack the confidence to move forward?

Based on fieldwork in Hong Kong and preliminary explorations in Mumbai and Dubai, the chapter combines macroeconomic and census data with ethnographic observations to explore the mobility tracks and vulnerabilities of a generation of Hong Kong residents who have middle-class aspirations. The chapter contrasts the city's long, multiethnic history and regional financial significance with the experiences of postwar baby boomers and their children who feel marginalized by the world's obsession with China. Turning inward against new immigrants from China, highlighting an essentialized set of core values, and unleashing frustrations in street protests and direct political action, the postwar backbone of Hong Kong's development seems to have dug in its heels.

These observations are counter-intuitive to those of other Asian cities, which are demonstrating unprecedented dynamism in their global reach and aspirations. One might expect that the horizons of Hong Kongers are dwarfed by turbocharged projects in Shanghai and Dubai (Aihwa Ong, Introduction, this volume), or even Dalian (Lisa Hoffman, this volume), and Vancouver (Lowry and McCann, this volume), but one must seriously examine Hong Kong's lack of dynamism when compared to the energies of a planned eco-village in northern China (Shannon May, this volume) and slum-dwelling African urbanites (Simone 2004). If the outward-looking capabilities of Hong Kongers need to be uplifted, a crucial question is whether the government's *laissez-faire* model in encouraging freewheeling entrepreneurship is still relevant. Policy-makers and businesses have been asking how the city should produce the necessary infrastructure and institutions for a globalized knowledge economy, as well as the cross-cultural professional skills and motivations among its population to navigate across Asia's mega-city environments, such as Mumbai, Dubai, Singapore, and Shanghai.[1]

Nonetheless, just as concerns are voiced over Hong Kong's increasing marginality in this Asian renaissance, and over its population's apparent lack of flexible positioning, a closer look shows that Hong Kong professionals at both ends of the human resource chain are enjoying new social and spatial mobility.[2] In the banking and finance sectors, a new breed of Hong Kongers have joined global processionals to provide services for Asia's new rich in asset management, in Sharia-compliant banking and migrant remittances as market demands have emerged in China, the Middle East, and South and Southeast Asia. Others, for example, are hired by Chinese state firms and private Hong Kong developers to design projects built by South Asian migrant laborers in the Gulf Region. At the lower end of the labor hierarchy, many have looked north. In personal terms, they increasingly settle their families across the border in South China. In work, they form the technical and managerial core for China's "post-world factory" development. If such border-crossing intensifies, may we perceive the present predicaments of Hong Kongers "precariously stuck in the middle" as anything but an interlude, a moment of being uncharacteristically grounded?

Historical Global and Cultural Bricolage

To understand Hong Kong's apparent decline and possible revival in worlding aspirations, it is important to appreciate the global historical linkages with which the city started. When European national powers came to the South China region in search of trade, in 1715 the British East India Company established its trading house in Guangzhou. The rest of the British Empire joined, creating ample opportunities for cultural and institutional inter-referencing. Various ethnic groups were heavily involved with the China–India–European trade in Guangzhou and later Hong Kong until the early twentieth century. Although small in number, Parsee merchants used Hong Kong as a base to connect with Shanghai and other regional cities in the cotton trade, construction, and the capital markets. They were also known as aggressive money-lenders.[3] When the Hongkong and Shanghai Bank was set up in 1864 by Scottish traders, three out of the thirteen board members were Parsee merchants (Leiper 1997; Guo 2005).

The thriving China Trade in the eighteenth and nineteenth centuries, centering on Guangzhou and later tied to Hong Kong, showed that "China as world factory" was by no means a contemporary phenomenon, nor was it limited to European traders. The sophistication and variety of goods made for the European, North American, and Middle Eastern markets were remarkable – silverware, European dining utensils, wallpaper, furniture, and presentations wares with Arabic, European, and American insignia. Such wares marked global economic connectedness, cultural fusion, and the mutual shaping of tastes and styles in everyday life (Crossman 1973; Ganse 2008).[4] China Trade paintings display similar cultural circulation. In the head office of the Hong Kong and Shanghai Bank today, one finds precious pieces from this genre of painting (some by George Chinnery), which the bank collected over the century. The popular oil paintings by Chinese artists (Lamqua, for example) who were commissioned by Chinese and European patrons in Guangzhou and Hong Kong of the same period showed tremendous mutual borrowing in cultural substance and artistic styles.

Where multiethnic merchants congregated, distinctive architectural connections continued to shape the urban landscapes of these historical world cities. The merchant quarters of Guangzhou, Mumbai, and Hong Kong, and the native places of overseas Chinese merchants in the Pearl River Delta (e.g., Shiqi, Jiangmen, and Taishan) shared the styles of late nineteenth to early twentieth century architecture in London and New York, some with a touch of the Islamic via Southeast Asia.[5]

On the Chinese political map, Guangzhou was distant and culturally marginal. Hong Kong, as it came into existence as a political entity after the Opium War in 1842, was even more so. However, the regional ecology linking the island to the Pearl River Delta and Guangzhou formed the basis for a concentrated urban experience for traders and political exiles from southern China and every corner of the British Empire (Ching and Liu 2004).[6] The merchant elites were worldly and unorthodox in their practice, but they were best situated to buy cultural orthodoxy in the form of literati degrees and imperial official titles. They also lavished money on community charities and religious rituals, and were active in political mediation. These pursuits allowed them to gain authoritative local positioning. The colonial office in London and the Chinese regimes on the mainland tolerated, compromised, and colluded (Sinn 1989).[7]

Historian Elizabeth Sinn argues that Hong Kong not only thrived as "a space of flow," of goods and services, but also for passenger traffic. Between the 1880s and 1939, over 6 million people passed through Hong Kong from China to other parts of the world. Another 7 million went in the opposite direction. The ability to facilitate through-movement made the growing city a predominant hub for Chinese migrants to circulate in the mid-nineteenth century, an indispensable "in-between place" in the Chinese Diaspora. With the openness of its borders, residents became accustomed to looking beyond conventional barriers and seeing China and the outside world as equally accessible, thus positioning Hong Kong *centrally* as the hub for circulation (Sinn 2008).[8]

Although Shanghai, as Asia's world city in the Republican era, dominated the region with cosmopolitan glamour, Hong Kong and Shanghai have had deep cross-cultural fertilization in business, politics, and material and cultural consumption. They have been nodes in the crossroads of trading empires, colonial encounters, religious traditions, industrial assembly lines, and now global finance capital, media, and consumption. The Hongkong and Shanghai Bank, for example, has straddled the two cities for more than a century. Established in Hong Kong in 1866 by Scottish business interests, it served as a banker for the Qing dynasty and then for the Hong Kong government during the entire twentieth century. On the eve of the Communist takeover of China, the Shanghai branch of the bank and the bulk of China's most prominent industrialists relocated their capital and businesses to Hong Kong, fueling the latter's postwar economic miracle. The Asian headquarters of the bank, designed by Sir Norman Foster in 1986, remains a center of gravity in the business district of Hong Kong. The bank's parent holding company HSBC, now headquartered in London, is the largest in Europe.[9] In the bank's renewed move north, its China subsidiary has recently rented luxurious offices in Shanghai, owned by a prominent Hong Kong developer.[10] The bank's former headquarters at the Bund stands to mark Shanghai's skyline, then and now. To prepare for the bank's reentry into China, it has acquired shares in major Chinese banks and is preparing for listing on the Shanghai Stock Exchange.

In culture and the media, scenes from Ang Lee's recent film *Lust, Caution* illuminate another stage of urban experiments and inter-referencing. The film is a tale of two cities in the late 1930s and early 1940s. Hong Kong and Shanghai, competitors and partners linked by historically global networks, shone behind the grim shadows of war and political terror with charged commercial energies. Taken for granted were the circulation of cosmopolitan populations and their brashly luxurious cultural styles – film, opera, fashion, cuisine, markets, and the underworld of crime and political intrigue.[11] Such mutual modeling has continued in the non-fictional commercial world today. Shanghai Tang, a Hong Kong-based fashion chain founded by Cambridge-educated Sir David Tang, stands out in the global consumer market. It specializes in re-orientalizing Shanghai chic at the high end, with a colonial touch and a postmodern twist.[12]

Grounding a Mobile Population

The term "Hong Konger" is an elusive concept, because it defines not a static target population but one that has circulated in and out of the territory at different historical junctures (Siu 2008a).[13] Their varying sense of belonging has made Hong Kong a place full of diverse meanings, emotions, and family histories. Furthermore, they may not be physically or administratively bound to Hong Kong. Until a postwar generation of baby-boomers passes on, Hong Kong's cemeteries do not contain many Hong Kongers. Instead, most of the native places of the deceased, carved in stone, are claimed to have been elsewhere (Sinn, pers. comm.).[14]

Like many port cities of the British Empire, Hong Kong was a meeting place for adventurous sojourners, with cultural styles drawn from Britain's former colonies and from the mainland. Massive waves of refugees from China came after the war and in 1949 (Wong and Wong 2008). From the 1970s onward, when Hong Kong was transforming itself into a regional business and service hub, professionals from Europe, America, and South and Southeast Asia filled the executive ranks of transnational businesses.[15] In the 1990s, with the accelerated growth of China, they were joined in the finance and trading sectors by Chinese returnees. Moreover, dependent spouses and children of Hong Kong men at the lower end of the social economic hierarchy constituted the largest group of immigrants. From 1991 to 2001, the number of persons who had not resided in Hong Kong for more than seven years jumped from 2.6 to 4 percent of the whole population (Siu 2008a). Census figures also show that in 1996, 40 percent of Hong Kong's population was born outside the territory (Lam and Liu 1998). In the 2006 by-census, over half of the registered marital unions in Hong Kong involved a partner from outside the territory (HKSAR 2007).

Outward movement from the territory was also intense. The number of Hong Kongers, largely professionals, who applied to migrate to Canada, Australia, the United Kingdom, and North America was estimated to be around 374,500 in the 1990s. Their motivations were mixed, but anxiety toward Hong Kong's change of sovereignty was a major factor. Many have since returned, but their careers have been truncated, and family linkages attenuated (Salaff, Wong, and Greve 2010). The extent to which their sojourning experiences have impacted on Hong Kong society remains unexplored.

In view of such population movements, who are the immobile? In Hong Kong, political attention since 1997 has been focused on local-born people who came of age in the 1960s and 1970s. As Hong Kong transformed from a land of immigrants to an urban postindustrial economy and regional financial hub, they have become Hong Kong's middle class – the technical and administrative backbone of its modern energies. The popular television series *Below the Lion Rock* is their cultural icon. It denotes social mobility through educational aspirations, hard work, family commitments, and political detachment. As I noted in 1996, the identity and cultural orientations of this generation are quite different from those of the global expatriates and new immigrants from the mainland. Most significantly, the baby-boomers and their families have nurtured a strong sense of belonging to the territory.

They identify with its cultural and professional icons and are proud of their "can-do" spirit. Given unique historical junctures, they have experienced unprecedented social mobility in the postwar decades. However, they seem to have the least confidence to reposition themselves in post-1997 Hong Kong. Their children, coined by scholars and the media as the post-1980s generation, have also emerged as a political force today, characterized by their social concerns and confrontational civic actions.[16] Sociologist Tai Lok Lui has argued that mobility opportunities (both physical, social, and mental) are not lacking in Hong King, but the population mix in Hong Kong may not be equipped to take them. Social unrest is increasingly triggered by the young generation's perceptions of immobility rather than income polarity.

Why are the postwar generations of local-born Hong Kongers unable to capture China's new energies? There is heavy political baggage (Siu 1996, 1999, 2009). Scholars have explored why a great many Hong Kongers find it difficult to belong to a nation (Matthews, Ma, and Lui 2008). Coming of age at a time when China was politically and socially remote, these Hong Kong residents had the most to consider when the Sino-British negotiations over Hong Kong began in the early 1980s. What this generation learned from books and media and experienced first-hand from China has not always been comforting – the land reform, the Great Leap Forward and famine, the hungry refugee populations who poured across the border in the years from 1959 to 1961, the food packages sent to relatives in China from every corner store, and the upheavals of the Cultural Revolution in 1966 and 1967 that spilled violently onto the streets of Hong Kong. Last but not least, there was the Tiananmen incident in 1989. As China accelerated its economic reforms in the 1990s, the media was filled with scandals of corruption, accompanied by negative images of yet another massive wave of immigrants from the mainland. In these decades, every turn of the Sino-British negotiations leading to the changeover added pressure to family and career dilemmas. Unlike families with established wealth and connections, who could leave the territory at their leisure, and unlike working families who had little to lose, Hong Kong's middle-class families had a great deal to consider, but their choices were limited. Those who chose to vote with their feet and emigrated faced unpromising career prospects. Those who decided to stay wondered if they could dance to their own tunes after the changeover (see Faure 2003). They sought assurances for the rule of law, freedoms, and professionalism they had taken for granted. In their eyes, these qualities are particularly lacking in China, thus discouraging the proactive pursuit of opportunities even since the economic border between Hong King and the mainland has become blurred.[17]

Granted that many refugee families from China and their locally born children rose to middle-class circumstances in a relatively short time, their worldly engagement was superficial. Subsidized education through a diverse range of schools produced a small, meritocratic elite. For the rest, functional English and vocational training turned them into a technically efficient workforce (Luk 2008). Accelerated globalization has not generated the flexible worlding energies that would have turbocharged a majority of these Hong Kongers toward the twenty-first century.

For the professional elite, positioning for the new millennium has not been difficult. This top tier has been able to compete with the global talents (China's returnees included) who dominate the finance and trading sectors at the high end of the economic hierarchy. There is a great demand for their professional expertise in Singapore, Beijing, and Shanghai. Not only are corporate headquarters moving to these cities to capture the growing strengths of sovereign wealth but, also, individual family decisions are increasingly based on concerns beyond employment – environmental health and school choices among them.[18] This has led businesses to pressure the Hong Kong SAR government to be more aggressive and holistic in formulating population policies and recruiting talents so that business opportunities can be effectively captured (Eldon 2006; Kwoh 2006).

Below the top tier, the prospects are less certain. When China was poor and isolated, these Hong Kongers found a strategy to thrive. But their functional links to trade and the world assembly line have given them the false impression that they are global and modern. Decades of prosperity for a Hong Kong-born generation have also fueled a "localized" culture – expressed through its movies, language, media, and Canto-pop music. Their knowledge of China is thin. They relate to the world outside through a limited range of material symbols rather than through deep cultural engagement.

With such historical baggage, the intensifying financial flows and geopolitical changes in Asia have special meanings for these Hong Kongers and the returnees, localized in orientation and yet unsettled. An additional worry for them is the prospects for their children. Competition to get into the territory's international schools is tough and expensive. Even for those who were successful in enrolling in the territory's top local schools, parents would strategize to send them abroad at an increasingly young age. Low English standards in the local schools, they claim, are the major problems. If the children are stuck in the local education system, their mobility opportunities in a global society are circumscribed. The fate of being "grounded" would thus extend to the next generation of Hong Kongers.

That "Sinking" Feeling in Post-1997 Hong Kong

The term "sinking middle class" emerged in the early 2000s in sociological works on Hong Kong (see Wong *et al.* 2002; see also Lui and Wong 2003). The works of the Japanese writers Atsushi Miura (2005) on downward mobility and Ohmae Kenichi (2006) on the formation of an M-structure society in Japan have been widely circulated and publicly debated in Hong Kong.[19] Has the downward mobility of the middle class widened the gap between the wealthy and the poor? Why, in the public mind, has the backbone of Hong Kong's success become the city's urgent problem? In the wake of the July 2003 demonstrations, when half a million took to the streets to protest against government policies, President Hu Jintao was among those who immediately urged the Hong Kong government to pay particular attention to the middle class and pledged timely support.

There are structural reasons beyond Hong Kong's control, such as the volatile forces of neoliberal globalization and China's rapid liberalization. It might have also involved a mindset, an attitude, and unexpected political pressure. Trouble started in the 1980s when industrial jobs moved across the border. By the 1990s, technical support and white-collar jobs were shifting north as well.[20] In the last 10 years, a painful economic restructuring has been complicated by a culture shock caused by the blurring of the border between Hong Kong and the mainland. Going north to engage with China is a necessary move, but few Hong Kongers have the cultural compass to navigate with a map that has changed beyond their imagination.

The Asian finance crisis in 1997 and the collapse of the property market scored a direct hit on middle-class families. It is estimated that in 2002, over 150,000 families fell into the category of those having negative assets. The unemployment rate soared from a mere 2 percent in the pre-1997 decade to 8 percent that year. Even the once secure and protected civil service shed jobs. Bankruptcies rose, from 780 recorded cases in 1996 to a high of 26,922 cases (see Siu 2007: 77).

Avian flu and SARS further crippled the city. For almost six months in 2003, when SARS- related deaths mounted in the public hospitals, the once bustling city became ghostly. Real-estate values, a major source of middle-class status and security, dived further. Cathay Pacific, Hong Kong's proudly profitable airline, was counting its days toward closure. Although the government tried to be as transparent as possible in dealing with the crisis, panic and sadness were mixed with a declining confidence in the ability of the government to function in the public's interest. Amid debates about the balance between privacy and the public's right to know, the media respectfully reported a steady flow of funerals of medical professionals who had fallen in the line of duty. It was symbolic of a city shaken to the core (Siu 2007; see also Loh 2004).

The economy rebounded by 2006, but the fortunes and confidence of most Hong Kong families have been further polarized (Figure 5.1). The government by-census of 2006 showed that households with monthly incomes

Figure 5.1 Hong Kong white-collar workers during lunchtime
Source: photograph by Helen F. Siu, 2008.

between HK$10,000 and HK$40,000 had dropped from 61 percent 10 years
ago to 55 percent in 2006. Those with monthly incomes below HK$10,000
had risen from 23.9 percent to 27.9 percent. Those at the top, with monthly
incomes above HK$40,000, had risen from 15 percent to 17 percent. This
trend continued in the subsequent years and the local media saw this as a
structural problem in the contemporary global age. In a knowledge-based
economy, those without the necessary education or professional skills face
declining incomes and structural unemployment (especially after reaching
middle age), and falling out of the middle-class ranks. Those riding with the
global economy at the high end prosper because there is fierce competition
for their talents, but the global financial tsunami in 2008 reversed their fortunes as well.[21]

In sum, for families with middle-range incomes and education in Hong
Kong, the world has shifted under their feet (Lui 2007c).[22] As the world
speeds past them at the beginning of the new millennium, there is sadness
and resignation (Chow 2007; Wong 2007).[23] Business leaders have also wondered if these Hong Kongers have lost their "global outlook" and "can-do"
spirit (Siu and Ku 2008).[24]

Renegotiating Identities

When besieged by uncertainties, some people hold onto the past. In the cultural/historical realm, this began before 1997. Scholars have described an entire industry that produces the "nostalgia of disappearance." Moreover, for a younger generation of the locally born, the search for cultural roots rests more in a familiar city space than a remote rural "native place" on the mainland. Debates about core values, collective memories, and historical preservation efforts highlight the need by a generation to rethink its positioning when established boundaries can no longer be taken for granted (*South China Morning Post* survey 2007).[25] Fights over which public sites to preserve have exploded into a social movement – *baoyu yundong* (保育運動) – in the streets. Highly politicized events, such as protesting against the demolition of the Star Ferry, the Queen's Pier, and the wedding card street, were led by the Local Action Group. They captured a lot of media attention (Chen 2007; Lu 2007).[26] A more subtle movement to emphasize the social dimension of "locality" has also sprung up. Community literature highlights personal narratives linked to meaningful city spaces – Temple Street, Shanghai Street, Wing Lee Street, open wet markets, *dai pai dang* (大牌檔), herbal medicine shops, pawnshops, public housing estates, and other landmarks that have been an intimate part of a generation's coming of age and extraordinary social mobility in the postwar decades. This might explain why experiences of locality associated with a narrow time frame are invested with such intense emotions.

A fixation that conflicts with historical preservation has also arisen in business and policy communities. Writer Lung Ying-tai (2004) terms it "the value of Central District" (*zhonghuan jiazhi*, 中環价值). Anthony Cheung, an academic in the policy circle, aptly highlights it as a quest by the city's new administrators for positive identity. "Its impulse is to 'create a new Hong Kong' and build a Hong Kong brand," he says, "a project akin to nation-building in other post-colonial societies" (Cheung 2007). In the name of making Hong Kong into a leading world city in China and Asia, many of the accumulated details of the lives of generations are lost in policy blueprints. Old neighborhoods together with their colonial pasts will be erased, replaced by essentialized "Chinese" cultural icons or signature landmarks on the grandest scales. They are planned for the city to signify super (post)-modernity and global engagement. Skeptics readily point to the government's agenda for the West Kowloon Cultural District as a prime example of borrowed hardware, without human substance or cultural sensitivity.[27] Critics claim that there are plenty of grand projects in China's cities. With bare concrete and marble wasting away in the sun and rain, these public spaces have no character or vibrancy (*ren qi*, 人氣), only the shallow vanity of local officials.

A more politically oriented group of the locally born Hong Kongers focuses its preservation energies on Hong Kong's inherited institutions – the rule of law, clean and efficient government, civic values, and increasingly, universal suffrage and democratic representation. Since 1997, the pan-democrats, composed of several young political parties, have made their voices heard both in the Legislative Council and on the streets. On July 1, 2003, half a million spilled onto the streets to protest against what they considered to be a draconian national security bill proposed by the government (Figure 5.2). Since then, each year on July 1, and on June 4, when candlelight vigils are staged to remember the victims of the 1989 crackdown in Tiananmen Square, tens of thousands have gathered in Victoria Park, the symbolic home for pro-democracy movements in Hong Kong (Siu 2009).

A third group of Hong Kongers comes "from the left field." Small businesses, former students, employees, and cadres of the Chinese establishment in pre-1997 Hong Kong have never fitted comfortably into mainstream Hong Kong society. During the riots of 1967, when the violence of the Cultural Revolution spilled over the border, leftist activists fought the police and took a strong political stance against the government. If they were not true believers in Chinese socialism, they were at least ardent patriots. Over the years, they have been loyal supporters of China's policies in Hong Kong. They continue to subscribe to China's master narrative to define Hong Kong's identity and culture. In their view, Hong Kong is a colonial product, a cultural hybrid, a symbol of national humiliation; its reunification with the Motherland is to be lauded; those who demand democracy and seek world connections are subversives and traitors. Branded by pro-democracy Hong Kongers as "leftists" who have not moved with the times, they have drawn a hard line against those they consider unpatriotic. The fixated images, the crude accusations, and the tactics they have used to demonize the cosmopolitan mainstream have proven to be the government's liability.

Moreover, as China speeds up its embrace of the global market and big businesses, the cultural and political positions of these people have become awkward. At times, the pro-business moves of the SAR government go against their grassroots sentiments. The loss of credibility of the pro-government labor union in the 2007 metal-bar benders strike is a case in point. However, these political groups have accumulated tremendous organizational capacities among working families, new immigrants from China, and mass organizations.[28] Since 1997, they and the political party that represents their interests (the Democratic Alliance for the Betterment of Hong Kong) have moved into mainstream Hong Kong politics.

These are numerous examples that constitute an impasse among broad categories of "Hong Kongers." Their lives and career trajectories are often intertwined, but hard lines are repeatedly drawn. Since 1997, charged emotions have generated a vicious cycle of polarization and paralysis, preventing any bold rethinking of Hong Kong's positioning and of ways to move forward

Figure 5.2   Hong Kong's middle class marched for democratic reforms
Source: photograph by Helen F. Siu, 2010.

(Cheung 2007; Lui 2007c).[29] Each group's historical baggage weighs heavily on how it deploys its cultural capital to define who the Hong Konger is, what his/her entitlements are, and what "collective memory" and "public interest" should be. The negotiation for cultural and social identity within

Figure 5.3 The Bank of China building in Hong Kong, a symbol of China's rising power in the global economy.
Source: photograph by Helen F. Siu, 2010.

the political formula of "One Country, Two Systems" is far from a simplistic reading of pro-democracy leanings pitched against pro-Beijing, pro-government loyalties. A question poignantly asked in the past 10 years of the HKSAR is how to balance the priorities and anxieties of "one country" with the complicated histories and emotions attached to "two systems." The emergence of China as a global economic magnet combined with its heightened nationalistic mindset has sharpened the cultural dilemma of many Hong Kongers (Figure 5.3). Feeling marginalized and grounded, they may not be able to reactivate the inter-referencing processes that have made Hong Kong relevant to China, Asia, and the world for over a century.[30]

The New Silk Road: Worlding Activities at the High End

Hong Kong's tense relationship with its national space is probably echoed in Mumbai and Dubai. As hubs for the intense flow of capital, people, goods, and cultural orientations, these cities are at once facilitators, competitors, and challengers to one another and to their respective national agendas. Despite the volatilities, the allure of the new financial landscape that links them is irresistible. These cities are in the limelight for new brand-naming. Another round of outward-looking activities for the cities' residents is emerging. This section focuses on the energies of professional Hong Kongers who have seized the moment to charge ahead.

Businesses in Hong Kong have blazed the trail. HSBC and Standard Chartered Bank, representing the power of Hong Kong's "Central District," and of professionals at the high end of the social hierarchy, have long sunk roots in East Asia, India, and the Gulf region.[31] In September 2004, Cheong Kong Holdings, the flagship of Hong Kong tycoon Li Ka-shing, joined forces with a bank in Dubai to set up a fund to facilitate investment in Asian real-estate properties (see Swire 2004). In November 2005, David Eldon, then Chairman of the Hong Kong General Chamber of Commerce, led a group of members of the Chamber to Dubai and Tehran to promote mutually beneficial business opportunities.[32] The China – Middle East Economic Summit organized by the *Financial Times* in January 2007 highlighted "The New Silk Road." There would be potholes, warned Eldon, chairman of the Dubai International Finance Authority, as institutions designed to monitor and regulate the flow of capital, and the cultural sensitivities needed for business decisions have yet to be developed and refined. Moreover, professionals with multicultural experiences linking the two regions are lacking (Eldon 2007).[33]

A crucial ingredient of the New Silk Road is Islam, which connects the Middle East to Southeast Asia. In a study by Richard Pyvis, a director of CLSA BV, the Hong Kong-based global banker points to the need to better understand the development of Islamic finance for the Asian region. He and his team explore Islamic attitudes to capital markets, and how globalization is fundamental to Islam and may provide a new code for sustainable and equitable economic practices beyond neoliberal ordering frameworks. They set the direction for the business community to move from a Eurocentric focus to Islamic opportunities in a broadly defined Asia (Pyvis and Braun 2009).

The Hong Kong SAR government has followed business interests to forge this route. Frederick Ma, then Secretary for Financial Services and the

Treasury, led a delegation of business and policy-makers to the China –
Middle East Summit held in Dubai in January 2007. In his speech to that
conference and subsequent ones, he stressed the core institutional strengths
of Hong Kong – the rule of law, clean government, freedom of information,
the stable currency, the sophisticated banking infrastructure, and mature
capital markets and professional practices. He and his colleagues in the
financial services sector have repeatedly articulated the government's enthusiasm to provide the necessary administrative environment for Hong Kong
to traverse the New Silk Road.[34]

For eight days in January 2008, the Chief Executive of Hong Kong led a
prominent delegation of business leaders and government officials to Kuwait,
Saudi Arabia, and the United Arab Emirates (UAE), to promote Hong
Kong's capacity to develop Islamic banking.[35] He was, as expected, accompanied by David Eldon, a former chairman of the Hongkong and Shanghai
Banking Corporation (Asia), David Li, chairman of the Bank of East Asia,
and Laura Cha, a former vice-chair of China's securities commission. The
Hong Kong Mortgage Corporation, a subsidiary of the Monetary Authority,
whose function is to stabilize the mortgage debt market in Hong Kong, also
actively devises ways to reduce legal and other structural barriers to Islamic
debt financing with Malaysia.[36]

Enthusiasm is two-way traffic. The Gulf Research Center in Dubai, boasting
multinational professionals and researchers, conducts a Gulf–Asia Research
Program with the explicit goal of stressing the need to reinvigorate the two
regions' mutual economic reliance beyond oil and energy, and to overcome
the barrier of "information asymmetry."[37]

The enthusiasm for connectivity is probably justified. Trade statistics show
that trade between Saudi Arabia and China has reached a new height. In
2006, bilateral trade reached US$20 billion, a jump of 25.3 percent from
the previous year, and that with UAE rose 32 percent to $14.2 billion.[38] In
Dubai, the governor of the Dubai International Finance Center predicted
that the Middle East would invest US$200 billion in Asia (see *Wen Wei Po*
2007a). The new Dragon Mart – the largest trading hub in the UAE – comprises 4,000 shops in a dragon-shaped mall and displays a large range of
Chinese-manufactured goods for wholesale buyers, and restaurants and cultural heritage sites for tourists. China Southern, a major airline listed on the
Shanghai and Hong Kong stock exchanges, operates daily flights from
Beijing and Guangzhou to cities in the Middle East and Lagos. Real-estate
advertisements showcasing Dubai's super, postmodern skyline are introduced to eager Chinese buyers. Mega-state construction companies, highly
subsidized by China's wealthy state funds, outbid most competitors from
Europe and North America for infrastructural projects in the Gulf. Sovereign
funds in Abu Dhabi, Dubai, and Saudi Arabia are buying major stakes in
Asian banks. In May, Dubai International Capital announced that its Global

Strategic Equities Fund had bought a large percentage of HSBC, following in the footsteps of Maan al-Sanea (Saudi Arabia), who bought 3.1 percent of the bank's shares (Treanor 2007; see also *Wen Wei Po* 2007b). The financial tsunami of 2008 and the debt problems of Dubai World might have dampened enthusiasm somewhat, and real-estate speculators from Wenzhou, China have suffered heavy losses. However, the crisis has caused expatriates from Europe and North America to retreat from the region. The economic downturn has made China's presence there more prominent.

Following China's global engagement, the Hong Kong government and business community have taken the lead in shaping possibilities for the territory's professional institutions and talents. The signing of a memorandum of understanding between Hong Kong's Securities and Futures Commission and the Dubai Financial Services Authority is a most recent example to signify Hong Kong's positioning – to serve as a gateway for Asian business interests into China, and also to service China's capital formation needs in its global march (SFC 2008).[39] The Hang Seng Bank, the second largest in Hong Kong and a subsidiary of HSBC, has recently established several funds for Islamic bonds that are Shariah compliant.[40] According to a report by Reuters in June 2008, the Airport Authority in Hong Kong planned to follow with its own Islamic bond for institutional and individual investors (see Reuters 2008).

Professional training is also on the agenda. Laura Cha, Chair of the University Grants Committee, that advises the government on the funding of Hong Kong's eight universities, has negotiated a US$2 billion endowment for the support of academic research.[41] She has set up a special committee to consider revising the rule that government funding cannot be used outside of the territory. She believes that with Hong Kong's economy "crossing borders" in multiple ways, research activities also need to be cross-regional as well. This is especially applicable to Hong Kong's relationship with the dynamic Pearl River Delta. Along a similar line of thinking, when the ruler of Saudi Arabia established the new King Abdullah University of Science and Technology (KAUST) for the training of top-level academics and professionals, the publicly funded Hong Kong University of Science and Technology was among those invited to bid for hundreds of millions of funds to set up research centers in energy, environmental studies, engineering, and health delivery. Exchanges among the top administrators of the two institutions correspondingly increased.[42]

The New Silk Road is hot in Hong Kong, but has institutional building to create opportunities inspired Hong Kong professionals to reach beyond the territory? How would the new positioning of Hong Kong trigger the next round of self-fashioning among its residents, compared to the efforts of their counterparts in Shanghai, Mumbai, and Dubai? Would these energies remap an increasingly connected "Asia?"

A few personal cases illustrate the global paths of a different kind of professional. The volatility of finance capital and trade in these emerging markets means that jobs attached to them no longer nurture long-term career commitments and mobility up the corporate ladder. As members of the postwar baby-boomer generation in Hong Kong with middle-class means, John and Michael both went abroad for college and professional degrees. John returned to Hong Kong and spent almost an entire engineering career working for several local developers. Before early retirement, he managed the building of a container port. In his mid-fifties, he was sought out by a headhunter who persuaded him to take a 14-month contract in Dubai to build a port in the city's free trade zone. Managing a multicultural team of Europeans, Emirates, Chinese, and South Asians, with distinct hierarchies based on class, gender, and ethnicity, was an eye-opening experience. He took the opportunity to travel through the Gulf region, and returned to Hong Kong with fresh perspectives on new career maps and the necessary skills to navigate through them. He found the two years of sojourn personally lonely and difficult, because he was away from family and friends, and had few opportunities to interact with local society. However, the experience broadened his horizons and added confidence. When the next opportunity arises, he might get involved again. John has managed to step out of a comfortable, inward-looking Hong Kong experience which has "grounded" many of his peers and colleagues.

Michael's career trajectory seems to have headed a different direction, although he finds himself navigating along the New Silk Road as John has done. After college and professional training in architecture and structural engineering in Canada, he worked his way up a CDME career (Consulting, Design, Management, Engineering) with major firms in North America. His portfolio includes projects with world-class architects – Zeidler on the Eaton Centre and Ontario Place, and Barrett on Calgary International Airport. In the mid-1990s, however, he made a drastic career choice to move back to Hong Kong and then Suzhou and Shanghai. Again, he worked with big names – I.M. Pei on the Shanghai Trade Center, and K.M. Ma on the Shanghai TinAn Tower. For the past few years, he has been vice president and design director for a state-owned corporation, China Construction Design International Ltd., based in Shanghai. His work, however, has remarkable global elements. The company bids for projects not only in China, but in the Middle East. He manages design teams with colleagues from Europe and Hong Kong, backed up by junior engineers and construction workers from China. Heavily subsidized by the Chinese government, the company often outbids global competitors for project in Dubai and other parts of the Gulf Region. Such experiences make him increasingly attractive to engineering corporations. With an offer from a globally positioned engineering firm to head a division in Shenzhen, he finds himself, for the first time in a 32-year career, close to "home." However, his home-coming was short lived. The financial crisis of 2008 compelled him to move back to Shanghai after a year, to head his own consultancy.

Joining them is a generation of "Hong Kong returnees" – those whose parents were emigrants to North America and Australia during the decade before 1997, and who returned to Hong Kong after college to work in the finance services sector (Salaff *et al.* 2008). Another group of bilingual, bicultural professionals comes from China. Labeled "returnees" as well, many have spent a number of years studying and working in North America and Europe. Increasingly, they fill the professional and executive ranks of global financial institutions, legal consultancies, and media companies which are headquartered in Hong Kong but actively moving their businesses into China. With the government's plans to expand the tertiary education sector by 25 percent in 2012, the returnees are filling the academic ranks in all disciplines.

The Strategic March to the North

Today, the towering presence of Shanghai cannot be ignored by businesses in Hong Kong. The two cities have been partners and competitors for over a century. The only time that Shanghai's worldly dominance faded into the background was during three decades of Maoist closure. Apart from being the country's leading manufacturing and service metropolis, Shanghai's dramatic reentry into world trade and finance in the post-reform era dwarfs the record of any other city in Asia. Since 2005, the Port of Shanghai has become the world's busiest in terms of cargo tonnage. In the short two decades since its reestablishment in 1990, the Shanghai stock exchange has listed some of the world's largest companies by market valuation, such as PetroChina, the Industrial and Commercial Bank of China, and the Agricultural Bank of China, with HSBC waiting in the wings. Despite surveys and league tables placing Shanghai far behind Hong Kong and Singapore in business competitiveness and attractiveness, the State Council in China announced in the spring of 2009 its plans for Shanghai to become the country's lead finance centre by 2020. The news sent fresh jitters to the financial and policy communities in Hong Kong.

Furthermore, since the financial tsunami, China has accelerated its plans to globalize its currency in world trade. The difference in worlding capabilities of Shanghai's capital market compared to those of Hong Kong has been heightened. China's ability to draw FDI continues to top the world, and most of it is channeled through the capital markets in Shanghai. In recent years, many of China's most successful state-owned enterprises listed in Hong Kong (the red chips) have returned to be listed in Shanghai. The

Hong Kong banking system held *renminbi* deposits of 84.7 billion in May 2010, a mere trickle in the estimated 65 trillion circulated in the Chinese capital markets. Scholars and practitioners have wondered if Hong Kong's lead as the region's financial center will soon disappear, because the city lacks the backing of a nation's domestic economy or the force of political will (Holland 2010; Yam 2010). Moreover, the resurrected Bund, the sky-scrapers in Pudong, the new airport and high-speed rail, and lately the Shanghai Expo all point to the city's spectacular worlding energies in a fast-forward mode. The talk of Hong Kong's rapid decline against the rise of Shanghai has become daily news in the media.

Shanghai's rise makes it a magnet for the most energetic and adventur-ous. Again, Hong Kong has lagged behind Shanghai and other major Chinese cities that flaunt their own worlding ambitions. Between 1991 and 2001, Hong Kong's growth in population was 16.9 percent, close to that for cities in advanced industrial (or postindustrial) countries, such as New York (9.4 percent) and London (7.5 percent). In Beijing, the rate of increase for the same period was 25.4 percent. Shanghai had an increase of 23 percent, Guangzhou 57 percent, and Shenzhen, 320.3 percent. In view of the fact that all of these cities have low birth rates, based on personal preference or policy, the extraordinary population growth in Chinese cities was due largely to in-migration (Wong and Wong 2008: 95).

Shanghai's worlding capabilities are boosted by the wealthy and adven-turous from Hong Kong. Vincent Lo, founder of the Shui On Group in Hong Kong, enriched Shanghai's cityscape with the luxuries of Xintiandi in 2001. The US$150 million project converted a historical neighborhood with *shicumen* architecture of the early twentieth century into trendy boutiques, galleries, haute-cuisine, bars, cafés, and clubs. Xintiandi has become the entertainment icon for Shanghai's global rich and expatriate consumers.[43] Sun Hung Kai Properties, the second-largest developer in Hong Kong, specializes in building Shanghai's luxury hotels, malls, and commercial landmarks. Its International Finance Center in Pudong, opened in 2009, houses the new headquarters of HSBC, as well as the Ritz–Carlton Hotel and the conference center of the Harvard Business School. The Hong Kong-based Esquel Group, global producer of the world's leading brands in cotton apparel, and with family ties to some of the wealthiest textile manu-facturers in Republican Shanghai, has established its China headquarters in Shanghai. This is a simultaneous act of going global and returning home (Yang 2007).

While policy attention is conspicuously focused on the global tracks of upper- and middle-class professionals, it is useful to explore how the dra-matic growth of China's economy provides unexpected mobility at all levels of Hong Kong's labor hierarchy. Over the years, the Hong Kong govern-ment has negotiated with Beijing to provide Hong Kong-based businesses and professionals an advantage in the maturing China market. CEPA (the Closer Economic Partnership Arrangement), signed between Hong Kong and China in June 2003, includes free trade arrangements for a wide range of Hong Kong products. It also encourages trade in services by mutual recognition of professional qualifications and the reduction of regulatory barriers. Although the numbers using the CEPA arrangements have not been overwhelming from the Hong Kong side, CEPA has in fact benefitted Chinese corporations and professionals in their global march. Hong Kong has become a valuable springboard.[44]

More significant is the fact that this mobility is not limited to the globally minded businesses and their supporting professionals. For Hong Kongers at the lower end of the labor hierarchy, border crossing means tapping into China's position as world factory. The foreign-owned factories and the influx of massive numbers of migrant workers to southern China are well documented (Lee 1998; Pun 2005). In the 1980s and 1990s, managers, technicians, and transport and sales personnel have followed the factories in their strategic march north. The "One Country, Two Systems" formula has enabled dramatic increase in cross-border flows of capital, goods, people, and images. In 2007, the government revised the number of Hong Kongers residing in China upwards, from 290,000 in 2005 to 460,000. Nearly half of this group was between 30 and 49 years of age. Over 40 percent of them had attained post-secondary education, with 80 percent engaged in professional and managerial positions.[45] While the business and policy communities have focused on the infrastructural links between Hong Kong and the South China region, less attention is paid to the ways in which such developments have changed the social and cultural landscape.

Cross-border marriages between Hong Kongers and Mainlanders have deeply affected family strategies and labor mobility. Historically, working men in Hong Kong looked across the border for affordable spouses. An immigration scheme worked out between Hong Kong and China since the 1950s permits an average of 150 persons per day to legally enter the territory, mostly on the basis of family reunion. A large number of adult Chinese men from rural Guangdong and Fujian entered Hong Kong in the late 1970s and early 1980s, when post-Mao China suddenly relaxed its border controls. The labor participation rates for these laborers were high, as many were employed as construction and transport workers in Hong Kong's expanding infrastructure projects. They returned to their native villages to marry. After years of waiting, they were able, in the 1990s, to bring their families to Hong Kong as permanent residents. Census data from Hong Kong shows that in the decade from 1990 to 2000, the number of new arrivals (those who have settled in Hong Kong for less than seven years) increased from 2.6 to 4 percent of Hong Kong's population.

Local-born Hong Kongers have reacted negatively to the influx, labeling them "new immigrants" and seeing them as poor, uneducated, rural, and a societal burden. However, changes in the cross-border social landscape have accelerated since 1997. The "new immigrants" are no longer the rural, dependent spouses and children of older, structurally unemployed Hong Kong men. Instead, they are younger, more educated, and more likely to have migrated to South China from other cities and provinces to work in factories and services. Frontline social workers and community agencies find them culturally attuned to life in Hong Kong and socially resourceful (Siu 2008b).

The government by-census in 2006 shows a trend of intensified cross-border marriages. That year, 28,000 Hong Kong men married women from the mainland, an increase of 14 percent from 1996. The by-census also shows that Hong Kong women have joined their male counterparts to look for cross-border spouses. Numbering 6,500 in 2006, such marriages jumped by a factor of 2.5 compared with 1996 (HKSAR 2007; see also *Mingpao Daily* 2007b). The marriages are not without difficulties, as societal discriminations are still deeply felt, and the government wavered in the provision of services for these new arrivals. The local media often play up the sensational aspects of family trauma and sadness (Newendorp 2008).[46]

In 2005, an interdisciplinary team of academics strongly recommended the government to incorporate the concept of "circulation" in its population policies (Siu and Ku 2008).[47] The best use of this human resource at the lower end of the labor hierarchy is to create maximum flexibility for the young families to cross the border at different stages of their life trajectories. If social services for Hong Kong residents are made more portable, the study argues, one might expect this generation of new immigrants to become the technical and service backbone of an interconnected metropolitan region that comprises Hong Kong, Shenzhen, Guangzhou, and the Pearl River Delta. The analytical point to stress is that if China's economy continues to surge, engagement with its global march will indirectly allow Hong Kongers at the lower end of the labor hierarchy to be translocal in employment and cultural orientation. Comprised of newer immigrants from China, and mostly working class, this group has fewer cultural or political barriers to engage China than the city's entrenched middle-class residents.

The Historical Global and the Asian Postmodern

The twenty-first century, as the authors of this volume argue, will be a century of Asian urbanization. There is intense inter-referencing among Asia's urban nodes – economic linkages, cultural borrowings, competitions, and collaborations. Governments, elite actors, circulating professionals, and migratory laborers are cultivating new positions in their own resourceful ways. Hong Kong, like its counterparts in Asia, is trying to reinvent itself as a world city in this volatile process. This chapter has explored the historical baggage that its major stakeholders carry to engage with this emerging inter-Asia environment.

The chapter has tried to treat Hong Kongers as a moving analytical target. It has focused on the multiethnic groups who came to Hong Kong in the last century in search of entrepreneurial opportunities. Their aspirations, energies, and cultural practices gave Hong Kong its historically global character. These early "Hong Kongers," as citizens of the colonial city and Chinese subjects, were ungrounded in the territory. However, several generations of Hong Kong residents have matured in the postwar decades. For the first time, there is a real sense of place-based identity among the locally born. They have excelled in Hong Kong's education system and have taken for granted unprecedented upward social mobility. They claimed entitlements from the colonial government and have continued such claims after Hong Kong's sovereignty reverted to China in 1997. In the ensuing economic downturn, a sinking and shrinking middle class have dug their heels in, and have drawn hard lines against new immigrants from their entrenched "citizenship" positions in the territory.

Has such provincializing continued in the present decade? This chapter has argued that with the forging of "the New Silk Road," and strategic participation in an emerging Chinese market, some of the territory's residents have taken the initiative to seek global opportunities. Joined by professional and entrepreneurial immigrants from China and abroad, they have overcome a fortress mentality and are changing Hong Kong's work structure and cultural styles. If their enhanced footprints contribute to the inter-referencing processes across the dynamic cities in the region, they will become a substantial part of Asia's urban renaissance.

Notes

1 I thank Aihwa Ong and Ananya Roy for raising some of these important issues. See policy-relevant treatment in Siu and Ku (2008).
2 On the concept of flexible positioning and citizenship among global professionals, see Ong and Nonini (1999) and Ong (2006).
3 According to local sayings, "big earlobes" were given to these ethnically distinguished money lenders because they wore large earrings. The term is generally used today for usury.
4 On items produced in Guangzhou and Fujian for the China Trade, see Ganse (2008) and Crossman (1973). See also the catalogue of the exhibition jointly mounted by the Guangzhou Museum and the Victoria Albert Museum, in Guangzhou (Wilson and Liu 2003). The Peabody Museum at Salem, Massachusetts displays one of the world's best collections of such wares.

5   In the 1990s, I visited the ancestral home of a Chinese merchant in Chaozhou, who made his fortune in the trading of Chinese herbs in Thailand and North America. The Chen family house, with its pretentiously Chinese literati-style chambers and halls, was connected by numerous courtyards and alcoves. Their walls were lined with ceramic tiles bearing elaborate Arabic/Islamic motifs and colors (field trip in 1992 with Dr. Choi Chi-cheung in Chenghai of Chaozhou).

6   On how the China Trade affected the cultural styles of merchant families in Guangzhou, see Ching and Liu (2004).

7   For example, the Tung Wah Hospital, established in the colonial legal framework in the 1860s under the British Hospital Ordinance, was a charity, and its Chinese merchant elites who served as board members anchored their authoritative presence upon a Man Mo Temple. The charity dominated the governance of Hong Kong for almost a century and has continued to function as a major charity today (Sinn 1989). On state–merchant relationships in late imperial China, see Siu (2000). On similar state–society relationships in the regional city of Hankow in the eighteenth and nineteenth centuries, see Rowe (1985).

8   This paragraph is taken from Sinn's chapter in *Hong Kong Mobile* (2008). The concept "space of flow" originally came from Manuel Castells. For recent theoretical works concerned with the reconfiguration of urban space in the modern and postmodern eras, see Harvey (1989), Sassen (2000), Hannerz (1996), and Holston and Appadurai (1999).

9   See a special issue of *Forbes Magazine* (2008).

10 The developer is Sun Hung Kai Properties, the second-largest developer in Hong Kong and the owner of high-end business real estate such as the IFC in Hong Kong and Shanghai.

11 See also Lee (2000) on Shanghai modern. The life of talented writer Ailing Chang and her novels (*Love in a Fallen City, Lust Caution*) are illustrative of the intimate worlds between Hong Kong and Shanghai.

12 Two recent studies substantiate our appreciation of the region's historical cosmopolitanism, centering on the close ties between Shanghai and Hong Kong. *The Age of Openness* by Frank Dikötter (2008) shows that Republican China was far from being a period of decay and political implosion. Instead, his chapters stress "open governance, open minds, open borders, and open markets." The country's engagement with the world was multifaceted and dynamic, and its urban social landscape brashly worldly. Leo Ou-fan Lee, in *City Between Worlds* (2008), highlights Hong Kong's past and present, "perched on the fault line between China and the West," and how generations of residents – expatriates, locals, and itinerants – continue to churn a cultural kaleidoscope that exuberates intense energies, glamour, and also sad memories. It is *bricolage* in every sense of the word, allowing Lee, a converted Hong Konger, to play local *flâneur*. These cities and their residents might not always be comfortable with the imposition of hard political borders or rhetoric. Economically useful to their national spaces but culturally ambiguous and politically suspect, their worlding capabilities problematize governmentality and citizenship.

13 The following sections are adapted from Siu (2008a). I have used a history of "border" crossing to highlight three categories of "Hong Kongers" whose lives and identities are linked, but whose sense of citizenship are worlds apart. In the 10 years since the return of Hong Kong's sovereignty to China, pro-democracy middle-class

professionals, patriotic working families, and new immigrants have negotiated their respective places along multiple political fronts.

14 This observation was related to me by Hong Kong historian, Dr. Elizabeth Sinn.

15 It is interesting to note a similar influx of migrants to Mumbai from the rest of India in history and in recent years (Appadurai 2001). In Dubai, over 80 percent of its residents are expatriates. Although most of the migrant workers come from the GCC region, there is an elite European and Australian community. The middle ranks are filled by Indians and Chinese entrepreneurs. At the lower end of the labor hierarchy, there are massive numbers of migrant workers from the Philippines, Pakistan, Southeast Asia, and Islamic North Africa (see Janardhan n.d. a,b; provided by the author). The financial crisis in 2008 might have diminished the number of foreign workers at the top and bottom ends, but the groups in the middle (especially Chinese entrepreneurs and service workers) have maintained their presence. During my visit to Dubai in March 2007, I noticed that these workers filled the construction sites in groups. At the end of the day, buses transported them back to the neighboring emirate of Sharjah (as Dubai City is too expensive for residence). On the eastern bank of the Dubai Creek, where the gold and spice markets stand, multiethnic traders congregate in cheaper guest houses.

16 Sociologist Lui Tai Lok (Lui 2007a) has written a great deal on four generations of Hong Kongers.

17 On some HK businessmen compiling a journal to chronicle the problems of operating in China, see *Mingpao Daily* (2010).

18 Expatriates who have moved to Singapore often cite the push factor in Hong Kong (deteriorating quality of air and water, inadequate education facilities, high rents), and the pull factor in Singapore (pleasant environment, good schools, multilingual capabilities).

19 See the debates in 2007, in *Mingpao Daily* and the *Hong Kong Economic Journal*. The scholars include Lui Tai Lok, Nelson Chow, Wong Chack Kei, and Lui Ting-ming. The issue was also raised in forums and workshops organized by the Strategic Policy Commission, the Central Policy Unit.

20 Those who could move with the jobs did so. In 1998, only 52,000 Hong Kongers worked on the mainland. By 2005, the number was 237,000.

21 A low unemployment rate can mask structural issues in the labor hierarchy. Although businesses at the high end are pressuring the government to import more professional talents and create the proper incentives and environment, labor at the low end cannot be fully employed. See the government statistics (http://www.hkeconomy. gov.hk/en/pdf/08q2_ppt.pdf) on the difference. Newspaper editorials have urged the government to think outside the box and take drastic action to address the imbalance of the labor market.

22 Lui Tai Lok and Anthony Cheung suggest that for over 20 years, this generation of Hong Kongers might have been too complacent, and has not reached beyond old ordering frames to enrich its localized experiences. See Lui's "Yau lok, hou sou" ("Time to get off"), the postscript to a new edition of the book, published by Oxford University Press in Hong Kong (Lui 2007b). See a summary of the postscript in Lui (2007c).

23 See Chow (2007: 11) and Wong (2007). See also Chow (2009) on a social breakdown of the poor who received public assistance in Hong Kong.

24 On competitiveness and the Hong Konger's mindset, see Siu and Ku (2008).
25 See a public opinion survey, "Historical Conservation" (*South China Morning Post* 2007). A large percentage of opinion leaders interviewed feel that the government has not done enough.
26 See a recent sample of public sentiments on the issue in Chan (2007b) and Lu (2007). The leaders of the Local Action Group comprise many students and young professionals.
27 See essays by cultural activists in Lung *et al.* (2004).
28 On every significant date involving China, the leaders are able to mobilize large numbers. Every year, for example, they have organized tens of thousands of working families on July 1 to celebrate the return of Hong Kong to her motherland.
29 See comments by Cheung (2007) and Lui (2007c).
30 See a speech delivered by Siu at a Hong Kong Asia Society luncheon (Siu 2004).
31 The annual reports of these two banks clearly show these as major regions on which to focus business attention.
32 See the Hong Kong General Chamber of Commerce website (Faces and Places 2005) for more detailed descriptions of the trip.
33 See Eldon (2007). The full program of the summit can be found on the web archive of the *Financial Times* for 2007. Other keynote speakers included Cheng Siwei (Chairman, Standing Committee, National People's Congress, China) and H.E. Dr. Omar Bin Sulaiman, Governor of the Dubai International Finance Center. A following summit was held in Riyadh, Saudi Arabia on May 5, 2008, displaying a similar array of world financiers and political luminaries. For a program of the China – Middle East Summit in Riyadh, organized by the *Financial Times*, go to www.ftconferences.com.
34 See the efforts by John Tsang, Finance Secretary of the HKSAR, and K.C. Chan, Ma's successor after Ma retired in 2008. In a tour of the United States, Chan says "We are reaching out to tap business opportunities in emerging markets such as Russia, Vietnam, India and the Middle East. Our market infrastructure and regulatory regime are being upgraded to align them with the evolving global market. As a new initiative, we are working to put in place an Islamic financial platform to harvest market opportunities in the Middle East" (*Hong Kong Digest* 2008).
35 See *South China Morning Post* (2008) on the trip and on the advantages of Hong Kong that Donald Tsang stresses.
36 See the 2007 Annual Report of the Hong Kong Mortgage Corporation Limited and its recent agreement with its counterpart in Malaysia, Cagamas Berhad. Ms. Susie Cheung, General Council and Company Secretary, articulated some of the legal and cultural barriers (e.g., definitions of interest, debt, and insurance) that need attention.
37 See the *Gulf-Asia Research Bulletin*, published tri-annually by the Gulf Research Center, Dubai, UAE. Dr. Samir Ranjan Pradhan, an Indian national and senior researcher at the Center, is the editor of the *Bulletin* (www.grc.ae).
38 See Dueck (2007), in the *South China Morning Post* (May 18); see also *Wen Wei Po* (2007c,d).
39 See the press release by the Securities and Futures Commission (2008); see also a circular by the Hong Kong Trade and Development Council (2008), commenting on the MOU signed between The Hong Kong Monetary Authority and the Dubai International Financial Centre Authority in May 2008.

40 See Chan (2007). John Tsang, finance secretary of HKSAR, intends to level the territory's role as international finance hub to lure Middle Eastern investors.
41 It is a significant commitment from the government, as it constitutes 15.5 percent of the government's surplus in 2008 (see *Mingpao Daily* 2008b).
42 See *Mingpao Daily* (2008a). The Vice Chancellor of Hong Kong University of Science and Technology, Professor Paul Chu, led a small delegation to Yale to introduce the university to senior postgraduate students. He and his senior administrators were on their way to attend the ground-breaking ceremonies of KAUST in Saudi Arabia, and had high hopes for linking research programs in Hong Kong with developments in the Middle East.
43 See the web site of Xintiandi for history, photographs, and happenings.
44 See CEPA data for 2008.
45 For statistical data on Hong Kongers who live and work in China, see *Mingpao Daily* (2007a).
46 See a recent study by Newendorp (2008).
47 See Siu and Ku (2008). The study was commissioned by the 2022 Foundation in Hong Kong to look into the software of Hong Kong's competitiveness; in particular, Hong Kong's human resources. Hong Kong's population is aging. With a rather restrictive immigration policy that allows largely family reunion, the mismatch between the needs of the economy and the available labor power has been serious. There is a need to create a workforce that will allow Hong Kong to reposition itself in the rapidly changing political and economic environment.

References

Atsushi Miura (三浦展) (2005) 下流社會：新的階層集團的出現 (Downward mobility: the emergence of a new social group) (translated from Japanese). Kao Pao, Taipei.
Chan, M. (2007) Tsang unveils Islamic bond push. *South China Morning Post*, September 11, p. B10.
Chen Yun (2007) Huanghou (Queen). *Hong Kong Economic Journal*, August 9, p. 36.
Cheung, A. (2007) Defining ourselves. September 17; www.scmp.com (accessed September 17, 2007).
Ching May Bo and Liu Zhiwei (2004)《18、19世纪广州洋人家庭的中国佣人》(Chinese servants in the homes of Europeans in 18th and 19th century Guangzhou).《史林》(*Shilin*), 第4期, 第1–11页 (no. 4, pp. 1–11).
Chow, N. (2007) Zhongchan jieji de beiai he wunei (Hong Kong middle class, sadness and resignation). *Hong Kong Economic Journal*, February 1, p. 11.
Chow, N. (2009) Huigui 12 nian duole 22wan qiongren (The poor increased by two hundred and twenty thousand, twelve years after the return of sovereignty). *Hong Kong Economic Journal*, September 17; www.hkej.com (accessed September 16, 2009).
Crossman, C. (1973) *The China Trade: export paintings, furniture, silver, and other objects.* Princeton, NJ: The Pyne Press.
Dueck, C. (2007) Dubai courts mainland firms in week-long tour. *South China Morning Post*, May 18.
Eldon, D. (2006) The talent we need. *The Bulletin*, Hong Kong General Chamber of Commerce, April 6.

Eldon, D. (2007) The New Silk Road: an opportunity with an asterisk. Keynote speech at the Financial Times China – Middle East Summit, Dubai, January 30.

Faure, D. (2003) *Colonialism and the Hong Kong Mentality*. Centre of Asian Studies, The University of Hong Kong, Hong Kong.

Forbes Magazine (2008) Forbes 2008 guide to the biggest companies in the world (excerpted by HSBC Private Bank). April 21; www.forbes.com (accessed April 21, 2008).

Ganse, S. (2008) *Chinese Porcelain: an export to the world*. Hong Kong: Joint Publishing (in Chinese).

Guo Deyan (2005) *Qingdai Guangzhou de Basi shangren* (Parsee merchants in Canton during the Qing Period). Beijing: Zhonghua Shuju, p. 134.

Hannerz, U. (1996) The cultural role of world cities. In *Transnational Connections*. London: Routledge, pp. 127–39.

Harvey, D. (1989) *The Condition of Postmodernity*. Oxford: Blackwell.

HKSAR (2007) *2006 Population By-Census*, February. Census and Statistics Department, HKSAR.

Holland, T. (2010) Hubris, not Shanghai, is Hong Kong's greatest threat. *South China Morning Post*, April 7.

Holston, J. and Appadurai, A. (1999) Introduction: cities and citizenship. In J. Holston (ed.) *Cities and Citizenship*. Durham, NC: Duke University Press, pp. 1–18.

Hong Kong Digest (2008) Secretary for Financial Services and the Treasury visits U.S. April–May; http://www.hketony.gov.hk/ny/e-newsletter/08apr/SFST.htm

Hong Kong Trade and Development Council (2008) Islamic finance deal an important milestone. July 2.

Janardhan, N. (n.d. a) *Gulf–Asia Ties: time to convert East–East opportunity into strategy*. Dubai: Gulf Research Center.

Janardhan, N. (n.d. b) *Redefining Labor Market Rules*. Dubai: Gulf Research Center.

Kwoh, L. (2006) Talent gap hits businesses. *The Standard*, May 2.

Lam Kit Chun and Pak Wai Liu (1998) *Immigration and the Economy of Hong Kong*. Hong Kong: Hong Kong City University Press.

Lee Ching-kwan (1998) *Gender and the South China Miracle*. Berkeley, CA: University of California Press.

Lee, Leo Ou-fan (2000) *Shanghai Modern*. Cambridge, MA: Harvard University Press.

Leiper, S. (1997) *Precious Cargo: Scots and the China Trade*. Edinburgh: National Museums of Scotland.

Loh, C. (ed.) (2004) *At the Epicentre: Hong Kong and the SARS outbreak*. Hong Kong: Hong Kong University Press.

Lu Qiang (2007) Jia zixun, helai zhen gongleng (How can real impact be produced from faked consultation?). *Hong Kong Economic Journal*, August 9, p. 14.

Lui Tai Lok (2007a) *Sidai Xianggang ren* (Four generations of Hong Kong people). Hong Kong: Step Forward Multimedia.

Lui Tai Lok (2007b) *Wu gai, mai dan: yi ge shehuixue jia de Xianggang biji* (Checks please: the diary of a Hong Kong sociologist), 2nd edn. Hong Kong: Oxford University Press.

Lui Tai Lok (2007c) Yau lok, hou sou (postscript in Lui 2007). Excerpted in *Apple Daily*, July 22, p. A18.

Lui Tai Lok and Wong Chi Tsang (2003) *Xianggang zhongchan jieji chujing guancha* (Observations on the predicaments of Hong Kong's middle class). Hong Kong: Joint Publishing.

Luk, B. *et al.* (2008) Education reforms and social mobility: rethinking the history of Hong Kong education. In H.F. Siu and A.S. Ku (eds.) *Hong Kong Mobile: making a global population.* Hong Kong: Hong Kong University Press.

Lung Ying-tai *et al.* (2004) *Wenhua Qiyi* (Cultural revolt). Hong Kong: CUP Publishing.

Mathews, Gordon, Eric Kit-wai Ma and Tai Lok Lui (2008) *Hong Kong, China: learning to belong to a nation.* London: Routledge.

Mingpao Daily (2007a) 470,000 Gangren ju neidi duo gao xueli (Four hundred and seventy thousand Hong Kongers live in the Mainland and mostly with higher education attainment). September 29; www.mingpaonews.com (accessed September 28, 2007).

Mingpao Daily (2007b) Gang nan qu neidi nü nianling chaju zeng (The age gap between Hong Kong husbands and Mainland spouses rises). April 23; www.mingpaonews.com (accessed April 23, 2007).

Mingpao Daily (2008a) Keda jingtou Shade Daxue 2 yi yanzhi (HKUST bids 200 million research funds from the University in Saudi Arabia). January 5; www.mingpaonews.com (accessed January 5, 2008).

Mingpao Daily (2008b) Shi Meilun wei neidi Gang sheng zheng daiyu (Laura Cha fights for resources for Hong Kong students in China). March 5; www.mingpaonews.com (accessed March 5, 2008).

Mingpao Daily (2010) Gang shang chu zazhi jiang xueleishi (Hong Kong merchant founded journal to voice bitter histories of doing business in China). August 9; www.mingpaonews.com (accessed August 9, 2010).

Newendorp, N.D. (2008) *Uneasy Reunions: immigration, citizenship, and family life in post-1997 Hong Kong.* Stanford, CA: Stanford University Press.

Ohmae Kenichi (大前研一) (2006) *M型社會: 中產階級消失的危機與商機／*(M-shaped society: the dangers and opportunities of middle class demise) (translators Liu Jinxiu and Jiang Yuzhen; 劉錦秀, 江裕真), 商周出版 (Shang Chou Publishing), Taipei.

Ong, A. (2006) *Neoliberalism as Exception.* Durham, NC: Duke University Press.

Ong, A. and Nonini, D.M. (eds.) (1999) *Ungrounded Empires: the cultural politics of modern Chinese transnationalism.* New York: Routledge.

Pun Ngai (2005) *Made in China: women factory workers in a global workplace.* Durham, NC: Duke University Press.

Pyvis, R. and Braun, P. (2009) *Islam and Economics: a productive partnership?* Hong Kong: CLSA Books.

Reuters (UK) (2008) HK airport operator set to sell Islamic bond-report. Thursday June 5, 2:36 a.m. BST.

Rowe, W. (1985) *Hankow: commerce and society in a Chinese city, 1796–1889.* Stanford, CA: Stanford University Press.

Salaff, J. *et al.* (2008) Like sons and daughters of Hong Kong: the return of the young generation. In H.F. Siu and A.S. Ku (eds.) *Hong Kong Mobile: making a global population.* Hong Kong: Hong Kong University Press, pp. 199–222.

Salaff, J., Wong, S.L., and Greve, A. (2010) *Hong Kong Movers and Stayers: narratives of family migration.* Urbana, IL: University of Illinois Press.

Sassen, S. (2000) Spatialities and temporalities of the global: elements for a theorization. In A.M. Simone (ed.) *Public Culture: globalization,* vol. 2. Millennial Quartet, pp. 215–32.

SFC (Securities and Futures Commission) (2008) SFC Signs MOU with Dubai Financial Services Authority. Press release, April 3.

Simone, A.M. (2004) *For the City Yet to Come: changing African life in four cities*. Durham, NC: Duke University Press.

Sinn, E. (1989) *Power and Charity: the early history of the Tung Wah Hospital, Hong Kong*. East Asian Historical Monographs. Hong Kong: Oxford University Press.

Sinn, E. (2008) Lessons in openness: creating a space of flow in Hong Kong. In H.F. Siu and A.S. Ku (eds.) *Hong Kong Mobile: making a global population*. Hong Kong: Hong Kong University Press, pp. 13–41.

Siu, H. (1993) Cultural identity and the politics of difference. *Daedalus* (Spring), pp. 19–43.

Siu, H. (1996) *Remade in Hong Kong*, weaving into the Chinese cultural tapestry. In Taotao Liu and D. Faure (eds.) *Unity and Diversity: local cultures and identities in China*. Hong Kong: Hong Kong University Press, pp. 177–97.

Siu, H. (1999) Hong Kong: cultural kaleidoscope on a world landscape. In G. Hamilton (ed.) *Cosmopolitan Capitalists: Hong Kong and the Chinese Diaspora at the end of the 20th century*. Seattle, WA: University of Washington Press, pp. 100–17.

Siu, H. (2000) The grounding of cosmopolitans: merchants and local cultures in South China. In Wen-hsin Yeh (ed.) *Becoming Chinese: passages to modernity and beyond*. Berkeley, CA: University of California Press, pp. 191–227.

Siu, H. (2004) Hong Kong's strategic march to the north: a cultural narrative. A talk given at Asia Society Hong Kong, February 16.

Siu, H. (2007) Eulogy and practice: public professionals and private lives. In D. Davis and H. Siu (eds.) *SARS: reception and interpretation in three Chinese cities*. London: Routledge, pp. 75–102.

Siu, H. (2008a) Hong Kong mobile: redefining the Hong Konger. In C. McGiffert and J.T.H. Tang (eds.) *Hong Kong on the Move: 10 years as the SAR*. Washington, DC: CSIC Press, pp. 192–206.

Siu, H. (2008b) Positioning "Hong Kongers" and "new immigrants," in H.F. Siu and A.S. Ku (eds.) *Hong Kong Mobile: making a global population*. Hong Kong: Hong Kong University Press, pp. 115–46.

Siu, H. (2009) Positioning at the margins: the infra-power of middle class Hong Kong. In D. Madsen and A. Riemenschnitter (eds.) *Diasporic Histories: archives of Chinese transnationalism*. Hong Kong: Hong Kong University Press.

Siu, H. and Ku, A. (2008) Introduction. In *Hong Kong Mobile: making a global population*. Hong Kong: Hong Kong University Press.

South China Morning Post (2008) Hong Kong good bet, Tsang tells Kuwait staff reporter. January 28.

Swire, M. (2004) Cheung Kong Holdings teams up with Dubai bank to launch Islamic property investment trust. Tax-News.com, Hong Kong, September 9; http://www.tax-news.com/news/Cheung_Kong_Holdings_Teams_Up_With_Dubai_Bank_To_Launch_Islamic_Property_Investment_Trust____17234.html (accessed September 9, 2004).

Treanor, J. (2007) Dubai fund buys into HSBC. *The Guardian*, May 2.

Wen Wei Po (2007a) Lengyuan mouyi xin shilu zhanchengxing (New Silk Road on oil trade is taking shape). March 9, p. A6.

Wen Wei Po (2007b) Sade fuhao cheng Huikong di er dai gudong (Saudi tycoon becomes the second largest holder of HSBC stocks). April 17.

Wen Wei Po (2007c) Zhongdong kaolong Yuandong zhijin juantou Zhongguo (Middle East leans towards the Far East, investments switch to China). March 9, p. A6.

Wen Wei Po (2007d) Zhongsha mouyi qunian jisheng 25.3% (Trade between China and Saudi Arabia rapidly increased 25.3%). March 9, p. A6.

Wilson, M. and Liu Zhiwei (2003) *Souvenir From Canton: Chinese export paintings from the Victoria and Albert Museum.* Guangzhou: Victoria and Albert Museum/Guangzhou Cultural Bureau.

Wong Chack Kei (2007) Zhongchan jieji de ruohua ji yuanfen (The weakening and frustrations of the middle class). *Hong Kong Economic Journal*, January 31.

Wong, R. and Ka-fu Wong (2008) The importance of migration flow to Hong Kong's Future. In H.F. Siu and A.S. Ku (eds.) *Hong Kong Mobile: making a global population.* Hong Kong: Hong Kong University Press.

Wong Siu-lun *et al.* (2002) Hong Kong identity and social cohesion. Unpublished report for the Central Policy Unit, Hong Kong SAR Government.

Yam, S. (2010) A tale of two cities and their abiding suspicions. *South China Morning Post*, January 23.

Yang, M. (with Feng Xiaocai) (2007) *Tsai Hsiung: a biography.* Private publication.

6

Cracks in the Façade: Landscapes of Hope and Desire in Dubai

Chad Haines

Introduction

Prior to the economic crisis of 2009, Dubai was seen everywhere, even from space. Extensive media coverage of the city, Dubai-based investments in all corners of the world, and as home to migrants from Afghanistan and Bhutan to Yemen and Zaire – all of this transformed Dubai into one of the most visible spaces. Dubai achieved a presence on the world stage as a global city.

In 2007, as one drove south from New Delhi into the satellite city of Gurgaon,[1] looming large along the motorway there stood a billboard for Emaar – the largest real-estate development corporation in Dubai. The billboard read "Palm World: Unique Living Experience; Emaar – Building a New India." Similarly, driving along the October 6th flyover in downtown Cairo, amidst the billboards advertising the latest clothing fashions and mobile phones was a billboard for "Hyde Park, An Oasis in the City, Built by Al Futtaim," being one of the other major Dubai-based real-estate corporations. In Islamabad, Pakistan, Pak-Gulf Properties, a partnership of Sardar Builders of Pakistan and the Saudi real-estate developers Al-Tamimi, is constructing a seven-star hotel that claims to be "The Identity of Pakistan" while "Crafting New Lifestyles." Simultaneously, Dubai-based Al-Ghurair Ltd. and Emaar are undertaking partnerships in the construction of gated communities on the edge of the planned city, built in the 1960s.

The billboards, the real-estate projects they advertise, and the new lifestyles they market reflect strategic aspects of Dubai as a global city. The idea of Dubai is intentionally manufactured as a brand, rooted in its project of presence; brand Dubai is about being visible, engendering global visibility and wealth visibility. Brand Dubai is circulated and consumed throughout

Worlding Cities: Asian Experiments and the Art of Being Global, First Edition.
Edited by Ananya Roy and Aihwa Ong.
© 2011 Blackwell Publishing Ltd. Published 2011 by Blackwell Publishing Ltd.

Asia, Africa, and the Middle East, crafting new forms of urban presence, new means of being wealthy, and new markers of global success. Dubai's worlding presence is engendered in the interweaving of multiple processes, produced, circulated, and consumed in a diversity of locales, from small villages in Pakistan to Cairo, from New York to Tokyo. Focusing on two ways in which Dubai is imagined and lived, this chapter analyzes the multiple ways in which Dubai is inter-referenced in the urbanscapes and emergent lifestyles of people. The first focus is on the production and circulation of brand Dubai; the selling of a particular global dream of high-class consumption and luxurious lifestyles. Brand Dubai is an image that lives beyond and outside Dubai itself. It is produced as well as consumed in countries such as Pakistan, India, and Egypt, framed within the complex and multiple contexts in which it is produced and consumed. Brand Dubai has multiple lives, engaging in dialogue with nationalist projects in different countries.

The second focus is on the lived realities of Dubai, the grounding of the Disneyesque landscape of the city, enticing migrants, tourists, and capital to invest and spend in the unique urban accomplishment. Dubai is not just an image, but a lived reality, an everyday experience for those who make Dubai home or visit there, and for millions more buying into the Dubai-inspired dream of gated communities and endless consumption possibilities in their own cities. Dubai reshapes everyday lives near and far.

Each of these presencing projects re-landscapes the hopes and aspirations of the emergent middle classes throughout Asia, Africa, and the Middle East. In India, for example, the "new India" marketed by Emaar plays upon the global aspirations of Indians seeking out lifestyles that mark them as having made it in the global economy. The idea of a "new India" is an expression of an emergent "global nationalism" that is taking root in India as the nation attempts to redefine its place in the world. The "new India" trope shifts India's image as a Third World country to a major world player. Comparatively, in Pakistan, brand Dubai feeds upon the growing insecurities of the failed state structured by the US "war on terror." For many Pakistanis, as well as many Arabs, Dubai is an articulation of a Muslim modernity, an alternative to blatant "westernization."

In this perspective, Dubai is more than an Emirati or Gulf Arab city; Dubai is simultaneously an Indian, Pakistani, Filipino, Malay, Egyptian, Palestinian, and a Kenyan city. Dubai defies our commonsense geographies and moves us beyond an analysis of "the urban" as something transpiring within the bounds of a particular spatial unit (e.g., Davis 2006) or established global networks (e.g., Sassen 2001) that ignore the complex inter-referencing between Dubai and other cities, nations, and gated communities. While much of Dubai, particularly its malls, gated communities, and airport, can be recognized as "non-places" (Auge 1995) it is important not to slip into free-floating notions of disconnected, alienated people and spaces; the everyday

lives of the migrant laborers of those non-places, the professional expatriates, and the lifestyle aspirants dreaming of being global are very much
grounded in territorialized spaces, defined by state projects as much as by
global capital flows. Dubai's global multi-sitedness transforms but does not
erase state powers and national interests and their control over the spaces
through which we traverse in our everyday lives.

The emergence of Dubai as a worlding city, in its Emirati formation as
well as the shape it takes in Pakistan, India, and elsewhere, cannot be sepa-
rated from the neoliberalizing project of the past few decades. Just as the
Industrial Revolution was predicated on the "freeing" of labor from the
land, the neoliberal revolution is rooted in the "freeing" of labor from
public-sector employment that was the hallmark of the socialist-oriented
regimes of states such as India and Egypt. The structural readjustment and
privatization enforced by the neoliberal regime of the World Bank and IMF
led to severe un- and under-employment in many Third World countries.
The proliferation of stock exchanges and deepening forms of corporate fundamentalism are leading to the generation of extreme wealth for some,
tantalizing others, and leaving most behind as the gap between rich and
poor increases at an exponential rate.[2] Mass migration to the Arab Gulf
region and the ensuing real-estate boom in certain cities around the world
cannot be disconnected from these national, globalizing projects.

These processes, then, are not just about the emergence of new images,
new brands to consume, but the restructuring of people's lives. The new
"world-class aesthetic" (Asher Ghertner, this volume) informs a neoliberal
promise, as compared to earlier nationalist promises rooted in socialist agendas of development and social equality. The promise is of a planned, secure
and luxurious lifestyle; aspired to be landscaped in the new urban spaces of
cities such as Gurgaon. It is a promise, a project, not a reality. As individuals
strive to find their own place in the "new India" and create a globalized
lifestyle, be it in Gurgaon, Bangalore, the Silicon Valley, or Dubai, they
often find themselves trapped within new structures of power; their hopes
squashed within modes of control inherent in neoliberal globalization – from
the workplace and the naturalization of corporate rights as taking prece-
dence over human and labor rights to the endless cycles of consumption and
personal debt. The labor markets and the flows of global capital are constantly shifting at rapid paces, creating vulnerability for middle-class, global
aspirants. Controls over visas, threats of deportation, global capital shifting
to seek out new markets, and downturns in the global economy all encode different ways in which workers in the global workforce are controlled through
insecurity. While migration is a strategy of realizing personal hopes for a
better future for oneself or one's children, the mechanisms of control over
middle-class professionals create personal insecurities that become manifest
in everyday lives. The worlding city is given presence as "structured chaos,"

playing upon the insecurities of laborers; the spaces of the neoliberalizing city are constantly planned and replanned, investments shifted from one sector to another, projects often being left incomplete as new dreams and desires are chased.

Structured chaos was most acutely experienced with the global financial crisis of 2008 and 2009. In the early months of the crisis, the leaders of Dubai maintained denial of its impact on the city-state, playing up the image of Dubai as exception. By early 2009, however, reality sunk in – Dubai was just like every other global site, impacted by global economic processes. Despite the collapse of the real-estate market and the loss of billions of dollars in unfinished projects and speculative developments, Dubai embraced the crisis, transforming the economic downturn into a silver lining for brand Dubai.

Reports of abandoned cars on the streets and at the airport, left by laid-off workers who could no longer afford the fees, exposed the harsh realities of the crisis. For Dubai, it meant a strategic realignment of its demographic character. For years, Dubai had expressed an anxiety over long-term residents; the economic crisis was a wake-up call to many who now recognized that Dubai was not their economic Mecca. The personal insecurity of the crisis led many to rethink their place in Dubai and for others to imagine different destinations. Simultaneously, however, the extensive news coverage of the impact of the crisis on Dubai bolstered the image of Dubai as a special place, unique and different from other global cities; a strategic aspect of the place branding process, discussed below. The crisis did force Dubai to lessen its egoism, most clearly expressed in the renaming of the tallest building in the world from the Burj Dubai to the Burj Khalifa, the Emir of Abu Dhabi who bailed out Dubai by lending the city-state $10 billon. But, Dubai is not returning to the desert, it is being scaled back; real-estate prices are more affordable, and the city continues to attract capital investments, particularly as a major base for feeding the US wars in Iraq and Afghanistan, being home to countless companies of contractors, most famously Halliburton. Dubai's staying power feeds off the structured chaos of globalization, shifting markets from South Asia, to East Asia, the United Kingdom to the United States. Now becoming, increasingly, an American city, Dubai continues to be marketed as a desirable destination.

To analyze Dubai's presencing project, this chapter offers a comparative focus on Gurgaon, India; a satellite city of New Delhi, home to countless new businesses servicing the global economy. Gurgaon is a new city, offering distinct lifestyle opportunities based on apartment living, malls, and a distinct form of urbanism.

By drawing upon ethnographic research in Dubai and Gurgaon, the chapter traces the multiple ways in which symbolic capital is constructed, through place branding, and how symbolic violence, through structured chaos and differentiation, is encoded and acted out on the streets of global cities. By shifting between different global sites, the chapter highlights the processes of claiming global status, focusing first on the idea of place branding, then situating it in the particular historical and cultural contexts of the United Arab Emirates (UAE) and India, and finally seeing the different ways in which everyday lives are transformed as global migrants aspire for their own place in the globalizing world.

Dubai-as-Brand: Imagining Desirable Landscapes

Why do you want to spend 10 days in Dubai? Four days is too long!

It's the kids, all their friends have been; they insisted we spend the vacation there. Besides they can go on a desert safari, go skiing; it has so much more to offer than Cairo ... They've all been to Europe, Dubai is the new spot; it's like getting the latest mobile phone; now it is Dubai, in a few years they'll probably insist on going somewhere else ... It is important for the kids to see, it's an Arab city, its part of their culture, unlike Paris or London. It should make them proud.[3]

In the symbolic marketplace, cities compete for status and prestige, structuring a dialectical relationship between the place and its residents, each gaining legitimacy, prestige, and status from one another; there is an exchange of symbolic capital, employed to foster one's place in the global marketplace.[4] Dubai becomes a global city by being the destination of individuals from around the world, who themselves become global citizens by circulating through Dubai. Place branding is a means of attracting capital, investments, businesses, residents, talent, tourists, events, prestige, and influence, creating at once competition between places while simultaneously creating networks of interconnecting places through capital investments and the production and exchange of symbolic capital. Symbolic capital of cities is engendered by the extent of their presence in the global arena, the success of their imagineers in marketing the brand. Symbolic capital is interreferenced between cities; the success of one provides legitimacy to another. By investing in places like Gurgaon, Islamabad, and Cairo, Dubai affirms its global status and passes on symbolic capital of globalness to those cities in return. Further, cities such as Dubai transfer their global status to those working and visiting; a major means of marking one's self as global is by circulating through global cities. In return, the more global visitors circulating through a city, the more symbolic capital it gains as a global destination. Each process feeds the other, crafting simultaneously global cities and global consumers.

Unlike corporations competing for markets and profits, global cities are interdependent, each affirming the status of others as truly global; global branding of cities is inherently inter-referencing. Dubai needs Indian and Pakistani middle-class aspirants to migrate and it needs successful workers from Gurgaon and Karachi to visit as tourists, affirming its status as global. In addition, Dubai, where there is deep anxiety over long-term residents, needs to develop global cities in India and Pakistan to attract migrants back home. Dubai does not want to be a place of permanent residence and is constantly shifting labor markets from where it draws migrant laborers. Gated communities, malls, and seven-star hotels in the cities of migrant sending countries provide a place for Dubai émigrés to return to without giving up the lifestyle they grew accustomed to while residing in Dubai. Emaar's investments in places like Gurgaon benefit Dubai through the profits from investments and as creating global symbolic capital. I would add a third benefit as providing sites that guarantee labor circulation into and out of Dubai. Cities like Gurgaon create a class of tourists to visit Dubai, as well as offering a lifestyle for Indians who migrated to Dubai years earlier to move back "home."

Rarely are places marketed to laborers; however, for neoliberal global cities like Dubai and Gurgaon, much of their success is their ability to attract all levels of workers, from construction laborers to middle-class professionals and the multitude of service workers (domestic servants, drivers, sales clerks, etc.) to cater to their needs. Indeed, it is the availability of an extensive service economy catering to the interests of the emergent upper and middle-class aspirants that helps allure them in the first place, plus attractive salary packages that allow them to afford such luxuries as are usually reserved for upper-middle-class and upper-class families. The images constructed of Dubai feed upon such aspirations and hopes, creating the cities as places where dreams come true.

Place branding has two facets, the first of which is the visible, surface image, including the name, logo, and advertising campaigns. The second facet is having the infrastructure to deliver on the promises of the brand image: the facilities, resources, and expertise. It is in this sphere of what lies beneath the brand image that we discover cracks in the façade and shortcomings in the mimicking projects of neoliberalizing cities like Gurgaon, Islamabad, and Cairo.

The brand images produced and circulated involve multiple processes that, at their most basic, are about landscaping hope and desire. Thus, marketing campaigns from around the world include "Magical Kenya" and "Enchanting Finland," while Thailand promises "Happiness on Earth" and Samoa is "The Treasured Island of the South Pacific." In imagining desirable places, branding engages and counters negative stereotypes, histories, and other unsightly discourses and blemishes. Branding is more than just about an image of a place, it is also about the authority to speak, to represent. Branding is an affirmation of power. In the case of Dubai, it is the power of

"making history" and defining "where the future begins"[5] that catapults the
city-state onto the global arena.

Mapping urban status

There are multiple sources in the production and circulation of place branding.
Municipal governments and bureaucratic agencies such as tourism ministries,
along with chambers of commerce, are seen as the most active and responsible for creating images. In India, the India Brand Equity Foundation
(IBEF) is most active in producing images to attract global investments and
symbolic capital. IBEF is based in Gurgaon and managed by the Deputy
Director of the Confederation of Indian Industry.[6] As much as governments
or business leaders attempt to construct a particular image, other voices
respond to the images, to the brand. Journalists play an important role in
validating or questioning a particular brand image. In the case of India, and
much neoliberal globalization, *New York Times* columnist Thomas Friedman
(2005) is one of the principal cheerleaders (Hertz and Nader 2005).

But individuals too have a say, a voice. Though far from democratic,
there are distinct channels of communication through which different global players validate and critique place brands. For tourists, internet web
pages such as *tripadvisor* and *virtualtourist* provide forums to share information
and insights. While mostly focused on the mundane (good hotels, worthwhile sites to see, etc.), many of the comments also directly engage representations of destinations. Blogs are another source of engagement with
place brands. The UAE community blog, comprised mostly of Western
expatriates residing in Dubai, is a major place of engagement, debate, and
critique of brand Dubai. Personal blogs, such as "secretdubai," "onebigcon-
structionsite," and "grapeshisha," also provide extensive insights into personal experiences and attitudes of life in Dubai – although, in Dubai,
extensive monitoring and censorship (governmental as well as self) of access
and content does limit the extent to which diverse voices participate in the
representational process.

Though not solely a centralized endeavor, branding of neoliberal cities
occurs in limited discursive spaces defined by commercial interests. The
dictatorial nature of the political structure of Dubai furthers the interests
of Dubai through strict controls over creative processes, various forms of
censorship,[7] and vast amounts of money to invest in countering any negative
images. Despite the lack of creative and individual voices as dissent, other
forms of exposure of the harsh realities of life in Dubai for many do exist.
In the case of Dubai, it is international non-governmental organizations that
offer the greatest challenges. In particular, the reports of *Human Rights Watch*
(2006) and the International Labor Organization (Sabban n.d.) confront
directly Brand Dubai as an opulent life of leisure, exposing the extent of

exploitation of unskilled laborers, particularly in the construction industry. Journalism plays another role in producing and circulating alternative images of Dubai; however, as discussed below, nationalist and ideological lenses frame the images, tainting their portrayals.

Control over Brand Dubai by the corporate rulers is not absolute, but highly effective. India faces a very different reality. The lack of control over images produced about India creates extensive anxiety, seen, for example, in the confused nationalist responses to the success of the film *Slumdog Millionaire* during the 2009 Oscar awards. At once jubilant for the international acclaim, newspaper editorials and politicians criticized the movie as focusing solely on the negative. The success of *Slumdog Millionaire* simultaneously confirmed India as a global site of cultural productions, feeding India's global nationalism, while simultaneously tainting the image of "Incredible India!" by forefronting poverty, corruption, the gangster underworld, and religious communalism. While the state has little control over the production of alternative images in India, as compared to Dubai, an emergent global nationalism frames for the Indian public a whitewashed image that erases the realities of exploitation, poverty, and discrimination that are part and parcel of the Indian social landscape; and, as argued by Asher Ghertner (this volume), entails a shift in aspirations of slum dwellers in Delhi, buying into the worlding project.

India's branding growth, leaving the Third World

Branding is an attempt to limit and control access to speak with authority about a commodity. As such, place branding directly engages other representations and discourses in attempting to package a destination. In the cases of India and Dubai, their brand images are posited against the negative landscape of their pasts and their sociocultural milieu. Branding in these two places simultaneously erases particular, unsightly, qualities of their social landscapes and celebrates their successes of overcoming obstacles in their striving to be global. Brand India is "incredible" by ignoring the major social and economic chasms that exist in India, but also because its successes as a global player are achieved despite the country once being defined as "Third World." India as a nuclear power and India's new economy based on outsourcing make India that much more "incredible" in the eyes of its imagineers.

Unlike India, Dubai's image is not burdened with a history; however, it confronts its Muslim and Arab setting in its attempts to brand itself as the global destination for the wealthy of the world. Generally speaking, many Western analysts perceive being Muslim and Arab as counter-opposed to neoliberalism and globalization.[8] Brand Dubai thus simultaneously attempts to erase its Muslim milieu though simultaneously celebrating it, creating a particular modality of Muslim modernity. The brand image is not about rejecting or denying their pasts and cultural milieu, but asserting their successes in spite of such perceived handicaps. India and Dubai are exceptional because they have created neoliberal success despite being Third World and Arab/Muslim.

India's construction of being a global power is produced and circulated contra the image of India as a poor Third World country. India's claims to a seat on the UN's National Security Council, to being a nuclear power, and to having a rapidly growing economy feed a new self-image, a "global nationalism." Brand India is about India not being Third World. Gurgaon, along with Bangalore in southern India, plays an important role in the new self-image. As a modern, global city, symbolically, Gurgaon feeds brand India by its lack of history. As an urban center, Gurgaon is new, a product of the new India, where old "stereotypes about India and Indian culture are beginning to break" (IBEF 2008). But in so doing they also ignore the significant anti-government militant movements in thirteen of its twenty-eight provinces; the extensive communal violence, and the violent displacement of farmers to make room for India's neoliberalizing efforts in the construction of Special Economic Zones (Ananya Roy, Chapter 10, this volume). Despite the erasures, the marketing campaign is successful both in India and abroad in creating a façade of India as a global force. In 2004, *Newsweek* "heralded [India] as the Best Country to be an Investor" (quoted from IBEF) just two years after the devastating pogrom against poor Muslims in the state of Gujarat, under which the country was still reeling.

IBEF marks India as the "fastest growing free market democracy" (IBEF n.d.), playing upon two of the three dominant images of brand India: that India is the world's largest democracy, and India's sustained and high levels of economic growth in the early 2000s. The third image is the touristic branding of "Incredible India!" that portrays India as a harmonious cultural mosaic. Gurgaon, as a city of middle-class, globalized, multicultural Indians, is the perfect setting for re-landscaping the new India. Gurgaon is constructed as a middle-class city; its apartment/residential complexes, its malls, and its lack of public transportation all cater to the Indian emergent middle class. Thomas Friedman's writings romanticize the growing middle class of India (Fernandes 2006: xxviii), naturalizing the image of India as a world economy ripe for neoliberal, entrepreneurial "advancement" and "growth" – key ingredients of brand India. The idea of "advancement" and "growth" provides India a discursive shift away from "development", an idea closely associated with Third Worldness, an image brand India attempts to shed. Brand India is constructed in direct relationship to India's former status as a Third World country, a country of "snake charmers" (*International Herald Tribune* 2006) attempting to imagine India as a major world power.

Strategically, brand India is in direct dialogue with brand Dubai, partners in building the "new India." As discussed below, brand Dubai is imagined both as a global as well as a modern Muslim place. While the Muslim modernity constructed by Dubai feeds into branding projects in countries like Pakistan and Egypt, it is ignored in India. Rather, in India Dubai is imagined as an urban wonderland and a shopping mecca, and it is this side of brand Dubai from which India gains symbolic capital. The Muslim connection, however, is problematic, creating tensions in the transfer of symbolic capital. One example of the tension is Dawood Ibrahim, a notorious mafioso from the Indian city of Mumbai, who supposedly resides in Dubai; Ibrahim is held responsible for a series of bomb blasts in Mumbai, particularly in the early 1990s. However, the UAE's alignment with the US "war on terror" and the fact that it is a major hub for US privatized security forces and redevelopment efforts in Iraq and Afghanistan softens the relationship between India and Dubai.

Brand Islam or brand "Do Buy"?[9]

Unlike India, Dubai lacks an established cheerleading squad. While many celebrate the successes of Dubai and validate brand Dubai as an urban playground for the "Davos man" (Ramamurthy 2003), Dubai is more often than not portrayed in a negative light in Western media. The excesses of development – particularly its man-made island real-estate developments (The Palms, The Palms II, and The World) – are often discussed with deep cynicism; Dubai is portrayed as a "sinister paradise" striving for excess, realizing the vision of a benign despot, and being built upon labor exploitation (Davis 2005, 2006). While much of the criticism is based upon serious cracks in the façade of Dubai, much of it is also rooted in anti-Muslim bias. The idea of a "sinister paradise," "enlightened despot" (Davis 2005), a "prophet of modernization" (Davis 2006: 68), an "Islamic Disneyland" (Brooks 2006), or reports on an "emir who once backed the Taliban" (Sheer 2006) all allude to Dubai as a Muslim country, playing upon American audience stereotypes and knee-jerk jingoism, even in an American liberal guise.

Unlike the neighboring Emirate of Sharjah (which affirms itself as a Muslim place, with close ties to Saudi Arabia), Dubai's rulers and "imagineers" have a complex relationship with their Muslim identity. On the one hand, Dubai is imagined as a neoliberal extravaganza, open to all, including human traffickers, South Asian Mafiosos, illegal arms dealers, and male sex tourists.

On the other hand, as part of a Muslim country that is achieving unprecedented economic growth (though much of it is bankrolled and guaranteed by the personal wealth of the ruler of Dubai, Sheikh Mohammad), Dubai is often seen, by both its imagineers and Muslim émigrés, as a model for a Muslim modernity. Leaders gathered for the meeting of the Organization of Islamic Countries (OIC) affirmed this version of brand Dubai, when meeting there in October 2006.[10] Many British

Pakistanis also buy into this vision. Many feel that following the 2005 "7/7" bombings in London, they are no longer comfortable in the UK. Many British Pakistanis find Dubai a happy medium, realizing that after years of living in the West it is too difficult to return to Pakistan. Dubai provides a place in the Muslim "East," but still allows them to be Western-oriented. They imagine Dubai as a place where they can affirm themselves as both modern and Muslim, be close to Pakistan, and live without their Muslimness being under daily attack.[11]

While brand India struggles to overcome India's Third Worldness, brand Dubai struggles with the UAE as a Muslim country in the Arabian Peninsula. While there are many facets to brand Dubai, one of its major components is a veiling of its Muslimness. Indeed, great strides are made for Dubai not to become an Islamic place. Brand Dubai's focus on wealth, conspicuous consumption, excess, and its "liberal" acceptance of "immoral activities," including alcohol, co-habitation of unmarried couples, and prostitution, are partly statements of Dubai's rejection of being defined as Muslim. Most important in brand Dubai is its rapid growth "being fuelled by the launch of spectacular and innovative mega real-estate projects and other investment opportunities, which have exceeded expectations" (bin Ayat 2007).

Except for the Jumeriah mosque, built in neo-Mamluk architectural style borrowed from Cairo (Elsheshtawy 2006: 247), there is very little about the urban landscape of Dubai that expresses a Muslim orientation. The many skyline pictures of Dubai published in the *Dubai Strategic Plan (2015)* (Government of Dubai n.d.) do not include any minarets. The efforts to downplay Islam goes further than just representations; they are structured into the physical landscape. The skyline of Dubai is a testament to iconization of modern high-rise architecture, without a single reference to Arab or Muslim architectural design. For example, in the area known as the Marina, where hundreds of new apartment complexes have been built in the past five years, there is not a single mosque. In the Springs, a series of residential gated communities, there is only one mosque, which was built only recently, despite the area being home to thousands of residents. On the other hand, there is constant reference to the creation of Islamic financial institutions in Dubai. The contradiction informs the responses of many British Pakistanis toward the city, as it falls short of their hopes in finding a truly modern, truly Muslim place.

Brand Dubai as not Muslim is in direct contrast to the construction of the neighboring emirate of Sharjah, consciously branded as a Muslim space. In Sharjah, alcohol, shisha/hookah, and co-habitation between unmarried people of the opposite sex are all illegal. As a result, there emerges a deep segregation of communities within the UAE, based on religious orientations, nationality, and class. Segregation is an important component of the neoliberal city, structuring a diversity of hopes and desires, all landscaped within distinct spaces. Segregation allows brand Dubai to play upon multiple hopes and aspirations in its globalizing efforts. Brand Dubai, then, is not just about selling Dubai, but constructing segregated landscapes and asserting power through the control over labor/migration.

Dubai-as-Lived: Landscapes of Urban Desires

Dubai, through branding and through the built environment, attracts an array of investors, each seeking out fulfillment of particular aspirations and hopes. Movement to and through cities like Dubai is structured by individual aspirations – geographic mobility is directly linked to social mobility. Middle-class professionals seeking jobs, tourists in search of leisure and entertainment, businesses chasing profits, and investors speculating for high returns are all banking on Dubai to deliver. What is being delivered is multiple. It is not just wealth being sought, but also status, security, and validation.

There are multiple manners in which people act out their hopes in the global city of Dubai. Of particular interest is the crafting of status, transferred from the success of brand Dubai and Gurgaon onto the individuals living and visiting the cities. Another consideration, just as in place branding, is an erasure or repackaging of one's history. In Dubai, many migrants from Pakistan, Egypt, Indonesia, Malaysia, and elsewhere grapple with their Muslimness. Some find in Dubai a place to craft secular selves; others find comfort in defining themselves as simultaneously modern/global and Muslim; while others move toward a more religiously orthodox orientation.

Inherent in the chasing of the global dream is a transformation of self, through wealth, through status, and through the encoding of a rationalist, neoliberal self (Miyazaki 2006). That is, participation in the global sphere implies adopting particular rationalist modes that include planning for one's future and centering the self through status seeking and consumption. Globalization can thus be seen as an attempt to craft a rationalist individual making choices in the free market of goods and ideas. In this perspective, globalization is about the crafting of a particular type of self, not just an economic network of linkages. The "global self" is crafted in a variety of milieus. Of particular importance are educational institutions and vocational training centers, which dot the landscape of Dubai, located in "Knowledge Village" (a literal strip-mall of neoliberal "universities"). The global self is also acted out on the streets of Dubai – well, not the streets, but in the malls and workplaces where "best practices" are instituted and extensive regimes of surveillance are implemented.

Seeking global status

For many global migrants, social mobility is most clearly acted out at home. Remittances are obviously a key ingredient to marking one's self as having "made it." The construction of new homes and the payment of tuition for children in private schools are clear markers. Home countries of migrants to Dubai are full of grand stories of wealth accumulation. Besides stories of social mobility, global status is visibly performed in the trip home when migrants carry with them an array of gifts, often electronics, and cash to invest in property and new constructions. The status is achieved through the display of their newfound wealth, but it is also carried with them, by residing in Dubai. For many, Dubai itself is a marker of status and mobility, of having "made it". Living in Dubai, or going there on vacation, creates status; Dubai's brand as a global city, a shopping mecca, and a playground for the rich is transferred to those living and visiting there. For Indians, though, the idea of Dubai does not carry the same status that it did a decade earlier. India's own global nationalism asserts that there is no requirement to migrate abroad to seek status; rather, it is achievable in India itself. A higher status for Indians is achieved by traveling to Dubai as tourists rather than migrants. Having the capacity to afford a trip to Dubai, or more recently, Bangkok, Singapore, or Hong Kong, affirms a global status on individuals.

The global self gains social capital by hyping up brand Dubai's image as a playground for the rich, while others longingly look on.[12] Recognizing how Dubai sells itself to a particular audience, though dependent on laborers and professional migrants from different countries to keep it afloat, engenders a multiplicity of hopes and desires structured within complex frames through which people move in the global sphere, including national and ethnic identity, religious orientations, lifestyle choices, social class, and gender.

As with branding, migration can be seen through the prism of status seeking. Place branding is about creating status – India is global, not Third World; Dubai is modern, not Muslim backwardness. Individuals also seek status in migrating to Dubai. Indeed, one of the hopes articulated by many South Asian middle-class migrants in Dubai is that the global status of Dubai will rub off on them. By living in Dubai they are automatically transformed into global citizens; there is a transformative hope. Thus their own identity becomes intricately connected with the success of Dubai, not as a national identity, members of an "imagined community," but rather as individuals seeking status from being located in Dubai. If brand Dubai is a success, so is their transformation to becoming global selves.

This new sense of identity feeds into global nationalism in India, where both ideas of identity, as tied to community as well as to neoliberal success, merge. The success of NRIs (Non-Resident Indians) overseas is headline news in India. The global self and the nation are fused in India, re-crafting the national self as the global, corporate, neoliberal self. The "Davos man," manifested in corporate leaders such as the late Dhirubhai Ambani (founder of Reliance Industries) or Narayana Murthy (founder of Infosys), becomes the national ideal rather than Gandhi. The nationalism promoted by Gandhi was submission of the self to the needs of the country; the Davos man's nationalism is that promotion of the self will benefit the nation.

Indeed, the predominate vision of Dubai as circulated in Pakistan and India is as a place where the streets are paved in gold.[13] When visiting home, migrants to Dubai play out this image, often feeling forced to "be wealthy" even if not. Through remittances, and more importantly, gifts to hand out during visits home, they create status for themselves by acting out wealth. Many migrants have expressed extreme pressure and stress around visits home, as they are required to play a role that is far from their everyday reality. While many migrants to Dubai have achieved financial gains through much higher salaries, the cost of living in Dubai forces many to live highly constrained everyday lives.

In the early 2000s, the British American Tobacco Company (BAT) offered a promotion to consumers of its cigarettes, mostly South Asian laborers. A drawing was to be made and the initial idea for a grand prize was to bring the family of the winner to Dubai for a one-week visit. Upon taking an initial survey, it was learned that no one wanted such a prize. In the end, BAT offered the winners a paid trip home. The reason for the rejection of the visit of one's family was that the migrants had no home space to put up their own family.[14] Most share small apartments with several other "bachelors" and cannot afford social activities. They did not want their own penury to be exposed.

Indeed, the lifestyle of many South Asian middle-class aspirants in Dubai is very constrained. The norm is shared accommodation in crowded neighborhoods and an inability to fully participate in the consumer culture of Dubai. Neighborhoods such as the Marina and the Springs are reserved for the upper echelons of migrants, mostly Westerners. While salaries are much higher in Dubai than back home, the salaries do not necessarily translate into an improved lifestyle, due to cost-of-living and racist policies and practices that structure salary differences and segregated communities.[15] Despite their penury, many migrants act out wealth when they visit home, by bringing gifts, loaning money to family members, and through their remittances. In so doing, they also reproduce the idea of Dubai's streets as paved in gold. They cannot expose the façade for fear of losing their own status.

Often what one observes is not social mobility of individual migrants to Dubai, but of their children back home. Dubai can affect generational social mobility. Though far from the norm, one example is a Pakistani truck driver who migrated to Dubai in the early 1980s. Being uneducated himself and from a rural agricultural family, his daughter is now pursuing her MBA in Pakistan, a son is in law school, and another studied medicine and migrated to Canada. In the 25 years during which he lived in Dubai, he saw his children on average for about two weeks in every two to three years.[16] Most stories are not so successful, if indeed one considers such a story "successful". Yet the idea of "Dubai *chelo*" (Let's go to Dubai)[17] looms large with the hope of such social mobility, if not for oneself, for one's children.

In Gurgaon, similar yet distinct processes occur of creating status and feeling constrained. While Gurgaon is populated by people from all over India, particularly North India, many people from the northeast region of India have found great success working in the corporate service economy, referred to as business processing organizations (BPOs): companies that provide outsourcing services to predominately US- and UK-based corporations. Many communities from the "tribal" fringe of the northeast (e.g., Nagas, Mizos, and Khasis) are Christians and were educated in missionary schools, learning English at an early age. Their skills as English-speakers are highly sought after in the BPOs, particularly call centers. While India itself is attempting to shed its image as a Third World country, different "tribal" people find working in Gurgaon a way of overcoming their lowly status in the hierarchically social and political structures of India. Working in a call center is a means of moving from a backward status to playing a leading role in India's global economy.

The mall culture of Gurgaon and the distinct lifestyle structured by apartment living in "societies" (condominium-like home-owners' associations of small, gated communities) also infuses residents and visitors with a particular status. A move to Gurgaon is a move to being part of the new India, of being global. One woman, with a PhD in sociology from Jahalwar Nehru University in New Delhi, first worked as a researcher for a national labor research institution. She ended up quitting her position as her parents, with whom she resided, were uncomfortable with the practice of her often working late into the evening and then having to return home. Her parents admitted to her that a neighbor once questioned them on why their daughter was always out so late, insinuating that she was out partying. She is now working for a call center, working the entire night, returning home in the early hours of the morning. For her parents, this is acceptable, as not only is she earning three times more in salary, but also she is working for a BPO in Gurgaon. Her job creates a new kind of status for her parents, having a daughter working for a multinational corporation rather than a semi-government institution, which is no longer seen as a prestigious position – her PhD irrelevant to the crafting of status in the new India.[18]

Controlling desire

While technologies of surveillance are inherent within the project of modernity, within neoliberal global cities such as Dubai and Gurgaon, the control and surveillance in the workplace and in places of leisure is extensive and varied. The surveillance state is not unique to the neoliberal moment, but the way in which state surveillance overlaps with corporate interests and power in controlling and pacifying the workforce is a hallmark of policing in both Dubai and Gurgaon. There are various mechanisms of overt and covert control that become manifest through a state of fear; fear not of corporal punishment, but of loss of status. In Dubai, any migrant worker found guilty of violating laws, be they anything from minor traffic violations to more serious crimes, could lose his or her work visa. One's presence in Dubai is dependent on a work visa, as there is no system of permanent residency or naturalized citizenship. All migrants remain migrants, even if born in Dubai.

As a workforce of national citizens, Gurgaon does not have the same power to deport as Dubai. Indeed, much of the "failure" of Gurgaon in its mimicking project is due to the fact that India is a democracy and workers have a degree of rights, though serious roadblocks exist in union organizing of BPO employees – one of which is the lack of interest among employees, not due to the lack of exploitation or need, but rather the so "utterly unglobal" image of a labor union.[19] Despite the greater sense of rights, it does not mean they are not without mechanisms of control and surveillance.

Within the neoliberal paradigm, the workplace is a space of extensive control, often through mechanisms of self-policing. In the same way, self-censorship keeps many from speaking out too negatively about the realities of life in Dubai; a successful employee is constructed as one who self-polices their behavior and creates an atmosphere of control, even where there is no overt mechanisms of surveillance. In many workplaces though, surveillance is extensive. Employees in call centers in Gurgaon are extensively policed through CCTV cameras, computer checks, eavesdropping on phone conversations, and body searches on entering and leaving the workplace. Such practices are justified as means of assuring "quality control."[20] A security guard in a shopping mall in Dubai matter-of-factly points out that the CCTV cameras are not to spy on potential shoplifters but on mall employees, to keep track of their performance, the bathroom breaks they take, who and for how long they talk with someone, and if they are ever out of position.[21]

A third means of social control in Dubai is the holding of one's passport by the company one works for. Though illegal, it is extensively practiced. The vast majority of migrant workers are hired within their home countries through employment contractors. Companies pay for new hires to travel to Dubai, arrange for their work visas, provide or subsidize housing for the first month or so, and may even lend money to employees to settle in. In return, they become virtual indentured servants. They cannot travel outside of the UAE without seeking permission from the company, a request that is often denied within the first year of employment.

When quitting or if fired from a job, one becomes immediately a non-person in Dubai. One informant recounted a horror tale of their visa being near expiration, but of the company refusing to return his and his wife's passport (though she was not an employee of the company, they still insisted on holding it), meaning that they would be arrested on their attempt to leave the country for overstaying their visa. The day before the visa expired, the company gave them their passports and they were able to head back to their home country. Such stories are rampant, and part of the lore of the street of middle-class migrants in Dubai.

Mechanisms of control are multiple; relying on direct surveillance, fear over deportation and loss of status, self-policing, and corporatized "best practices" to assure a pliable and passive workforce. Technologies of control wed state and corporate interests, crafting a defining feature of neoliberal global cities: emplacement of corporate fundamentalism. In their work and in their social lives, middle-class migrants to Gurgaon and Dubai surrender their personal hopes to those of the city and the success of its global status-making and its corporate leaders.

Segregating self

While Dubai is dependent on migrants of all classes to construct and maintain the brand image, not all migrants are equally welcome. Dubai is inherently a racist and classist city that attempts to whitewash exploitation and discrimination through a variety of discreet practices. The exploitation of migrant laborers, particularly in the construction industry, has been well documented by the ILO and *Human Rights Watch*; and middle- and upper-middle-class migrants encounter outright discrimination as well as structurally discriminatory practices. While many discriminatory practices are officially illegal, they continue to be an inherent aspect of the everyday experiences of life in Dubai for a majority of its residents. Some forms of discrimination, such as differentiated salaries, define the socioeconomic structure of life in Dubai, classifying lifestyle options based on one's country of origin rather than on one's skills and professional class.

One of the defining ideas of Dubai circulated throughout the world is that its streets are paved in gold; it is a place where one can earn undue riches. The illusion of wealth draws many to seek out their millions in Dubai. Though one rarely does earn millions, the myth of riches to be had is based on the salary structure. In order to attract a skilled, professional, educated workforce, salaries in Dubai are from two to four times higher than in one's home country. While the increase in salary is offset by higher everyday costs, the attraction is compelling for many.

In short, one's salary package is not based on merit or position, but rather on the salary structures of one's home country. Thus, two individuals in the same position, working for the same company, do not have the same salary; indeed, if one is from the United Kingdom or the United States and the other is from India or Pakistan, for example, the former will be earning four times more than his or her colleague. In addition, the salary package for many white Westerners includes subsidized housing, transportation, and schooling for children; such benefits are rarely provided for Asian, African, and Arab white-collar professionals, even if they are migrating from the United Kingdom or the United States. Given the salary structure, one Pakistani informant pointed out how his British (white) secretary earned twice as much as him, despite the fact that he had an MBA degree from the United States.

The government of Dubai regulates that no resident can sponsor family members to live with them unless they earn more than 3,000 Dirhams (approximately US$800) per month. While many mid-level corporate managers earn twice this amount, they still cannot afford to bring their wives and children with them. Thus many live alone in corporate housing or shared apartments with several other "bachelors,"[22] in poorer neighborhoods of Dubai such as Satwa or Deira. In comparison, many of their British and American colleagues live in upscale-gated communities such as Arabian Ranches or the Springs, with their families.

The position of "bachelors" in Dubai is a precarious one, and the government has made various efforts over the years to control and limit their very visible presence on the streets of Dubai. "Bachelors" as employed in Dubai refers to men, whether married or not, who are in Dubai on their own. The vast majority of bachelors are South Asian. Many white, Western men also live in Dubai, but rarely are they addressed in discussions by the state, media, and the blogosphere. While no statistics are available, it is estimated that at least 60–65 percent of Dubai's population are men. As well, many women, particularly from South and Southeast Asia, work as domestic servants and thus are mostly invisible on the streets of Dubai. As such, the streets are predominately a place of men.

Starting in 2006, the Dubai government banned bachelors from living in villas. Marwan Abdulla, head of the Municipality's Building Inspection Section, explained the measure as a way of creating "a secure and clean environment in residential areas" (Ahmed 2007). The ban excluded "service apartments" that are rented out to companies for the use of their executives, predominantly white, Western men (many such apartments are villas, located in gated communities). What was being "cleaned" from view was brown-skinned men.

In 2008, the Municipality banned bachelors altogether from living in the Satwa area as it neighbors Jumeira, one of the upscale neighborhoods along the coast. The Municipality is forcing employers and landlords to document that all tenants are married, with their families living with them.

In addition, from 2006 on, the Municipality is contracting to various developers to rebuild the older locales of Dubai, namely Deira and Satwa. Both residential areas are home to many Asians, from laborers to junior managers, from sales clerks to bus drivers. In tearing down older buildings and constructing new residential communities, rents are doubling or tripling, making it impossible for many to continue to live in the area. The increase in rent forces the Asian residents to seek out rental properties elsewhere; only there is no elsewhere.

Increasingly, many who provide the vital services of Dubai, catering to the rich, find themselves no longer welcomed, being forced to move to Sharjah, where rents are generally lower. From salary structure to arbitrary rental laws, many Asians are openly discriminated against. There is a general pattern to hide the majority population, the ones who Dubai is dependent on, from public view. One can even see the construction of the metro system in Dubai as another mechanism of hiding its brown-skinned workers, by transporting them below ground, rather than having them horde around bus stops on the streets, visible to all.

Conclusion

As both a brand and a lived space, Dubai creates a presence; as an urban form and as a lifestyle, Dubai's presence is inter-referenced in cities throughout Asia, Africa, and the Middle East. In creating a presence, there is also a structuring of invisibility, an erasure of unsightly blots on the brand image. The inter-referencing projects of both self as well as urban landscapes take on diverse forms in different countries; each feeding, inter-referencing, the other, crafting legitimacy and global acknowledgment. While the forms may be different, they interconnect in seeking out global presence as individuals buy into a particular lifestyle that is predicated on constructing and maintaining a façade; marketing one's self as a global citizen, a Davos man. In so doing, the negative aspects of life are erased, ignored, apologized for. The structural racism of Dubai is forgotten, the extent of labor exploitation ignored, the degree of insecurity and structured chaos explained away – all masked by the claim to being global.

The global presence constructed by and in Dubai as an idea and a lived experience becomes a whitewashing. Somewhere between the imagined paradise and the constructed dreamland, migrant employees in the global service economies of Dubai, as well as in emergent global sites like Gurgaon, become stuck in a hypermarket of hope and desire. Behind façades of glitz and glamour lie multiple cracks, fractured selves, mapped by displacement and disillusionment.

Acknowledgments

This chapter is based on field research conducted in 2006 and 2007 in Dubai and Gurgaon, with support from the American University in Cairo and the American Institute of Pakistan Studies. I am grateful to many people for their assistance, particularly Javed Ahmed in Gurgaon and Sajjid Ghazi in Dubai. In addition, I wish to thank Aihwa Ong and Ananya Roy for organizing the SSRC workshop, as well as the other participants for their critical engagement. I am also grateful to Ahmed Kanna, Michael M.J. Fischer, and Neha Vora for enlightening discussions and for sharing their critical insights.

Notes

1 Though with a longer history, Gurgaon has emerged in the past 10 years as one of India's leading global cities, being home to countless multinational corporations, call centers for US and UK companies, consumer malls, new architectural styles, and distinct lifestyle options.

2 A glimpse of any of the annual *Human Development Reports* published by the UNDP affirms these processes.

3 Interview with a resident of Maadi, Cairo on their family's winter-break vacation plans; October 23, 2008.

4 I draw upon the work of Pierre Bourdieu, seeing symbolic capital not as the product of hierarchical power, but as a claim to a status, and relate it directly to processes of branding, a marketing of place and self in the global economy.

5 "Making History" is part of Emaar's advertising campaign in the construction of the Burj Dubai (renamed to the Burj Khalifa), the tallest building in the world; while "Where the Future Begins" is the official slogan of the *Dubai Strategic Plan (2015)*, available at www.dubai.ae.

6 I am deeply indebted to the insights shared with me by Jayanta Bhuyan, the former CEO of IBEF.

7 The "uaecommunity" blog operates under a severe cloak of self-censorship; fear of the site being blocked by the government-controlled internet provider looms large in various discussions and in the extent of control of the moderators over posts.

8 A virtual industry of self-proclaimed experts on the Muslim world has emerged since 2001, many claiming the incompatibility of Islam and neoliberal ideas. Many such works take their cue from Huntington (1993).

9 *Do Buy! A Dubai Documentary* is the title of a documentary on Dubai filmed by Omair Bakhatulla, in 2006, available at http://www.youtube.com/user/omairways.

10 Personal interview with journalist Ahmed Rashid.

11 This sentiment was articulated consistently by many British Pakistanis now residing in Dubai.

12 This sense of being on-lookers is most clearly articulated in the documentary *Do Buy!*

13 This allusion was in fact articulated to me several times by Pakistanis who had never been to Dubai when talking about their vision of what Dubai is. Through Bollywood films and the media, this image gets replayed continuously.

14 This story was related to me by a Pakistani working for BTC.
15 Salaries in Dubai are not based on one's qualifications, but rather on one's passport. Salaries and benefit packages are used to attract wanted workers; thus salaries must be higher than anyone can earn in their home country. Thus a British manager in a hotel earns four times more than his Pakistani counterpart, despite the fact that they both do the exact same job. See below for further explanation.
16 Personal interview, March 19, 2007, Dubai.
17 The name of a popular Pakistani TV drama in the late 1970s and subsequently made into a movie.
18 Personal interview, June 26, 2006 (she desired that her name not be used).
19 As one employee put it so eloquently to me in an interview; April 12, 2007.
20 Insights into the workplace in call centers are based on an array of interviews conducted in Gurgaon in summer 2006 and spring 2007; including with employees, former employees, and human resource managers.
21 *Do Buy! A Dubai Documentary*, available at http://www.youtube.com/user/omairways.
22 A catch-all phrase that is used, predominately, for Asian males, whether young and single, or married, who live alone in Dubai.

References

Ahmed, A. (2007) Bachelors being evicted from villas. *The Gulf News*, August 9; http://archive.gulfnews.com/indepth/costofliving/Rent_x_Property/10145546.html (accessed November 7, 2007).

Auge, M. (1995) *Non-Places: introduction to an anthropology of super modernity*. London: Verso.

bin Ayat, A. HE, Secretary General of Dubai Executive Council (2007) Dubai Urban Development Framework Plan. Press release, August 27; http://www.urbisjhd.com/index.cfm?contentid=525 (accessed November 7, 2007).

Bourdieu, P. (1984) *Distinction: a social critique of the judgment of taste*. London: Routledge & Kegan Paul.

Brooks, R. (2006) Dubai's Islamic Disneyworld (originally published in *The Los Angeles Times*). March 3; http://www.commondreams.org/views06/0303-27.htm (accessed February 19, 2007).

Davis. M. (2005) Sinister paradise: does the road to the future end in Dubai? July 14; http://www.commondreams.org/views05/0714-31.htm (accessed February 19, 2007).

Davis, M. (2006) Fear and money in Dubai. *New Left Review* 41, September/October, 46–8.

Elsheshtawy, Y. (2006) From Dubai to Cairo: competing global cities, models, and shifting centers of influence? In D. Singerman and P. Amar (eds.) *Cairo Cosmopolitan: politics, culture, and urban space in the new globalized Middle East*. Cairo: American University in Cairo Press.

Fernandes, L. (2006) *India's New Middle Class: democratic poltics in an era of economic reform*. Minneapolis, MN: University of Minnesota Press.

Friedman, T. (2005) *The World is Flat: a brief history of the twenty-first century*. New York: Farrar, Straus and Giroux.

Government of Dubai (n.d.) *Dubai Strategic Plan (2015)*; www.dubai.ae (accessed January 7, 2008).

Hertz, L. and Nader, L. (2005) On *The Lexus and the Olive Tree*. In C. Bestman and H. Gusterson (eds.) *Why America's Top Pundits Are Wrong: anthropologists talk back*. Berkeley, CA: University of California Press.

Human Rights Watch (2006) Building towers, cheating workers: exploitation of migrant construction workers in the United Arab Emirates, *Human Rights Watch* 18(8[(E]), November.

Huntington, S. (1993) The clash of civilizations? *Foreign Affairs* 72(3), 22–50.

IBEF (2008) Brand India: telling the India story. India Brand Equity Foundation, Gurgaon; http://www.ibef.org/brandindia (accessed January 7, 2008).

IBEF (n.d.) *India*, IBEF brochure. India Brand Equity Foundation, Gurgaon; http://www.ibef.org/artdisplay.aspx?cat_id=431&art_id=13877&arc=show (accessed January 7, 2008).

International Herald Tribune (2006) India wants the world to see it as it sees itself. October 26.

Miyazaki, H. (2006) Economy of dreams: hope in global capitalism and its critiques. *Cultural Anthropology* 21(2), 147–72.

Ramamurthy, P. (2003) Material consumers, fabricating subjects: perplexity, global connectivity discourses, and transnational feminist research. *Cultural Anthropology* 18(4), 524–50.

Sabban, R. (n.d.) Migrant women in the United Arab Emirates: the case of female domestic workers. GENPROM Working Paper No. 10. Gender Promotion Program, International Labour Office.

Sassen, S. (2001) *The Global City: New York, London, Tokyo*. Princeton, NJ: Princeton University Press.

Sheer, R. (2006) Dubious Dubai deal (originally published in *San Francisco Chronicle*). March 1; http:// www.commondreams.org/views06/0301-23.htm (accessed February 19, 2007).

Websites and online sources

Do Buy! A Dubai Documentary, a documentary filmed by Omair Bakhatulla, in 2006; http://www.youtube.com/user/omairways

http://aethoughts.blogspot.com

http://bujassem.blogspot.com

http://secretdubai.blogspot.com

http://uaecommunityblog.blogspot.com

www.ibef.org

7

Asia in the Mix: Urban Form and Global Mobilities – Hong Kong, Vancouver, Dubai

Glen Lowry and Eugene McCann

Be Klahowya! Kloshe maika ko yukwa, ka towagh mitlite keekwullie illahee.
Greetings! Good you arrive here, where light be under land.

From Henry Tsang, *Welcome to the Land of Light*,
public art installation, Vancouver, 1997

Introduction

The skyline of downtown Vancouver, British Columbia has been markedly reshaped over the past two decades. In the 1990s, skinny glass and steel residential towers began proliferating, especially around the shores of the peninsula on which the downtown sits. This new urban form is epitomized by Concord Pacific Place, one of the largest urban mega-projects in North America (Figure 7.1). Pacific Place stretches along the north shore of False Creek, an inlet of the Pacific which was once the polluted heart of the city's manufacturing and wood processing industries, and is now a high-priced residential and recreational hub that has become a key element of the city's postindustrial identity (Olds 2001). The physical form of Pacific Place has become emblematic of Vancouver's contemporary urban landscape and, as such, is central to the city's promotional materials (Simons 2005). Carefully crafted marketing images feature its glittering towers, framed by the waterfront and a backdrop of snowcapped mountains, and highlight the development's waterfront walking paths and green spaces as visual representations of Vancouver's much vaunted "livability" (City of Vancouver 2003).

Worlding Cities: Asian Experiments and the Art of Being Global, First Edition.
Edited by Ananya Roy and Aihwa Ong.
© 2011 Blackwell Publishing Ltd. Published 2011 by Blackwell Publishing Ltd.

Figure 7.1 Concord Pacific Place, 2009
Source: Levin, Lowry, Tsang research document, digital photograph; courtesy of the artists.

The relationship between Pacific Place and the city's identity involves more than simply concrete, glass, and steel, however. The development, which was built on the dilapidated site of Expo'86 and purchased by Hong Kong investors, was designed to attract ethnic Chinese buyers at a time of social and economic uncertainty in Asia. In the wake of Tiananmen and in the lead-up to 1997, Vancouver became a safe haven for affluent, middle-class investors from Hong Kong who were looking for a place to which to move their families and business interests. Its regenerated urban waterfront and carefully constructed global image as the livable economic and social hub of "Beautiful BC" did fit – and still do fit – hand in glove with the federal government's new immigration policy and its drive to establish Canada among the leaders of an unfolding Pacific Rim economy. Thus, the built form and the changing identity of Vancouver were conditioned by flows of capital, people, architecture, and urban design knowledge from Asia. Developed and marketed as a high tech communications hub, where apartments would be linked into a global "network society" (Castells 1996) through fiber-optic communications, Pacific Place and its surrounding environs became a base for the growing class of wealthy, footloose, cosmopolitan, "flexible citizens" and "pied-a-terre" subjects (Ong 1999, 2007) that Vancouver's local elites were desperate to attract (Olds 2001; Mitchell 2004).

Figure 7.2   Emaar's Marina Promenade development, 2009
Source: Levin, Lowry, Tsang research document, digital photograph; courtesy of the artists.

The redevelopment of False Creek in the 1990s was only one moment in the ongoing "worlding" and "Asianization" of Vancouver. Evidence of the city's emergence as an "extraterritorial" Asian city and of the active role many of its elites play in influencing contemporary Asian urbanism – the "Vancouverization" of Asia, as one might say (Sharp and Boddy 2008) – came recently when local architecture critic Trevor Boddy (2006) reported that an "almost a perfect clone of downtown Vancouver – right down to the handrails on the seawall, the skinny condo towers on townhouse bases," was being built in Dubai, "around a 100-per-cent artificial, full-scale version of False Creek filled with seawater from the Persian Gulf" (Figure 7.2). The design of this "other False Creek" does not involve some inadvertent isomorphism. Rather, it is a product of another purposeful transfer of urban form, design knowledge, people, and capital. After a chance visit by its chairman to Pacific Place in 1997, the Dubai-based development corporation Emaar Properties enlisted a number of the Concord Pacific corporation's key executives to develop Dubai Marina as a high-rise waterfront way-station for footloose global elites (Campbell 2007). Thus, Vancouver's Hong Kong/ Waikiki-inspired model of the Pacific Rim residential urban form was de/reterritorialized once more to produce profit and "lifestyle" on the other side of Asia from Hong Kong – in the continent's southwest, where the desert meets what is known in Dubai as the Arabian Gulf.

These two moments in the production of and inter-referencing among Asian cities set the context for this chapter. Our purpose is to detail and interpret the mobilities, practices, and identities that tie Vancouver to Hong Kong and Dubai through networks of inter-Asian connection and referencing. Specifically, we employ a cultural and historical approach to these three distant and distinct (post)colonial cities. We suggest that global urban development and neoliberal statecraft can be analyzed in useful ways through critical cultural productions. Cultural or artistic production can, after all, be both an interpretive or representational practice and also a method in critical research. This approach builds upon and extends literatures on the production of cities in global-relational context (Massey 1991, 2005, 2007; Peck and Theodore 2001; Peck 2003; Ward 2006; Cook 2008; Guggenheim and Soderstrom 2010; McCann and Ward 2010, 2011; McCann 2011), on "mobilities" as a socio-spatial concept (Cresswell 2001, 2006; Hannam, Sheller, and Urry 2006; Sheller and Urry 2006; Urry 2007; McCann 2011), on the built environment as a key moment in wider social, political, and economic circuits (Harvey 1985; Goss 1988; Domosh 1989; McNeill 2009), on the analysis of global urbanization beyond the frame of solely Anglo-American theories and examples (Appadurai 1996; Ong 1999; Olds 2001; Mitchell 2004; Robinson 2006), and on the social production of False Creek specifically (Ley 1987, 1996; Olds 2001; Punter 2003; Mitchell 2004). Our primary contribution is to combine these urban geographic perspectives with literatures that address the role of cultural production (and cultural producers) in urbanism, particularly those in art history, cultural theory, and literary studies that focus on contemporary Asian Canadian culture (Miki 1998, 2000, 2001; McAllister 1999; Gagnon 2000; Kamboureli 2000; Wah 2000; Lowry 2006; Cho 2007; Mathur 2007; Lai 2008).

"Welcome to the Land of Light"

We draw on an example of cultural production in False Creek, Vancouver as an entry point into the case. Henry Tsang's 1997 public art installation, *Welcome to the Land of Light* (Figure 7.3), allows us to deepen, historicize, and problematize the development of False Creek as an extraterritorial Asian place and, in turn, it permits consideration of the implications of the inter-referencing and transfer of that place back to Asia through Dubai. Tsang's permanent public installation was commissioned by the City of Vancouver as part of its Public Art Program and, as such, it represents a point of convergence for various social processes and discourses germane to the regeneration of Vancouver's urban waterfront. Illuminating a 100-meter arc along Vancouver's False Creek walkway, *Welcome to the Land of Light* is at the physical and conceptual fulcrum of a complex urbanism that interlinks Asian

Figure 7.3   Henry Tsang, *Welcome to the Land of Light* (detail), public art installation, Vancouver
Source: courtesy of the artist.

investment, Canadian policy development, and global lifestyle marketing with the legacy of British colonialism. As we discuss below, Tsang's work speaks critically to and about those connections by invoking the historical palimpsest that is False Creek – a space that has been shaped by intercultural connections, translations, references, and transactions since at least the beginning of the colonial encounter.

In the remainder of this section, we will describe and interpret Tsang's work and outline what it says about False Creek as a global node. Subsequently, we will turn to the de/reterritorialization of the False Creek urban form in Dubai as a lens into the ongoing process of Vancouverization, Asianization, and mobility that characterizes these places. As site-specific artwork, Tsang's public art points to an obvious tension in the globalization of urban forms *vis-à-vis* the aporia of a local, which is itself already part of a complex negotiation with the colonial and postcolonial geographies of Asian Northern American identity. Reframing historical or cultural histories of "contact" in the fabric of Vancouver's urban development, writing it into the lines on the seawall, Tsang recalls and reworks a new hybrid language (based on Chinook Jargon) that speaks to the disparate investments brought to bear in worlding the new city. His work speaks directly to the double-edged worlding performed by and on mobile (Asian) subjects at the limits of the modern nation. Reading it against the mobilization of new urban forms it helps to frame, Tsang's *Welcome to the Land of Light* allows us to invoke a notion of cultural production that draws from Miki's (2000) notion of "Asiancy." In turn, this provides us with a way of interrogating the cultural characteristics and implications of this form of global-Asian urbanism. "Asiancy," as a cultural project that is self-consciously engaged with the investments of state-identified subjects, further allows us to argue for the crucial role of cultural production (art along with architecture and urban planning) in consideration of new global urban methodologies.

Installed along the edge of the seawall skirting the glass and steel towers of Pacific Place, Tsang's site-specific artwork (Kwon 2002) creates a participatory space for reflection on and discursive engagement with the emergence of Vancouver's new urban waterfront. Featuring a series of "translations" from English to Chinook Jargon and back, the two parallel rows of aluminum type that form the 100-meter sweep of the work effectively collapse the distances separating Vancouver's colonial past and its global future. Fixed to the walkway railing, underscored by pulsating colored light that courses through a thick fiber-optic cable at the base of the railing, Tsang's translations lead walkers along this section of seawall while inviting them to stop momentarily to contemplate off-beat messages of welcome and benediction before going on their way. The affect this site-specific experience produces is uncanny. The empirical reality of global urban development and technologization – solidity of concrete, steel, and glass – becomes ephemeral. Wandering through Tsang's hybrid text, viewers confront a conflation of present and past. A public counterpoint to the privacy of Pacific Place, this walkway installation activates the city's symbolic topography – towers, seawall, oceans, mountains – and reinscribes it in a psychic geography of trans-Pacific exchange and contradictory new-world desires that challenge both the sanctity of nationalist history and immediacy of globalization.

Vancouver's postcolonial, postindustrial waterfront has long been a place of global mobility and of collapsing historical and geographic distances, as Tsang's work suggests. Furthermore, the geo-historical perspective of his installation helps locate technologized communication (and virtual mobility) within larger systems of power and domination. Situating an emergent tele-communication hub within the historical space of Pacific Northwest trade, it recalls a period when Chinook Jargon was *lingua franca* up and down the coast from Oregon to Alaska. Chinook Jargon (a.k.a. *Chinuk Wawa, Wawa, lelang* – words, tongue, language (*le langue*)) was a pidgin of indigenous Wawashan dialects mixed with English and French, as well as other sources. Named after the Chinookan (*Chinuk* or *Tsinuk*) people of the lower and middle Columbia River basin, but based loosely on the aboriginal language, it was structured on the principle of inserting words and phrases from different linguistic sources into basic syntactic or grammatical units. Chinook Jargon was readily adaptable and *portable*, capable of facilitating exchanges among diverse cultural–linguistic groups and accommodating disparate regional demographics. Suggestive of a prototypical open source technology, Chinook lexicon reflects the use of Kannaksis (from Hawaii), Chinese, and Norwegian, in addition to Chinook, Nootkan, English, and French. In some regions, it became a creole and was spoken as a first language.

Adding layers of linguistic patina to the vernacular of the city's newest urbanism – a high tech, high-gloss "Vancouverism" that might even vie with an outmoded Manhattanism, according to Sharp and Boddy (2008). Tsang's playful, noisy translations gesture toward a complex history of cultural hybridity, experimentation, and colonial miscegenation that draws Vancouver past the brink of British and Canadian identities. Reworking the strains of the old trade language, which was spoken up until World War II, Tsang reappropriates the cultural specificities of a nineteenth-century Pacific Northwest in order to reflect on a new age of global communication. His site-specific identification with the forgotten innovators and adopters of Chinook Jargon activates three interrelated forms of site – geographic, social, and discursive – Kwon (2002), and informs the work's critical engagement with Vancouver's (real and meta-phoric) seawall as a space of racial and cultural mixing. On each of these levels, Tsang's installation speaks back to Vancouver's contested urban trans-formation – its Asianification (Miki 2000). Problematizing the primacy of Anglo-European cultural antecedents, *Welcome to the Land of Light* encourages viewers to think about their own movements through circuits of commerce and capital – both those that put British Columbia on the map of empire and also those reinscribing the site within the trajectories of twenty-first–century urbanization. The work spatializes the arrivals and departures of hundreds of thousands, now millions, of Asian migrants – Japanese, South Asian, and Chinese – seeking investment and lifestyle opportunities outside their home countries, including more than 100,000 people who came to Vancouver from Hong Kong in the run-up to 1997.

There is a significant self-referential element to Tsang's work. Self-consciously representing the historical antecedents underpinning transconti-nental migrations of actors and ideas, it grounds the unfurling communications networks that enable and direct global mobilities through specific geographic nodes. To the extent that it looks back to the colonial history of this trading ground, it looks forward to Vancouver's urban future or futures. Thus, it stages an engagement with the Concord development that draws on the social and material relations of the work's production and Tsang's involve-ment in Asian Canadian cultural politics. Commissioned by Concord in compliance with Vancouver's newly minted Public Art Plan, *Welcome to the Land of Light* functions on the level of the social in relation to the artist's cultural identity and his self-identification as a Hong Kong-born artist who migrated to Canada with his family in the 1960s. His activities as a culturally engaged artist, curator, activist, and organizer (Tsang and Chan 1991; Tsang and Lee 1993; Tsang and McFarlane 1997a) are an important element of the work, and would no doubt have been considered in the competition through which it was selected. Thus, Tsang's installation provides a significant insight into the Vancouver cultural policy and programming *vis-à-vis* an emergent diversity. Taking the opportunity to intervene or otherwise participate in the Concord redevelopment project, it chooses to read past and present through the legacies of British colonialism, the racist drive to build BC as a "white man's province" (Perry 2001; Roy 2003), and through the limited goals of contemporary Canadian official Multiculturalism (Day 2000; Mackey 2002). Interestingly, Tsang avoids obvious reference to Vancouver's Chinatown (a short distance from False Creek) and popular representations of the so-called Chinese or Chinese Canadian community. Focusing instead on questions of linguistic hybridity, the complex machinations of colonial trade networks, and questions of indigeneity or aboriginality, *Welcome to the Land of Light* creates an ideal site from which to revisit the transformation and mutations of one city into the next; to stop and reflect before walking on.

Along the Seawall – Mohamed Ali Alabbar Takes a Walk

Vancouver's urban form can be read in terms of a series of cultural, economic, and political flows, relations, intersections, and territorializations extending across space and time. It is a node in the mobilization of development and policy knowledge from place to place (McCann and Ward 2010, 2011; McCann 2011), and it is a key site in the creation of what Ong (2007) identifies as "pied-a-terre subjects" who fly from one urban space to another as part of global exchanges of expertise. This new urbanism might be read as a technique with which local governments negotiate the extra-local forces that comprise neoliberal economic development. Vancouverism involves, then, the mobilization of Hong Kong development capital and expertise, and this model of high-end, high-density, high-rise urban living has proven to be a catalyst for urban growth, especially for sites outside the dominant geography of world cities. The urban form is a portable technology capable of being mobilized and adapted to the needs of new and emerging middle classes. The advantage of the "Vancouver model," itself a hybrid of Hong Kong and Waikiki-style urban typologies, rests with its concentration on developing the residential real estate, and the ingenuity of Li Ka Shing and his team of executives, who were able to tap into international Asian markets while taking advantage of local conditions (Olds 2001). Key players from Li's Concord team were able to lobby local governments and orchestrate the purchase of a massive swath of Vancouver's urban waterfront at the bargain price of $320 million, financed over 15 years. The size and nature of this project meant that Concord could systematically leverage Vancouver's urban waterfront, repackaging it for offshore investors. In this way, Concord was able to generate a $30 billion project out of a polluted urban site that, in turn, has fueled an impressive market for international real-estate speculators.

It is in this neoliberal, globalized context that we come across a curious corollary to Tsang's seawall walker: Mohamed Ali Alabbar, Chairman of the Dubai-based development corporation Emaar Properties. Visiting the False Creek seawall walkway in 1997, possibly strolling by Tsang's installation, Alabbar became so impressed by Vancouver's new, Hong Kong-style urban landscape that he decided to adopt the model and transfer it to Dubai (Boddy 2006). Almost immediately, Emaar enlisted or employed many of the Concord Pacific's executive team. Seeing possibilities for Dubai's burgeoning urban economy, Emaar was able to identify and repurpose salient features of the Vancouver model for export/import. These included the exploitation of readily available, inexpensive urban real estate; the articulation of a mega-development into a growing market for global investors; the enrolment of an already amenable local government into the project; and the marketing of the development within shifting trade networks and local (cultural, social, economic) contexts in order to make it desirable to new urban elites. The result is an echo of Vancouver – similar, yet different. Certain design features, such as the curves of Dubai Marina, resemble those of False Creek quite closely, as do the railings that skirt the Emirati's version of the seawall walkway (Figure 7.2). Yet this walkway is wider, more socially diverse, more commercial, and in certain spots more lively, with various cafés and restaurants, than Vancouver's (field notes, Dubai Marina, February 2008). In comparison, Vancouver's seawall,

> looked a little stark and Presbyterian, a narrow band for walkers and bicyclists to pass through, a kind of aerobic expressway, but almost nowhere a place to linger, with barely a half dozen restaurants along its whole length. One small strip of the Dubai Marina seawall can have that many dining options at all prices serving up a baffling variety of global cuisines, along with waterparks for children, temporary art exhibitions, live musicians and strollers in every colour and cut of national dress ... Dubai Marina's seawall is an obliging urban festival; Vancouver's seawall is an obligation to exercise. (Boddy 2006)

This "festival" setting is surrounded by a growing number of condo towers, higher and architecturally more diverse than Vancouver's, but housing a similar class of pied-a-terre subjects.

The unlikely rise of the "other" False Creek at Dubai Marina allows us to think of Vancouver's Pacific Place not as a concrete and glass fetish but, rather, as one moment in an ongoing social process of mobility – the transportation and transformation of desire for a high-priced waterfront "lifestyle." Alabbar's decision to duplicate the development in Dubai involved not only the copying of design details and hiring of the same professionals to continue refining a desirable, or at least marketable, urban form, but also the creation of new consumers for this mobile urban dream, buyers conversant with a new hybrid language of urban leisure and unfettered enjoyment. In fact, shopping for waterfront, lifestyle condominiums became, until the global financial crisis, a pastime for Dubai's rapidly expanding affluent class, fed as it is from various locations across the globe. The process of de/reterritorializing this particular architectural typology was then a thoroughly social one, that is not only enacted through the practices of key experts but through the mobility of new global-urban subjects with the wealth and cultural capital needed to access liberalized nation/state spaces and by state agents, such as the Canadian consulate in Dubai that has helped facilitate the emergence of what Boddy (2006) calls a "Maple Leaf Mafia" of architects and developers in the United Arab Emirates (UAE) (interview with consular officials, Dubai, February 2008).

The story does not simply involve Canadian–Emirati connections, however. When we consider the socioeconomic conditions that have allowed Dubai to become a hub for Middle Eastern financial transactions, we must take into account not only the billions of dollars "repatriated" in Dubai following September 11, 2001, but also the UAE's historical trade relations with the Asian subcontinent, links to financial and ruling elites in the United States and the United Kingdom, and the function of Shariah law in creating the conditions for investment. The liberal, secular outlook of Dubai's Sheikh Mohammed bin Rashid Al Maktoum stands in stark contrast to the more repressive state policies of Saudi Arabia, Iran, and Syria, while providing an alternative to the uncertainty of Iraq (Davis 2006). We must also consider the ongoing role of race and ethnicity in the creation or destabilization of labor markets throughout the region. During its boom, the UAE proved its ability to capitalize on migrant workers from across the economic spectrum – the expatriate executives and experts from Europe and North America, middle managers from India and Pakistan, and massive numbers of laborers also from South Asia and from various other more economically impoverished countries. "Dubai Inc." (Fonda 2006) became a model throughout the region, influencing growth in Bahrain, Oman, Qatar, as well as elsewhere in the UAE. In fact, the growth of Dubai up until the end of 2008, and its continued efforts at development, rely on the ruler's skill in managing complex rights, responsibilities, and expectations and in translating North American – or, we might argue, Asian/North American – urban development for Arab/Asian consumers.

Cultural Production in, and in Critique of, Pan-Asian Urban Form

Much can be said about the important role innovation or creative thinking might play in twenty-first–century urbanization. In a general sense, culture – understood as social process (lifestyle) and material practice (literature, media, the arts, architecture, and design) – plays a significant role in many of the studies referenced in this chapter and culture, variously defined, is often acknowledged as an element of mobilities (Cresswell 2006). The populariza-tion of Richard Florida's (2002) "creative class" thesis, particularly among governments, points to a growing interest in culture and cultural producers as significant drivers of the contemporary urban economy (on the limits of this approach, see Peck 2005; McCann 2007, 2008). Among the mobile professional classes, cultural producers – educators, artists, curators, and consultants – have come to play key roles in urban development, not only in Canada but also in the UAE, by helping to refine and resituate the so-called Vancouver model (Boddy 2006). Thus, we argue that critical cul-tural productions provide a vital avenue into the analysis of global urban development and neoliberal statecraft, since cultural or artistic production can be both an interpretive or representational practice and also a method in critical research.

Local conditions, particularly in relation to colonial history and ethnic relations, are likewise integral to the development of Dubai in particular, and the Gulf region more generally, as a new economic hub – a goal that still drives Dubai's elites even after the downturn of 2008–9. In Hong Kong, Vancouver, and Dubai, culture and citizenship are dependent on and also in excess of state practices. In the UAE, we are beginning to witness serious interest and investment in "culture," especially in the sense of star-architect-designed centers and facilities. The most striking example of this is the $27 Billion Sadyat Island development in Abu Dhabi. The plans for this cultural hub include a new Guggenhiem and a Middle Eastern Louvre, among other museums and an opera hall. Given the size of the UAE, the flow-through of cultural producers from Abu Dhabi to Dubai and Sharjah, the third of the seven emirates and host of the 9th art biennial in 2009, is significant. Already, many Western curators, artists, and arts administrators, have been invited to work in the UAE. In the wake of the Concord Pacific executives who were hired to help with Emaar's Dubai Marina project, and an ex-city planner from Vancouver who is now special advisor to the Sheik in Abu Dhabi, we have seen a number of luminaries from Vancouver's art world (Jayce Saloum, Ken Lum, Roy Arden) working in the UAE.

Our point so far in this chapter has been to illustrate the mobilization and inter-referencing of a particular urban form from Hong Kong to Vancouver,

to Dubai. Our argument is that the proliferation of this built environment
must be understood not only in terms of the production of concrete landscapes, but also in terms of the obliteration or elision of the historical,
cultural, economic, political, and transnational connections through which it
is produced. We have suggested, by reference to Tsang's critical evocation
of the submerged layers and connections that constitute the Pacific Place
development, that cultural production can also constitute a powerful critique
of contemporary global urbanism. How might such a critical approach be
operationalized in the Asian context?

Asiancy: a critical cultural perspective on the inter-referencing of urban Asia

As we see in Concord's urban mega-project in Vancouver, the mobilization
of Asian Canadian actors was necessary in translating urban form back and
forth across the differences separating the investors, civic leaders, government,
and local and non-local communities. While there might be a tendency to
see these acts of facilitation as mundane exchanges between "native"
informants and internal and external stakeholders, it is crucial to recognize
that they occur within a dynamic of particularized and contradictory spa-
tializations that have involved large numbers of actors – artists, activists,
small business owners, students, and other social groups. These cultural
producers are vital to the scripting, depicting or portrayal of hegemonic
narratives capable motivating or influencing massive numbers of citizens –
voters, consumers, investors, and spectators. These actors are also instrumental
to the creation and transportation of ideals about the nature and meaning
of contemporary urban experience. To counteract local resistance and
entrenched anti-Asian sentiment, Concord Pacific was founded as a Canadian
company and availed itself of guidance and leadership from individuals who
were educated in Canada and the United States, and who developed
expertise in North American cultures (Olds 2001).

Therefore, Concord Pacific might be understood as an assemblage of
national or transnational interests; its ability to respond to the imperatives
of various levels of government, while assuaging the material and social
needs of local, diasporic, and global communities, is in part a function of
Asian Canadian culture and a long history of intricate negotiations between
"racialized" minorities and the state. In Vancouver, the extent to which
contemporary Asian Canadian writers and artists have been active in
imagining and creating alternative realities – "altered states" or "alter-
nations" (Miki 2000) – might be linked to the larger community or communities' ability to provide a platform for the flow of new (Asian) capital.
More than mere decoration, more than urban texture, Asian Canadian
cultural production seeds the promise of future engagements with the
forces of urban transformation. Tsang's work, like Miki's, might thus be

read in terms of the ongoing, multifaceted engagement of Asian Canadian subjects in the transformation of city and state.

To begin to work across the imaginative divide separating urban experiences in Hong Kong, Vancouver, and Dubai, Miki's work (1998, 2000, 2001) is of particular interest, particularly in light of our inquiry into the boundaries between critical and creative practice. Miki is a Vancouver-based, second-generation (Nikkei) Japanese Canadian cultural theorist, poet, and social activist, and his writing and scholarship works against the grain of racialized language and/or discourses of nation formation through careful attention to cultural forms that challenge the legacies of colonialism, on the one hand, and globalism, on the other. In response to the exigencies of a deterritorialized state, Miki calls for a renovated "ethics of reading Asian Canadian" that involves "critical practices that can negotiate the tension between the material conditions of textual [read knowledge] production ... and the normative conditions of reception"; that is, beyond the geo-political limits of the nation-state against which Asian Canadian identities come into being. In characteristically torqued diction, he calls for "an ethics of reading [that] can point towards a new 'ethnics'" (75). While Miki's language and focus is self-consciously literary, it pushes toward social engagement in which creative practice and knowledge production are inextricably bound with state relations. Miki goes on to argue that "the limits of existing critical frameworks are influenced by the always shifting and shifty contexts of racialization, sexuality, class and gender affiliations," which he defines as "historically-determined privileges and subordination, and ethnocentric frames of reference" (74). Against this, he posits a "condition" of reading (analysis, interrogation, interpretation) for both creative texts and institutional practices that "might be called 'minority-wise'" (75).

Linking Miki's work back to our earlier discussion of the development of Concord Pacific Place and Henry Tsang's artwork, as well as forward toward unfolding, deterritorialized hybrid or hyphenated Asian cultural subjects, identities, and places, we might say that Miki provides an important understanding of knowledge construction that is embodied and grounded in questions of political process. It builds on the perspective of those who have been marginalized and often violently excluded from the political process, but who nevertheless continue to exert pressures that transform and contest the space of social construction. His ethics of reading remains vigilant to a lengthy struggle over the rights of Asian Canadians and other dispossessed groups within or on the limits of the nation, and to the importance of recognizing this cultural history in the face of shifting global developments.

In response to the 1999 arrival of "four ships carrying 600 Fujianese people [from China's Fujian Province] seeking refuge ... on the west coast of

Canada" (Wong 2001: 105), Miki considers "the potential for the emergence of new cultural performances – and by implication new 'localisms' – that account for the 'spectral' effects of global uncertainties" (2000: 43). He takes issue with the media's ahistoricism, the so-called "'sudden arrival' of unidentified bodies in run-down ships." Borrowing Appadurai's notion of the mediascape, he rescales a shopworn nationalist trope: "the figures entering the Canadian mediascape in the summer of 1999 were instantly enmeshed in representations that occluded connections with a global economy in which bodies – often 'Asian'-identified bodies – are reduced to labour machines … in the logic of capital expansion, in other words, their 'arrival' had already been conjured across the oceanic divide to serve corporate agendas." These "queue jumpers" drew criticism from "the media and some Canadians, including some Chinese Canadians," but in so doing, they helped make visible Canadians' tenuous hold of its oft-proclaimed tolerance and internationalism. In contrast to the valued "economic migrants" Canadian immigration officials were courting in Hong Kong, Taipei, Singapore, and other prosperous Asian cities (for whom the glass and steel condos of Pacific Place were constructed), these refugees were treated as a threat, detained in BC's interior, and isolated from Chinese-speaking support workers and advocates in Vancouver.

For Miki, this event points to a "crisis in time" or deep-seated anxiety at the core of the modern nation-state that recalls Chinese railway workers: "an exploitable pool of 'Asian' bodies to provide the labour for nation-building." But, as Miki reminds us, even "[t]hese 'undesirables' would translate over time into Asian Canadians" (50), following the painful logic of cultural assimilation and appropriation by the Canadian nation. Asian Canadian thus becomes a fraught site. Visible and invisible within larger nationalist and global frameworks, representations of Asian and Asian Canadian subjects provide sites for radical reconceptions of the interdependence of political, geographic, and cultural zones and the multivalent investments flowing through them. Miki writes that "[t]he re-articulation of the past to account for the emergence of alterior narratives of the nation opens the possibility that 'Asian Canadian,' as one site of visibility can be read into the moment of alteration." It remains "a formation linked to the nation and simultaneously in excess of its border":

> "Asian Canadian," when dislodged from its foreclosures becomes a revolving sign which re-articulates and thus exposes discourses of both globalization (i.e., towards Asian markets and economies, for instance) and a reactionary nationalism (i.e., as a "yellow peril" that is asianizing white Canada). "Asian Canadian" then becomes both a localized subject – of research, cultural production, interrogation – and a double edged site: where relations of dominance threaten to be remobilized (more of the same), or where critiques of nation can posit future methodologies of resistance and collective formations. (53)

Miki's figure of the "Asian Canadian" as "revolving sign" or "double edged site" – "neither subject or object" – clears the way for an understanding of the complex social processes moving beneath or alongside the mobile forms and actors crossing back and forth across the globe among Hong Kong, Vancouver, and Dubai, as well as for the ethical obligations involved in "reading," or researching new (Asian) cultural formations and paradigm shifts.

Walking toward a Conclusion

Miki's argument for ethical engagement with these mobile localisms and their uneasy collisions with structures of an emergent globalism provides a useful corollary to contemporary research on the phenomenal growth of Dubai, and the Gulf region more generally.

Regarding Dubai

The amazing drive and apparent vision of Dubai's ruling elite has meant that the emirate has been able to take advantage of a series of global shifts. Not only has it been able to use its economic clout and geo-political position within the Gulf region to begin massive urban development but, more importantly, it seems to have captured the world's imagination, providing images about what a future city might or should be like. With the expansion of Dubai and its emergence as hub of international shipping (Dubai World Ports owns P&O, making it one of the largest shipping interests in the world) and passenger transportation (Emirates Air is quickly building the biggest fleet of aircraft in the world), the emirate receives significant coverage in European and North American media. Dubai is also generating interest among academics and cultural theorists (Katodrytis 2005; Davis 2006; Basar, Carver, and Miessen 2007; Davis 2006; Khoubtou and Koolhaus 2007). In both the media and academic studies, the Dubai phenomenon tends to be met with cynicism. The achievements of "Sheikh Mo" and his growing force of experts are framed within an important but somewhat obvious discourse of excess.

After inviting his readers to join him on a plane above Dubai, the better to see its plethora of architectural firsts and opulent urban consumption sites, Mike Davis (2006) asks rhetorically, "Is this a new Margaret Atwood novel, Philip K. Dick's unpublished sequel to *Blade Runner* or Donald Trump on acid?" "No," he answers, "It is the Persian Gulf city-state of Dubai in 2010" (49). Tellingly, Davis cultural examples hinge on the primacy of Anglo-American references. As we see in Davis's overview, much of the research on Dubai is characterized by a strong sense that the city itself is a vortex into which Western-style consumption is being poured by the barrel.

Dubai and its development is, thus, represented and analyzed in Anglo-American terms, from afar and from above, rather than in and through the city's own complex social spaces, where multiplicity can be identified in ways that might not be immediately evident. In part, readings of Dubai through an Anglo-American lens have been encouraged by the ruling elites' yearning to import the most desirable goods and services – products and people, from elsewhere, including Vancouver. But certainly a city of this size and with its complicated social structures and strata cannot be seen from the air or even on the drive in from the airport. These are the perspectives Davis offers in his dissection of Dubai. And undoubtedly the view from the air, conveying the vast sweep and frenetic activity that characterizes urban development in contemporary Dubai is worthwhile and insightful, as far as it goes.

Yet, on the other hand, it calls to mind Donna Haraway's (1988) admonition against the "god trick" of the objective, masculinized, all-seeing gaze. Furthermore, it also happens to be a favorite representational strategy of Dubai's developers themselves, a point which calls to mind another feminist critique of contemporary critical social analysis – J.K. Gibson-Graham's (1996) insightful argument against critical discourses about capitalist development that simultaneously serve to glorify and discursively strengthen it. But how, then, do we begin to move beyond the "flyover critique"? Attending to the situation on the ground, it is clear that the emirate is becoming a cultural hub with a growing capacity to develop and support Dubai-based artists and designers. Undoubtedly, the main event in Dubai is commerce, specifically real-estate development, and unlike neighboring emirates Sharjah and Abu Dhabi, Dubai has been slow to invest in cultural infrastructure. Nevertheless, recent events suggest that things are changing. The converted warehouses of the Al Quoz district have become home to cultural workers who are actively reshaping the face of city. Individuals such as Sunny Rahbar, director of Dubai's Third Line gallery, artist and filmmaker Lamya Hussain Gargash, who represented her country at the UAE pavilion in the 2009 Venice biennale, and Rami Farouk, founder/director of design-gallery Traffic and the British Council's International Young Design Entrepreneur of 2009 – to name but a few – represent a young, dynamic cadre of Dubai-based curators, artists, and designers who are gaining international recognition. Local cultural producers provide an important counterpoint to a flood of internationally recognized artists and star architects – the likes of Mona Houtoum, Zaha Hadid, and Rem Koolhaas – who have been brought to the UAE as part of a programmatic drive for cultural recognition and global legitimacy. Recent initiatives such as the Dubai Culture and Arts Authority, Art Dubai and the Abraaj Capital Art Prize, as well as significant art/design spaces (Tashkeel, Jam Jar, and Shelter) mark a significant change in the role of culture in Dubai and emergent shift in urban development across the region.

As we pursue our still nascent study of the Hong Kong – Vancouver – Dubai nexus, we suggest that cultural production, and its shifting and transformational role in the development of each of these urban spaces, provides both a useful lens into the production of cities in global context from the ground up, rather than through the view from everywhere and nowhere. This sort of situated knowledge might offer an analytical perspective that both complements and challenges some of the dominant perspectives on Dubai's development and on Asian and global urbanism.

Back to the Land of Light

The promise of a new, clean, cybernetic universe of unfettered mobility is enmeshed in a colonial geography of free trade and racialized exploitation, as Tsang's *Welcome to the Land of Light* demonstrates. Despite the influx of global capital, despite the promise of multicultural development and a shiny new urbanism, mega-developments in Vancouver and Dubai stage disparate social interactions that rework and reterritorialize Pratt's (1992) conception of a colonial "contact zone." Reciting phrases taken from sales brochures and other documentation produced by False Creek developers, including Concord Pacific, Tsang's Chinook–English translations (an early Chinglish?) are incommensurable with either standard lexicon. Instead, they belie a difficult irony about the primacy and transparency of communications: "*Chako kopa laly ka tillikums wawa huloima, keschi kloshe kunamokst.*" / "Come to time where people talk different but good together." The luxury lifestyle promised in this new Vancouver model of urbanism, with its shiny residential towers that seem to represent the possibility of unimpeded leisure beyond the shadow of the modern, industrial cities sits in difficult contrast with the specificities of ethnic encounter and compromise.

Thus, in Tsang's installation, the trope "light" functions materially and metaphorically. Incorporating the vaunted fiber-optic technology into his installation, Tsang represents the "land of light" as a code space that is simultaneously actual and virtual: "*Be Klahowya! Kloshe maika ko yukwa, ka towagh mitlite keekwullie illahee.*" / "Greetings! Good you arrive here, where light be under land." Exacting a pun on the transient nature of knowledge and technology, Tsang's "land of light" marks a threshold of new and old ways of knowing, of the digital/code-based technologies inextricable from the infrastructural developments through which they course. The artist's uncanny pairings of Chinook and English propose and evoke a kinetics of migration mirrored in the physical structure of the work. Each discrete phrase strung along the seawall invites viewers to walk as they read; because each phrase exists as a part of a semantic unit, however, this reading takes place moving from left to right or right to left. In other words, the work can be approached from east or west. It can also be read *in media res*. Resisting the lateral pull of the seawall, while also working with it, the structure of *Welcome to the Land of Light* encourages viewers to stop and reflect on the distance between individual phrases and to look between the lines of text and above. Here, translation becomes an act of spatial as well as cultural mobility. A kinetics of interpretation is taken up in the semantic reworking of the original text: promotional copy, hyping False Creek's high tech, luxury lifestyle, is mediated through Chinook and back into an uneasy English. Tsang's poetics of *ostranenie* ("defamiliarization") (Shklovskij 1998) troubles the spatial–temporal coordinates of object and subject. Coursing through this network of cultural interchanges, *au courant* dreams of urban luxury and state-of-the-art connectivity become enmeshed with pasts that submerged, literally and figuratively, below False Creek's reflective surface. Momentary fragments of comprehension speak of another time and place that is also here, also now. Drawing on advertising that is designed to attract buyers from elsewhere – other parts of the city, country, or globe – Tsang's work situates a virtual (promised) land within the particularities of a built environment; in it, commodification runs up against its own physical and geographic limits.

In moments of relative stasis, one's gaze is drawn out across the water, away from the steel and glass towers, without ever escaping their looming presence. The almost perceptible hum of cybernetic activity running under one's feet envelops viewers, staging the physical relocations, readings and subsequent re-readings, within the ebb and flow of digital information. This cybernetic context in turn suggests a counterpoint to the ebb and flow of Asian migrations that have helped shape the geography of Vancouver and BC – the Gold Rush, the building of the Canadian Pacific Railway, the Asian Exclusion Act, the Japanese Canadian Internment of World War II, and finally the hyper-urbanization that continues to transform Vancouver beyond the physical territory. The ground in which the fiber-optic cables run is marked by earlier channels of communication and exchange; as the work of Asian North American artists and cultural theorists suggests, the pristine reflections of sea and sky, of joggers and roller bladders, cannot completely occlude the deeper imprints of Empire and the violence of modern nation formation. Thinking global mobilities necessitates an engagement with structures, histories, and cultures of power that continue to underwrite a geo-political continuum that links Dubai to the events of Tiananmen Square, the collapse of the twin towers, and the wars in Iraq and Iran (Davis 2006). The exchange of ideas and experiences continues to reconfigure the double-edged brutality of yet another promised land (deal). This paper asks how the work of Asian North American artists and cultural producers, such as Tsang, might be picked up and moved to a seawall twelve time zones away. It invites speculation on the form of critical engagement such work might take beneath the bifurcating towers of what might be legitimately called the Dubai model. We are left to reflect on the role of mobilities theory in relation to an unfolding "geography of longing" (Cho 2007). How does the work of scholars and artists enter the waves of diasporic (un)settlement?

Looking forward to the coming decades, Tsang's installation nods and winks (or blinks) toward a future of globally mobile actors and ideas that will transport Vancouver beyond the confines of its place in the history and culture of nation formation. Tsang's strange new vernacular, pseudo-technologized, becomes charged by strains of a series of hybrid translations that might be seen to culminate during 1990s, and which suggest an unfolding Asia or plurality of Asias that might also lay claim to the particularities of this urban locale. The continuous waves of traders, explorers, laborers, and entrepreneurs who, for the past 150 years, have continued to develop and redevelop local cultures in the name of progress, colony, Empire, and nation remain connected with a long and complicated engagement with the fluidity of new cultural forms that continue to challenge the racialized yearnings of the nation-state – China, Canada or the UAE. Described as a "contemporary monument to the relationship between those who have lived on the False Creek waterfront and those who will arrive in the future to call this area their home," Tsang's artwork exemplifies a continued drive to transform cultural texts into spaces of negotiation in which readers/walkers/viewers strive to come to terms with their experience of and participation in urban regenerations that are both here and not here, now and not now.

Walking in places, rather than flying overhead, has its own analytical and artistic merits. It conveys one element of a multifaceted ethnographic moment. Yet, it also conjures notions of *flânerie* and its classed, ethnicized, and gendered power relations (Pollock 1988; Wolff 1990). With this danger in mind, we remain interested in the potential of what might be thought of as an "ethnographic–artistic moment" of inter-urban and inter-Asian research, representation, referencing, and articulation. In this regard, we will leave the closing word to Miki (2000: 59), who writes, "The mobility of [postcolonial Asian Canadian] articulations and re-articulations may offer a critical potential to expose and unravel homogeneities – of culture, identities, discourses – that cover over global/local indeterminacies in the production of aesthetic forms," of which the Asian city is a primary example.

Acknowledgments

Research for this chapter has been funded by a Research/Creation in Fine Arts Grant from the Social Sciences and Humanities Research Council of Canada and by a SSHRC Standard Grant. Additionally, we would like to acknowledge support from the Social Science Research Council for travel to Dubai and our participation in the Inter-Asian References conference. We are grateful to Ananya Roy and Aihwa Ong for organizing the "Urban Experiments & the Art of Being Global" workshop, and for their critical feedback and editorial direction. We would also like to acknowledge our colleagues who participated in the "Urban Experiments" workshop for their interest and engagement in the topic. We offer special thanks to Henry Tsang, with whom we co-authored and presented the initial draft of this chapter, and whose work – research, coordination, and critical-creative collaboration – is integral to our continued study of the Hong Kong – Vancouver – Dubai nexus. We would also like to acknowledge members of the Maraya Project team, especially M. Simon Levin, who travelled with us to Dubai and whose artistic and critical sensibilities frame our thinking about the Dubai phenomenon. Finally, we would like to recognize the support of the following writers, whose conversations and research have been vital to our research: Trevor Boddy and Deborah Campbell in Vancouver; Samia Rab and George Katodrytis at the American University of Sharjah; and Dalia Merzaban of Reuters in Dubai.

References

Appadurai, A. (1996) *Modernity at Large: cultural dimensions of globalization.* Minneapolis, MN: University of Minnesota Press.

Basar, S., Carver, A., and Miessen, M. (2007) *With/Without: spatial products, practices, and politics in the Middle East.* Dubai: Bidoun and Mountamarat.

Boddy, T. (2006) False Creek, Dubai. *BCBusiness*, September, 70–81.

Campbell, D. (2007) Magic kingdom or glass house. *The Walrus*, September.

Castells, M. (1996) *The Rise of the Network Society.* Malden, MA: Blackwell.

Cho, L. (2007) Diasporic citizenship: contradictions and possibilities for Canadian literature. In S. Kamboureli and R. Miki (eds.) *Trans.Can.Lit.: resituating the study of Canadian literature.* Waterloo, ON: Wilfrid Laurier University Press, pp. 93–109.

City of Vancouver (2003) *Vancouver's New Neighbourhoods: achievements in planning and urban design.* Vancouver, BC: City of Vancouver; http://www.city.vancouver.bc.ca/commsvcs/currentplanning/urbandesign/ (accessed February 5, 2011).

Cook, I.R. (2008) Mobilising urban policies: the policy transfer of US business improvement districts to England and Wales. *Urban Studies* 45(4), 773–95.

Cresswell, T. (ed.) (2001) Mobilities. Special issue of *New Formations* 43.

Cresswell, T. (2006) *On the Move: mobility in the modern Western world.* New York: Routledge.

Davis, M. (2006) Fear and money in Dubai. *New Left Review* 41 (September–October); http://newleftreview.org/?view=2635 (accessed February 5, 2011).

Day, R. (2000) *Multiculturalism and the History of Canadian Diversity.* Toronto: University of Toronto Press.

Domosh, M. (1989) A method for interpreting landscape: a case study of the New York World building. *Area* 21, 347–55.

Florida, R. (2002) *The Rise of the Creative Class: and how it's transforming work, leisure, community and everyday life.* New York: Basic Books.

Fonda, D. (2006) Inside Dubai Inc. *Time*; http://www.time.com/time/magazine/article/0,9171,1169886,00.html (accessed December 1, 2008).

Gagnon, M.K. (2000) *Other Conundrums: race, culture and Canadian art.* Vancouver, BC: Arsenal Pulp Press.

Gibson-Graham, J.K. (1996) *The End of Capitalism (as we knew it): a feminist critique of political economy*. Malden, MA: Blackwell.

Goss, J. (1988) The built environment and social theory: towards an architectural geography. *Professional Geographer* 40, 392–403.

Guggenheim, M. and Soderstrom, O. (eds.) (2010) *Re-Shaping Cities: how global mobility transforms architecture and urban form*. New York: Routledge.

Hannam, K., Sheller, M., and Urry, J. (2006) Editorial: mobilities, immobilities and moorings. *Mobilities* 1(1), 1–22.

Haraway, D. (1988) Situated knowledges: the science question in feminism and the privilege of partial perspective. *Feminist Studies* 14, 575–99.

Harvey, D. (1985) *The Urbanization of Capital*. Baltimore, MD: Johns Hopkins University Press.

Kamboureli, S. (2000) *Scandalous Bodies: diasporic literature in English Canada*. Toronto: Oxford University Press.

Katodrytis, G. (2005) Metropolitan Dubai and the rise of architectural fantasy. *Bidoun* 4.

Khoubtou, B. and Koolhaas, R. (ed.) (2007) *Al Manakh: Dubai guide*. Amsterdam: Stichting Archis.

Kwon, M. (2002) *One Place after Another: site-specific art and locational identity*. Cambridge, MA: The MIT Press.

Lai, L. (2008) Community action, global spillage: writing the race of capital. *West Coast Line 59* 42(3), 116–28.

Ley, D. (1987) Styles of the times: liberal and neo-conservative landscapes in inner Vancouver, 1968–1986. *Journal of Historical Geography* 13(1), 40–56.

Ley, D. (1996) *The New Middle Class and the Remaking of the Central City*. Oxford: Oxford University Press.

Lowry, G. (2006) Afterword. In *Roy K. Kiyooka's Transcanada Letters*. Edmonton, AB: NeWest Press.

Mackey, E. (2002) *The House of Difference: cultural politics and national identity in Canada*. Toronto: University of Toronto Press.

Massey, D. (1991) A global sense of place. *Marxism Today*, June, pp. 24–9.

Massey, D. (2005) *For Space*. London: SAGE Publications.

Massey, D. (2007) *World City*. Cambridge, UK: Polity Press.

Mathur, A. (2007) Transubracination: how writers of colour became CanLit. In S. Kamboureli and R. Miki (eds.) *Trans.Can.Lit.: resituating the study of Canadian literature* Waterloo, ON: Wilfrid Laurier University Press, pp. 141–52.

McAllister, K.E. (1999) Narrating Japanese Canadians in and out of the Canadian nation: a critique of realist forms of representation. *Canadian Journal of Communication* 24(1), 79–103.

McCann, E.J. (2007) Inequality and politics in the creative city-region: questions of livability and state strategy. *The International Journal of Urban and Regional Research* 31(1), 188–96.

McCann, E.J. (2008) Livable city/unequal city: the politics of policy-making in a "creative" boomtown. *Interventions Economiques* 37.

McCann, E.J. (2011) Urban policy mobilities and global circuits of knowledge: toward a research agenda. *Annals of the Association of American Geographers* 101, 107–30.

McCann, E.J. and Ward, K. (2010) Relationality/territoriality: toward a conceptualization of cities in the world. *Geoforum* 41, 175–84.

McCann, E.J. and Ward, K. (2011) *Assembling Urbanism: mobilizing knowledge & shaping cities in a global context*. Minneapolis, MN: University of Minnesota Press.

McNeill, D. (2009) *The Global Architect: firms, fame, and urban form*. New York: Routledge.

Miki, R. (1998) *Broken Entries: race, subjectivity, writing: essays*. Toronto: Mercury.

Miki, R. (2000) Altered states: global currents, the spectral nation, and the production of "Asian Canadian." *Journal of Canadian Studies* 35(3), 43–72.

Miki, R. (2001) Can Asian Adian? Reading the scenes of "Asian Canadian." In G. Lowry and S. Kong (eds.) *In-Equations: Can Asia Pacific. West Coast Line* 34(3), 56–77.

Mitchell, K. (2004) *Crossing the Neoliberal Line: Pacific Rim migration and the metropolis*. Philadelphia, PA: Temple University Press.

Olds, K. (2001) *Globalization and Urban Change: capital, culture, and Pacific Rim mega-projects*. Oxford: Oxford University Press.

Ong, A. (1999) *Flexible Citizenship: the cultural logics of transnationality*. Durham, NC: Duke University Press.

Ong, A. (2007) Please stay: pied-a-terre subjects in the megacity. *Citizenship Studies* 11(1), 83–93.

Peck, J. (2005) Struggling with the creative class. *International Journal of Urban and Regional Research* 29(4), 740–70.

Peck, J. (2003) Geography and public policy: mapping the penal state. *Progress in Human Geography* 27, 222–32.

Peck, J. and Theodore, N. (2001) Exporting workfare/importing welfare-to-work: exploring the politics of Third Way policy transfer. *Political Geography* 20, 427–60.

Perry, A. (2001) *On the Edge of Empire: gender, race, and the making of British Columbia, 1849–1871*. Toronto: University of Toronto Press.

Pollock, G. (1988) *Vision and Difference: femininity, feminism and histories of art*. New York: Routledge, pp. 50–90.

Pratt, M.L. (1992) *Imperial Eyes: travel writing and transculturation*. London: Routledge.

Punter, J. (2003) *The Vancouver Achievement: urban planning and design*. Vancouver, BC: University of British Columbia Press.

Robinson, J. (2006) *Ordinary Cities: between modernity and development*. New York: Routledge.

Roy, P.E. (2003) *The Oriental Question: consolidating a white man's province, 1914–1941*. Vancouver, BC: University of British Columbia Press.

Sharp, D. and Boddy, T. (2008) Vancouver, Vancouverize, Vancouverism: building an idea. In *Vancouverism: Westcoast architecture + city building* (online catalogue for an exhibition at Canada House, London); http://www.vancouverism.ca/vancouverism.php (accessed July 10, 2008).

Sheller, M. and Urry, J. (2006) The new mobilities paradigm. *Environment and Planning A* 38, 207–26.

Shklovskij, V. (1998) Art as technique. In J. Rivkin and M. Ryan (eds.) *Literary Theory: an anthology*. Malden, MA: Blackwell.

Simons, D. (2005) Impressive and interstitial space in Vancouver's False Creek. In B. Jeffries, G. Lowry, and J. Zaslove (eds.) *Unfinished Business: photographing Vancouver's streets, 1955–1985*. Vancouver, BC: Presentation House Gallery/*West Coast Line* 39(2).

Tsang, H. and Chan, L. (curators) (1991) *Self Not Whole: cultural identity and Chinese-Canadian*. Vancouver, BC: Chinese Cultural Centre.

Tsang, H. and Lee, K. (curators) (1993) *Racy Sexy*. Vancouver, BC: Chinese Cultural Centre.

Tsang, H. and McFarlane, S.T. (curators) (1997a) *City at the End of Time: Hong Kong 1997.* Artspeak, Access, Helen Pitt & Foto•Base Galleries, Vancouver Art Gallery, Simon Fraser University Harbour Centre.

Urry, J. (2007) *Mobilities.* Cambridge, UK: Polity Press.

Wah, F. (2000) *Faking It: poetics and hybridity.* Edmonton, AB: NeWest Press.

Ward, K. (2006) "Policies in motion," urban management and state restructuring: the trans-local expansion of Business Improvement Districts. *International Journal of Urban and Regional Research* 30, 54–75.

Wolff, J. (1990) The invisible *flâneuse*: women and the literature of modernity. In *Feminine Sentences: essays on women and culture.* Berkeley, CA: University of California Press, pp. 34–50.

Wong, R. (2001) Partial response to the global movement of people. In G. Lowry and S. Kong (eds.) *In-Equations: Can Asia Pacific. West Coast Line* 34(3), 105–19.

8

Hyperbuilding: Spectacle, Speculation, and the Hyperspace of Sovereignty

Aihwa Ong

The Chinese love the monumental ambition …. CCTV headquarters is an ambitious building. It was conceived at the same time that the design competition for Ground Zero took place – not in backward-looking US, but in the parallel universe of China. In communism, engineering has a high status, its laws resonating with Marxian wheels of history.

Rem Koolhaas and OMA (2004: 129)

Urban Spectacles

The proliferation of metropolitan spectacles in Asia indexes a new cultural regime as major cities race to attain even more striking skylines. Beijing's cluster of Olympic landmarks, Shanghai's TV tower, Hong Kong's forest of corporate towers, Singapore's Marina Sands complex, and super-tall Burj Khalifa in Dubai are urban spectaculars that evoke the "technological sublime." Frederic Jameson famously made the claim that the postmodern sublime has dissolved Marxian historical consciousness, but nowhere did he consider the role of architectural sublime in indexing a different kind of historical consciousness, one of national arrival on the global stage (Jameson 1991: 32–8). Despite the 2008–9 economic downturn, Shanghai's urban transformation for the 2010 World Expo will exceed Beijing's makeover for the 2008 Olympics.[1]

Spectacular architecture is often viewed as the handiwork of corporate capital in the colonization of urban markets. For instance, Anthony King and Abidin Kusno, writing about "On Be(ij)ing in the world," argue that the rise of cutting-edge buildings in Beijing is an instantiation of postmodern globalization transforming the Chinese capital into a "transnational

Worlding Cities: Asian Experiments and the Art of Being Global, First Edition.
Edited by Ananya Roy and Aihwa Ong.

space" (King and Kusno 2000: 41–67), a process driven by the apparent self-realization and development of capital. Such a perspective is based on the assumption that corporate power and Western technologies are creating a global space that is effacing national identity and undermining the capacity for a nation to control how it wants to be and how it wants to act in the world. Capital here thwarts national sovereign self-determination by subjecting "local" spaces to the overarching logic of a capitalist system with translocal or placeless determinations. Metropolitan studies have long been monopolized by Marxist perspectives that see capitalist hegemony as a determinative or agentive force in the shaping of urban landscapes and symbolism. There is, however, an urgent need to expand our analytical perspectives to include the analysis of sovereign rule and its control over the production of spectacle, speculation, and urban futures.[2] Sovereignty is not simply erased or replaced by the overwhelming power of capital, but is reconfigured through a variety of processes and practices whose outcomes cannot be determined *a priori*, or separate from the singular situated moments of particular forms of entanglement.

Rather than understand the development of new urban forms as merely the reflex of the expansion of capitalism or corporate power, this chapter proposes a theory of sovereign exception in shaping urban spectacles for political and economic ends. Asian cities and governments are neither merely the passive substrate on which capital erects and constructs itself, nor are they being reconfigured in a way that can be easily understood in terms on an implicit scale of "more" or "less" sovereignty. In emerging Asian countries, the rule of exception variously negotiates the dual demands of inter-city rivalries on the one hand, and the spectacle of confident sovereignty on the other. As I have argued elsewhere (Ong 2006), the rule of exception permits political flexibility in zoning practices for variable investments in property and citizen-subjects. Spaces are thus variegated, in a state of potential flux, and always potentially amenable to rezoning as a moment in the assertion and implementation of various forms of sovereignty. The global significance of a building frenzy in Asian cities requires an approach that explores the connection between the political exception and the variegated governmentality of urban spaces, where corporate towers and official edifices stand shoulder to shoulder. The variegation of the urban spectacle requires a more subtle analysis than has been attempted, and at least an exploration of the tensions between showy and flamboyant urban architecture embodying global capital on the one hand, and the spectacle of self-assured sovereignty on the other. In other words, the play of exception permits the spectacularization of urban success as well as of national emergence; that is, two modes of "hyperbuilding" that shape the urban profile in competition with other cities, and in the process, configure the global space of the nation, or configure the sovereign national space as one that is also emphatically and intractably global.

I borrow the term "hyperbuilding" from architect and thinker Rem Koolhaas, but use it more loosely. For Koolhaas, the "hyperbuilding" is the "anti-skyscraper"; that is, not defined by its exhilarating height, but by a striking and gigantic presence of the ground surface (*China Daily* 2004) (see Figure 8.2 below). I invoke hyperbuilding as both a verb and a noun to denote the two related urban trends in Asian cities. On the one hand, there is hyperbuilding as an intense process of building to project urban profiles. On the other, the hyperbuilding as a physical landmark stages sovereign power in the great city, or in cities aspiring, through these edifices, to greatness. The interactions between exception, spectacle, and speculation create conditions for hyperbuilding as both the practice and the product of world-aspiring urban innovations.

Hyperbuilding as worlding practice

My approach to urban spectacle centers on how different elements – a neo-liberal logic of maximization, the mobilization of political exceptions, and impressive development – are brought together to propel urban makeovers and leverage city futures. Political exceptions permit the varied and variegated use of metropolitan space, including the production of spectacular infrastructure that attracts speculative capital and offers itself as alleged proof of political power. Building a critical mass of towers in a new downtown zone animates an anticipatory logic of reaping profits not only in markets but also in the political domain. As Asian cities compete with other in the construction of ever more spectacular displays, it is not surprising that remarkable buildings become invested with contradictory symbolism about the nation itself.

Hyperbuilding as a hyperspace of sovereignty

While skyscrapers have long been associated with global capitalism, a different kind of impressive structure looms in the name of political futures. Whereas powerful architecture has long been associated with totalitarian rule (ancient Egypt, Nazi Germany, Soviet constructionism, Chinese communism), gigantic and spectacular buildings in contemporary Asian cities are associated with mixed symbolic meanings. State-commissioned edifices are planted closely alongside corporate skyscrapers. Rem Koolhaas' paradigmatic "hyperbuilding," the CCTV headquarters in Beijing, will be discussed later in its aspiration to be a connective structure that creates a public space that is not obliterated in a glutted concentration of tall buildings that, in other circumstances, would dwarf it or overshadow it. The CCTV media center

suggests the spectacular presence and power of Chinese sovereignty, and
offers itself as a potential index and manifestation of the power that brought
it to materialization – but it also engenders pornographic jokes that criticize
both the building and the agency it houses. Hyperbuilding, as both a process
and the set of monuments it erects, raises broader questions about the political
implications of the shift of the urban hyperspace to the Asian metropolis.

Hyperbuilding: Exception, Spectacle, and Speculation

Our reading of spectacular urban spaces has been dominated by a Marxist
focus on the proliferation of postmodern corporate forms that instill a sense
of disorientation and placelessness among ordinary people. In his landmark
book on postmodern culture, Frederic Jameson has influenced subsequent
views on urban spectacles as mirrors of the global circulation of corporate
sign-values; that is, hegemonic images that have a depoliticizing effect of
displacement and disorientation among urban-dwellers (1991: 43–5, 95–6).
Building on Jameson's claims, David Harvey remarks that the "stable aesthetics" of Fordist modernism gave way to an aesthetics of difference,
ephemerality, and spectacle – a kind of flexible aesthetic regime that paral-
lels and constitutes the accelerated commodification of cultural forms (1989:
156). More recently, Scott Lash and Celia Lury directly tie the function of
capitalist spectacles to urban strategies (2007: 141–8). They argue that zones
of spectacle are about city branding, a mode of value-making in symbolic
differentiation that makes a site stand apart from others. Branding intensifies
city associations with certain objects or indices of globality (often the insignia
of an increasingly globalized commercial sphere: Nike, Samsung, Coca-Cola),
thus improving the host city's capacity to mobilize and mediate among
things and actors. In this account, by amassing spectacles – associated with
certain industries and special events – urban centers are involved in the
creation of regimes of (capitalist) iconicity that influence the quality of
experience in these cities. Despite an interest in city branding, the focus is
again on the effects of corporate iconography on materializing and driving
our consumer imagination. This is an argument about the cultural hegemony
of corporations and the domination of their surroundings. At a broader
level, Guy Debord (1995) has argued that the spectacle society orders all
relations of accumulation, producing a momentary unity among spectators
who have become profoundly alienated by the processes of both the
production and the consumption of the commodity. In short, for Marxist
theorists, the spectacle is primarily associated with all aspects of capitalism,
including the use of modern media as a technology of manipulation that also
conceals the social fact of domination. The spectacle is thus taken to be
embedded in a set of technologies aimed at maintaining specific forms of

hegemony, creating the conditions of a dangerous and mystified political alienation and effectively thwarting the possibility of social change.

While the above analyses linking spectacle to disorientation and alienation are important, my approach looks at the state and its promotion of hyperbuilding and technologies of spectacle for political ends. These spectacles are thus productive, playing a constitutive and performative role in the assertion and realization of different political and politicized ends. Just as early twentieth-century Chicago stood as a potent projection of American dreams of being a rising industrial superpower, urban spectacles in Asia today play an aesthetic role in promoting future values and new political orientations. As Georg Simmel notes, value is not based on fixed, objective or enduring causes. Rather, economic, social, and aesthetic values are purely relational, emerging only in the context of specific exchange relationships and regimes of exchange (1900: 577–603). In other words, cultural values do not merely serve to reproduce an existing social system, but can expand geometrically through a proliferation of connections. In conditions of uncertainty, the spaces of spectacle animate an anticipatory logic of valorization; that is, speculations that anticipate economic, aesthetic, and political gains through circulation and interconnection. The political exception also engages value-making by permitting the spectacular zones that engender speculation in urban assets and thus accelerate the rise of a metropolis.

We can identify two the kinds of hyperbuilding logic at work in Asian cities. First, building frenzy helps to leverage gains beyond the market sector; that is, not only by inflating real-estate values, but also by raising hopes and expectations about urban futures and, by extension, the nation's growth. The hyperbuilding becomes part of an anticipation of a future that is asserted as a guarantee. Second, in a related phenomenon, hyperbuilding inter-references spectacular structures in rival cities, thereby fueling a spiral of increasing speculation in urban forms. The dynamic of this inter-referential practice constitutes competitive hyperbuilding as a parameter in which urban rankings will be understood, and, in this condition, hyperbuilding generates more hyperbuilding. A dynamic approach to spectacular cities thus shows that the stakes in urban spectacles go beyond mere capital accumulation to include the generation of promissory values about the geopolitical significance of the city and the country that it stands for in metonymic relation. The skyscraper megalomania of Asian cities is never only about attracting foreign investments, but fundamentally also about an intense political desire for world recognition.

From Shanghai to Dubai, cities in emerging countries are renovating at a furious rate, amassing glittering malls, museums, opera houses, and science parks. They have also been busy staging world events such as the Olympics, art biennales, world fairs, and scientific conventions. Visually stunning urban projects can be viewed as leveraging practices that anticipate a high return not only in real estate but also in the global recognition of the city. We must thus challenge Jameson's claim that the centrifugal proliferation of commercialized cultural forms destroys our sense of "critical space" shaped by history, class, and politics (1991: 43–5, 95–6). In fact, commodity signs articulate certain situated historical imaginaries and aspirations. While the commodity-saturated environments of a Ginza in Tokyo or of Wangfujing in Beijing can indeed induce disorientation, the proliferation of signs does not destroy a need for cultural hierarchy, or diminish a sense of critical spatial politics. One should point out that in developing countries, the critical spaces of the nation trump those of purported class mobilization (Jameson's concern). Indeed, the glittering surfaces of global capitalism are added value to the political emergence of the nation on the world stage, rather than the sign of their imminent replacement by a disembedded corporate-capitalist process.

Urban-dwellers in Asia's big cities do not read spectacles as a generalized aesthetic effect of capitalism, but rather as symbols of their metropolis that invite inevitable comparison with rival cities. Shanghai sees itself as the international gateway to China, and is therefore a critical site of China's urban representations, as well as its symbolic encapsulation of the world and the potential of globality. A city of 12 million, Shanghai has been trying to spread its ever-growing population beyond its city limits. It has constructed a ring of nine satellite cities to accommodate at least half a million residents. Given the craze for faux-European urban environments and lifestyles, each mini-city is designed by international planners and named after a Western country or town such as Weimar, Thamestown, London, Bellagio, and Santa Monica. Perhaps somewhat tongue in cheek, Shanghai authorities declared in 2002 that "foreign visitors will not be able to tell where Europe ends and China begins" (Beech 2005). In this series of developments, Shanghai is of course implicitly and sometimes explicitly rivaling Hong Kong, China's leading commercial center, and both cities are competing with Singapore, which is remaking itself as an international knowledge hub and casino center (Ong 2005).

Such inter-city competition drives the building frenzy that one encounters throughout East Asia, as well as putting at risk anticipated gains in the urban economy and/or in politics. Real-estate values are especially parasitic upon an excess of corporate signifiers. For instance, Hong Kong is home to dozens of corporate towers above 700 feet, the most important of which operate as part of a symbolic code for the port's commercial fortunes, especially since the return of the former British colony to mainland rule in 1997. Hong Kongers give their iconic buildings pet names, and tend view them like pieces in a chess game. The Cheung Kong Building is called "The Box that the Bank of China came in." Meanwhile, the nearby HSBC Building, a venerable colonial structure with roots in British imperialism, is seemingly being menaced by the I.M. Pei-designed Bank of China. Fondly referred to as the Cleaver Building, its sharp edges are interpreted as sending bad qi toward the HSBC building. The close juxtaposition of these warring buildings reinforces the palpable feeling of tension between the powers of the global financial world and of the Chinese state intersecting in Hong Kong.

Thus, far from merely serving as props of capitalist hegemony, Asian urban skylines advertise their own city brand of can-do-ism, providing a visual and infrastructural attraction that draws international actors, capital, and information and cultural flows to the city. Elsewhere (Ong 2007), I have analyzed the synergy between flamboyant cityscapes and the influx of "pied-a-terre" residents and international workers whose very presence adds further economic and cultural clout to Singapore or Dubai. Hyperbuilding as a mechanism to leverage global funds and status has been most obvious in inter-city rivalry to raise the tallest tower, build the sleekest airport, or set up the latest knowledge or design center.

Singapore's models of science parks and biotechnology hubs has spawned copycat projects in other cities (see Chua Beng Huat, this volume), but other urban templates are also being developed in East Asia. Recently, Seoul metropolitan authorities boasted of the city's innovative "Global Zones" plan to turn the metropolis into "a remarkably business-friendly − and business savvy − global city" for global actors.[3] As self-proclaimed "World Design Capital 2010," Seoul will design a "universal, ubiquitous, and unique" sustainable city dedicated to cultural, environmental, aesthetic, and social living. Architect Zaha Hadid will design a modern center for fashion and design. Clearly, the political ambition is to go beyond the old industrial model and become a world cultural city that hopes to rival or even surpass Tokyo or New York. Urban innovations in Asia are thus caught up in this larger game of translating spectacular towers into schemes for scaling political heights, but there are pitfalls in some attempts to bring about joint urban–national ascendancy.

There is, however, no certainty that hyperbuilding practices in any particular city can leverage global investments and draw global actors in significant numbers, or guarantee the rising fortunes of an ambitious nation. For instance, in the 1990s, Prime Minister Mohamed Mahathir of Malaysia spent lavishly on urban development, following the premise of "if you build, they will come." Unfortunately, the multimedia corridor, including a new cyber-capital, failed to blossom into an Asian Silicon Valley, and has been operating as a node in a second-tier circuit dominated by Indian cyber-firms (Ong 2005). The Petronas towers in Kuala Lumpur were for a few years the highest buildings in the world, until overtaken by Taiwan's Taipei 101 tower in 2004. Despite costing billions of petrodollars, the Petronas' telecommunications function is obsolete in an age of satellites, while its location contributes to a traffic gridlock in the capital's downtown area. This underused structure has become a white elephant, reminding citizens of their leaders' profligacy and desire for hollow symbols of national advancement. At the street level,

Malaysians casually refer to the Petronas towers as Mahathir's "double erections." The symbolism of these towers can stand for stalled attention-grabbing urban showpieces that stir the imagination of citizens about the danger of their governments grasping for glory beyond their reach (even with billions of lost dollars). In short, hyperbuildings cannot always leverage actual values, or realize a city's dreams for its nation. As Tim Bunnell has noted, the multimedia corridor's attempt to link up with the information age has merely "reaffirmed Malaysia's global peripherality" (2004: 3).

The hoped-for synergy between urban spectacle and speculation has been taken to an extreme in Dubai, the most flamboyant urban wonderland of the new century. Despite being the least oil-rich of the nine United Arab Emirates, Dubai has built a thousand skyscrapers in less than a decade. This brand new city is most famous for its indoor ski slope and offshore palm-shaped and globe-shaped manmade islands, all suggesting a level of ecological unsustainability and decadence in a desert redoubt. Beyond its skyrocketing rise as a global financial and transportation hub and a playground of the rich and famous, the city is made up of special zones with independent laws. There are also over a hundred independently master-planned commercial, industrial, and residential districts. The spectrum of mini-cities includes a financial center, an academic hub, an information-technology center, a free media zone, and even a humanitarian service site. Special jurisdictions cater to foreign professionals, with relaxed rules for drinking and lifestyles that are exceptions to laws imposed elsewhere in the city. The over-zoned city is a vivid example of the urban effects of graduated rule; that is, the constitution of variegated spaces for expatriates, guest workers and citizens, each zone regulated by different kinds of biopolitical investments and social controls (Ong 2006). During the boom years, this urban mirage in the desert attracted billions of investments from global banks as the city projected itself into the global stratosphere of international banking and living.

By the fall of 2009, a year after the global recession, Dubai had gone into free fall as its profligate borrowings created a debt of $3 trillion that it could not repay. Dubai has turned to oil-rich Abu Dhabi for a $10 billion debt-relief package. The completion of the Burj Dubai, renamed as the Burg Khalifa after Sheikh Khalifa of Abu Dhabi, has become a symbol of gratitude and of hope. As the world's tallest skyscraper at over 2,700 feet, the rocket-like tower is expected to stimulate and oversee Dubai's revival as a global business hub. Nevertheless, the gamble of betting on spectacular skyscrapers to draw in global capital has its limits, and the city has become a symbol of over-leverage. In contrast, Shanghai and Hong Kong are deeply anchored in the world's most dynamic economy, the so-called "banker to the world." But are there, even in Chinese mega-cities, political hazards to the leveraging powers of urban spectacles?

II. The Hyperbuilding: The Hyperspace Moves East

The role of the state in building exceptional structures and even entire cities has a long and venerated tradition in many Asian civilizations, and the current state-sponsored construction of hypermodern urban spaces reveals a political urgency that surpasses urban developments elsewhere. Among developing countries, political investments in architectural icons have been crucial in establishing a particular modern national identity. Postcolonial nations in earlier decades, however, have sought to imprint their global signature by building new capitals that spoke to universalist values. In *The Modernist City*, James Holston (1989) identifies how the internal contradictions of modernist urban planning were played out in the design of a futurist Brasilia. But Holston argues that this image of an ideal city and its utopian promises of democracy failed in the daunting social realities of an emerging nation. On the opposite side of the world, New York architect Louis I. Kahn designed a capital complex for Dhaka, the capital of post-Independence Bangladesh. Kahn's template blended elements of Bengali architecture with a modernist sense of governing and clarity; the complex was to be an island of rational governance in the midst of a chaotic city. The utopian urban projects in Brasilia and Dhaka both shared beliefs that the formal structure of modernist architecture had the capacity to transform the political structure and habitus of emerging countries in accordance with the purportedly universal principles of enlightened modernity.

By contrast, contemporary Asian countries seek eye-catching urban landmarks that cannot be easily read as bearing the imprimatur of democratic modernity or capitalist triumphalism. They do not stand as integrated material metaphors of a hoped-for single modernist future. Viewing urban aesthetics through the lens of what he understands as a unified global process, Jameson claims that in the "post-industrial era," the logic of multinational capitalism erases barriers between cultures, languages and nations in a "postmodern hyperspace" of capitalist mirage (1991: 44). Jameson's conception of a multicultural hyperspace where people lose the capacity to locate and orient themselves echoes Guy Debord's (1995) observation that in the image-saturated environment, the spectacle has come to mediate the relationship between people by inducing in them the false feeling of an imaginary commonality in apparently shared spectatorship. While one can easily agree that the hyperspace can have a disorienting effect and that a virtual world may reshape social relationships, it would be a stretch to thereby maintain that urban-dwellers also lose a sense of their ties to the nation. Especially in emergent countries, a surfeit of images, cultures, and peoples in the cities becomes an index of national development. Globalized urban milieus are by definition pulsating with the constant mixing and remixing of

Figure 8.1   The CCTV tower, Beijing
Source: courtesy of the Office for Metropolitan Architecture (OMA), The Netherlands.

disparate signs and symbols from business, media, culture, and politics. In China, the wildly entangled and discordant signs of unfettered capitalism, rampant consumerism, cosmopolitan lifestyles, and political authoritarianism are the expected mediated chaos that goes with *Chinese* urban growth. The kind of hyperspaces opening up in Shanghai, Shenzhen, and Beijing are distinctive from, say, postmodern Los Angeles in that the sexy handiwork of borderless capitalism bears the heavy imprint of China's state power, and cannot be understood outside a reconfigured aesthetics of this power.

At the beginning of this chapter, I quoted Koolhaas' remarks that since the 9/11 attacks on New York City, "the parallel universe in China" (and, one may add, Seoul, Singapore, etc.) has become the space of international architectural design. Koolhaas has long been interested in the potential of architecture and urban planning to contribute to the formulation of culture worldwide. He observes that "Beijing has become the staging ground for the definitive urban design for the twenty-first century" (Ellis n.d.). As the co-designer of the Chinese Central Television headquarters (see Figure 8.1), Koolhaas self-interestedly claims that the hyperbuilding will "revolutionize" the Asian city landscape, as well as the world of urban architecture. Such assertions have inspired questions about the role of radical architecture in a historical moment of emerging autocratic states. Will Koolhaas and his partner Ole Scheeren of the firm OMA (Office for Metropolitan Architecture, the Netherlands) participate in the opening of the forbidding Chinese state, or will they simply help build a spectacular hyperspace of sovereignty?

Post-9/11, East Asian countries are the ones with the deep pockets and the political will to commission revolutionary buildings. As Scheeren has remarked, without apology, "Historically, architects have built for those in power. How else are great buildings made? Or paid for?" But Asian sovereign wealth funds are only part of the explanation for artistic turn to Asian cities. The OMA architects defended what they considered to be rare opportunities for pushing the boundaries of global architecture, and using architecture to push open closed societies. For instance, the building spree leading up to the 2008 Beijing Olympics was viewed by an international cast of designers as an opportunity to inject, via avant-garde architecture, conditions of "accessibility," "accountability," "transparency," and a "new publicness" in a politically repressive society (Fong 2007). Western critics have asked whether these buildings both configure and symbolize potential freedoms that are denied by the state, or whether "starchitects" are engaging in a kind of propaganda for autocratic regimes (Zalewski 2005).

Another misgiving about Asian cities stocking up on impressive towers and structures is that the availability of huge funds and cheap labor in Asia marks a post-utopian opportunism that destroys the traditional character of the city. There are the ethics of building an extravagant foreign-designed spectacle (the CCTV project cost over $1 billion) in a developing country, and the eviction of hundreds of residents from the building site. Furthermore, only foreign firms were invited to bid for high-profile projects in Beijing, while established Chinese architectural firms that cut their teeth on socialist designs were bypassed. City planners and Chinese architects worry that such prestige structures have no connection to the surrounding landscape. For instance, the Chinese partner of a Shanghai firm complains, "When you have gargantuan projects created by administrative fiat, it looks spectacular in a photograph, but that's not the recipe for a livable city" (Frangos and Chang 2003). The criticisms echo objections by Jane Jacobs to plans for expressways that threatened to ruin the vitality of Manhattan neighborhoods in the 1960s (1993 [1963]). And unlike the Singaporean model, this project is not intended by officials to be replicable by other aspiring cities as a model for integrated urban development; its very unlivable and unwelcoming qualities, and the emphatic discord of the building from its site, are a mark of its unique character and role in Beijing's future.

Beyond the worry of preserving old urban character, critics making the post-utopian charge objected to its initiation by a repressive state. As a US-based architect, Sze Tsung Leong, notes, the CCTV structure can only be built in a country with an autocratic tradition of large-scale destruction and rebuilding of the urban landscape (while dislocating huge populations in the process) in order to mark regime change (Leong 2004). Koolhaas has, somewhat elliptically, defended the destruction of some districts of historical architecture (*hutong*) in the construction of the CCTV project as "sacrificial zones" that are necessary to allow other zones to be "tourist free" (Koolhaas and OMA 2004: 129). The sacrifice of antiquated districts is not taken lightly (as in land expropriated for the construction of condominium towers, as is the case elsewhere in Beijing), but to establish a new base of state power to which foreign tourists are not especially welcome. The attraction for OMA seems to be that only state-driven projects can secure the extensive funds, population clearance, and the mobilization of resources needed to break ground for a new kind of publicness! The CCTV center is a building of barbaric beauty that presides over four city blocks in China's capital, facing off with the towers of corporate capitalism. It gives material figuration to an autocratic state grappling with the global flows in and out of a distinctive kind of hyperspace. Let us take a brief look at the Koolhaas project as a design.

The CCTV hyperbuilding

The headquarters of the CCTV is giant colossus that appears to straddle Beijing's new Central Business District, outside the Third Ring Road. Unlike the Forbidden City model laid out in rigid symmetric enclosures, Koolhaas' design defies stability; "the scary aliveness" of his design displays "elasticity, creep, shrinkage, sagging, bending (and) buckling" (Koolhaas and OMA 2004: 129). The architectural forms play with the vertical and transversal possibilities of disjointed connections, combining features of vertical overlook, sky-bridges, and ground-level flows so that instead of two separate towers (of seventy stories each) there is "a single, integrated loop." The continuous series of vertical and horizontal sections links different realms of news administration, broadcasting, studios, and program production. The overhang between the two towers includes public spaces for canteens and a public viewing deck (162 meters above ground; see Figure 8.2). This "single, condensed hyperbuilding" houses 200 television stations and such a big population that it becomes an urban center in itself (*China Daily* 2004). An entire building as a self-enclosed city suggests something like the Pentagon, the largest office building in the world, which is only slightly bigger than the CCTV fortress.

Bert de Muynck (2004), a European architect, characterizes Koolhaas' architectural intervention in China as "not phallic but vaginal, one that contributes to the modernization of communist culture and to the definition of architecture." This interpretation registers a shift in the symbolism of modern architecture from a tower reaching for the stars to an enclosing structure that absorbs power into the body politic. Designed according to

Figure 8.2   The cantilever joining the CCTV towers
Source: courtesy of the Office for Metropolitan Architecture (OMA), The Netherlands.

the principles of "connectivity and opportunity," this hyperbuilding in downtown Beijing configures a kind of publicness that is circumscribed and enclosed within an immense trapezoidal loop. An army of media producers and protectors are gathered in a centralized infrastructure to manage the risks and security of information flows. Koolhaas' engineering skills in designing the building seems to achieve a diagnostic synthesis of the various information technologies and practices that will shape the Chinese picture and projection of the world. The very design of this outlandish structure broadcasts the state agency's role in regulating transnational flows while maintaining a network of enclosure.

CCTV and technological prowess

In 2006, Chinese Premier Wen Jiabao articulated a new policy that favors "independent innovation" (*zizhu chuangxin*) as a new emphasis in China's development project. The state recognizes that at stake in China's emergence as a global power is the production and control of ideas, information, culture, and invention that can be disseminated across the world. Part and parcel of this emergence, then, will be the terms in which this dissemination can be managed, stimulated, and controlled. In this broader context of China's desire to exert cultural influence at home and abroad, CCTV, as China's biggest state-controlled news organization, has spent billions of dollars not only on the construction of this revolutionary flagship building, but also on the expansion of facilities to launch respected international news organizations overseas.

CCTV, Chinese Central Television, is thus both a state mouthpiece and the largest conglomerate in China vested with the responsibility for controlling media in the name of "cultural security." Despite joining the World Trade Organization in 2001, CCTV has not significantly liberalized local content, but maintains control over the TV medium by defining "that which can be made commercial, that which cannot, and that which is in-between" (Wang 2008: 250). CCTV regulators favor non-controversial topics such as finance and economy, science and technology, leisure and lifestyle, but tend to control news and TV documentaries with domestic content. At the same time, CCTV is worried about the increasing presence of foreign media corporations such as CNN, CNBC, Bloomberg, and other global channels, whose broadcasting rights are limited to diplomatic compounds, elite hotels, and Guangdong Province. Nevertheless, the foreign media exerts its influence in mass market offerings such as game shows, talk shows, sports programs, and dramas that are accessible across much of the country (Wang 2008: 249–51).

The CCTV headquarters is therefore a gigantic state presence, symbolically and materially, in the world of global network media. The structure houses a hybrid state agency and commercial broadcaster, with 10,000 workers running the sixteen national channels, many broadcasting on a twenty-four hour cycle. The audience is estimated at over one billion people, and some Chinese intellectuals have charged the center with whitewashing the news, especially on the touchy issues of human rights and minorities, for a susceptible public. As a state-owned TV monopoly, it has been called one of the largest propaganda entities in the world. Indeed, the CCTV building was completed in time for the Beijing Olympics so that it could display the state's "charm offensive" by showcasing the games for an international audience. CCTV has gone global by opening a multilingual channel that broadcasts Chinese views to the world. The hyperbuilding thus materializes, in a dramatic way, the "evolving" nature of Chinese propaganda.

Premier Hu Jintao has called for "raising China's cultural propaganda abilities," which "have already become a decisive factor for a national culture's strength" (Feuerberg 2009). The new strategy is to have CCTV replace propaganda (*xuanchuan*) with explanation (*shuoming*) and a more "informational" approach to the news. Such declarations, especially in the midst of on-again, off-again crackdowns on artists, journalists, lawyers, activists, and ordinary dissenters, seem to teach the lesson that selective news is more sophisticated than sheer propaganda. With its immense digital network, the CCTV machinery permits the technicalization of information control as a way to depoliticize the content of propaganda, to control domestic cyber-activities, and deflect global Internet penetration.

The CCTV headquarters is thus central to the state defense of official conceptions of Chinese culture, values, and identity in the midst of ubiquitous digital and news flows, as well as disseminating the definitive normative judgment for Chinese publics on matters of official political correctness. The development of an elaborate communications apparatus facilitates the strengthening of censorship of information available to private citizens and corporations. Before and after the Beijing Olympics, minority protests led to the shutdown of Internet activities in parts of Xinjiang Province. Since the Olympics, there has been a severe tightening of electronic and Internet communications, mainly in the name of uprooting pornography, piracy, and other illegal activities, or activities deemed problematic for national harmony. The authorities have closed hundreds of web sites, including the blog of artist Ai Wei Wei, which had posted 5,000 names of children who died in the 2008 Sichuan earthquake. An anti-pornography campaign against netizens (web-based citizens) has been extended to controls on texting by cellphone users found to use "unhealthy" key words (LaFraniere 2010). The increased digital prowess of CCTV is reflected in extensive cyber-surveillance and interruptions of information flows that are viewed as detrimental to state authority.

CCTV is an emerging force as well in controlling the influx of foreign news, information, and entertainment, both on media networks and in cyberspace. Since 2006, Microsoft, Google, and Yahoo had complied with earlier demands to filter or remove political content in their China services. In mid-2009, the Chinese government demanded that all new computers to be sold in the country must carry pre-installed filtering software. The move to control free access to information is formally justified as an anti-pornography campaign by the Ministry of Health. The campaign is called "Green Dam Youth Escort" (*lvba huaji huhang*), a name that suggests the healthy protection of the young from informational pollution. Although the demand was later withdrawn by the Industry and Information Technology Ministry, the domestic charge was that pornography was easily accessed on cyberspace, and therefore search engines must be strictly regulated.

Beyond the state objective of controlling the content of foreign media, CCTV technological capacities are also deployed for generating economic gains. For instance, global media corporations such as Rupert Murdoch's News Corp, Disney, Time Warner, and Viacom, among others, have created vast new media markets and audiences in China. CCTV seeks to nurture the rise of a Chinese media world that can meet these challenges by promoting Chinese cultural content. At the same time, China's new communication technologies have been linked to the escalation of cyber-attacks on the security systems of Internet firms and other kinds of foreign companies. While it has been difficult to trace Internet sabotage to the Chinese state, in 2010 the mix of cyber-censorship and cyber-attacks prompted Google to withdraw from the Chinese mainland and relocate to Hong Kong.

But whereas foreign critics have focused on freedom-of-information issues, what is often overlooked is how cyber-attacks create a bigger space for Chinese media companies to expand their opportunities and influence. There are over 430 million Internet users in China, served mainly by private companies such as Baidu.com, Alibaba.com, and Sohu.com. Already, with Google.cn's departure from the mainland, many local cyber start-ups both mimic and seek to replace foreign web sites such as Facebook, Twitter, and so on. More important, the new CCTV center has laid the technological foundation for the creation of a government-run search engine as well as an online video site that will compete with Chinese cyber-companies in controlling the Internet in China. An official of Xinhua, the official state-run news agency, explains that the state-run search engine platform is "part of the country's broader efforts to safeguard its information security and push forward the robust, healthy, and orderly development of China's new media industry" (Barboza 2010). In other words, the CCTV complex is a singular expression of the state's desire to scientifically diagnose what it considers as a cultural security issue, and to effectively counter the powers of free-floating information managed by private Internet companies. The CCTV complex acts as a state filter for political news at home, and also a national battleground for China's fight against what it calls "information imperialism" by the West (Buruma 2001).

The new media technologies also help to extend China's global reach. CCTV is opening more news bureaus that publish and broadcast to international audiences by broadcasting in English, French, and Spanish, as well as other languages. There is a plan to create a twenty-four hour news channel modeled on Al Jazeera, a media outlet for the Arab-speaking world, that would reach the United States, Europe, and other regions. The CCTV headquarters stamps Beijing as a global media center, and in its technical and symbolic forms, enables China's competition with Western media outlets in shaping international news, spreading Chinese cultural values, and improving the nation's image globally. More broadly, China often views foreign arts and films as hostile to or inappropriately interfering in Chinese internal policies, and thus the new and expanded media agency plays the crucial role of patrolling the content of outside media production and its portrayal of matters deemed to be "Chinese."[4]

Whether intended or not, the surface of the CCTV monolith brilliantly displays this tension between propaganda and news, obfuscation and transparency. The net-like gridwork on the building's glassy façades seems to give expression to the flows of information that enter and leave the structure, not freely but as though through a sieve. On smoggy days, which are plentiful in Beijing, the latticework is even more visible, as a kind of political matrix, while the rest of the building dissolves into the polluted atmosphere.

The view from below

The sophisticated building design seems to have elicited a range of reactions from ordinary people. In China, public symbolism plays a big role in political culture, shaping ideas about politics in a way that can preempt public debates. The CCTV design is an especially rich target for all kinds of allusions about the staggering nature of state power. Western journalists have compared the building to a blank TV screen, a particle accelerator, and a deformed doughnut, and other rather decontextualized terms that reference Koolhaas' playful aesthetics that belie the media center's function in conquering the airwaves. What has been the reception of people in Beijing to this startling structure?

Chinese citizens have found the CCTV puzzling, and out of place or resonance with their notion of stable and staid modernist buildings. At the same time, however, to many others, the angled arch formed by conjoining the two towers suggests a grand gateway into the heart of political Beijing. Other metaphors the media center calls up include a twisted Chinese ideograph for "mouth" (*kou*); that is, a figuration that alludes to the building's role as the mouthpiece of the government. But to some Chinese netizens, the CCTV structure seems to frame a "knowledge window" (*zhichuang*) onto a new kind of architectural space.

Cultural theorists have argued that the legibility of the urban landscape often escapes the experiences of pedestrians and viewers. What is socially marginal ("the everyday, "the low life," the pornographic) can provide central symbols to the experience of urban life (cf., Stallybrass and White 1986). The CCTV center viewed from the street level or on the web site has generated a slew of transgressive jokes that poke fun at Koolhaas (who has become a household name among the urban elite), but also at the state's pretensions at media control. The squat and angled shape of the headquarters has inspired nicknames such as "big shorts" (*da kuzi*) or boxer shorts (*da kuzha*). Comparisons of the CCTV structure to a giant toilet or the public staging of a pornographic act mock an emerging psychic topography shaped by reconfigured relationships between foreign architects, the powerful state, and ordinary citizens. Cyber-jokes about Koolhaas' hyperbuilding trace the multiple displacements that cut local people off from massive urban transformations.

In June 2009, a Beijing architect, Xiao Mo, attacked the CCTV headquarters as "hindquarters." Xiao had earlier made a summary of posted netizen comments opposing the behemoth's design, and charged the media for not reporting dissenting opinions to the general public. With this design, was Koolhaas playing a cruel joke on "1.3 billion Chinese people"? Mo reports his shock at the finished building, which when viewed at an oblique angle, suggests a kneeling figure with its rear end (the overhang) poised in relation to a nearby annex tower (*Danwei* 2009; and see Figure 8.3). While Mo appears to be genuinely horrified by what he sees as Koolhaas' "genital worshipping" structure, netizens have had a field day posting pornographic CCTV images, some of them featuring a satiated Mao. Cyber-smuttery also takes a jab at the state, recasting CCTV as CCAV (Chinese Central Adult Video), thus suggesting that political vulgarity is part of the state broadcasting content.

The proliferation of building pornography compels the CCTV to undertake the embarrassing chore of stamping out cyber-jokes. In the run-up to the Sixtieth Anniversary of the nation's founding, in 2009, the Central Propaganda Department handed down directives to various departments to eliminate all web site and Twitter references to the "CCTV Porn Joke" the "CCTV big pants designer," "CCTV building, sex organ" and even "Koolhass, CCTV" (McCue 2009). The mixed reception to CCTV has made it Beijing's most controversial structure. Among Chinese architects, there are calls for rethinking the cultural trend of falling "in line with the West" (*Danwei* 2009). Furthermore, if viewed in non-pornographic terms, the mammoth building can seem, to passers-by below, a threatening presence looming above. Instead of hindquarters, the hawk-like angle of the cantilevered top can be experienced by pedestrians as symbolizing being put under state surveillance. As elsewhere in Asian cities, urban pornography rewrites the meaning of controversial architectural space, producing an underground narrative that subverts and overturns the symbolic hierarchy and dignity vested in overweening power structures.

The view from the West

Western critics view the flow of cutting-edge urban designs to Asia with a mix of hope and foreboding. The relocation of radical architecture to East

Figure 8.3 A view of the CCTV figure poised next to an adjacent tower
Source: courtesy of Ole Scheeren and the Office for Metropolitan Architecture (OMA),
The Netherlands.

Asian cities has been viewed as a blatant cooptation of architectural
innovation by repressive states. Shannon Matten notes that "[a]s the medium
of television grows increasingly decentralized through digitalization and
mobilization, and as China's state media faces increasing competition from
other media in other forms and from other places, the symbolic significance
of a huge, monolithic structure will become even more important in signally
the continuing power of this state institution" (Matten 2008: 869–908).
Edwin Heathcote of *The Financial Times*, while admiring the "staggering and
innovative" CCTV structure, bemoans that "China has co-opted architectural

and artistic radicalism in a manner that might be described as visionary, or perhaps as shrewd, or perhaps as coolly cynical." He calls the structure "modernism without utopia" (Heathcote 2007: 17). For Matten and Heathcote, it appears that whatever "cool" cynicism Koolhaas exhibited had been in seeking authoritarian sites to stage his outlandish designs, thus perverting the association between radical architecture and modern utopianism.

Koolhaas had expressed the desire to use risky architecture to open up authoritarian China, but has his experiment misfired in playing with the politics of opening and closure? The CCTV project is not widely viewed as a monument to transparency and openness, but rather as a condensed symbol of deep tensions as Beijing seeks to be simultaneously an open city and a forbidden capital. To many ordinary Chinese, the CCTV headquarters is experienced as a massive affront to their cultural sensibilities, a kind of collective urban shame that may induce a retreat from Western urban conceptions. For the Chinese state, however, the stunning hyperbuilding has established Beijing as a global stage, a hyperspace that is dominated by Chinese sovereignty.

Conclusion

This chapter has compared and contrasted two related sets of distinctive practices associated with the hyperbuilding in ambitious East Asian cities. A notion of exception allows us to identify the variable uses of spectacular spaces for accumulating capital and for raising the metropolitan ranking in the world at large. Hyperbuilding as a verb refers to the infrastructural enrichment of the urban landscape in order to generate speculations on the city's future. Hyperbuilding as a noun identifies a mega-state project that transforms a city into a global hyperspace. Hyperbuilding is about the world-aspirations of the state, and my approach challenges studies that disconnect urban transformations from the national environment and aspirations, or view spectacular spaces as the exclusive tool of global capitalism.

A focus on exceptional city spaces highlights the politics of urban transformations and the various processes and built forms that compete to position the metropolis on the global stage, and the nation as a global actor. However, there is no guarantee that spectacular zones will realize urban dreams of world conquest. The over-leveraged city of spectacle or the arriviste nation is especially susceptible to global market gyrations abroad, and subversive disruptions at home, or perhaps, as in the Malaysian case, to continue on unnoticed.

Frenzied over-building in Asian cities gives us a picture of what happens when powerful emerging countries configure their own hyperspaces of sovereignty. The pivotal urban spectacle is not global capital alone but also sovereign power. This should not be surprising, as massive public buildings were also erected at the peak of European empires. What is different about the contemporary emergence of an architectural hyperspace in Asian cities is the unease it has stirred among theorists of modernity. There is a new questioning about their capacity to interpret contemporary trajectories of monumental change when it happens outside the Western world. Radical architecture is responding to profound geopolitical shifts, and rapidly innovating Asian cities rupture conventional understandings of urban innovation as either modernist utopia or dystopia. While urban spectacles in Asia have been defined by international actors and designs, Asian cities and political codes are also shaping how we use and think through contemporary architectural forms and spaces.

Notes

1 Beijing was estimated to have spent US$3.5 billion on the Olympics, while Shanghai's preparation for the 2010 exhibition was estimated to have cost over US$4.2 billion.
2 There is no space in this chapter to discuss the synergy between spectacular spaces and spectacular events in promoting the urban standing of Asian cities.
3 For examples of this, see www.seoul.go.kr or http://wdeseoul.kr
4 For instance, the Chinese authorities have protested the showing, at home and abroad, of documentaries and films produced by foreigners that deal with sensitive topics such as Tibetan or Uyghur minorities, or the victims of the 2008 Sichuan earthquake, subjects that raise questions about the actions of the Chinese state.

References

Barboza, D. (2010) New China search engine will be state-controlled. *New York Times*, August 14, p. B4.

Beech, H. (2005) Ye olde Shanghai. *Times Magazine*, February 7; http://www.time.com/time/magazine/article/0,9171,1025219,00.html (accessed December 28, 2009).

Bunnell, T. (2004) *Malaysia, Modernity, and the Multimedia Super Corridor*. London: RoutledgeCurzon.

Buruma, I. (2001) Battling the information barbarians. *The Wall Street Journal*, January 30–31, p. W1.

China Daily (2004) Kool enough for Beijing? March 2; http://www.chinadaily.com.cn/English/doc/2004-03/02/content_31080 (accessed August 6, 2006).

Ellis, R., CB (n.d.) The CCTV tower: central icon of post-urban Beijing? See http://www.cbre.com/NR/rdonlyres/0B07294B-814C-450C-9A6E-C1DA079AE7D0/0/CCTVTowerMay07.pdf (accessed July 1, 2009).

Danwei (2009) Rem Koolhaas and CCTV architectural porn. August 20; http://www.danwei.org/architecture/rem_koolhaas_and_cctv_porn.php (accessed December 28, 2009).

de Muynck, B. (2004) The end of the skyscraper as we know it: from CCG to CCTV. *Archis* 5.

Debord, G. (1995) *The Society of Spectacle.* New York: Zone Books.

Feuerberg, G. (2009) Commission hears how China's propaganda is evolving and expanding. *The Epoch Times,* May 20; http://www.theepochtimes.com/n2/content/view/17100/ (accessed December 28, 2009).

Fong, M. (2007) A deformed doughnut? No, China's TV tower. *The Wall Street Journal,* November 7, pp. B1, B8.

Frangos, A. and Chang, L. (2003) Architects go east. *The Wall Street Journal,* December 17, pp. B1, B8.

Harvey, D. (1989) *The Condition of Postmodernity.* Oxford: Blackwell, p. 156.

Heathcote, E. (2007) Modernism without Utopia. *Financial Times,* December 20, p. 17.

Holston, J. (1989) *The Modernist City: an anthropological critique of Brasilia.* Chicago: The University of Chicago Press.

Jacobs, J. (1993 [1963]) *The Death and Life of Great American Cities.* New York: Random House.

Jameson, F. (1991) *Postmodernism, or the Cultural Logic of Late Capitalism.* Durham, NC: Duke University Press.

King, A. and Kusno, A. (2000) On Be(ij)ing in the world: postmodernism, "globalization," and the making of transnational space in China. In A. Dirlik and X. Zhang (eds.) *Postmodernism and China.* Durham, NC: Duke University Press, pp. 41–67.

Koolhaas, R. and OMA (2004) Beijing manifesto. *Wired 08/2004,* 1, 122; http://www.wired.com/wired/archive/12.08/images/FF_120_beijing.pdf (accessed December 28, 2009).

LaFraniere, S. (2010) China to scan text messages to spot "unhealthy content." *The New York Times,* January 20, p. A5.

Lash, S. and Lury, C. (2007) *Global Culture Industry.* Cambridge, UK: Polity Press, pp. 141–8.

Leong, S.T. (2004) The traditions of Chinese cities. *32 Magazine,* Winter; http://www.szetsungleong.com/texts_traditions.htm (accessed December 28, 2009).

Matten, S. (2008) Broadcasting space: China Central Television's new headquarters. *International Journal of Communication* 2, 869–908.

McCue, W. (2009) The latest directives from the Ministry of Truth. Working paper, US Embassy, Beijing, China, August 31.

Ong, A. (2005) Ecologies of expertise: assembling flows, managing citizenship. In A. Ong and S.J. Collier (eds.) *Global Assemblages: technology, politics, and ethics as anthropological problems.* Malden, MA: Blackwell, pp. 337–53.

Ong, A. (2006) *Neoliberalism as Exception: mutations in sovereignty and citizenship.* Durham, NC: Duke University Press.

Ong, A. (2007) Please stay: pied-a-terre subjects in the megacity. *Citizenship Studies* 11(1), 83–93.

Simmel, G. (1900) A chapter on the philosophy of value. *American Journal of Sociology* 5, 577–603.

Stallybrass, P. and White, A. (1986) *The Politics and Poetics of Transgression.* Ithaca, NY: Cornell University Press.

Wang, J. (2008) CCTV and the advertising media. In *Brand New China: advertising, media, and commercial culture.* Cambridge, MA: Harvard University Press, pp. 249–51.

Zalewski, D. (2005) Intelligent design. *The New Yorker,* March 14; http://www.newyorker.com/archive/2005/03/14/050314fa_fact_zalewski

Part III
New Solidarities

Figure 9.1 Water worlds: Infosys's oasis pools in contrast to the contaminated water canals of Bangalore
Sources: left, photograph by Michael Goldman, 2007; right, photograph by Wesley Longhofer, 2007 – used by permission of the author.

9

Speculating on the Next World City

Michael Goldman

If you believe in the India story, the outlook for real estate, which is a critical part of the whole development process, is bright.

Anurag Mathur, Cushman & Wakefield, 2008

Deutsche Bank was only being more explicit than most when it advertised that it "needed" a 25% rate of return annually – from economies growing in single digits.

Robert Wade, 2009

The city, as a domain of immanence, thus remains an open-ended provocation to government.

Osborne and Rose (1999)

Introduction: Believing in the India Story

In spite of the recent global financial crisis, capital is flooding India's cities like never before. Curiously, much of the surge has come from US hedge and derivative funds, the chief antagonists of the recent global economic collapse. Those who believed in the "American story" – that the US economy was taken down by overly extended new homeowners – have come to realize that the adjustable rate mortgage market reflected only a tiny fraction of the whole speculative bubble that burst across the world; US mortgage debt was worth about $10 trillion, a drop in the bucket as compared to the $700 trillion derivatives and hedge fund market. Once it became clear that large-scale speculation was the foundation on which the world's banks, investment firms, and insurance companies stood, governments had little choice but to offer multi-billion dollar bailouts or risk total economic collapse.

Worlding Cities: Asian Experiments and the Art of Being Global, First Edition.
Edited by Ananya Roy and Aihwa Ong.
© 2011 Blackwell Publishing Ltd. Published 2011 by Blackwell Publishing Ltd.

By mid-2009, these investors were looking elsewhere for "value," and one of their first stops has been India (Figure 9.1). In short time, foreign investment firms have created multi-billion dollar infrastructure funds in support of World Bank and Government of India plans to transform India's problem-ridden cities into "world cities," purportedly to catapult India into the top tier of the global economy. As India's Planning Commission has recently stated, India hopes to raise $1 trillion in the next five years on infrastructure, half of which must come from private investors.[1]

This chapter highlights a set of interrelated phenomena occurring in the name of world-city making both within Indian cities and across aspiring cities throughout Asia and the Arabian Gulf, where the imperative to speculate, and the incitement to overcome the "stasis" of urban life with a globalized and virtuous entrepreneurialism, meet. We can call this trend *speculative urbanism*. A prime example of this is the way in which competing cities have leveraged their urban infrastructure – housing complexes, water-fronts, city centers – to attract the capital to improve city life. Just as specu-lative profits often come from perceived confidence in that market, these worlding practices too rely on the confidence that rates of return can be high for investments, *at different stages of* the urban worlding process. Since the "hot capital" of hedge funds is never invested for more than the short term (e.g., weeks, months), national governments and international finance institutions are creating the institutional apparatus of guarantees to insure that investors will continue to come long after the hot-capital players have moved on. New urban planning takes as its starting point the imperatives of the rapid turnover of capital, and thus, new mechanisms of governance are being developed in anticipation of such turbulence, as we shall see below. In this chapter, I argue that networks of financiers investing billions of dollars across portfolios of urban projects have had a demonstrable influence on the way in which local urban governments are retooled for integration into the culture and practices of the global economy. This string of overlapping practices, forces, and events can be understood as a new form of transna-tional urbanism, a speculative urbanism.

This process of luring and tying down investors, while also anticipating their imminent departure, has shaped the type of world-city projects being financed as well as the informal regulatory structure and citizen–state relations in these rapidly urbanizing worlds. As investors play one city off another, so too do governments, trying to out-*Shanghai* Shanghai. The sacrifices of residents of Shanghai and its periphery are ones that are invoked for other to follow, creating a conduct of conduct for world-city citizenship (Lin 2007; Ong and Zhang 2008). In Bangalore, residents are both asked to sacrifice as the Chinese have, as well as try to fit into the idealized imagery of the "Bangalore model" being mobilized in far-flung sites such as Dalian, China, and Glasgow, Scotland – one that few Bangaloreans would recognize from their own experiences (*Business Standard India* 2008; Press Trust of India 2008; Goldman forthcoming). In sum, the contours of this phenomenon of speculative urbanism can be understood through the tracing of four tendencies.

The first is a new *architecture of investment capital*. In India, in 2007, Dubai's largest developer and real-estate firm, Limitless LLC, committed $15 billion to finance and build India's first privately owned small city, India's "Knowledge City," the first of five multi-billion dollar private "greenfield" cities on the newly urbanizing rural periphery of Bangalore. Using foreign capital to build – and govern – private cities is only one dimension: similar to Karen Ho's thesis from her ethnography of Wall Street (Ho 2009), I argue that speculative investors (and their shareholders) are not only demanding higher rates of return on public infrastructure investments, but that they are also inculcating a *culture of liquidity* in the expectations of the way such capital-intensive projects are set up and run. Keeping capital liquid and mobile not only reflects the size, pace, and intensity of movement of capital from one project to another; it also affects the culture of government and its technologies of urban management.

Hence, we find a new volatility to speculation, with conditionalities. World-city projects are being designed so that large institutional investors can remain vested long enough to capture the initial speculative spike in value, and leave. Consequently, urban managers must package a string of deals along the life of a large-scale project so that different types of investors can gain differently. Since many projects on the drawing board never make it to the building stage, early investors expect the highest profits, as they are assumed to have taken the biggest risk. Yet projects at the building stage can often be delayed for years due to numerous social, political, and environmental obstacles. Although we tend to focus on the on-the-street public protests against large projects that displace thousands of people, we often fail to note that major investors also make major demands.[2] Since the mid-2000s, some key pension, hedge, and derivative fund managers have shifted investments to global South cities, albeit only under the conditions (i.e., government guarantees) that their rates of returns will be larger than those in the "less risky" West.

Second, a new *architecture of urban governance* is rapidly emerging. Although the scholarly literature on displacement has focused primarily on the rural, city building has now overtaken the center of mass displacement in the global South, as the idea of world-city construction has become global, and land has become viewed by planners and investors as the key obstacle.[3] Chinese and Indian cities, for example, are no longer receiving their budget allocations from their central governments; instead they must generate public resources from the direct sale or long-term lease of land (Lin 2007; Ong and Zhang 2008).[4] Hence, the practice of selling land and displacing denizens to finance public goods and services has become one of the primary jobs of world-city government. In Bangalore, this is changing the business of, and people's relations with, government, in which a *speculative government* has become the new political rationality, and their primary interaction with government agents is over land, whether it is the new agency with oversight over the airport, or older ones overseeing water, sanitation, or education. As many people must adapt, cope, and mobilize new opportunities in order to become viable world-city citizens, one sees tensions emerge over the process of world-city subject formation (i.e., how one can conduct oneself in order to survive the pressures of speculation-based change).

Third, these investment strategies reflect an intensification of *inter-urban competitiveness and inter-referencing* (see Aihwa Ong, Introduction, this volume). As global expertise on world cities suggests, it has become necessary for policy-makers to enter the competitive bidding process which pits cities against each other, making one's city attractive to global investors even as it may compromise people's rights locally. Spectacular endeavors in Dubai generated huge profits by 2007, and reinvestment strategies for "dreamland" urban projects in India, Jordan, Saudi Arabia, Vietnam, Russia, Turkey, Lebanon, and Egypt (Elsheshtawy 2010). But by early 2009, the Dubai market had lost three-fourths of its value, skyscrapers stood empty, and grand designs in Moscow and Bangalore have been scrapped. Although volatility and market crashes drew investors from the United States and the Arabian Gulf to a whole new tier of world cities, they have also caught those captive populations off guard. These new inter-urban dynamics, when combined with those discussed elsewhere in this volume, produce a frenzied exuberance and undulating social turbulence across urban landscapes.

Fourth, these urban worlding strategies do not emerge from thin air, but from the peripatetic hard work of transnational policy networks (Goldman 2005, 2007), creating a *global architecture of expertise on cities*, led by consultants (e.g., McKinsey, PricewaterhouseCoopers), UN agencies (e.g., UN Habitat, the UN Development Program), international finance institutions (e.g., the World Bank, the Asian Development Bank), and global forums (e.g., the World Cities Summit [Singapore in 2010], the World Bank's Cities Alliance, the Global City Forum, the Global Cities Dialogue, the C40 Cities Mayors Summit), often co-sponsored by a combination of the above institutions and firms (e.g., Siemens, Philips, Veolia, Accenture, Limitless, Tamouh, Emaar). On one end of the spectrum, the World Bank and bilateral agencies are advocating the "urban turn" in lending and global managerialism; at the other end, environmental NGOs and experts have deemed cities as the new site of green innovation for carbon-cutting built environments, living spaces, transport systems, and the future of reduced greenhouse gas effects. Whereas 15 years ago, these actors deplored the violent and stagnant mega-cities of the Third World, today cities have become the fount of innovation and "best practices" for "ending poverty," sustainable lifestyles, and more. Indeed, the constellation of transnational policy actors from the Global Cities Forum and the Cities Alliance to the World Bank and PricewaterhouseCoopers have crystallized such claims into governance models and lending strategies, as the World Bank's influential 2009 report *Systems of Cities: harnessing urbanization and poverty alleviation* (World Bank 2009) duly notes.

But when China plans to build 100 global cities in the next two decades and India hopes to spend $1 trillion on infrastructure in the next five years – half from foreign market investors – the definitions of governance, green sustainability, and the urban take on new meanings. As we take a closer look at the sponsors and voices at these fora, the movers behind global policies and loan packages, and the investors and designers of world-city projects, we begin to see convergences worthy of further exploration.[5] The rationale for these urban worlding practices starts with the assumption that global South cities have been dying under the weight of mega-city problems such as overcrowdedness, virulent poverty, violence, corruption, and a culture of ineptitude that has made it hard for any national government or financial market to expect that cities such as Delhi or Rio could become drivers of an economy. Yet, against all odds, select cities are becoming economic power-houses that urban boosters are suggesting as models for learning and replication: Singapore and its city-state model of capital accumulation (as Chua Beng Huat notes in this volume), Shanghai and its massive infrastructural transformation, Dubai and its capital-flush real-estate sector, and Bangalore and its phenomenal IT industry. These "models" of urban transformation – when bolstered by key regulatory changes by states and new investment strategies by private equities and debt-financing firms – have incited ambitious master plans to *world* urban landscapes.

In a keynote speech in the Global Investors Summit in Delhi in July 2010, a prominent fund director declared that what we're seeing is a world of investment that is no longer "developed" (i.e., the West) versus "emerging" (i.e., Third World) markets, in which the latter is too risky for investors; on the contrary, it is a new world of "declining" in the cases of the U.S. and Europe versus "growth" markets in which most opportunities for high returns are in the Global South.[6] The question, this British fund manager presents with a flash of irony, is not just who wants to invest in India, but who is still willing to invest in the dying markets of the West. Large pension funds from California and Washington, Abu Dhabi, and China, he claimed, have plenty of capital and are eager to invest *if* urban governments offset huge risks of world-city projects with guarantees for attractive rates of return.

Hence, as Aihwa Ong argues in the Introduction, the *worlding of cities* is not a phenomenon derived, or trickling down, from the European experience;

world-city projects throughout Asia and the Middle East exhibit new dynamics across and within cities, even if, to some investors, such binaries as West versus East are comforting and strategically useful (Simone 2001). For example, an Asia-based North American pension-fund manger explained at this Delhi Summit that her clients require a much higher rate of return if they are to invest in India: If they get 12 percent in the United States, why should they expect anything less than 20 or 25 percent in India, to offset what she called the volatile "India risk" of doing business on the subcontinent? In response, this chapter asks: What political and discursive shifts have occurred such that the Indias of the world *can* now offer, and transnational investors *expect* to receive, such exorbitant profit rates from projects? What happens when the promise to "end poverty" and improve the quality of public services for all gets enacted through these investments?

Subsequent sections will introduce an alternative reading of recent Bangalore history, and present a schematic on how a world-city discourse gets constructed, travels, and gains traction. This chapter will then explain the nature of governmental changes occurring, review Bangalore's main world-city projects and their displacements, and explain how India's engine of urban growth – the phenomenal IT sector – may be contributing more to the permanence of a volatile and speculative urbanism than to an urban dreamscape of social opportunity and justice.

Provincializing "Old" Bangalore

In thinking through Bangalore's transformation, it is useful to start by asking from where this specific impetus of contemporary world-city-making came: How did certain discursive strategies bubble up to dominance, while many other alternative planning narratives became *provincialized?* Initially, Bangalore did not shift into world-city mode as part of a larger moral panic to refashion the Third World "mega-city," teeming with uncontrollable violence, wrenching poverty, and fetid living (Srinivas 2001). Until the IT explosion starting in the late 1980s, Bangalore was a comfortable middle-class town with secure union jobs in large public-sector research and manufacturing firms that fed into the high-end functions of the Indian state and economy (e.g., radar and satellite systems, telecommunications and space research, manufacturing equipment). A few years into the IT boom, Bangalore was not "burning" or a planet of slums. Instead, world-city making started when firms such as Texas Instruments asked for substantial upgrading of Bangalore's pleasant but small-town public facilities in order to survive in the fiercely competitive global IT sector.

Bangalore's largest employers, many opening in the early 1900s, were BEL (Bharat Electronics Ltd.), HAL (Hindustan Aeronautics Ltd.), ITI

(Indian Telephone Industries), HMT (Hindustan Machine Tools), BHEL (Bharat Heavy Electricals Ltd.), and Mysore Industrial and Testing Laboratory, which alongside the nation's top science institutes, such as the Indian Institute of Science, produced the "first wave" of India's IT revolution in the 1950s, in aeronautics, space research, radar and remote sensing, military equipment, and factory tool-making (Vyasulu and Reddy 1984; Heitzman 2004; Nair 2005). Bangalore's urban landscape had been shaped by the housing and industrial colonies for these plants and their workers and managers, with English medium schools, accessible and affordable housing, health clinics, shopping areas, bus lines, parks, and community centers where local organizations used to meet. As Bangalore-based economist Narendar Pani (2009) writes: "These townships [since incorporated into Bangalore city] covered hundreds of acres of land each, and in the case of the Aircraft Township of Hindustan Aeronautics, 2,847 acres (Nair, 2005: 89). These units attracted workers of varying skill levels from technologists to unskilled labor. A strongly unionized labor force meant that the lowest paid public sector employees fitted easily into the lower middle class of the rest of Bangalore. The children of all public sector workers then had access to Bangalore's English based technical education."[7]

The phenomenal growth of India's recent IT revolution led to the in-migration of the world's most profitable and innovative IT firms, plopping themselves down in cow pastures, spinach fields, and drained irrigation tanks on the southern and eastern outskirts of the city. Since most of what the IT sector produces is software coding and data management (Parthasarathy 2004), all of which can be transported globally via satellite and fiber-optic cables, firms could function and prosper on very little urban infrastructure.[8]

Ironically, it is only since the mid-1990s, *through the actual process* of making Bangalore into a world city, that Bangalore has developed "mega-city problems" rife with rapidly escalating social inequality, mass displacement and dispossession, the proliferation of slum settlements, increased community and ethnic violence and tensions, and epidemic public health crises due to severe water supply and sewage problems occurring in poor and working-class neighborhoods. Roads are over-the-top congested and vehicles spew such high levels of pollution that many motorcyclists travel around with bloodshot eyes and respiratory problems. How did India's "garden city" and "pensioner's paradise" become such a world-city nightmare?

The key movers and shakers for urban transformation in India's largest cities include coalitions of local business elites (e.g., the Confederation of Indian Industry and NASSCOM, the software industry's chamber of commerce), professionals from the IFIs and bilateral aid agencies, Indians living abroad, internationally connected NGOs, and India's elite urban bureaucrats and officials. Their approach overlaps with other globally circulating efforts promoting a "master plan" agenda, often privileging a single sector of the economy as an engine of rapid accumulation coupled with large infusions of external loans and investments for world-class urban infrastructure (see Bombay First and McKinsey 2003; PricewaterhouseCoopers 2005, 2007).[9]

At one public meeting in a middle-class neighborhood (February 2007), the city commissioner brashly declared what he considered it would take to turn Bangalore into a European-style world city: clear the city of its slums and bring in world-class amenities such as pubs and theaters. Meanwhile, city commissioners from other Indian cities have called for massive investment to convert crowded and run-down parts of town into entertainment complexes by tapping undervalued public spaces for privatized value creation that benefits what they imagine to be the new urban citizenry. These plans reflect more than discrete individual confessions, revelations, and logics; one finds them articulated in PowerPoint presentations from Pricewater houseCoopers staff, in bureaucrat training courses, urban planning exercises, and international fora on "urban futures," and in Asian Development Bank loan portfolios (Robinson 2011).

Together, they reveal a sequence of events unfolding recently in India, which can be summarized in the following way. First, the career trajectory of an ambitious administrative civil servant has changed, such that it is now imperative that one's resumé includes training programs run by interna tional agencies such as the World Bank and those at the Administrative Staff College of India's Urban Management program, originally designed by the World Bank Institute.[10] Second, whereas previously only national govern ment ministries could expect to borrow from the IFIs, now local government agencies are being asked to bid for international finance loans and grants, situating these local agencies with new powers but also new risks that are extraordinary for a small service-providing bureaucracy. Hence, officials are being retrained and aided by consultants from transnational firms ensconced in this transnational arena of world-city making.

Third, the central government of India has initiated its own world-city investment strategy – the J. Nehru National Urban Renewal Mission, or JNNURM – that channels more than US$11 billion over seven years to cities that must bid for a slice of this money, with conditions attached that encourage corporate partnerships between foreign service providers and public goods managers in state agencies, borrowing capital from interna tional markets and financing debt through municipal bonds, and other steps that convert these small bureaucracies into competitive and "responsibi lized" agents (Rose 1999) of new urban financial and governance norms.

These changes come with a political and economic rationality. To convert "dead capital" into high-value "liquid capital," city officials have embarked upon a new way of managing the urban public: *worlding through speculation and liquidation.* This adjusted aperture helps planners visualize the transformation of old city markets into central business districts, clusters of small shops and street-vending locales into downtown shopping malls, and irrigation tanks (small lakes) and village fields into glass and steel corporate campuses of the new Googles of the business world. There is much to be gained and much that will change in this process of envisioning a world city. This world- or global-city approach attributes economic stagnation to the failure of the command-and-control state to nurture freedom of investment and the entrepreneurial spirit amongst the whole population, right down to the ready-to-be-unleashed poor.[11] Rural peasants need not continue to play the static role of handcart pushers, selling vegetables and herbs in and out of city neighborhoods. According to the logic, peddlers, vendors, and "slumdogs" also desire an opportunity to leverage their participation in city life and capitalize on the transformations of city economic life. The poor should expect more from their cities, and these globally integrating projects are precisely the vehicle to meet such expectations. Following from this world-city logic, rural communities can be more than mere suppliers of (cheap) city food products, but also landlords and providers of higher-end services to world-class IT engineers, what many city projects on the outskirts of Bangalore promise.

Building upon Hernando de Soto's notion of how the Third World poor sit upon a surfeit of untapped capital, one can see how acres of underutilized or dilapidated public infrastructure signify thrice-ignored capital reserves: dead infrastructural capital sitting on dead land capital, overseen by dead managerial capital (de Soto 2000; World Bank 2009). The world-city idea has brought a renewed vigor to city officialdom, as if city leaders had discovered oil reserves under crowded open-air markets, debt-burdened farming villages, and even their own office desks.[12]

Speculative Government

These speculative endeavors are being supported by, and are spearheading, major changes in the practices of government (Foucault 1991; Rose 1999) and in daily government–citizen interactions. One can shrug one's shoulders at these dream projects and see them as purely speculative, pie-in-the-sky; yet, they have their institutional effects, whether or not they are built as planned. The idea of making a world city in Bangalore has become a constant "provocation to government" (Osborne and Rose 1999). The first dramatic shift has been the privileging of local government agencies called parastatals, agencies largely financed by IFIs and buttressed with foreign loans, debts, and investments, whose job is to oversee and support particular world-city projects that existing government agencies are ill-equipped to undertake. For example, the public water agency (BWSSP) worked with the parastatal airport authority (BIAAPA) to insure that its first big effort to provide water to consumers was at the airport, where no one lives, and that less than 4 percent of the city population utilizes, for only a short time per visit. (Elsewhere in town, most receive "BWSSB water" for only a few hours every third day.) The responsibilities of these two types of government agencies – public and parastatal – have begun to blur, as Bangalore's public water agency now outsources 70 percent of its most basic tasks to private operators, and its financing depends upon IFI and world-city project infusions.[13]

In 1993, a pivotal set of legislation was passed that suggests a national turn in Indian government toward decentralization and democratization: the passing of the 73rd and 74th Amendments to the Constitution in 1993 to decentralize power from national- and state-level authorities to rural *panchayats* (local multi-village councils) and urban municipal corporations. Yet, their enactment on the ground is undermining democratization processes: many of Bangalore's key nodal agencies for world-city making are the newly empowered parastatal agencies, accountable only to their lending agencies (such as the Asian Development Bank) and to the chief minister of Karnataka (the state in which Bangalore is situated). Decision-making has jumped scale, leaving very few formal mechanisms for local control.[14] Parastatals have become "single window," one-stop shopping sites for the expedited approval and disbursal of permits for projects financed by foreign capital, ostensibly blending efficiency with "professionalized" good governance, ditching the slow-churning and much-maligned Indian state bureaucracy (Fuller and Benei 2000; Harriss, Stokke, and Tornquist 2004; Harriss 2006; Baindur and Kamath 2009). The most powerful city agencies, shaped and financed by IFIs, are the Bangalore Development Authority (BDA), overseeing the Comprehensive Development Plan; the Karnataka Urban Infrastructure Development and Finance Corporation (KUIDFC), distributing IFI funds; and the Karnataka Industrial Area Development Board (KIADB), which negotiates land acquisitions for world-city schemes. Hence, new government initiatives have not led to a uniform path of democratization; on the contrary, attempts to bring democracy to the city are being undermined by the development technologies of these semi-autonomous and debt-financed agencies (as well as by a new form of voluntarism and civil-society participation, as we will see below) (Benjamin and Bhuvaneswari 2001; Nair 2005; Ghosh 2006b).

The world-city project, however, is no steamroller. Solomon Benjamin (2008) explains the "porous" nature of this bureaucratic maze, which enables working-class and poor constituents to make demands upon their own brethren staff at the lowest reaches of the bureaucracy, gaining them access to a wide range of government services such as electricity, water, and the use of abandoned lands for makeshift homes and workshops (Benjamin 2000a). Yet this highly localized set of political maneuvers – what Benjamin and also Simone (2004a,b) argue is part of large phenomenon called "subaltern urbanism" – do suffer from seismic ruptures such as the creation of world-city projects described here, which can destabilize and force new alignments of these necessary survival strategies and practices.

For example, the sole elected urban local body for Bangalore city, Bruhat Bangalore Mahanagara Palike, or the city corporation, is comprised of councillors elected from the 198 wards of the city (BBMP 2009). But because of the 2007 city mandate to expand the city's limits to include seven surrounding towns and 110 villages, increasing the area threefold, the city council was suspended from September 2006 until a much-delayed election held in December 2009, and the city had been run solely by the bureaucratic arm of BBMP.[15] As the only democratically elected body in Bangalore, their responsibilities have historically been quite limited, responding to complaints from citizens about storm drains, solid waste management, roads, schools, stray dogs, and health services. Yet, wherever the city expands into surrounding villages and towns, and local ruling bodies are replaced by BBMP councillors, and representation shifts from the 300 to 30,000 denizens for every elected official, there has been a reduction in official representation at the same time as local issues of sovereignty over land have become much more contentious, dispossessing locals from city land (Kamath, Baindur, and Rajan 2008).

Three other significant institutional shifts have occurred in the governance arena: first, as Baindur and Kamath (2009) have astutely noted through their research, most of the key World Bank and Asian Development Bank policy reforms on urban governance that have been recommended have been subsequently instituted as requirements for access to their loans as well as to those offered by JNNURM (Baindur and Kamath 2009). Starting in 2001, IFI recommendations have included the repeal of the Urban Land Ceiling Regulation Act, phased reduction of stamp duties, the phasing-out of rent control laws and indexing rents of municipal properties to market rents, the unbundling of municipal services to create user charge revenue streams for each public service, rapid increases in tariffs for water and utilities, and the introduction of double-entry accrual accounting. All have been incorporated into JNNURM guidelines for urban local bodies, and have shaped the creation and work of new urban parastatals. These reforms are separating historically weak government agencies overseeing very small maintenance budgets from newly autonomous agencies; the latter have become swollen with large budgets and yet also made volatile, as their work is defined by high-risk, multi-million dollar international loans and large-scale obligations of debt finance.

Second, expert commissions and taskforces have, since 1999, played a critical role as an institutional apparatus that could "meet demands that the present system of elected corporators [or city councillors] does not adequately fulfill," and to "help citizens make 'informed and effective decisions that truly represent citizen's priorities', a direct call to 'take ownership and get to participate in governance'" (Nair 2005). That apparatus was the Bangalore Agenda Task Force (BATF), a fifteen-member nominated body of elites from the IT and biotechnology industries, such as Infosys CEO Nanden Nilekani, from the business community; Naresh Malhotra, of the international consulting firm KPMG; and NGO leaders such as Ramesh Ramanathan, former New York-based Citibank trader who started Janaagraha, and Samuel Paul, former World Bank official and director of the Public Affairs Centre. The latter two organizations have played the lead role of citizen-participation/government-watchdogs in town. The BATF office and many of its initiatives, before it closed down in 2004, were funded by Nilekani's private foundation, Adhaar Trust, which also offered seed grants for entrepreneurial projects that would help BATF's main initiatives: Swachha Bangalore, or Clean Bangalore; and Swayam Ghoshane, or Self-Promotion (Heitzman 2004; Ghosh 2005).[16]

BATF hoped to be the citizen-based vehicle for de-politicized, audit-based, anti-red tape, urban initiatives. It wanted a no-nonsense approach to urban development, based on the Singapore model of cleanliness and efficiency. Its biggest success was its construction of well-adorned bus stops and clean public toilets in select sites. But their attempts to institutionalize the taskforce approach to governance met resistance from a variety of citizen groups, as well as from civil-servant suspicion. Whereas BATF was started by the newly elected Congress Party's Chief Minister S.M. Krishna, who unabashedly wanted to turn Bangalore into Singapore, BATF's successor, "ABIDe Bengaluru," was started by the Bharatiya Janata Party's (BJP's) Chief Minister B.S. Yeddyurappa, once he was elected in 2008, with its members from the Hindu nationalist BJP, together with senior government and industry officials, and Ramesh Ramanathan from Janaagraha, again.[17] One of ABIDe's flagship projects may become a 60 km monorail system (*Times of India* 2009). Although specific taskforces seem to come and go with each election, as the Janata Dal (Secular), Congress, and BJP parties have exchanged the reins of power over the past decade, the trend of placing elite corporate and citizen leaders in positions of power to circumvent existing forms of government decision-making seems to have stuck in Bangalore, as it has in Chennai, Mumbai, and New Delhi (Chamaraj 2009).

Third, elite citizen action groups have been working under the premise that only when citizens participate, if not take the lead, will local governmental bodies modernize. Social audits are a key technology for forcing government agencies to become more transparent and responsive. Samuel

Paul's PAC created the "citizen's report card" – opinion surveys asking consumers to rate their public utilities and service-delivering agencies. PAC actively publicizes the results, enters into dialogues with the agency, and mobilizes professionals to push for better services. PAC has run high-profile public fora for English-speaking, professional-class audiences, and worked closely with parastatals and the IFIs to insure that its citizen constituents are heard in the shaping of projects. Attracted to this type of citizen activism, the World Bank and the Asian Development Bank have since hired Paul and PAC to consult on their behalf in world-city initiatives across Asia and Africa. India's central government has hired Ramanathan to promote citizen participation across India.[18] By 2008, BATF had long vanished, replaced by the BJP-led ABIDe, and Ramanathan and most of his staff had shifted to Delhi, doing citizen's participation work for JNNURM's sixty-four city lending program.

In sum, local state agencies have privatized more of their public tasks and responsibilities, focused their efforts on world-city projects, and transferred the responsibilities of government to a tight-knit but expanding group of elite local/transnational networks of "citizen" actors. Not only has the art and practice of government become more widely dispersed; it has required a speculative sensibility that puts into question, and requires action on, everything once taken for granted as stable. Debt-financed parastatals, betting heavily on hedge-fund investments that demand world-class profit rates, require tremendous ingenuity but also risky behavior by eminent-citizen taskforces and citizen NGOs, as well as the people who expect that the streets they walk to work on, and the informal workshops and sidewalk services they provide, will be there tomorrow. When the land under their lanes and shops becomes capitalized based on Dubai-sized expectations, the rules of the street and city hall shift, as we shall see, in unpredictable and highly speculative ways.

Speculative World-City Projects

In order to understand how political rationalities and institutions change through their articulation with these high-risk, large-scale world-city projects, this section introduces a few mega-schemes currently being executed: the Bangalore–Mysore Infrastructure Corridor (BMIC), the IT corridor, and the Bangalore International Airport and its surrounding development area (BIAL). Here, I will only highlight two elements: the size of each project relative to its perceived public good, and the cumulative world-city projects' physical impact on the region. As we can see from Figure 9.2, these three projects alone comprise a substantial proportion of the new land under the expanded Bangalore, and the overall area is much larger *in toto* than the

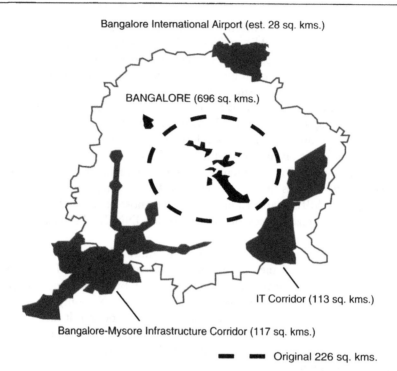

Bangalore International Airport (est. 28 sq. kms.)

BANGALORE (696 sq. kms.)

IT Corridor (113 sq. kms.)

Bangalore-Mysore Infrastructure Corridor (117 sq. kms.)

━━ ━━ Original 226 sq. kms.

Figure 9.2 The new Bangalore has grown by threefold since 2007 and yet sits in the shadows of its expanding world-city projects
Source: produced by Wesley Longhofer.

original city of Bangalore prior to 2007. If we add to these projects the road-widening project which leaders perceive as a solution to the doubling of cars every five years (e.g., 400 km of roads to be widened), plus the dozens of small lakes and reservoirs drained in the past two decades for construction, we find that much of the complex urban terrain of Bangalore has been transformed by world-city building (*Times of India* 2006; D'Souza 2008).

The International Airport, which opened in May 2008, was built and is being run by a consortium led by the Unique Zurich Airport firm and Siemens, receiving highly subsidized land from the government 30 km north of the city, large enough to build two and a half (London) Heathrow airports. The IT corridor on the city's eastern periphery is yet to be fully built, on land not yet fully acquired; planned to be one and a half times the size of Paris, it will be subsidized by the government and designed with the help of a Singapore-based firm. It will have its own local government, but it will tap into the Greater Bangalore's refinanced power and water grids. The IT corridor and airport will be connected by a world-class monorail built to transport IT professionals back and forth between airport and work, flying above the traffic jams and nuisance of the city below.

Following the model of regionalized expansion, the Bangalore–Mysore Infrastructure Corridor (BMIC) intends to spread development out from Bangalore's interior in order to alleviate urban density and expand the overall space of Greater Bangalore to include new and old townships, small cities, village clusters, and agricultural land. Operated by a US-based investor, NICE, this project starts with the construction of a six-lane *privately* owned toll expressway between Bangalore and the second-largest city in Karnataka, Mysore. The 130 km expressway will become a catalyst for regional urbanization with NICE building five new *private* townships and multiple industrial parks on agricultural, village, and forested land. The project's advertised main goals are to reduce the travel time between the two cities from three and one-half hours to ninety minutes, alleviate the crowding of Bangalore's IT sector, and allowing it to expand geographically. In 2005, Mohandas Pai, then director of human resources at India's major IT firm Infosys (with large campuses in both cities), said in the press: "It's the single most important project for Bangalore. It will not only provide more employment, but also improve the quality of life of the people of Bangalore."

At an estimated cost (so far) of more than $1 billion, the 7,000 acres required for the toll-based expressway will be surrounded by another 21,000 acres on which NICE can develop these new townships, each affiliated with a corporate center, industrial center, farming/marketing center, ecotourism center, or a heritage center that would preserve in a museum the rural lifeworlds that the thoroughfare and malls may pave over. Besides reducing travel time, it will also denude up to 7,000 acres of forested land and drain eight lakes. The government chose to lease the land at a controversially low subsidy of Rs.10 per acre per year (in 2010, Rs.45 equaled US$1).

While the toll expressway will be owned by the government after the 30-year lease expires, the townships created along the road will be privately owned and managed; not the thoroughfare, but the "unleashed value" converting rural Karnataka into urban real estate is the ingredient that attracted the US investor, along with one of India's largest corporations (Anil Ambani's ADAE) to the scheme. Just as New York, Singapore, and Dubai real-estate firms have hoped to set up their own townships outside India's cities, in 2007 a Dubai firm closed a $15 billion deal (with DLF of New Delhi, an investment partner with Lehman Brothers – until they went bankrupt in 2007, rocking DLF's fidelity) to build/own/operate and *govern* a prototype township known as "Knowledge City" on 9,000 acres surrounding the town of Bidadi, alongside the planned infrastructural corridor (Forbes. com 2007).

Since there are no vast open spaces *out there* to build upon, land must be acquired from rural denizens, many of whom are engaged in agriculture and live in villages. For a developer to receive 28,000 acres from the state government, states have industrial areas development boards (such as the KIADB in Karnataka) charged with the task of purchasing land from rural owners and villages, building up basic infrastructure – that is, water and electricity, and in some cases, a physical plant or campus for an auto factory or software company – and then selling or leasing it to businesses. By and large, Indian farmers are not allowed to sell agricultural land for non-farming purposes, ostensibly to preserve the national treasure of farmland and protect vulnerable farmers from "land vultures" who might prey on them. This is especially true for the Dalits (India's lowest-caste communities) who have received land under land-to-the-tiller programs since the 1970s. Yet, in this case, the government has bypassed these rights and legal remediations. Consequently, more than 200,000 rural people will be displaced by this Mysore–Bangalore corridor project – people who farm the land, who live in the villages, and who work in rural service and small-industry sectors supporting the regional economy.[19]

Under the law of eminent domain, based on the colonial Land Acquisition Act of 1894, the government can acquire land from farmers if it is for a project that is for the "good of the nation," but it must offer a fair market price (D'Rozario n.d.). The state-level Karnataka Industrial Areas Development Board (KIADB), however, offers a relative pittance to the non-elite members of rural communities, exercising its right to choose the depressed rural market price and not the upscale world-city market price as its marker. The difference comprises "the rent" that shapes and fuels the new urban economy and its governance structure. The rationale for offering farmers a low price relative to land's new urban value is based on the belief that many of Karnataka's farmers have become quite poor, in debt, and judged as uncompetitive. But this is true less because of the failure of the land, the people, or the crippled rural economy than because of the post-1991 liberalization shift in priorities by the government in price supports from the rural to the urban service sector. Whereas, in the past, the government would subsidize agriculture in order to keep both a national food surplus and some of the 70 percent of the nation's population engaged in rural work employed and compensated (some political moments have been better than others), since the early 1990s, the policy has shifted from rural subsidies and supports, and away from social welfare provisions in general. In other words, world-city investments depend upon widespread *disinvestment* from other local economies, such as the diverse rural, and the urban informal. Significantly, most of the urban and rural population works for the multifaceted "informal" economy (including textiles, apparels, silk processing, mechanical fabrication, plastic parts manufacturing, floriculture, food processing, and a varied service sector), which employs most of the population and generates between 55 and 75 percent of Bangalore's GDP (Benjamin 2000a,b, 2008). World-city projects, with their large appetite for land, devalue these small and medium-sized enterprises, as the latter's political clout has diminished by comparison.

This historical convergence of neoliberalization and world-city urbanization has empowered parastatal agencies such as the KIADB to become brokers of large-scale public and private land transfers. In fact, world-city land brokering has become *the* biggest growth sector for the regional economy. The management of this land acquisition process has become the main source of revenue and wealth accumulation in Bangalore today, and the main political tussle amongst political parties and parastatal agencies.[20] In the lengthy and laborious process of master planning, mapping out the specific plots of land to be acquired, notifying the land owners, and handling the land users, and the final purchase and transfer to investors, a lot of money changes hands.

It is estimated that for the Bangalore–Mysore Industrial Corridor (BMIC), only a small fraction of the rural denizens notified by the government will be compensated, and compensation will be much below market prices. Those who will be compensated will not be treated justly, as dozens of court case filings and protests in the area reveal. Since the promotional world-city literature on "cities of the future" sells social imaginaries, let us too imagine a different scenario. Imagine that in the name of development and India's rising, the 200,000 people who live in the way of this urban development plan were given market value for the land in exchange for their lives being upended – that is, not the depressed land price, but the market price that got generated once Dubai and US real-estate firms began to invest their capital (but before markets went bust). Then the major "value" component of the scheme – *making real estate* – would be socially dispersed amongst diverse land users. Farmers and non-deed-holding villagers alike could own smaller plots of land along this new expressway to set up shops, small apartment complexes, and own a share in the factories and the new townships. Conceivably, they could enjoy a share of the prosperity of these new projects. Their children could afford to build a solid house, own a small business, go to school, and be trained in areas other than poorly remunerative work. But then the road builder, US-based NICE, would be reduced to the role of a public-like agency, producing improved infrastructure, housing, transport, commercial sites, and generating income and public spaces for the majority to use. It may sound like "development" in some abstract roman-ticized sense, and certainly what the rural poor deserve as their rightful share of "India rising," but this is not how world-city-style development unfolds. Without this high-risk speculation and highly rewarding capital accumulation, neither institutional investors nor IFIs seem interested.

Similar to the BMIC toll expressway, it is not the airport with its one runway that will be the profitable investment: land is not being acquired for the Unique Zurich consortium to build numerous runways to compete with the world's largest airports, but to transform the land surrounding it into high-value gated residential communities, seven-star hotel complexes, "medical tourism" hospitals, and business centers (John 2005). Whose land is being purchased or taken for these world-city transformations, and to what effect on the local economies (especially the de-subsidized rural and farming sectors) are key questions that the development industry and world-city boosters have largely ignored. They are also avoiding the possible causal connections of mass dispossession with the alarming farm-related suicide rates occurring in rural Karnataka and the growth of slums populated with displaced rural farmers and workers (*The Hindu* 2008; Gandhi 2009).

As Bangalore's world-city master plan calls for the incorporation of dozens of villages and towns on its periphery in order to grow, it is becoming clear that much more money can be made from the conversion of undervalued rural and urban economies into world-city projects than from the actual infrastructure projects. Consequently, most Bangaloreans must become speculators of one sort or another, taking extreme risks, and must gamble on when government agents or land brokers will tag their possessions next for acquisition, and act before it is too late. What, then, is happening in the growth sector that is buoying up these urban ventures?

IT as the Urban Growth Machine

The transformation of Bangalore into a world city rests on the rather large assumption that its extraordinary IT sector will become a permanent growth machine, and as such, can be the collateral for these large loans and long-term investments in urban infrastructure (Parthasarathy 2004; Dittrich 2007). With that in mind, it is useful to better understand what fuels Bangalore's IT sector and how the IT star firms (e.g., Infosys, TCS, Satyam, Wipro) are reinvesting their surpluses and ingenuity. Are they, as the World Bank and PricewaterhouseCoopers hope, providing exceptional leadership, innovation, and the telematicization of governance – the world-*classing* of the cities of India (Ananya Roy, Conclusion, this volume)? Will they be here tomorrow, when the projects are complete, and the bills come due?

The dream team of Indian IT started from humble entrepreneurial origins: a few young talents offered California computer firms an attractive outsourcing proposition during the Y2K crisis. They could hire Indian software engineers at a fraction of the cost of US and European ones, and fix the Y2K problem before midnight on January 1, 2000. As one of its managers explained to me, India's premier firm, Infosys, offered to do the tedious job, promising it could pay its workers $15 per hour, and not the $30 per hour which US firms were paying their local engineers; the fledgling Infosys instead paid Indian engineers $2 and kept $13, and made millions instantly. Infosys eventually took on other mundane tasks of Northern banks, insurance companies, and health firms, coding and data processing on the night shift and cutting the local fee structure substantially (interviews in January 2007; see also Heitzman 2004; Parthasarathy 2004; Upadhya and Vasavi 2008).

Infosys grew quickly, from a small $75 million firm, to a $2 billion firm in 2005, and $3 billion in 2006, and had expected to grow into the double-digits by 2010, before the 2009 downturn. Although the largest competitor is IBM Global, with revenues at $40 billion, IBM's profit margin hovers around 15 percent, whereas Infosys had a 46 percent margin in 2005. Most of its work is customer analytics, payroll processing, and back-office work; in some cases, Infosys has taken over as much as 70 percent of US firms' work. For mail-order companies (such as Amazon), insurance, finance, and credit-card companies (such as American Express), whose main tasks are data processing behind the scenes, Bangalore has become an offshore boon.

But to the question of how much IT firms invest locally, aside from their well-paid programmers and their high consumer spending, most firms are not active investors or innovators. Although world-city advocates argue that IT firms could use their smarts of computers and telecommunications to support new systems of state-of-the-art e-government – transparent, democratically accessible, efficient, and competitive – the reality is quite different. As one Infosys manager explained to me, 98 percent of Infosys's work is business from outside of India, and 65 percent is US based: "Our offshore rates are too high for local Indian clients, and we make our large profit margins from the difference between our local costs and what western companies are willing to pay." We cannot afford to hire ourselves to local governments, he explained, and government agencies really have no use for what we offer.

Instead, surpluses are invested in mergers and acquisitions of competitors in Europe and the United States. In early 2008, Infosys invested in two major mergers and acquisitions in Europe and Australia, to increase its market share and reduce competition, and become more vertically integrated into more arenas of business. Flush with cash during the economic down-turn of 2008, Infosys was, according to the business press, looking to buy more undervalued/underperforming European firms (Venkat 2008).

Domestically, IT's main investment is in real estate, which has now surpassed IT itself as the most profitable industry in India. As competition stiffens in the global IT industry, the most lucrative place to invest IT surpluses has been in land: converting cheap (by international market standards) public and undervalued private or community lands into real estate (CNN/IBN 2006). As land values have skyrocketed, one of Infosys's strategies has been to buy up land in and around many of India's cities, creating high-value "land banks" (Rediff 2005). According to the 2006 Annual Report of Infosys, "creating land banks was a key challenge" of the year.[21]

Infosys is not alone. Once the fourth largest Indian IT firm, the darling of Hyderabad, Satyam chairman Ramalinga Raju admitted to police in January 2009 that he had set up 275 real-estate holding companies in the names of his family members for handling numerous land transactions, while lying in Satyam's accounting books about more than $1 billion of non-existent assets.[22] While Satyam worked for more than one-third of the Fortune 500 companies in sixty-six countries, as well as for the World Bank, most of its surplus had been diverted to real-estate deals throughout Andhra Pradesh, with close links to the chief minister and large development projects related to Hyderabad's emergence as India's next world city (affectionately called Cyberabad). In a public confession, former chairman Raju said he had set up this out-of-control scam not for private gain, but as the only way he saw Satyam *could be globally competitive* (Aaftaab 2009).

It therefore appears that real estate is keeping the struggling IT industry afloat, not innovation or competitiveness, and the real-estate market in India has grown at 30 percent per year since the mid-2000s (Shrivastava 2008). Unitech, one of India's largest real-estate firms, reported a 3,190 percent increase in net profits from 2006 to 2007, and its market capitalization grew by almost 12,000 percent, before stagnating in 2008. In the third quarter of 2009 alone, more than $7 billion of foreign direct investment has flooded into India. Although much of it flows into infrastructural funds set up by large US firms such as Morgan Stanley, Citigroup, Goldman Sachs, Blackstone Group, and DE Shaw, owners of the hedge and derivative funds that crippled the global economy in 2007–8, much of that financing is based on the acquisition of large banks of land.[23] This money will only be invested if government is able to free land from India's rural landed population, which has, and will, create a massive displacement crisis. Yet these deeply political concerns aside, in making India an urban giant, real estate is where the action is, and the IT sector has profited greatly from its rise, intertwining what at first blush seems to be the stable foundation for world-city building with a highly unstable sector. As we learn from observing the interactions among India's top IT and real-estate firms, neither is as stable or secure as they appear. Neither seems to sustain itself without the other, and yet both are referred to as the "secure foundation" on which these remarkably speculative world-city projects are being built.

Conclusion: No Exit (Strategy)?

This *worlding* of Indian cities has triggered shifts in new technologies of government that affect urban and rural people who have "given it all up" in the name of world-city making. There is sufficient uncertainty built into these endeavors that the city and its periphery is engulfed by a collective social angst over whether or not one's domicile or informal workshop will be taken over to build the new highway, the Metro, widen a city road, construct a housing complex, or develop a special export zone. This social anxiety in turn generates large flows of cash as a normal practice to reduce the chances of personal and community bankruptcy. That is, everyone must pay what he or she can in order to influence the outcome, even though outcomes are often determined by class, caste, and gender inequities when it comes to who will get displaced and whose land can be, for a price, avoided by world-city project planning. In Bangalore, rising urban anxiety is not about traffic, congestion, pollution, filth, or too few good pubs; the most palpable urban anxiety is focused on official land theft and the speculative nature of routine decision-making in a rising world city (Figure 9.3). Even as highly lauded middle-class civic associations hold regular public meetings

Figure 9.3 The writing on the wall: anxiety and anger spread across the political/ cultural spectrum
Source: photograph by Michael Goldman.

calling for transparency, participation, and accountability, drawing up "report cards" on the performance of each government agency, marching in line with the global mandate for *audit culture as politics*, the omnipresent practices of world-city making – land theft and the legitimating governance structure being built up around it – are treated as anomalies or part of the age-old problem of corruption (Strathern 2000; Ghosh 2006a,b), and yet they have become as common as the logo of 'India Rising'.

World-city projects are not only large-scale, place-altering capital infusions from Dubai, Singapore, and the IFIs, and they do more than merely facilitate the restructuring of governance institutions for improved access to public goods and services for international capital (i.e., privatization of township governance, special citizenship rights, and privileged rules for special export zones). They also trigger new political rationalities of government and technologies of rule that emerge *in situ* as bureaucrats and political officials broker jackpot deals for external clients who are themselves brokering inter-urban deals, all of which contribute to these institutionalized forms of land and wealth redistribution.

Hence, we find a confluence of four processes remaking Bangalore: a new global architecture and legitimacy of urban expert networks selling the idea of large-scale re-capitalization of cities; the expansive use of new instruments from the world of investment capital to finance and transform public sectors, landscapes, and politics; and the rise of new forms of urban governance that not only force urban dwellers to rethink their legitimate claims to the city and to government, but also get shaped and empowered through inter-urban competitions and inter-referencing across the south and north. That nation-states today are confronted with the immutable fact that there is no alternative to world-city building suggests the depth, vitality, and hegemony of this phenomenon we can call speculative urbanism. The recent transformation of Bangalore can best be understood both in its relationship to these processes and as they become realized through the remaking of cities transnationally. Such an analytical approach invites an innovative methodology that reaches beyond conventional inquiries into the urban and the global (Roy 2009; Simone 2010).

By December 2008, much of the miraculous side of Asian city real-estate value had begun to vanish. As one real-estate executive explained of the Dubai real-estate market in early 2009: "What real estate market? There isn't a market at all. Value has dropped by 75% and nothing is moving."[24] In fact, she only captured half the "moving" story in Dubai: in March 2009, 30,000 seats were booked by the United Arab Emirates government on India-bound jumbo jets to fly home the low-paid Indian building construction workers, passports returned to them at the gate (*Human Rights Watch* 2006; ArabianBusiness.com 2009). As the leaking real-estate bubble in Dubai required large bailouts from Abu Dhabi, disappearing dollar remittances from construction workers in the Gulf States to local Indian economies severely undercut the Indian government's ability to support its urbanization loans. Moreover, the most audacious real-estate ventures in India are disappearing: Bangalore's Knowledge City has been scrapped as Lehman Brothers went bankrupt, and Limitless, LLC pulled out because its creditors were calling on their capital. Unable to pay its monthly bills, Limitless had to postpone or drop its other schemes (e.g., Palm Jumeirah, The World Island Resort, and The Universe) from its $110 billion portfolio of fantasy dreamscapes in Dubai.[25]

By early 2010, India's largest urban developers quickly sold off assets, desperate for liquid capital as their projects had run aground: no credit, no land banks, no capital.[26] Their last hope, to calm creditors and state officials, was to borrow the "hot capital" of hedge and derivative investors who prey and profit off the desperation of near-bankrupt firms and public agencies, much the way they had in the United States and Europe. Because India's banks were not allowed to invest in the risky global transactions that caused Western banks to collapse, India escaped the worst of the 2007–9 global economic crisis. But because its city administrations are now able to borrow globally, and most urban "development projects" have become speculative real-estate ventures financed by undulating flows from unregulated capital sources, Indian cities have begun to reel from the shocks of the global speculative market.

In sum, the financial meltdown revealed its world-city speculative opportunities and risks: new parastatals were created on the basis of international borrowing and municipal bond marketing; they have been fueled by speculative projects and financed by other world-city real-estate ventures. Since the ability of the Indian government to provide services and goods is now based on rents from these promised external capital flows, when these flows run dry, so do the essential urban services and goods. As Sameer Nayar, Managing Director, Head of Real Estate of Asia Pacific, Credit Suisse, explains in the clearest terms, "Every time you have a developing market in the early stages, it is high risk." To prepare for risks, he warns, you must "*have a good exit strategy*" (Nayar 2009, emphasis added). Unlike Credit Suisse, for many Bangaloreans left standing in the detritus of a passing speculative storm, there is no good exit.

Acknowledgments

A substantially revised version of this chapter appears in the *International Journal of Urban and Regional Research* (2011); both are based on research conducted in Bangalore and at global meetings on cities and their financing, since 2006. My gratitude goes to Ananya Roy, Aihwa Ong, and the SSRC Dubai workshop participants, as well as my colleagues working on global cities at the University of Minnesota, NIAS and ISEC in Bangalore, and the generous intellectual and research help of Vinay Baindur, P. Rajan, Wes Longhofer, and Sinan Erensu. Financial support came from a research fellowship from the American Institute for Indian Studies (University of Chicago) and funding from the University of Minnesota.

Notes

1 My research over the past five years has included participant observation and ethnographic research at meetings, workshops, in offices of government agencies, and interviews with local leaders, urban planners, real-estate developers, academics, and activists. Some of the discussion here on "global investors" comes from my participation at PEI's Global Investors Summit in Delhi, in July 2010, where the latest Planning Commission's report on financing infrastructure was presented and discussed in great detail by investors and government officials.
2 This chapter does not introduce the realm of protest – from roadblocks to the filing of hundreds of court claims – to slow and stop many of these world-city and land-dispossession schemes.
3 Early development displacement literature focused on mainly rural processes from green revolution, dam-building, and World Bank mega-projects; see, for example, Chris de Wet's work (2006).
4 These recent turns of events were discussed by Chinese scholars at an international workshop, "Global Cities and the Global Economic Crisis" in Shenzhen, China, in January 2010.
5 Here are a sample of reports reflecting the converging mandate from TPNs of making cities as the solution to our global problems: the World Bank's *Eco² Cities: Ecological Cities as Economic Cities* (Suzuki, Dastur, Moffatt, *et al.* 2010) and its Eco² Cities program; the OECD's *Competitive Cities and Climate Change* report and meeting, Milan, October 9–10, 2008 (OECD 2009); OECD Secretary-General Angel Gurria's speech at the Copenhagen Climate Summit on December 15, 2009 (Gurria 2009); and the World Wide Fund for Nature's *Reinventing the City* (2010). On policy and "model" transfers and convergences, see Peck, Theodore, and Brenner (2009), Robinson (2011), and Bunnell and Das (2010).
6 I paraphrase his speech. As noted earlier, these discussions and interviews come from my participation at PEI's Global Investors Summit in Delhi in July 2010.
7 According to Janaki Nair (2005), services were provided within these industrial colonies but not to the neighborhoods that built up around them, which reflected the class- and community-based nature of public service provisions.
8 As the story goes, the customs agents, so used to receiving a cut from all goods passing through their offices being shipped in and out of India, demanded that Indian IT firms physically "show" their goods that they were exporting via satellite. So, in the first few years, IT officials had to *also* put their software on CDs and allow for the agents to see the products, and get their fair cut.
9 As Bunnell and Das (2010) explain it, the "Vision Mumbai" report (2003) by the international consultants McKinsey & Company, having produced similar reports for city governments elsewhere, explicitly models its world-city design for Mumbai from the experience of Hyderabad, which is an acknowledged emulation of the Malaysian

development plan for Kuala Lumpur. Hyderabad's IT city was renamed Cyberabad after Malaysia's new IT city was named Cyberjaya. "Vision Mumbai" was also the basis for Bangalore's "vision report," designed by the same international consultants.

10 For example, a 2009 workshop on strengthening urban management, co-sponsored by the Administrative Staff College and World Bank Institute, featured modules such as "Creating Creditworthy Cities and Urban Systems," "Good Urban Governance and Decentralisation," and "Change Management."

11 See the World Bank (2008) and the Bank's urban strategy web site: http://www. wburbanstrategy.org/urbanstrategy/. One can read more on this perspective from the development guru Hernando de Soto, in his publications, and workshops around the world with the World Bank.

12 Besides the motivation to cultivate a synergy with these high-end service firms, the World Bank has its own reasons to support this shift to world-city building; a consequence of the anti-privatization response to its policies has been widespread "disinvestment" from the World Bank by national ruling bodies, such that by the early 2000s, the Bank and IMF were losing its client base across Latin America and what the Bank calls its middle-income countries of Asia. It found a source of new clients through its lending either directly to weak urban local bodies, ill-equipped to borrow international loans and incur international debt, or to parastatals designed for the task, both at the local and regional levels, less accustomed to borrowing from and negotiating with the IFIs and capital brokerage firms.

13 The IFIs have tried unsuccessfully to lease the water agency's goods and services to European firms; each time, their plans have been met with resolute public (and agency) opposition.

14 These parastatal agencies reflect a broader trend of building what PricewaterhouseCoopers (2005) consultants call "democratic capital," or establishing various public–private partnerships in an effort to enhance accountability and civic participation; as noted here, the opposite, however, is occurring. See Chamaraj (2009).

15 On the interminable election delay, see Idiculla (2009).

16 BATF focused assiduously on what scholars researching different Indian cities call the bias of "middle-class urban aesthetics" – attempts to eliminate some of the more repugnant elements of Indian cities that hold them back from world-city prominence: smells of urine and unsightly slum "muck" (Fernandes 2004; Ghosh 2005; Baviskar 2006; Ghertner 2008).

17 ABIDe stands for Agenda for Bengaluru Infrastructure Development; but it is also, of course, an acronym that expresses professional-class frustration with the ways in which *other* urbanites are not abiding by the "rules" and aesthetics of decent (middle-class) world-city living, *à la* Singapore, but also perhaps of Hindutva (the Hindu nationalist claim on the proper way of being a Hindu).

18 Paul's Report Card technology has been replicated for many Bank loan recipients, including the Philippines and Gambia.

19 Leading the opposition against the project is the Environmental Support Group, a Bangalore-based NGO that dubbed the BMIC the "Enron of road development" (http://www.esgindia.org/campaigns/bmic/docs/BMICP%20short%20note.htm). See Saldanha (2007) and the hundreds of pages of raw documentation about BMIC "irregularities," on the web site www.hiddentruthofbmicp.com.

20 The key beneficiaries of these land transactions have been the new class of real-estate moguls. In acknowledgment of the fact that the market value and legitimacy of these contentious land acquisitions are often determined, in one way or another, through politics, the biggest winners from these land deals have quickly gotten into politics. In the 2008 state-wide elections, twenty-three of the thirty local MLAs (legislators) elected to represent Bangalore received much of their recent wealth from the real-estate industry. Ten to fifteen years back, when such land deals were not a possibility, many of these MLA positions were filled by trade unionists, farmers' union activists, and progressive political party leaders.

21 Infosys's Annual Report for 2006; see also Srinivasaraju (2008). Another strategic move by Infosys and others is to invest in their own offshore production sites where labor and operating costs are lower; in the Philippines, for example, hourly wages are half the Bangalore rate.

22 See *Statesman* (2009) and the *New York Times* (2009).

23 In 2009, Morgan Stanley, with partners, set up a $10 billion urban infrastructural fund, Goldman Sachs a $7.5 billion fund; Citigroup and Blackstone a $5 billion fund; and DE Shaw a $1 billion fund.

24 "Even Illustrious Dubai is Suffering a Devastating Real Estate Crash," Deutsche Welle TV, February 17, 2009. From 2004 to 2008, 200 luxury residential skyscrapers were built on Dubai's main harbor; in 2010, many of the residences remained empty.

25 See the fascinating catalogue from the exhibit in 2010 at the Centre Pompidou, Paris, "Dreamlands: Des parcs d'attractions aux cités du future" ("From amusement parks to cities of the future").

26 Social protest against these forms of institutionalized land theft has also been a major deterrent and is a major part of investors' calculus of the "India risk" they are trying to avoid, for which they are demanding substantial government guarantees. It is normal procedure for the World Bank to help borrowing countries write political-risk guarantees into their loan agreements, and it has trained government officials, including local urban bureaucrats, in these contractual practices (Goldman 2005).

References

Aaftaab, N. (2009) A quality worker: IT workers and adapting to new global economics. In *38th Annual Conference on South Asia*, University of Wisconsin, October 14–17.

ArabianBusiness.com (2009) 20,000 Indian workers to be flown out of UAE. February 8; http://www.arabianbusiness.com/20-000-indian-workers-be-flown-out-of-uae-80215.html (accessed September 25, 2010).

Baindur, V. and Kamath, L. (2009) Reengineering urban infrastructure: how the World Bank and Asian Development Bank shape urban infrastructure finance and governance in India. *Bank Information Centre*; http://www.bicusa.org/en/Article.11410.aspx (accessed September 25, 2010).

Baviskar, A. (2006) Demolishing Delhi: world-class city in the making, *Mute* 2(3), 88–95.

Benjamin, S. (2000a) Governance, economic settings and poverty in Bangalore. *Environment and Urbanization* 12, 35–56.

Benjamin, S. (2000b) Urban land transformation for pro-poor economies. *Geoforum* 35, 277–88.

Benjamin, S. (2008) Occupancy urbanism: radicalizing politics and economy beyond policy and programs. *International Journal of Urban and Regional Research* 32(3), 719–29.

Benjamin, S. and Bhuvaneswari, R. (2001) Democracy, inclusive governance and poverty in Bangalore. University of Birmingham Urban Governance, Partnership and Poverty Working Paper 26; http://www.idd.bham.ac.uk/ research/Projects/urban-governance/resource_papers/ stage2_casestudies/ wp26_Bangalore.pdf (accessed March 12, 2008).

Bombay First and McKinsey (2003) *Vision Mumbai: Transforming Mumbai into a world-class city*. Mumbai: McKinsey & Company.

BBMP (Bruhat Bangalore Mahanagara Palike) (2009) *Proposed Capital Investment Plan for Bangalore City (2009–2112)*. Office of The Commissioner.

Business Standard India (2008) Chinese city aims to do a Bangalore, June 30.

Chamaraj, K. (2009) Parastatals and task forces: the new decision-makers. *India Together*, February 22; http://www.indiatogether.org/2009/feb/gov-parastate.htm (accessed September 25, 2010).

CNN/IBN (2006) Real estate at a surreal price. March 27; http://www.ibnlive.com/ news/real-estate-at-a-surreal-price/7366-3.html (accessed March 27, 2006).

de Soto, H. (2000) *The Mystery of Capital: why capitalism triumphs in the West and fails everywhere else*. New York: Basic Books.

de Wet, C. (2006) *Development-Induced Displacement*. London: Berghahn Books.

Dittrich, C. (2007) Bangalore: globalization and fragmentation in India's high-tech capital. *ASIEN* 103, 45–58.

D'Rozario, C. (n.d.) Urban sprawl and decentralization. Alternative Law Forum, Bangalore, a survey of urban legislation and laws affecting land acquisition in Bangalore.

D'Souza, R. (2008) *Impact of Privatization of Lakes in Bangalore*. Bangalore: Centre for Education and Documentation.

Elsheshtawy, Y. (2010) *Dubai: beyond an urban spectacle*. New York: Routledge.

Fernandes, L. (2004) The politics of forgetting: class politics, state power and the restructuring of urban space in India. *Urban Studies* 41(12), 2415–30.

Forbes.com (2007) DLF surges on township deal with Dubai. October 3.

Foucault, M. (1991) Governmentality. In G. Burchell, C. Gordon, and P. Miller (eds.) *The Foucault Effect: studies in governmentality*. Chicago: The University of Chicago Press.

Fuller, C.J. and Benei, V. (eds.) (2000) *The Everyday State and Society in Modern India*. New Delhi: Social Science Press.

Gandhi, D. (2009) No compensation for these airport-displaced tillers. *The Hindu* (Karnataka edn.), March 19.

Ghosh, A. (2005) Public–private or a private public: promised partnership of the Bangalore Action Task Force. *Economic and Political Weekly* 40(47), 4923–30.

Ghosh, A. (2006a) Banking on the Bangalore dream. *Economic and Political Weekly* 41(8), 689–92.

Ghosh, A. (2006b) Working of the BATF. *Economic and Political Weekly* 41(14), 1376–77.

Goldman, M. (2005) *Imperial Nature: the World Bank and the struggle for social justice in the age of globalization*. New Haven, CT: Yale University Press.

Goldman, M. (2007) How "water for all!" policy became hegemonic: the power of the World Bank and its transnational policy networks. *GeoForum* 38(5), 786–800.

Goldman, M. (forthcoming) Speculative urbanism and the making of the next world city. *International Journal for Urban and Regional Research.*

Ghertner, D.A. (2008) Discourse of slum demolitions. *Economic and Political Weekly* 43(20), 17–21.

Gurria, A. (2009) Cities matter to the global climate policy agenda. Conference opening remarks, Copenhagen Climate Summit for Mayors, Copenhagen, Denmark, December 15, 2009,

Harriss, J. (2006) *Power Matters: essays on institutions, politics, and society in India.* New Delhi: Oxford University Press.

Harriss, J., Stokke, K., and Tornquist, O. (eds.) (2004) *Politicising Democracy: local politics and democraticisation in developing countries.* London: Palgrave.

Heitzman, J. (2004) *The Network City: planning the information society in Bangalore.* New York: Oxford University Press.

The Hindu (2008) KIADB to acquire 1,200 acres for SEZ near Bangalore: farmers protest against acquisition bid. October 25; http://www.hindu.com/2006/10/25/stories/2006102509770400.htm (accessed September 25, 2010).

Ho, K. (2009) *Liquidated: an ethnography of Wall Street.* Durham, NC: Duke University Press.

Human Rights Watch (HRW) (2006) Building towers, cheating workers: exploitation of migrant construction workers in the United Arab Emirates. *Human Rights Watch* 18.8(E).

Idiculla, M.P. (2009) Why BBMP elections are not happening. *Citizen Matters*, Bangalore, October 29; http://bangalore.citizenmatters.in/articles (accessed October 29, 2009).

Infosys (2009) *Annual Report 2008–2009.* Bangalore: Infosys.

John, J. (2005) Bangalore Airport: real estate matters. *Economic and Political Weekly* 40(11), 1015–16.

Kamath, L., Baindur, V., and Rajan, P. (2008) Urban local government, infrastructure planning and the urban poor: a study of periurban Bangalore. *Civic Bangalore and CASUMM*, March.

Lin, G.C.S. (2007) Reproducing spaces of Chinese urbanization: new city-based and land-centered urban transformation. *Urban Studies* 44(9), 1827–55.

Nair, J. (2005) *The Promise of the Metropolis: Bangalore's twentieth century.* New York: Oxford University Press.

Nayar, S. (2009) Moving forward: the long term growth prospects of Indian real estate. *Cityscape Intelligence*, December 9; http://www.cityscapeintelligence.com/moving-forward-the-long-term-growth-prospects-of-indian-real-estate (accessed December 9, 2009).

New York Times (2009) Satyam chief admits huge fraud. January 7.

OECD (2009) *Competitive Cities and Climate Change.* OECD Conference Proceedings, Milan, Italy, October 9–10, 2008. Paris: OECD; http://www.oecd.org/dataoecd/12/38/42554913.pdf

Ong, A. and Zhang, L. (2008) Introduction: privatizing China: powers of the self, socialism from afar. In L. Zhang and A. Ong (eds.) *Privatizing China: socialism from afar.* Ithaca, NY: Cornell University Press.

Osborne, T. and Rose, N. (1999) Governing cities: notes on the spatialisation of virtue. *Environment and Planning D* 17, 737–60.

Parthasarathy, B. (2004) India's Silicon Valley or Silicon Valley's India? Socially embedding the computer software industry in Bangalore. *International Journal of Urban and Regional Research* 28(3), 664–85.

Peck, J., Theodore, N., and Brenner, N. (2009) Neoliberal urbanism: models, moments, mutations. *SAIS Review* 29(1), 49–66.

Press Trust of India (2008) UK expert bids to set up "Scottish Bangalore." July 1; http://www.expressindia.com/latest-news/Top-outsourcing-expert-bids-to-set-up-Scottish-Bangalore/329787/ (accessed September 25, 2010).

PricewaterhouseCoopers (PwC) (2005) *Cities of the Future: global competition, local leadership*; http://www.pwc.com/extweb/ pwcpublications.nsf/docid/940ABE55AB5865A6852570F400722582/$FILE/cities-final.pdf (accessed September 25, 2010).

PricewaterhouseCoopers (PwC) (2007) *Cities of Opportunities*; http://www.pwc.com/extweb/pwcpublications.nsf/docid/CEDFBB47FF120D5B8525729F006CCEAE/$File/cities_of_opportunities.pdf (accessed September 25, 2010).

Pani, N. (2009) Resource cities across phases of globalization: evidence from Bangalore. *Habitat International* 33(1), 114–19.

Rediff (2005) Farmers' prayer: "May Wipro and Infy biz drop!" January 25; http://www.rediff.com/money/2005/jan/25spec.htm (accessed September 25, 2010).

Robinson, J. (2011) Mobility and differentiation in international urban policy: the case of city development strategies. In E. McCann and K. Ward (eds.) *Mobile Urbanism: cities & policy-making in the global age*. Minneapolis, MN: University of Minnesota Press.

Rose, N. (1999) *Powers of Freedom: reframing political thought*. Cambridge, UK: Cambridge University Press.

Roy, A. (2009) The 21st century metropolis: new geographies of theory. *Regional Studies* 43(6), 819–30.

Saldanha, L. (2007) A nice road goes dangerously off-course. *Indian Architect and Builder (IA&B)*, May, 97–104.

Shrivastava, A. (2008) Toward corporate city-states? *Seminar: A Monthly Symposium* 582; http://www.india-seminar.com/2008/582/ 582_aseem_shrivastava.htm (accessed September 25, 2010).

Simone, A.M. (2001) On the worlding of African cities. *African Studies Review* 44(22), 15–41.

Simone, A.M. (2004a) *For the City Yet to Come*. Durham, NC: Duke University Press.

Simone, A.M. (2004b) People as infrastructure: intersecting fragments in Johannesburg. *Public Culture* 16(3), 407–29.

Simone, A.M. (2010). *City Life from Jakarta to Dakar: movements at the crossroads*. London: Routledge.

Srinivas, S. (2001) *Landscapes of Urban Memory: the sacred and the civic in India's high-tech city*. Minneapolis, MN: University of Minnesota Press.

Srinivasaraju, S. (2008) *Keeping Faith with the Mother Tongue: the anxieties of a local culture*. Bangalore: Navakarnataka.

Statesman, The (2009) Raju had 275 firms for land deal. January 25.

Strathern, M. (2000) *Audit Cultures: anthropological studies on accountability, ethics, and the academy*. London: Routledge.

Suzuki, H., Dastur, A., Moffatt, S., Yabuki, N., and Maruyama, H. (eds.) (2010) *Eco²
    Cities: Ecological Cities as Economic Cities*. Washington DC: World Bank.
Times of India (2006) Bellandur Lake plays villain. January 12; http://timesofindia.indiatimes.
    com/city/bangalore/Bellandur-Lake-plays-villain/articleshow/1368108.cms
    (accessed September 25, 2010).
Times of India (2009) Monorail: a reality? July 3.
Upadhya, C. and Vasavi, A.R. (eds.) (2008) *In an Outpost of the Global Economy: work and
    workers in India's information technology industry*. New Delhi: Routledge.
Venkat, A. (2008) Infosys scouting for buys in Europe, US. *Hindu Business Line*, April 17;
    http://www.thehindubusinessline.com/2008/04/18/stories/2008041851940400.
    htm (accessed April 17, 2008).
Vyasulu, V. and Reddy, A.K.N. (eds.) (1984) *Essays on Bangalore*. Bangalore: Council on
    Science and Technology.
World Bank (2008) *World Development Report 2009: reshaping economic geography*. Washington,
    DC: World Bank.
World Bank (2009) *Systems of Cities: harnessing urbanization for growth and poverty alleviation*.
    Washington, DC: World Bank.
World Wide Fund for Nature and Booz & Company (2010) *Reinventing the City: three pre-
    requisites for greening urban infrastructure*, March; http://assets.panda.org/downloads/
    wwf_reinventing_the_city_final_3_low_resolution.pdf

10

The Blockade of the World-Class City: Dialectical Images of Indian Urbanism

Ananya Roy

In India, the turn of the century has been marked by a violent expansion of the urban frontier, a making way and making space for the new Indian middle classes, through the smashing of the homes and livelihoods of the urban poor. Such forms of violent urbanization are evident in Delhi, Mumbai, and Bangalore. This is also the case in Kolkata. Here, the long-standing Left Front government, led by the Marxist wing of the Communist Party of India, has sought to aggressively remake the city as a "world-class" urban environment. Such urban development has followed the predictable formula of elite enclaves of residence and leisure, economic zones to attract mobile capital, and civic campaigns to insure beauty and order in the city. In the Indian context at least, Kolkata belies any argument about Leftist exceptionalism. Neoliberalism has been as much at home in this Marxist-ruled region as it has been elsewhere in the country.

Yet, it is also in Kolkata that the ambitious project of making the world-class Indian city has been repeatedly blocked. Faced with fierce peasant uprisings and electoral challenges by opposition parties, the Left Front's efforts to claim land and space for urban and industrial development have been stymied. Such a blockade calls into question the primary instruments of state power: eminent domain, zoning strategies, geobribes. But the blockade is also a lived experience, a part of the texture of everyday urban life in Kolkata, where infrastructures of circulation – roads, highways, trains, buses – are constantly subject to demonstrations, marches, shutdowns, and curfews. The imagined dynamism of the world-class city, a space inserted into global circulations of capital, thus comes to be "*gheraoed*," or "encircled," by protest. The world-class city is made to stand still.

In this essay, I examine these practices of protest and also demonstrate how they ultimately embolden rather than erode the hegemonic icon of the

Worlding Cities: Asian Experiments and the Art of Being Global, First Edition.
Edited by Ananya Roy and Aihwa Ong.
© 2011 Blackwell Publishing Ltd. Published 2011 by Blackwell Publishing Ltd.

world-class city. I am interested in the making of consent to the world-class city because I think it is important to understand this icon as more than a fetish, as more than a commodity-on-display or a commodity-in-circulation. Instead, following Walter Benjamin, I conceptualize the world-class city as a phantasmagoria, the dream world of postcolonial development. Yet, this phantasmagoria is also a "dialectical image," containing within it the radical potential of disenchantment and critique. In particular, I am interested in how the blockade of the Indian world-class city conjures up what Benjamin (1935: 10) titled "the law of dialectics at a standstill." As Robinson (2004: 715) has noted, the methodology of a "dialectics at a standstill" makes possible an understanding of the phantasmagoria (of urban life) as "as a site which potentially exposes the range of alternative future and past possibilities for organizing social life." It is in this spirit that I turn to the discourses and practices that constitute the Indian world-class city and pay careful attention to its blockade.

"India Poised"

Homegrown neoliberalism

The urban question has not featured prominently in the plans that have guided the many decades of development in postcolonial India. It is the liberalization of the Indian economy, enthusiastically adopted by the Indian state, in the 1990s, that cast attention on India's cities. A bold new national urban strategy, the National Urban Renewal Mission, launched in 2005 and named to pay homage to India's first postcolonial modernizer, Jawaharlal Nehru, makes the case for investments in urban infrastructure. Its founding documents predict a massive increase in India's urban population – from 28 percent in 2001 to 40 percent in 2021. It also yokes India's economic future to this urban sector, stating that "by the year 2011, urban areas would contribute about 65% of gross domestic product." These predictions are repeated in a recent report on Indian urbanization issued by McKinsey & Company. The report claims that between 2008 and 2030, "urban India will drive a near fourfold increase in average national income" and "unlock many new growth markets," from infrastructure to health care (McKinsey & Company 2010: 17).

The mission statement of the national strategy argues that such productivity can only be insured through "reforms and fast track planned development of identified cities." The reforms are meant to insure "an investor-friendly environment" through the repeal of existing regulations such as India's Urban Land Ceiling and Regulation Act, which until now imposed a ceiling on vacant land in large cities and empowered the state to acquire land in excess of the ceiling. Alongside the deregulation of urban space is an emphasis on "efficiency in urban infrastructure and service delivery mechanisms."

The National Urban Renewal Mission is not necessarily the most potent force in Indian urbanization today. Other state-led processes, such as the formation of Special Economic Zones, have decisively restructured the management of space. Nevertheless, the national mission establishes a new hegemony for neoliberal models of urban planning. Particularly significant is the casting of urban development in the dominant language of "private-sector efficiencies." But other hegemonic constructions are also worth noting. For example, while the national strategy promises services for all, including the urban poor, it does so in the rather circumscribed language of financial discipline, community participation, and transparent and accountable local governance. Such norms strengthen emergent forms of urban middle-class politics that are organized around the concerns of "consumer-citizens" and weaken the claims of the urban poor, those that must often be put forward in terms of survival or justice. Or for example, the national mission identifies a geography of urban development, both the "congested" city center that must now be reformed through urban renewal and the peri-urban margins, a frontier for new, planned cities.[1] The latter is enabled by mandates such as the following one, written into the Memorandum of Agreement between the national mission and the Kolkata Metropolitan Development Authority: "simplification of legal and procedural frameworks for conversion of agricultural land for non-agricultural purposes."[2]

Above all, the national mission makes a case for the activist state, one that is able to bundle immense amounts of financing, deploy powerful instruments of planning to deregulate space, and – above all – tackle the problem-space of the city. If Chatterjee (2004: 141) notes that in Nehruvian India, "no organic idea of the Indian city of the future was available," then now such a model has been constructed by the neoliberal state.

In particular, different levers of the state have deployed three socio-spatial technologies to implement the world-class city: slum evictions, Special Economic Zones, and peri-urban new towns. These do not constitute a unified and homogenous urban strategy imposed by a central government on the cities of India. Instead, they are undertaken in discrete and disparate ways by various scales of the state, including municipal and metropolitan authorities. But such heterogeneity only amplifies a national common sense about world-class cities and their productive economies. Take, for example, the following scenes.

In 2004–5, Mumbai's city authorities sought to implement their "Vision Mumbai" plan through the eviction of 300,000 slum-dwellers. Such brutal displacements were only the precursor to what is now a vast urban renewal scheme meant to reclaim the city center through the redevelopment of the Dharavi slum.

In Delhi, there has been a speeding up of "slum clearance," authorized and legitimized by a series of judicial rulings issued by the Delhi High Court and the Supreme Court of India. Steeped in the discourse of world-class cities, these rulings present Delhi as a "show window to the world" that must be protected against "degeneration and decay" (Bhan 2009). They also reinforce a broader criminalization of urban poverty that is at work in India, one formally inscribed in a 2000 judicial ruling that framed slums as usurpations of public land and likened slum-dwellers to pickpockets.

In Kolkata, the Left Front government has promoted the rapid urbanization of the city's rural eastern periphery through the development of new towns. Gavin Shatkin (this volume) argues that such "urban integrated megaprojects" are examples of "privatopolis," district-scale development projects that constitute a privatization of urban planning. Such urban districts have been formed, of course, through the erasure of the land and livelihood claims of squatters and sharecroppers and through the enclosure of wetlands, fisheries, and other commons.

Nationwide, India's Ministry of Commerce and Industry has facilitated the formation of Special Economic Zones, thus creating what, following Ong (2006), can be understood as spaces of economic and political exception. Meant to attract foreign investment, India's Special Economic Zones offer numerous tax exemptions and infrastructural incentives. But, most important, they provide land. The freeing up of such land has turned out to be a violent process, a land grab by the state that is best understood as "primitive accumulation." A forced expropriation and expulsion of direct producers, this is as an instance of what Harvey (2005) has termed "accumulation by dispossession." As in the case of the slum evictions and peri-urban new towns, the Special Economic Zones reveal how neoliberalism in India has been driven by an activist state seeking to open up new spaces of capital accumulation. It is here that characterizations of a "weak" Indian state fall apart. Not only does the Indian state seek to undertake "strong" action, often modeled after the Chinese experience, but also the seeming absence of effective government is itself a state strategy. As I have argued in previous work (Roy 2003, 2007, 2009), regimes of urban rule in India often function through an "unmapping" of cities. This in turn vests considerable powers of territorialized flexibility in the state. Such an informalized state, actively deploying ambiguity and uncertainty, is not a weak or absent state. It is an activist state.

Such state practices can be usefully conceptualized as homegrown neoliberalism. The term "homegrown" can be understood to mean the ways in which global circulations of market rule find a home in national contexts of development. In the Indian case, for example, these circulatory practices are evident in the restructuring of urban governance by the World Bank and the Asian Development Bank (see Michael Goldman, this volume), a process that is a soft-power version of structural adjustment and its harsh conditio-nalities. However, I use the term "homegrown" to mean something more than the local habitat of neoliberalism. The signifier refers to the discourses and practices through which a multitude of heterogeneous social forces in urban India actively produce and take up the norms of market rule and thereby the blueprint of the world-class city. It is thus that Asher Ghertner (this volume) shows how the "world-class aesthetic" is not only an "observa-tional grid" used by the state to govern space, but also a "form of self-government" among the urban poor "who identify with the desirability of world-class urban improvements." Or, Vijayabaskar (2010) shows how in some parts of India, the protests against Special Economic Zones have been feeble, since farmers have been eager to sell their agricultural land and have seen, in such land markets, new opportunities for accumulation and urban livelihood. Inevitably embedded in global circulations – such as the practices of referencing Asia that I describe later in this chapter – homegrown neoliberalism is thus a multiply determined, unstable conjuncture. Homegrown neoliberalism is engendered through this multiplicity of sites and through a variety of aspirations.

As an instance of homegrown neoliberalism, the making of the Indian world-class city is inevitably a normative project. It requires the valorization of worlding aspirations and the devalorization of claims that may block or stall such forms of worlding. Such is the case of an unusual branding campaign launched by the *Times of India*. Anchored by the Bollywood superstar, Amitabh Bachchan, the campaign seeks to brand not a consumer product or even a city, but in fact India itself. The "India Poised" campaign tells the story of "India vs. India," celebrating the India that can insert itself into global prosperity and rejecting the India that expresses doubt:

> One India is straining at the leash, eager to spring forth and live up to all the adjectives the world has been showering recently upon us
>
> The other India is the leash ...
>
> An India whose faith in success is far greater than its fear of failure.
>
> An India that no longer boycotts foreign-made goods, but buys out the companies that makes them instead ...
>
> [O]ne India, a tiny little voice at the back of the head, is looking down at the bot-tom of the ravine, and hesitating. The other India is looking up at the sky and saying, "It's time to fly."

In the YouTube video that promotes the campaign, Amitabh Bachchan is set in a curious landscape, an unfinished highway along the Arabian Sea. The construction site is reminiscent of the urban–industrial edifices of modernization and above all it is devoid of people, of the messiness of those who may be in the way of development. Such branding campaigns are central to homegrown neoliberalism.

Referencing "Asia"

The worlding practices of Indian urbanism make reference to key icons of urban development. Thus, Mukesh Mehta, the architect who is leading the redevelopment of Mumbai's Dharavi slum, argues that through urban renewal this space could become India's "Canary Wharf," an allusion to London's docklands that have been transformed into a global financial center (Tutton 2009). The 2010 Commonwealth Games, held in Delhi, were billed not only as a sporting event but also as a "city make-over," an event that "will leave behind a city much more beautiful and charming than it currently is."[3] Such forms of referencing are common practices of authorization in the production of urban space. They implement what, following Robinson (2002), can be conceptualized as the "regulating fiction" of the global city. Nor are such practices new. Colonial urbanism, for example, involved a heavy traffic in referents, be it the French model of Haussmann's modernized Paris or the British model of Ebenezer Howard's Garden City. Indeed, the colonies served as a space of urban experiments unlike any other (Rabinow 1989). Here, models-in-circulation were not so much applied as tested, often in extreme fashion, facilitated by the monopoly of power and advantage that colonialism afforded. It is in this sense that colonial cities were also worlding cities.

But what is distinctive about contemporary Indian cities is that their plans and designs increasingly make reference to "Asian" models of development. "Vision Mumbai," the plan devised for Mumbai by global consulting firm McKinsey & Company, promised that Mumbai could become the next Shanghai. India's Special Economic Zones are modeled after those in China. During the passage of India's Special Economic Zones Act in 2005, a Member of Parliament thus stated: "China is a shining example of a country which has developed through its special economic zones" (Gopalakrishnan 2007: 1492). The practice of "referencing Asia" is not confined to the state. As Bunnell and Das (2010: 280) note, global consulting firms such as McKinsey & Company play an important role in forging such routes of "urban emulation" and in thus creating "geographies of serial seduction." Also important is the work of an emergent urban civil society dominated by elite think tanks and middle-class associations. It is thus that Bombay First, an organization of Mumbai's wealthy and powerful, which endorsed the "Vision Mumbai" report and the attendant slum evictions, explicitly references Shanghai as a model for Mumbai. On its web site, the following quote from a former Indian Prime Minister is prominently displayed: "When we talk of a resurgent Asia, people think of great changes that have come about in Shanghai. But we can transform Mumbai in the next five years in such a manner that people will stop talking about Shanghai and Mumbai will become a talking point." Such a vision of a "resurgent Asia" anchored by world-class cities such as Mumbai not only references cosmopolitanism and worldliness, but also distinctive "Asian" features of urban life, particularly those that are seen to be entrepreneurial. Bombay First celebrates Mumbai as a center of global finance. But it also celebrates another type of entrepreneurialism: Mumbai's taxi drivers: "The taxi driver: You don't need GPS with him around. He knows every nook and cranny of the city."[4] Here, then, is a narrative of Asian creativity, resilience, and ultimately success – features that seem to defy the plotted coordinates of Western capitalism.

Referencing Asia is, of course, more than the circulation of referents. It is also the circulation of capital. The Dubai-based real-estate conglomerate Emaar Properties operates in India in partnership with MGF Developments Limited. Emaar-MGF's motto of "creating a new India" is territorialized in their signature lifestyle enclaves, those that promote the ability to "live, work, play" in "world-class" environments. Emaar-MGF billboards lining the streets of Delhi put on display Emaar's showcase project in Dubai, the massive development called Downtown Dubai, at the center of which is the Burj Dubai tower (now renamed the Burj Khalifa tower). The billboards read: "Burj Dubai, the World's tallest tower. The only thing taller is our dream for India." More is at stake here than Dubai-style manicured and gated prosperity; it is the very nature of urban planning in India that is being transformed. Today, it is actors such as Emaar-MGF that create "integrated master planned communities," their actions enabled and sponsored by the activist state. Can such "corporate economies," to borrow a term from Benjamin (2000), serve the dense terrain of slums and squatter settlements that house a substantial proportion of India's urban humanity? Or are these private enclaves a stark reminder of an urban world that is "splintered," one where the elite can secede from the larger urban fabric while the rest of the city must make do with a deteriorating public grid of infrastructure and services (Graham and Marvin 2001)? As Bose (2007) has argued, "state policies … have underscored the cultural importance of the mythic Global Indian," granting special privileges to Non-Resident Indians and enabling their investments in India. It is in the name of the Global Indian that the splintered world-class Indian city is being made.

But the story of Indian cities is more than that of splintering urbanism and secessionary citizenship. Indeed, the making of the Indian "world-class" city is engendered through claims of integration, public interest, and urban democracy. It is a reclaiming of the city, of the urban commons, rather than a retreat to gated enclaves. Such a reclamation is taking place not only under the sign of the "Global Indian," but also increasingly in the name of the "middle class consumer-citizen" (Fernandes 2004: 2427). Fernandes and

Heller (2006: 500) note that such class interests are at once distinct from those of the poor and the working class, as well as from those of the propertied classes. Yet, organized as neighborhood associations and reform movements, the middle class has taken up the cause of spatial order in Indian cities. An endeavor broader than the defense of property values, these interventions invoke the idea of the good city. Of course the urban poor have no place in the good city. In short, they "represent class projects of spatial purification" (Fernandes and Heller 2006: 516). Analyzed incisively by Baviskar (2003) as "bourgeois environmentalism," in Delhi, environmental and consumer rights groups have led the battle against slums and squatter settlements. Through the filing of public interest litigation, they have managed to criminalize poverty and assert the values of "leisure, safety, aesthetics, and health" (Baviskar 2003: 90). In the case of Kolkata, Chandra's (2006) research similarly shows the role of middle-class environmental NGOs and neighborhood associations in evicting squatters, often by invoking the pollution of ponds and local water bodies by the urban poor. Following Ong (2006: 6), such forms of bourgeois environmentalism can be understood as "technologies of subjectivity," those that animate rather than regulate. Such claims to the urban commons do not oppose, but rather align with, the world-class city of the Global Indian.

In other words, the making of the Indian world-class city cannot be simply understood as an elite project or as the interests of property capital, or even as the practice of an activist state. Rather, it is an ideal to which there is broad subscription. In earlier work (Roy 2009), I have identified this ideal as "civic governmentality," one that produces governable subjects and governable spaces through norms of civility and civic virtue. These norms are not necessarily imposed by the activist state; rather, they are produced and disseminated through middle-class politics.

They also anchor the discourses and practices of pro-poor federations, such as Mumbai's famous SPARC (Society for the Protection of Area Resources). Celebrated by anthropologist Arjun Appadurai (2002) as an instance of "deep democracy," SPARC works in solidarity with Mumbai's slum-dwellers and pavement-dwellers. Yet it also insists that the poor must make peace with the world-class city. Take, for example, a recent essay on "voluntary" displacement by two SPARC interlocuters:

> Millions of people in Mumbai's narrow island confines depend on the north–south railways to reach their places of work each day ... A critical problem was the sheer number of people living close to the tracks. Wherever shacks were within 30 feet, trains were required to slow down to 5 kilometres per hour ... When Indian Railways and the Government of Maharashtra embarked on long-planned improvements, these 18,000 households, with support from SPARC, planned and managed their own resettlement ... As cities grow and new or

improved infrastructure becomes necessary, some displacement inevitably occurs. (Patel and Bartlett 2009, 3–4)

SPARC has argued that such a strategy of "community-led resettlement" is dictated by pragmatism, which is derived from the actions and demands of poor women, the "core of the politics of patience" (Appadurai 2002: 34). As an infrastructure of populist mediation, SPARC thus maintains the dominant narrative of the poor as encroachers. In doing so, it reinforces rather than challenges the hegemonic icon of the world-class city. In her introductory essay to this volume, Aihwa Ong thus rightly makes note of "the apparently paradoxical interdependence of calculative practices of political entrepreneurialism and the progressive language of 'anti-neoliberalism'."

The Blockade

Unmaking consent

In 2006–7, the making of the Indian world-class city ground to a halt, at least in Kolkata. Two uprisings – one in Singur and the other in Nandigram – presented a blockade to the plans of the activist state. Singur, a site on the edge of Kolkata, was to house the Tata Corporation's flagship Nanocar factory. Billed as the world's cheapest car, the Nanocar itself is a phantasmagoria of middle-class consumption, marking a democratization of the automobility once reserved for India's elites. To make way for the factory, the Left Front government had procured land from local peasants and sharecroppers, and had also provided massive subsidies – "geobribes," to use Harvey's term (1989) – to the Tata Corporation. But here political opposition, led by the fiery Mamata Banerjee, mobilized the displaced and called into question the state's primary instrument of eminent domain. At Nandigram, a village in the state of West Bengal, of which Kolkata is the capital, the Left Front government sought to put into place a Special Economic Zone. Village land was to be transformed into a chemical hub owned and operated by the Salim Group, an Indonesian conglomerate. Here, a peasant uprising refused entry to the armed functionaries of the state. Despite brutal state repression, the peasant movement held its ground, becoming an important cause for national anti-displacement movements.

The Singur and Nandigram movements have altered the landscape of electoral politics in the region, with the Left Front losing ground to opposition parties in subsequent elections. Long a politically dominant force in West Bengal, the Left Front government now finds itself hemorrhaging seats all the way from village councils to the Indian Parliament. The blockade itself has held. In 2008, the Tata Corporation, seeking respite from the protests and strikes, abandoned its Nanocar factory at Singur. In the face of peasants with scythes and hoes blocking entry to their village, the Nandigram Special Economic Zone remains impossible to implement. The Left Front government is seeking new mechanisms of development, offering "cash incentives" to its officers if they are able to "locate" land for industrialization. As Gavin Shatkin (this volume) notes, the struggles in Singur and Nandigram have had a chilling effect on many other development projects in the region.

At first glance, the Singur and Nandigram movements seem to present a challenge to the very brand of "India Poised." They call into question the multiple exclusions and displacements of the modern nation and city; they defy primitive accumulation. They challenge the referents that underpin postcolonial spatial order, including the colonial 1894 land acquisition law that has served as the juridical framework for displacement and dispossession in contemporary India. It must then be asked: Does the blockade represent an unmaking of consent to the world-class city?

If the "Chinese model" of development once served as an important referent for India's worlding strategies, then today this model is under scrutiny. As protests against Special Economic Zones have proliferated in India, so state policy itself is being revised. In a seeming reversal of discourse, India's Secretary of Commerce, Gopal Pillai, has admitted that China is not the appropriate development model for India: "India is a democracy. People own the land. If we wanted a zone the size of Shenzhen it would take us 30 years" (Wonacott 2007). While Pillai's statement sounds like a lament, other critics undermine the myth of Chinese "success" and its replicability. In particular, they draw attention to the "land grabs" that facilitated development in China, and that have rendered the land rights of Chinese farmers fragile and tenuous (Gopalakrishnan 2007; Sarkar 2007). "The recent incidents of Nandigram and Singur ... clearly point to the fact that in a functioning democracy, the coercive method of land acquisition is untenable, not only from a moral standpoint, but also as a matter of practical policy" (Sarkar 2007: 1441). In a new version of referencing, media reports now cite the Chinese case, but do so to expose the "ugly truths" of glittering new cities and to celebrate the protests of Chinese "dispossessed peasants" against "state intimidation" (Pocha and Chakrabarti 2007).

The "Chinese model" is not the only development truth under attack. So are the key instruments of statecraft: eminent domain, geobribes, and indeed urban planning itself. The development deals at Singur and Nandigram required the acquisition of land by the state for "public purpose." This could only be achieved by defining industrialization as public purpose. Nirupam Sen, Minister of Industries, West Bengal, justified the public purpose thus: "If a particular industry wants a big chunk of land in a contiguous area for setting up a large plant there, it is not possible for the industry to purchase land from each and every farmer, particularly in West Bengal where fragmentation of land is very high ... will the State government not acquire it for the project? And, of course, it is a public purpose. Industrialisation means employment generation, it means development of society; the entire people of the State will be benefited" (Chattopadhyay 2006). The Singur and Nandigram movements called into question this "public purpose," thereby thwarting the state's prominent instrument of eminent domain. They also drew attention to the massive geobribes, or state subsidies, that underwrite private investment. Critics have thus noted that at Singur, the Tata Corporation, India's largest corporate group, was not only getting land for free but also was to enjoy interest-free loans and tax subsidies (Mitra 2007; Sarkar 2007). In comparison, the compensation for displaced peasants and sharecroppers was meager.

If the geobribes were justified in the name of "public purpose," then displacement was justified in the name of "consent" and "compensation." These twin concepts – public purpose and consent-based compensation – lie at the heart of what I have earlier demarcated as "civic governmentality." They mark a making of peace with the world-class city. The movements at Singur and Nandigram broke up this peace and challenged the norms of consent and compensation. Did those being displaced consent to the land acquisition and to the terms of compensation? Was this seeming voluntary displacement a sign of the rational rather than violent state? The struggles at Singur and Nandigram revealed that the concept of consent can ring hollow in a liberal democracy – that where the poor are subject to the sheer material and symbolic violence of socioeconomic inequality, they cannot grant or withhold consent to displacement.

The challenge to civic governmentality in Kolkata is embodied by a poignant symbol: Quarter no. 4/11. Occupied by Shambhu Prasad Singh, this factory quarter was the last hold-out in a tract of factory land that had been converted into the city's upscale South City retail and residential complex. The workers were evicted from their living quarters with no prior notice and with meager compensation. As documented by filmmaker and artist Ranu Ghosh, Shambhu Prasad Singh refused to make way. For a while, with the towers of South City rising around him, he was the blockade.

It is interesting to place Singh's struggle in juxtaposition to the Singur and Nandigram movements. Taken together, they manifest the mandates of India's new urban mission: on the one hand, the rapid urban renewal of the deindustrialized inner city through property capital and, on the other hand, the deregulation of the peri-urban edge to insure the freeing up of agricultural land for property and production capital. But as the Singur and Nandigram movements called into question the instruments of eminent domain and geobribes, so Shambhu Prasad Singh's blockade triggered important scrutiny of urban planning in Kolkata. Soon, it became evident that the South City complex had been built in violation of environmental laws and through the enclosure of some of southern Kolkata's largest water-bodies. Such forms of elite informality and illegality are commonplace in Indian cities today. While urban poverty is criminalized, elite informality is often legitimized and even practiced by the state. Thus, the new towns on the peri-urban edge of Kolkata exist in direct violation of the state's own proclaimed policies of protecting agricultural land and wetlands (Roy 2003; Dasgupta 2007). But rarely are they seen to be informal or illegal. Shambhu Prasad Singh's blockade made visible the South City complex as "towers of violation," thereby disrupting the consent that has hitherto accompanied elite informality and illegality.

The heroic subaltern?

The Left Front regime responded to the uprisings in Singur and Nandigram with considerable violence. The repression of the state came to be severely critiqued by Leftist intellectuals hitherto sympathetic to the agenda of the Left Front. Eminent historians returned literary awards once bestowed on them by the West Bengal government; world-renowned filmmakers and artists marched in the streets of Kolkata; accomplished poets and authors held public hearings for those who had been beaten, raped, and pillaged at Singur and Nandigram. If the Left Front had once been seen as a force of land reforms and socioeconomic justice, then it was now portrayed as a brutal, neocolonial force, waging war against its own people. In a strange turn of events, it is a group of international Leftist scholars – Noam Chomksy and Howard Zinn among them – who put forward a statement in support of the Left Front. They argued that in the face of American imperialism, any protest against this democratically elected communist regime would "split the Left." The response from India's Leftist intellectuals was fierce: "To 'share similar values' with the party today is to stand for unbridled capitalist development ... and the Stalinist arrogance that the party knows what 'the people' need better than the people themselves. Moreover, the violence that has been perpetrated by CPI(M) cadres to browbeat the peasants into submission, including time-tested weapons like rape, demonstrate that this 'Left' shares little with the Left ideals that we cherish. Over the last decade, the policies of the Left Front government in West Bengal have become virtually indistinguishable from those of other parties committed to the neoliberal agenda."[5]

But in whose name was such a critique launched by the Indian Left against the global Left? Who, then, was to speak on behalf of history and its dialectics? A closer look indicates that the struggles at Singur and Nandigram took place under the sign of the "peasant." This was the heroic subaltern to be represented and rescued in this movement. At the Singur public hearing held on October 27, 2006, activists presented "project-affected" men and women as "landholders, ... sharecroppers, ... agricultural laborers, ... artisans, and small traders." They argued that "the project cannot be more important than agriculture," that industry cannot replace a fertile, irrigated tract of multi-cropping, that it must instead utilize vacant "wastelands" of abandoned factories. Theirs was a claim to the "right to life" and to the agrarian settings that were seen to constitute the "natural environment" for such life (Kumar *et al.* 2006).

The blockade presents a moral challenge to the enclosures of primitive accumulation. It seeks to recuperate the "dispossessed villagers" who are being "lost to history." But the blockade also privileges the figure of the "peasant-owner" over that of the urban squatter, informal vendor and day laborer, the figures whose claims to space remain criminalized by the Indian judiciary and the aspirations of an urban middle class and elite to world-class cities. There are no such public hearings by Leftist intellectuals for the urban poor. Where does the urban subaltern fit in the teleology of historical materialism? Is this not what haunts Mike Davis's (2006: 28) anxious consideration of the slum's "surplus humanity": "To what extent does an informal proletariat possess that most potent of Marxist talisman 'historical agency'?" Davis argues that "uprooted rural migrants and informal workers have been largely dispossessed of fungible labour-power, or reduced to domestic service in the houses of the rich" and that thus "they have little access to the culture of collective labour or large-scale class struggle." It can be argued then that urban squatters and slum-dwellers are the new "awkward class," not fully proletarianized or dispossessed, tenuously tethered to property and petty bourgeois production. They cannot be defended as the heroic subaltern. They cannot be the subject of history. They remain at the awkward margins of the blockade. This too is "dialectics at a standstill."

A recent essay makes the case that the Singur struggle must be seen as a "popular effort to civilize rather than substitute contemporary forms of capitalist development" (Nielsen 2010). My argument goes further, for I wish to assert that the struggles at Singur and Nandigram do not challenge the making of the world-class city. Framed through a Marxist nostalgia for dispossessed peasant-owners, they trivialize the brutality of urban development and the displacements thus engendered. They mount a defense for a "*Sonar Bangla*" – a Bengal of fields of gold. In earlier work (Roy 2003), I have argued that such pastoral motifs are commonplace in elite Bengali ideology or what, following Sartori (2008), can be called "Bengali liberalism." *Sonar Bangla* is a powerful agrarian myth, for it evades the long history of concentrated landownership and pervasive landlessness in Bengal. But other evasions are also at work. Pastoral radicalism can only advance one critique of urbanization: the loss of an agrarian world. It cannot challenge the phantasmagoria that is the world-class city; it has no political vocabulary to do so. The denial of a place in history to the urban dispossessed and displaced makes possible a distinctive subject of history: the Indian world-class city, a project claimed by both the Indian Left and its critics.

There are other limits as well to these struggles in and around Kolkata. The blockade represented those displaced at Singur as "dispossessed villagers," only some of whom could become "wage-slaves" for the Tata Corporation. Yet, powerful counter-narratives soon circulated. In withdrawing from the Nanocar factory at Singur, Ratan Tata, CEO of the Tata Corporation, wrote an open letter to the people of West Bengal. In it, he explained the withdrawal as one where Tata's "dream of contributing to the industrial revival of West Bengal [was] shattered by an environment of politically motivated agitation and hostility." He posed a question to the young people of the state: "Would they like ... to build a prosperous state with the rule of law, modern infrastructure and industrial growth, or would they like to see the state consumed by a destructive political environment of confrontation, agitation, violence and lawlessness?" (*Financial Express*, October 18, 2008). The theme was echoed by India's corporate leaders in other cities and states. In Bangalore, Narayana Murthy, chairman of Infosys, noted that "what has happened in Singur is unfortunate for ... all progressive Indians" (*Financial Express*, August 31, 2008). Amidst a deindustrialized and informalized economy, Ratan Tata's open letter dangled that most rare of dreams: factory employment. In 2008, a new round of protests took place at Singur, this time by those who had relinquished land for the Nanocar factory in the hope of factory jobs. Their banners read: "Welcome Ratan Tata. We want industry, we do not want confrontation." This too was a blockade, this time in defense of "industrialization."

Echoes of such a defense could also be heard at Nandigram, where critiques were now launched against the movement and its efforts to block the dispossession of villagers. Here is one such indictment of the Bhumi Ucched Pratirodh Committee (a committee to prevent land dispossession):

> A number of women, from families of the labouring poor in Nandigram who had been ousted from their villages by the violence unleashed by BUPC, told me that there was a dearth of livelihood opportunities in the area; some of them were even sending their young children to Delhi as domestic labour and were forced to marry off their daughters at a very young age. They felt that if there was industrialisation in the area, this might give them more opportunities for employment. (Bhattacharya 2007, 1895–8)

As the public hearings had gathered testimonials of the heroic and dispossessed subaltern, so now a new set of counter-testimonials called into question the declaration of "the victory of the peasants at Nandigram against the combined forces of state and corporate power" (Sarkar and Chowdhury

2009). Cast in the language of choice and consent, such investigations claimed to speak truth on behalf of the subaltern. Above all, they put forward the subaltern dream of livelihood, especially that of factory jobs.

Amidst persistent structural violence, it is impossible to assert that the subaltern has consented to the wage-slavery of the world-class city. Yet it is equally impossible to assert that industrialization and urbanization are elite interests imposed on the poor. The making of consent – be it through the norms of civility and civic virtue or through the hope of factory jobs – remains central to the project of homegrown neoliberalism and its world-class cities.

After pulling out of Singur, the Tata Corporation relocated its Nanocar factory to Sanand, a town on the outskirts of the Ahmedabad metropolitan region in Gujarat. Flanked by the Gujarat Chief Minister, Narendra Modi, Ratan Tata declared it to be a "homecoming," made sweet by the "condu-cive and industry-friendly environment." The Gujarat government had provided ample "geobribes" for the relocation, including 1,100 acres of prime land freed up by the state for purchase by the Tata Corporation. But more is at stake here than an evasion of the blockade erected at Kolkata. Ratan Tata's "homecoming" referenced a nationalism that the Tata Corporation has long claimed: in this case that during colonial rule, Jamshedji Tata, the founder of Tata & Sons, had mitigated a severe drought in Gujarat through the establishment of a cattle farm. A century later, Ratan Tata was to declare (in Gujarati): "We belong here and so we have come back here" (*Business Standard*, October 8, 2008).

But if colonial Gujarat was the land of Gandhi and the ideal of *swadeshi* (economic self-sufficiency), then postcolonial Gujarat sounds a different register of nationalism. Narendra Modi, always eager to put on a show that Gujarat is open for business, is also the architect of the 2002 riots waged against Muslims. Carefully planned and implemented by the instruments of the state, the Gujarat pogroms killed and maimed hundreds. Bidwai (2008) calls this the "Gujarat model of development" – that of rapid industrialization with ruthless disregard for both human rights and environmental costs, now "sanctified" by Ratan Tata. The House of Tatas, Bidwai notes, was meant to be different: an "enlightened" and "ethical" industrial group with a storied history of pioneering *swadeshi* enterprises and thus Indian industrialization. Today, it is Modi who is the keeper of the phantasmagoria of postcolonial development. In his proud declaration about the Tata factory relocated from Singur to Sanand, he claimed the Nanocar itself: "I am supporting it in national spirit … Several countries had invited the Tatas to set up the project. If that would have happened, it would have been bad for the whole country" (*Business Standard*, October 8, 2008).

It is thus that the Nanocar stands at the confluence of Hindu fundamen-talism and neoliberal nationalism. So too, perhaps, does the Indian world-class city. But the mobilizations against such a city cannot be read in the simple register of heroic subaltern action. A multiplicity of aspirations – the dream of factory jobs and fast-paced "swadeshi" economic growth, the promise of a bourgeois city of order and beauty, even the fascist utopia of a Hindutva nation – conjoin to mark the limits and contradictions of resistance.

Standing Still

The blockade of the world-class city takes different forms. There are the civil insurrections of Singur and Nandigram that halt car factories and chemical hubs. There are hold-outs such as Shambhu Prasad Singh who refuse to make way for the towers of urban development. But there is also the block-ade that can be understood as "standing still." This too confounds the project of the world-class city. Following Peck, Theodore, and Brenner (2009: 49), the blockade can be understood to be "serial policy failure" and "resistance to neoliberal programs of urban restructuring," processes that are particularly evident in cities and that indicate the limits and frictions that accompany neoliberalism.

I borrow the term "standing still" from a photographic exhibit by artist Simryn Gill. The Standing Still exhibit is made up of photographs, taken in Malaysia between 2000 and 2003, of "ambitious development projects ... abandoned before completion." These are the "shells of what would have become large shopping centers or apartment blocks or private mansions or even mini towns" (Figure 10.1). Devoid of human figures, the photographs are a powerful articulation of space and time, of what Gill (2004) calls a "place in time": "A place in time, where, one might say, the past lies in ruins, unkempt and untended, and the future also somehow has been aban-doned and has started to crumble. No way forward, no way back."

Gill's photographs have the allegorical quality that Benjamin so avidly sought in art and literature. For Benjamin, allegory, unlike myth, makes evident the fleeting and the transitory, thereby eroding the certainty of progress. "Because these decaying structures no longer hold sway over the collective imagination, it is possible to recognize them as the illusory dream images they always were" (Buck-Morss 1991: 159).

Such is the case with the new towns that line the eastern periphery of Kolkata. Ambitious public–private partnerships meant to serve the "Global Indian" and embodying the urban dream of the middle classes, many of these are now spaces of "standing still." They are haunted by the sheer failure of planned development. There is Infospace, an Information Technology park, which is described as "perhaps the only Special Economic Zone in the country which is running entirely on diesel generators ... The state power utility, which was to supply power to Infospace, has not been able to lay cables." The head of the West Bengal State Electricity Board has

Figure 10.1 Standing still, 2000–2003; type c photograph, from a series of 116, 12.4 inches by 12.4 inches
Source: courtesy of Simryn Gill and Tracy Williams Limited.

argued that the power cables could not be laid because "locals would not let power utilities erect distribution towers on their land" (Datta 2009). Once again, the geobribe – in this case, the promise to companies of cheap and abundant power – has been frustrated by a blockade.

There is the city's showpiece township, New Town. It is here that Kolkata's middle class had hoped to find a world-class urban lifestyle, with many investing their entire savings or pensions in apartments and condominiums. Today, New Town is described as a "nightmare without an end" – bad roads, dirty water, poor drainage, insufficient electricity. In many of the housing complexes, there is no water supply or no connection to the power grid. Residents are quickly moving out and the area is becoming deserted. Those who remain survive in the ways in which slum-dwellers and squatters do in poor, informal settlements – by buying water from vendors, using diesel generators, and making do with unpaved streets (Mitra and Chakraborti 2008). New Town is the ghost town of homegrown neoliberalism, one where the ruins of the suburban middle-class dream are starkly visible.

This too is a blockade, not one erected by the unruly subaltern, but one that exists at the very heart of the activist state that lacks the capacity to fulfill its promises to the Global Indian and to the middle-class consumer-citizen. Here, the urban plan, crafted in the image of a Dubai or a Singapore or a Shanghai, becomes impossible to implement, marking a crucial gap in homegrown neoliberalism. Here, the world-class city stands still.

The ghost towns of homegrown neoliberalism return us to Benjamin's notion of a "dialectics at a standstill." Ruins of a world-class future, they expose the ideology of progress and rupture the enchantment of development. In doing so, they bear witness to history – as did the arcades of Paris for Benjamin's analysis of urban modernity. At such a site of standstill, is a different politics possible? At such a site, can alternative futures be imagined?

Yet, it is my contention that in Kolkata the gap – between urban plan and blockaded reality – does not sabotage homegrown neoliberalism. Rather, it emboldens it, strengthening the call issued by the new Indian urban middle class as well as the elite Global Indian for a world-class city. It inaugurates a phantasmagoria more mythic than that anticipated by Walter Benjamin. The blockade reproduces, rather than erodes, the icon of the world-class city. The abandoned factories, stalled condominium projects, and fleeing investors become the occasion for a new dream image of urban-industrial development and economic prosperity. This overpowering and seemingly impenetrable enchantment is the referent, Asia. Transformed from geography into history, as the epoch that follows, Asia is the citation and re-citation that remakes consent to the world-class city. Singapore. Dubai. Shanghai. Surely, elsewhere in Asia, urban dreams come true. Surely, elsewhere in Asia, with just the right dose of authoritarian power and free-market rule, the good city is being built and lived. Surely, it is therefore possible to reform and transcend this place in time, to transform the Asian city itself into the subject of history.

Notes

1 See http://www.jnnurm.nic.in/nurmudweb/toolkit/Overview.pdf
2 See http://jnnurm.nic.in/nurmudweb/MoA/Kolkata_MoA/Kolkata_MoA1.PDF
3 See http://www.cwgdelhi2010.org/Template3.aspx?pageid=P:1015
4 See www.bombayfirst.org/
5 See http://kafila.org/2007/11/24/response-to-noam-chomsky-howard-zinn-et-al-on-nandigram/

References

Appadurai, A. (2002) Deep democracy: urban governmentality and the horizon of politics. *Public Culture* 14(1), 21–47.
Baviskar, A. (2003) Between violence and desire: space, power, and identity in the making of Metropolitan Delhi. *International Social Science Journal* 55, no. 175, 89–98.

Benjamin, S. (2000) Governance, economic settings, and poverty in Bangalore. *Environment and Urbanization* 12(1), 35–56.

Benjamin, W. (1999 [1935]) Paris, the capital of the nineteenth century: exposé of 1935. In R. Tiedeman (ed.) *The Arcades Project*, transl. H. Eiland and K. McLaughlin. Cambridge, MA: Harvard University Press.

Bhan, G. (2009) "This is no longer the city I once knew": evictions, the urban poor and the right to the city in millennial Delhi. *Environment and Urbanization* 21(1), 127–142.

Bhattacharya, M. (2007) Nandigram and the question of development. *Economic and Political Weekly*, May 26.

Bidwai, P. (2008) Nano from Gujarat: Legitimising Moditva? October 20; http://us.rediff.com/money/2008/oct/20tata2.htm (accessed January 15, 2009).

Bose, P. (2007) Dreaming of diasporas: urban developments and transnational identities in contemporary Kolkata. *Topia* 17, 111–130.

Buck-Morss, S. (1991) *The Dialectics of Seeing: Walter Benjamin and the Arcades Project.* Cambridge, MA: The MIT Press.

Bunnell, T. and Das, D. (2010) Urban pulse – a geography of serial seduction: urban policy transfer from Kuala Lumpur to Hyderabad. *Urban Geography* 31(3), 277–284.

Business Standard (2008) Modi's Gujarat bags Tata's Nano. October 8; http://www.business-standard.com/india/news/modi%5Cs-gujarat-bags-tata%5Cs-nano/336735/ (accessed January 20, 2009).

Chandra, M. (2006) Grassroots environmental claim making and the state: the 74th Constitutional Amendment Act in Kolkata, India. Unpublished PhD thesis, University College London.

Chatterjee, P. (2004) *The Politics of the Governed: reflections on popular politics in most of the world.* New York: Columbia University Press.

Chattopadhyay, S. (2006) Land reform not an end in itself: interview with Nirupam Sen. *Frontline* 23, no. 25 (December), 16–29.

Dasgupta, K. (2007) A city divided? Planning and urban sprawl in the eastern fringes of Calcutta. In A. Shaw (ed.) *Indian Cities in Transition*. New Delhi: Orient Longman.

Datta, A. (2009) IT hub survives on diesel as Bengal Government trips on power. March 1; http://www.livemint.com/2009/03/01224042/IT-hub-survives-on-diesel-as-B.html (accessed April 11, 2009).

Davis, M. (2006) *Planet of Slums.* New York: Verso.

Fernandes, L. (2004) The politics of forgetting: class politics, state power and the restructuring of urban space in India. *Urban Studies* 41(12), 2415–30.

Fernandes, L. and Heller, P. (2006) Hegemonic aspirations: new middle class politics and India's democracy in comparative perspective. *Critical Asian Studies* 38(4), 495–522.

Financial Express (2008) Ratan Tata's open letter invites mixed reactions. October 18; http://www.financialexpress.com/news/ratan-tatas-open-letter-invites-mixed-reactions/374941/ (accessed January 11, 2009).

Gill, S. (2004) Matrix 210: Standing still. Exhibit at the University of California, Berkeley Art Museum; http://www.bampfa.berkeley.edu/images/art/matrix/210/MATRIX_210_Simryn_Gill.pdf (accessed November 5, 2009).

Gopalakrishnan. S. (2007) Negative aspects of Special Economic Zones in China. *Economic and Political Weekly*, April 28.

Graham, S. and Marvin, S. (2001) *Splintering Urbanism: networked infrastructures, technological mobilities, and the urban condition.* London: Routledge.

Harvey, D. (1989) From managerialism to urban entrepreneurialism: the transformation in urban governance in late capitalism. *Geografiska Annaler* 7(1), 3–17.

Harvey, D. (2005) *A Brief History of Neoliberalism*. New York: Oxford University Press.

Kumar, A. *et al.* (2006) Public Hearing, Singur; http://aidindia.org/main/content/view/348/169/ (accessed October 20, 2008).

McKinsey & Company (2010) *India's Urban Awakening: building inclusive cities, sustaining economic growth*. McKinsey Global Institute.

Mitra, A. (2007) Santa Claus visits the Tatas. *The Telegraph*, March 30.

Mitra, P. and Chakraborti, S. (2008) Life in Bengal's dream township turns into a nightmare. *Times of India*, December 15.

Nielsen, K. (2010) Contesting India's development? Industrialisation, land acquisition and protest in West Bengal. *Forum for Development Studies* 37(2), 145–70.

Ong, A. (2006) *Neoliberalism as Exception: mutations in citizenship and sovereignty*. Durham, NC: Duke University Press.

Patel, S. and Bartlett, S. (2009) Reflections on innovation, assessment, and social change: a SPARC case study. *Development in Practice* 19(1), 3–15.

Peck, J., Theodore, N., and Brenner, N. (2009) Neoliberal urbanism: models, moments, mutations. *SAIS Review* 29(1), 49–66.

Pocha, J. and Chakrabarti, A. (2007) Fields of conflict: from Beijing to Bengal, people are opposing industrialization. *The Telegraph*, March 20.

Rabinow, P. (1989) *French Modern: norms and forms of the social environment*. Cambridge, MA: The MIT Press.

Robinson, J. (2002) Global and world cities: a view from off the map. *International Journal of Urban and Regional Research* 26(3), 531–554.

Robinson, J. (2004) In the tracks of comparative urbanism: difference, urban modernity and the primitive. *Urban Geography* 25(8), 709–23.

Roy, A. (2003) *City Requiem, Calcutta: gender and the politics of poverty*. Minneapolis, MN: University of Minnesota Press.

Roy, A. (2007) *Calcutta Requiem: gender and the politics of poverty*. New Delhi: Pearson Books (2nd Indian edn. of *City Requiem*, Calcutta).

Roy, A. (2009) Civic governmentality: the politics of inclusion in Mumbai and Beirut. *Antipode* 41(1), 159–79.

Sarkar, A. (2007) Development and displacement: land acquisition in West Bengal. *Economic and Political Weekly*, April 21.

Sarkar, T. and Chowdhury, S. (2009) The meaning of Nandigram: corporate land invasion, people's power, and the Left in India. *Focaal* 54(16), 73–88.

Sartori, A. (2008) *Bengal in Global Concept History: culturalism in the age of capital*. Chicago: The University of Chicago Press.

Tutton, M. (2009) Real life "Slumdog" slum to be demolished. CNN News, February 23; http://www.cnn.com/2009/TRAVEL/02/23/dharavi.mumbai.slums/index.html (accessed March 1, 2009).

Vijayabaskar, M. (2010) Saving agricultural labor from agriculture: SEZs and the politics of silence in Tamil Nadu. *Economic and Political Weekly* 36(6), 36–43.

Wonacott, P. (2007) Land mine: in India, clashes erupt as industry expands. *The Wall Street Journal*, May 21; http://www.wsj-asia.com/pdf/opc_award/LAND_MINE.pdf (accessed October 20, 2008).

11

Rule by Aesthetics: World-Class City Making in Delhi

D. Asher Ghertner

Planning without Plans

From 2003 to 2007, news headlines in Delhi closely followed a story pitting a local environmental group against seven of India's top land developers. In 2003, the Ridge Bachao Andolan (Save the Ridge Movement) submitted a petition to the Supreme Court of India challenging the construction of India's largest shopping mall complex for being built on Delhi's southern ridge, a protected green space, in the up-and-coming South Delhi colony of Vasant Kunj. This constituted a land-use violation of the statutorily binding Delhi Master Plan. Expert testimony by the Delhi Development Authority (DDA) – the agency that drafts and is legally bound to implement the Master Plan – defended the project in the Court for being "planned" and thus legal because of the involvement of professional builders, its high-quality construction, and its strategic function in boosting Delhi's architectural profile. Showing architectural blueprints and artistic renderings of the proposed development (see Figure 11.1), emphasizing the project's US$300 million price tag, and describing the mall as a "world-class" commercial complex, the DDA suggested that the visual appearance of the future mall was in itself enough to confirm the project's planned-ness. How could a project of such strategic importance in Delhi's effort to become a world-class consumer destination *not* be planned, the DDA's lawyer argued. Even after its own "Expert Committee" found the complex in "flagrant violation" of planning law,[1] the Court concurred in early 2007, allowing construction to go forward based on the mall's capital-intensiveness and associated world-class appearance.[2]

During the course of the mall proceedings in the Supreme Court, an adjacent multigenerational slum settlement in conformance with the land-use

Worlding Cities: Asian Experiments and the Art of Being Global, First Edition.
Edited by Ananya Roy and Aihwa Ong.
© 2011 Blackwell Publishing Ltd. Published 2011 by Blackwell Publishing Ltd.

Figure 11.1 An artistic rendering of the DLF Emporio, one of the seven malls in the
Vasant Kunj shopping mall complex[3]
Source: reproduced with the permission of DLF Limited.

designation listed in the Master Plan was declared "unplanned" and illegal
by the DDA for being a "nuisance" to the neighboring middle-class residential
colonies. Based on a set of photographs showing the "unsightly" conditions
in the slum, and despite the absence of a survey or scientific evaluation of
its so-called "nuisance-causing activities," the DDA demolished the settlement
without compensation, an action upheld by the Court.[4]

In these two examples, "planned-ness," an attribute of urban space key to
the determination of legality, was defined as that which looks planned,
regardless of its formal standing in planning law or any correspondence
between actually existing urban development and expert paper representations of the city (e.g., the Master Plan).[5] According to this aesthetic mode of
governing, which I will show to be widespread in Delhi today, if a development
project looks "world-class," then it is most often declared planned; if a
settlement looks polluting, it is sanctioned as unplanned and illegal.

In preparation for Delhi's hosting of the 2010 Commonwealth Games
and as part of the government's officially declared plan to make Delhi into
a "world-class city" (see DDA 2007), public finances in the early 2000s were
gradually shifted away from education, public housing, health care, and
food subsidies toward large, highly visible, and "modern" infrastructure
developments such as the Delhi Metro Rail, more than twenty-five new
flyovers, two new toll roads to Delhi's posh, satellite cities, and the
Commonwealth Games Village – prestige projects built "to dispel most
visitors' first impression that India is a country soaked in poverty" (Ramesh
2008). In the late 1990s, the DDA also began aggressively privatizing the
approximately 35 percent of Delhi's land that had been public, much of
which had been acquired for, but never developed as, low-income housing.[6]

While these changes in Delhi's regulatory landscape and public policy priorities have been central to recent transformations of Delhi's physical landscape, I argue here that the making of world-class cities is not instantiated solely (or even primarily) through an economic calculus of cost–benefit or through a juridical redefinition of property; rather, it also takes shape through the dissemination of a compelling vision of the future – what I will here call a world-class aesthetic – and the cultivation of a popular desire for such a future – the making of world-class subjects.

This chapter examines this process in two parts. In the first two sections, I look at how a world-class aesthetic – a distinct observational grid used for making normative assessments of urban space – has been codified through law in Indian cities, making aesthetic judgments such as that in the Vasant Kunj case increasingly central to the delineation of state policy and practice. My analysis here draws from three data sources: orders, judgments, and petitions filed in the Delhi High Court and Supreme Court of India; observations of court hearings in the Delhi High Court; and newspaper and television reports on land-use and slum-related matters. In the next two sections, I examine how slum residents – those being displaced from public land and thus those with seemingly the least to gain from the world-class redevelopment of Delhi – both oppose and take up the vision of the world-class city, advancing the dream of a privatized city at the same time as they posit their own claims to the global future. Based on extended ethnographic research in a single slum settlement, I consider how the vision of the world-class city establishes clear aesthetic criteria for self-evaluation; that is, how a socially produced aesthetic – which I define, following Ranciere (2004), as "a distribution of the sensible" that lays down boundaries between the beautiful/ugly, visible/invisible, legal/illegal – operates as a normalizing urban quality, inducing a form of self-government among those who identify with the desirability of world-class urban improvements. Through a discussion of the decorative posters that residents hang on their walls and the stories of city and self they convey through them, I show, specifically, how residents of this slum have begun to adopt world-class aesthetics as a basis for both locating themselves in the changing city and for framing their own world-class aspirations.

While this world-class aesthetic does offer particular "norm(aliz)ed interpellations through which urban subjects come to inhabit space" (Ananya Roy, Conclusion, this volume), so too does it operate as a contested arena, allowing those subjects to fashion new political demands and visions. Just as the urban elite launches ambitious experiments to advance new norms and forms of the urban, so too do the informal poor engage in cross-class appropriations, stepping inside these norms and forms to try to leverage, negotiate, or happen upon improved life prospects. In attempting to carve out a space for the expression of their individual and collective desires – be it by centering the slum as a space of hope or by celebrating their potential to become property owners – these residents too engage in worlding practices. Thus, in contrast to Davis's (2006: 201) assessment of global slums as mere containers for "warehousing this century's surplus humanity," I show slum residents to be integral vectors in Delhi's worlding efforts, their aspirations central to both the material and symbolic transformation of the cityscape.

Taken together, the two parts of this chapter examine the world-class aesthetic as a form of governmental legibility that: (i) provides "an overall, aggregate, synoptic view of a selective reality" (Scott 1998: 11), enabling state intervention into an otherwise ungovernable terrain; and (ii) is deployed via governmental programs to guide "the population's" conduct toward certain "suitable ends" (Foucault 2007: 96) – in this case, a system of private property and a world-class visual landscape. But, rather than reading the world-class aesthetic as either producing or not producing "governable subjects" – that is, rather than seeing slum residents' appropriation of world-class aesthetics as consent or resistance – I want, in line with a broader argument of this book, to "trouble the subject-power of the subaltern" (Ananya Roy, Conclusion, this volume) by considering the contradictory ways in which subjects participate in the world-class city making project. Insisting that slum residents' desires are simultaneously a constitutive part and an effect of this project, I locate their political agency at the intersection of how they partake in both ruling and being ruled (Ranciere 2001). This means asking how the world-class aesthetic is made sensible to slum residents – how they step into its field of vision and take up the aspirations it sets before them – but also how they might mobilize that aesthetic for different ends.

Calculative Deficiencies and the Turn to Aesthetic Norms

By the late 1990s, state officials and politicians in Delhi had begun to articulate the goal of turning Delhi into a "slum free city," giving it a "world-class" look, promoting an efficient land market, and converting the "under-utilized" public land occupied by slum-dwellers into commercially exploitable private property (DDA 1997). These were all part of the policies of economic liberalization initiated by the Finance Ministry in 1991 and concretely implemented in Delhi in the late 1990s (Jain 2003; Ghertner 2005). But despite the clear mandate from above to remove slums, the practical means of doing so were limited. Through the 1990s, for example, various programs were launched to upgrade or relocate slums, but the slum population nonetheless increased from 260,000 to 480,000 families between 1990 and 1998 (MCD 2002).

During this period, the decision to remove a slum lay almost entirely in the hands of the state agencies upon whose land slums were settled. Thus, if a slum on DDA land was to be removed, for example, the DDA was charged with notifying the slum residents, surveying the households to determine resettlement eligibility, collecting fees from those offered resettlement, purchasing and/or allocating the necessary land for establishing a resettlement colony, obtaining support from the police for protection during the demolition, hiring the demolition team for the appropriate day, and coordinating the resettlement exercise with the Slum Wing of the Municipal Corporation. Not only was each of these steps bureaucratically challenging, but the elaborate patronage relations extending from slums into the lower bureaucracy, what Benjamin (2004) calls India's "porous bureaucracy," made the assembly of accurate survey registers – a requirement before a demolition could be carried out at the time – nearly impossible. Surveys were tampered with, false names were appended, and between the time when the survey was completed and when the agency obtained the necessary clearances and land appropriations (usually years), the number of people residing in the slum had changed, thus demanding a new survey and setting much of the same process in motion again (cf., Hull 2008). Furthermore, through the 1990s, the cost of obtaining and preparing land for resettlement colonies escalated (DDA 1997), creating a strong disincentive for land-owning agencies to remove slums in the first place. In addition, the legal status of most slum settlements was ambiguous, with various forms of *de facto* regularization over the years (e.g., state-issued ration and voting cards, state-funded infrastructure improvements, the presence of government-run schools) making slum removal a charged political issue. In short, the procedure for removing slums was costly, slow, and contentious.

In the early 2000s, however, there was a huge increase in public interest litigations (PILs) filed against slums by resident welfare associations (RWAs) (Chakrabarti 2008) – property owners' associations mobilized around quality of life and neighborhood security issues. Combined with the 2003 announcement of Delhi's successful bid to host the 2010 Commonwealth Games, this placed the state and municipal governments under increasing pressure from both above and below to "clean up" the city. In the late 1990s, the courts had increasingly begun to take notice of "the dismal and gloomy picture of such jhuggi/jhopries [slum huts] coming up regularly"[7] and in 2002 observed that "it would require 272 years to resettle the slum dwellers" according to existing procedures and that the "acquisition cost … of land … and development … would be Rs.4,20,00,00,000/– [~ US$100 million]."[8] This set of conditions was incompatible with Delhi's imagined world-class future, so the courts, in response to the PILs filed by RWAs, began intervening in slum matters and increasingly rebuked the DDA and other land-owning agencies for failing to address the "menace of illegal encroachment" and slums.[9] However, when the courts pushed these agencies to act more aggressively to clear slums, judges were befuddled by messy ground realities, missing government records, ambiguous tenure statuses, and incomplete surveys. The courts found themselves in a position where they were unable to even assess the size of the problem, not to mention issuing informed action orders. For example, in a case against a slum in South Delhi, the High Court stated, "There are several controversies, claims and counter claims made by the learned counsel for the parties. The records are, however, scanty and the said claims and counter claims cannot be decided on the basis of existing material and documents on records."[10]

Such an absence of cadastral precision is widespread in slum-related cases, which led to the absence of a synoptic vision by which upper-level bureaucrats and the courts could "survey a large territory at a glance" (Scott 1998: 45) and "govern from a distance" (Rose 1999). For Latour (1987), such "action at a distance" relies on a "cascade" or relay of measurements and inscriptions (e.g., survey registers) that can be combined and simplified into more generalizable and thus legible representations of the territory (e.g., maps and statistical tables) as they move up the chain of administrative command to "centers of calculation," such as courtrooms and centralized government offices. The absence of accurate baseline surveys in Delhi, however, broke this cascade, rendering knowledge of slum space highly localized rather than abstractly knowable and manipulable from above. As a result, land-owning agencies could easily delay slum-related court decisions for years by postponing court hearings in order to survey and reassess the ground situation. Until accurate visual simplifications of slum space were secured (i.e., until the "cascade" of inscriptions was complete), bureaucrats sitting in state offices and judges in courtrooms had their hands tied, or so it seemed.

In many instances, the ownership of the land occupied by slums was itself ambiguous, putting the court in the strange position of being prepared to order a slum demolition, but not knowing which agency was obligated to carry out the order. In a case that ultimately resulted in more than 2,800 homes being razed in 2006, one party claimed that the land in question belonged to the Municipal Corporation, but "Thereafter it was difficult to find out as to who was [*sic*] the owner of the land as all the land-owning agencies abdicated their responsibilities and none was prepared to own the land."[11] This recalls Roy's (2002, 2004) discussion of the "unmapping" of Calcutta and the regulatory ambiguity/informality to which it gave rise. But, whereas the absence of maps and numbers in the Calcutta context increased the state's ability to arbitrarily and selectively deploy power, distribute benefits, and dodge previous duties and promises, in Delhi such a calculative deficit or absence of map-based legibility rendered slums ungovernable, for it limited both the court and the upper-level bureaucracy's ability to see and manage slum space, and left the implementation of court orders and state mandates to the "porous" lower-level bureaucracy that slum residents have historically been able to "work" through cultural and political ties (Kaviraj 1991; Benjamin 2008).[12]

The ambiguity in property records in Delhi is even more complicated by the fact that, according to the Municipal Corporation, 70 percent of Delhi is "unauthorized," meaning that it violates land-use codes or building bye-laws in some way or another.[13] What is more, as the former Commissioner of the Slum Wing of the Municipal Corporation told me, "the rich have unauthorizedly grabbed far more land in Delhi than the poor. The total land under squatters and slum-dwellers is far less than the illegal land held by the rich and famous, it's just that nobody sees those violations."[14] If the court were to begin removing all unauthorized land uses, most of Delhi would have to be razed, including those developments central to Delhi's worlding strategy – for example, the Vasant Kunj shopping mall complex discussed in the introduction. Thus, strict enforcement of the Master Plan or development codes, which had been avoided for almost 50 years since the first Master Plan was implemented in 1962, would lead not just to a "slum-free" city, but also a business-, mall-, and industry-free city. Recognizing this dilemma, the Municipal Corporation submitted in the High Court that the problem of unauthorized constructions and slums is "mammoth in nature – and cannot be controlled by simply dealing under the existing laws or under the provisions of [Delhi's] master plan" (Biswas 2006).[15] That is, it called upon the judiciary to exceed existing law – that is, to exercise the rule of exception (Schmitt 2006) – in carrying forward what had become the agreed-upon *telos* of Delhi's development: a world-class future.

The courts did so by abandoning the previous bureaucratic and statutory requirement that land-owning agencies create calculative, map- and survey-based simplifications of slum space. Through the 1990s, government surveys were conducted to summarize slums according to the duration of the slum population's occupation of the land in question, residents' eligibility for resettlement, the land-use category of the occupied land, and the density and size of the population settled thereupon. Only then would summary statistical tables and maps that simplified messy ground realities into compact "planes of reality" (Rose 1991: 676) be relayed up the bureaucratic chain so that state decision-makers and judges could assess their legality. But, as shown above, assembling such calculative and "scientific" simplifications was slow, inefficient, and contentious. So instead of requiring these complex calculative procedures, the courts started using a surrogate indicator to identify illegality: the "look" or visual appearance of space. In lieu of accurately assessing (i.e., creating paper representations that correspond to) physical space, a set of visual determinants began to be used to render slums legible and locatable within the new, predominantly aesthetic "grid of norms" (Rose 1991). How was this transition from a calculative to a more aesthetic regime for evaluating physical space carried out?

World-Class Aesthetics and the Nuisance of Slums

In the early 2000s, the courts began making widespread mention of Delhi as a "showpiece," "world-class," "heritage," and "capital" city. In a landmark judgment from 2000, the Supreme Court stated,

> In Delhi, which is the capital of the country and which should be its showpiece, no effective initiative of any kind has been taken by the numerous governmental agencies operating there in cleaning up the city … Instead of "slum clearance" there is "slum creation" in Delhi. This in turn gives rise to domestic waste being strewn on open land in and around the slums. This can best be controlled … by preventing the growth of slums.[16]

The court thus established the presence of slums as the clearest obstacle to Delhi becoming a clean, showpiece, or world-class, city, a link made even clearer when the Delhi High Court noted that at the current pace, it would "require 1,263 years to demolish the illegal constructions carried out over the last 50 years, and convert Delhi into a world-class city."

Court documents from this period show that the growing concern for the city's world-class appearance increasingly came to be expressed through an environmental discourse of cleanliness and pollution (cf., Baviskar 2003). Popularized through the phrase and public campaign launched by the Delhi Government called "Clean Delhi, Green Delhi," this discourse tied deficiencies in environmental well-being and appearance to the presence of slums, largely through the legal category of "nuisance." For example, in 2001, the Delhi High Court stated: "Delhi being the capital city of the country, is a show window to the world of our culture, heritage, traditions and way of life. A city like Delhi must act as a catalyst for building modern India. It cannot be allowed to degenerate and decay. Defecation and urination cannot be allowed to take place in open at places which are not meant for these purposes."[17] Before 2000, nuisance-causing activities such as open defecation or unhygienic living conditions did not provide sufficient justification for demolishing a slum. Unsanitary conditions in slums and general slum-related public nuisances were legally considered the responsibility and fault of the municipal authorities through the 1980s and 1990s: slums were dirty because the state did not provide them with basic services.[18]

However, as I have argued elsewhere (see Ghertner 2008), the early 2000s introduced a new legal discourse of nuisance that reconfigured the parameters and mechanisms by which slum-related nuisances were to be remedied.

The juridical category of "nuisance" is broadly considered any "offense to the sense of sight, smell, or hearing" (Jain 2005: 97) and is as such directly linked with aesthetic norms. In Indian law, nuisances are of two types, public and private, where the former is an "unreasonable interference with a right common to the general public" and the latter is a "substantial and unreasonable interference with the use or enjoyment of land" (Jain 2005: 97). Because slums are almost entirely settled on public land, slum-related nuisances have always been addressed through public nuisance procedures. The definition of public nuisance, according to statute and precedent, had until this time included only particular *objects possessed* or *actions performed* by individuals or groups that interfered with a public right. Aesthetically displeasing, annoying, or dangerous actions or objects could only be addressed by improving municipal services or fining individuals for their violation.[19]

The inability of the DDA and Municipal Corporation to improve, clean up, or remove slums, as well as the court's failure to efficiently provide order to the city by removing slums through existing statutes, led to two gradual shifts in how public nuisance was interpreted in the early 2000s. First, the courts increasingly began accepting petitions under *public* interest litigation from *private* parties (mostly RWAs, but also hotel and business owners) claiming that neighboring slums were interfering with their quality of life and security. That is, concerns of a distinctly *private* nature were granted legal standing as matters of *public* purpose or, as Anderson (1992: 15–17) noted of colonial jurisprudence in India: "Propertied groups were able in many instances to invoke public nuisance provisions against anyone threatening the value of their property," making nuisance "the coercive arm of property rights." This elevation of the concerns of propertied residents, or blurring of public and private nuisance, was based on the High Court's 2002 distinction between "those who have scant respect for law and unauthorisedly squat on public land" and "citizens who have paid for the land."[20] This ruling established land-ownership as the basis of citizenship as such, thus rendering the preservation and security of private property a public priority and setting the conditions for a broader reworking of nuisance law.

The second shift in the interpretation of public nuisance made the *appearance* of filth or unruliness in and of itself a legitimate basis for demolishing a slum. This change took place by redefining the categories of nuisance such that not only *objects* or *actions*, but also *individuals* and *groups* themselves could be declared nuisances, a shift carried out by equating slum-related nuisances with slums themselves (see Ghertner 2008) – that is, slums do not just improperly dispose of "matter" (e.g., trash, sewage), but are themselves "matter out of place" (Douglas 1966). This vastly expanded the range of procedures that could be administered to remove nuisance: no longer by stopping nuisances through imposing fines and penalties, but by displacing entire populations.

Once the interpretation of nuisance was expanded to include categories of people or entire population groups, the legal (and calculative) basis for slum demolition was simplified. Demolition orders no longer require complex mapping and survey exercises to determine the nature of land use or demand even the confirmation of land-ownership in slum cases. Today, courts ask for little more than the demonstration by a petitioner (who is usually a neighboring RWA) that the slum in question is (i) on public land (which is the definition of "slum" and has never been a sufficient condition for demolition orders in the past) and (ii) a nuisance. Evidentially, this is most commonly and effectively done by furnishing photographs that show the slum's "dirty" look and poor environmental conditions: open defecation, overcrowded living conditions, children playing in and "taking over" the street, stagnant water, municipal waste, and so on.[21] Since approximately 2002, the courts have considered such photographs sufficient evidence to confirm that the slum in question does not conform to the aesthetic and civic codes deemed "normal" in Delhi and have, in the majority of such cases, issued demolition orders. For example, in a case in South Delhi, an RWA pleaded to the High Court "for better civic amenities and for nuisance caused by open wide drain [*sic*]" without making a single mention of the neighboring slum in its petition. Only in the petition's annexures containing photos with such captions as "Jhuggi [slum] dwellers defecate in nallah [drain]" was it revealed that a slum existed beside the drain. Nonetheless, the court observed that "Photographs were filed of the area showing the filth at site and encroachments in and around the nallah" and ordered that "The area should also be cleaned and the encroachments removed."[22] Without initiating an inquiry into the settlement's size, location, history, or legal basis – not to mention the settlement's contribution to water pollution in the drain – the court ordered the slum's demolition.

Over the past 10 years, close to a million slum-dwellers have been displaced in Delhi[23], the vast majority thanks to court orders equating slum clearance with environmental and visual clean-up (Ramanathan 2006; Ghertner 2008). This new aesthetic ordering of the city, in which the legality and essential features of space can be determined entirely from a distance and without requiring accurate survey or assessment, marks a clear shift away from the previous approach to carefully surveying, monitoring, and assessing the land-use status of areas under question. In this new, more aesthetic framework, the law crafts fields of intelligibility by disseminating standardized aesthetic norms. Spaces are known to be illegal or legal, deficient or normal, based on their outer characteristics. A shopping mall, even if in violation of planning law, is legal because it looks legal. A slum, even if its residents have been formalized at their current location, is illegal because it looks like a nuisance. Here, the visuality of urban space itself is a way of knowing its essential features and natural standing within the "grid of norms" on which government can operate. The ability to look at a building, plot of land, or population and immediately locate it within such a grid is an entirely different way of knowing and evaluating urban space than the calculative, inscriptive approach typified in much of the governmentality literature. This more aesthetic approach allows government to overcome the (political and bureaucratic) difficulty of translating messy "reality out there" (e.g., population densities, land-use designations, territorial area, settlement history, etc.) into a numeric or cartographic legibility. Thus, instead of having to inscribe the population and its complex relation with things into standardized, abstractable forms that can be aggregated, compiled, assorted, and then calculated,[24] this "aesthetic governmentality" (Ghertner 2010), or rule by aesthetics, works to ascribe an aesthetic sense of what ought to be improved and what ends achieved. Governmental legibility is achieved today, then, not by (statistically) simplifying territory into easily intelligible representations, but rather the reverse: it takes an idealized vision of the world-class city gleaned from refracted images and circulating models of other world-class cities (a little Singapore here, a little London there) and asks if existing territorial arrangements conform to this vision. But, while world-class aesthetics effectively establish norms for urban life and order, these norms are only effective (under a consent-based and not purely coercive form of rule) to the extent that they produce corresponding desires and subjectivities for directing Delhi residents to "do as they ought" (Scott 1995: 202, citing Bentham). It is to this domain of the everyday experience of world-class aesthetic discourse that I now turn.

Slum Surveys and Aesthetic Training

Due to the scale of slum demolitions today, the avenues by which slum-dwellers can remain and participate in the city are dwindling. As the government auctions off public land for private real-estate development, occupation of public land has become increasingly precarious. Thus, slum residents' primary means to retain access to land today is to earn government resettlement. This means that after a family's home is demolished, it is offered a resettlement plot – undeveloped, usually with minimal service provision and transportation options – somewhere on the outskirts of the city. While less than a third of displaced households end up receiving resettlement plots (Leena 2007), this does not prevent the government from depicting resettlement as a pathway to improvement. The Delhi Government frequently announces new housing schemes for the poor – advertised through images of serviced flats in multi-storey apartment buildings – few of which are ever implemented. In addition, a wide range of popular stories about successful slum relocation programs in the 1970s and 1980s, when land and resources were more widely available, mythologize resettlement plots as equal in standing to private plots. Furthermore, the DDA and Municipal Corporation run slum surveys prior to removing a slum to establish resettlement eligibility, which, in addition to enumerating and registering slum households, construct a compelling image of resettlement colonies as fully serviced, permanent, and integrated residential spaces, something akin to a private plot.

While attending three of these slum survey exercises implemented by field engineers and surveyors in the DDA, I observed how the survey process trains slum residents to see the city through the lens of world-class aesthetics – to see themselves as "illegal" for being outside the "normal" visual order. Over the course of these multi-day exercises, surveyors constantly narrate – both in their formal introduction to the survey process and in informal interactions with residents – the aesthetic impropriety of the slum and reference slum deficiencies to the aesthetic norm established by nuisance law and the repertoire of media and government representations of world-class urbanism. For example, one surveyor told an angry resident, "In the whole world, no settlement that looks like this is legal," and suggested that the resident's demand to remain settled at his current location is at odds with the interests of the rest of the city. "Can't you see that nobody wants this type of slum? ... You bother [*pareshan*] these people," he said with a gesture toward the neighboring middle-class colony. The slum's physical conditions thus get tied to a notion of illegality and are, in part, the deficiencies of the population that must be corrected: as another surveyor said to a group of residents, "once this place is cleared, the whole area will improve, and so will you." These deficiencies, surveyors either directly stated or indirectly intimated, include overcrowding, congestion, unhygienic living conditions, lack of property ownership, and other presumed environmental and public health risks.[25]

A clear effect of the slum survey is that it makes use of what slum-dwellers already know about the slum – that it is dirty, congested, *kachcha* (constructed in a "temporary" fashion), unserviced, on public land – to produce a vision of slum space as illegal and lacking the characteristics necessary for "normal" citizenship. Spaces that look like slums, that look dirty and over-crowded, are learned to be illegal, despite their far more complex political, residential, and legal histories. Thus, participants in the slum survey learn a way of seeing and identifying the essential traits of urban space and are, in the process, trained to conceptually link locations in the city that share these same traits. That is, "slum space" across the city, as a category, is rendered imaginable and intelligible through the survey. The slum survey thus operates as one of many[26] "technologies of perception" (Rajagopal 2001) to redistribute the aesthetico-political field of possibility – in this case, to make the division laid down by nuisance law between clean/polluting, private/

public, legal/illegal *sensible* in the sense of both (i) easily perceptible and (ii) logical, sensible, and natural (see Ranciere 2004). A key effect of the survey, then, is to recruit slum residents into the new visual regime premised on world-class aesthetics.

By offering resettlement in conjunction with disseminating this vision of slum space, the survey shows slum-dwellers that the government is attempting to improve this category of space; that individual slum-dwellers are part of a larger deficient population whose improvement is necessary for the city's improvement; and that it is in their interest to cooperate with this process so as to gain resettlement-cum-private property. That is, unlike previous uses of the survey oriented toward assessing the legality of slum residents (discussed in the second section), the survey today is used to construct the slum-dweller not just as an "illegal," but also as a subject eligible for improvement, resettlement, and thus propertied citizenship. Thus, the slum population's identity itself becomes a key target of governmental practice. While such governmental efforts at "refashioning the human subject from the inside, informing its subtlest affections and bodily responses" (Eagleton 1990: 43) are never complete, as I will now examine through a case from West Delhi, the relationship between slum-dwellers' sense of self and their urban imaginary powerfully shapes how they engage in the "art of being global" and the futures they anticipate.

Shiv Camp: Picturing Private Property

I first entered Shiv Camp shortly after the Municipal Corporation razed about a third of its huts. The demolition, however, stopped before the demolished homes could be fully cleared because an infant was crushed under a hut as it was toppled by a bulldozer. The residents subsequently rebuilt their brick huts, but the Municipal Corporation returned four months into my research to again demolish the same homes, this time permanently.[27] I thus had an occasion to study the lead-up to and aftermath of the demolition, in addition to the two-day demolition exercise itself.

My research in Shiv Camp began by asking residents why they thought their settlement was being demolished. What seemed to me to be a straightforward line of questioning ended up producing extremely contradictory responses. On the one hand, residents expressed anger and sadness that their houses (or those of their neighbors) were being destroyed. Most of the homes were multigenerational, with the earliest residents having arrived in 1968 as government labor contractors. Dislocation therefore threatened not only their livelihood, but also their social networks, family history, and sense of belonging. On the other hand, they understood that the government and local RWAs were trying to improve the city's image by removing slums; and that the preparations for the 2010 Commonwealth Games, when tens of thousands of foreign tourists would arrive in Delhi, required an urban facelift. Therefore, when I asked residents why the government had demolished part of their settlement, the most common responses I heard were "because slums are dirty," "because slums spread filth," or, as one man put it, "Because we are dirty and make the city look bad ... Nobody wants to step out of his home and see us washing in the open or see our kids shitting."

To be sure, residents did not want to be displaced, but most understood and many even empathized with those who wanted them removed. One woman named Kishani, for example, stated: "I have lived here for 30 years. This is my home. It is wrong to remove us from here," expressing a clear opposition to slum demolition. However, when I asked her what she thought Delhi would look like in 10 years, she calmly and without sarcasm said, "Delhi will be a beautiful city, totally neat and clean. All the slums will be removed and there will only be rich people." Shiv Camp residents often expressed such a desire for Delhi to become "neat and clean," despite their knowledge that this would require removing "dirty and polluting spaces" such as slums. When I pushed residents to clarify how they could want a world-class city even if it required their displacement, I noticed that we often reached a point at which my interlocutor would, almost in exasperation, talk about slums in a different voice. If she earlier described her experience in slums in the first-person voice, as when Kishani told me, "After we built our huts, we thought the land was our own," or in second-person voice, as when she said, "When you are given a ration card, you become a permanent resident of Delhi," she would shift and start talking about slums "in general." Thus, while Kishani had earlier been describing her personal hardships in Shiv Camp, when I asked why slums were being demolished, she said, "Slums are dirty. They aren't permanent. Slum-dwellers don't live on their own land." Where is the subject located in this third-person description? From where does this omniscient, distant voice depicting "dirty slums" come?

One day, upon entering Shiv Camp, I met Shambu, who called me to his house, as he had many times before. Shambu, a 50-year-old Rajasthani man who was a construction worker until he fell ill, was one of the first residents of Shiv Camp to invite me into his home for regular conversations about his life and city. Our previous talks over *chai* and a *bidi* had followed a familiar script, which we quickly settled into again on this occasion. I asked some variation of the question, "Do you think your slum will be demolished?" And he responded, "Look, one day we're going to have to leave this place. Such slums have no place in Delhi. Our future isn't here." Shambu built his one-room, brick hut (see Figure 11.2) in Shiv Camp 25 years ago, before his children were born and married, and well before residence in a slum was considered illegal. Even though this hut nurtured his family and livelihood,

Figure 11.2 "Our future isn't here," February 2007
Source: photograph by Asher Ghertner, 2007.

he now anticipates the day when it will be razed to the ground, sending him in search of "his future."

Shambu was describing here what I had heard other residents of Shiv Camp articulate dozens of times before: the inevitability of slum demolition.[28] On this particular day though, when Shambu said "Our future isn't here," I pressed him, asking: "If your future isn't this hut, then what is it?" Sipping his *chai*, and perhaps sensing that I wanted something more concrete this time, he said, "Only God knows, but we hope it will be like this," as he turned to the back corner of his hut and pointed to a small paper poster nailed to the wall (see Figure 11.3). The poster shows a house, unlike any

Figure 11.3 "It is a proper house," February 2007
Source: photograph by Asher Ghertner, 2007.

I have seen in India, nestled in a surreal landscape. Although it looked photographic at first, it is actually a computer-generated collage, with an
enhanced, orange sunset-like skyline, a cartoonish foreground of landscaped
trees, flowers, and a pond, and something of a hybrid American ranch and
Swiss chalet styled home depicted as the image's central object. In the backdrop to the left, a second house is shown, making it clear that the main
house is just one within a larger terrain of private, plotted homes. After
asking Shambu what the poster shows, he replied, "it is a beautiful place.
There is no noise or filth there. It is a proper [*sahi*] house." I sought
clarification on what the word "proper" meant to him, and he said it: "It is
one's own [*khud ka*] house. A private [*niji*] house."

I had noticed the decorative posters in Shiv Camp homes before. How
couldn't you? They adorn the walls of most huts, with some enthusiastic
interior decorators hanging more than a dozen in their small, usually one-
room, homes. But, the significance of the images displayed had never struck
me. When Shambu indicated that his aesthetic choice to hang a poster of a
house was linked to his desire for private property, I realized that these

posters might provide a useful device for talking with residents about their future, both imagined and feared.

Devotional posters depicting deities, typically amidst lush pastoral landscapes, have been long-standing decorative and functional fixtures of slum residents' huts. Christopher Pinney's (2004) study of the production and politics of Indian poster art describes the engrossing quality of such Hindu devotional pictures, through which the beholder is enlisted to partake in the scene. These images' "fecund claustrophobia," compressed depth of field, "increased stress on the surface," and frontal religious figures produce a relationship between viewer and viewed in which "The viewer is immediately hailed by his [the god's] gaze" and "commanded to reciprocate" (96). As ritual objects, popular devotional posters have a *darshan*[29] function, permitting mutual recognition and affection between divine and devotee. The gods in these images, then, are not placed within a surrounding landscape (foreground and background). Instead, that landscape and everything shown in the image is aligned to the god. Beyond their functional utility, Pinney argues that this aesthetic renders the images' central religious figures as the source of the religio-national landscape, constructing India as the divine territory of the gods.[30] The lush, pastoral aesthetic found in these posters, he goes on to suggest, lead viewers during the nationalist movement to imagine the utopian space of the nation as springing directly from the divinity shown and experienced within the image. In Shambu's poster shown in figure 11.2, the river Ganga flows from the locks of the god Shiv, producing the nation's territory as Hindu territory. Pinney (1995: 96–9) elsewhere suggests that non-religious Indian calendar art too is typified by a pictorial style in which the landscape emanates from the central figure, as if the presence of the object shown carries with it the power to transform or produce surrounding social and physical space.

In Shiv Camp, posters of gods remain the focal point of people's homes, especially as personal temples. But, in addition to these "photos of gods," a large number of the homes are also dressed in what are popularly called "house posters." House posters retain the rich, pastoral landscapes found in devotional posters: both are characterized by vivid colors, overly floral foregrounds, shimmering water, anachronistic and lush foliage, and radiant skylines.[31] Yet, these posters replace the central figure of a deity with a private, bungalow-style house. Are these private homes – like gods – similarly seen as productive of the surrounding landscape, exuding goodness outwardly and ordering social space?

After Shambu's description of his house poster, I made sure to ask about such posters whenever I encountered them in Shiv Camp. This always surprised people. When I asked why they hung a particular poster, they would say, "I like it," "it is pretty," or "it is nice to look at." These seemed to them to be obvious answers to a stupid question. This was not the response they gave, however, when I asked about devotional posters, or even film posters.

If I asked why they hung a poster of Shiv, for example, their reply was a description of who Shiv is, when they pray to him, and why he is important. In the case of Shambu, whose poster of Shiv we saw above (Figure 11.2), his son makes an annual pilgrimage to the mountains near Haridwar to pray to Shiv, thus the poster in his house. Similarly, when I asked about a poster of Shah Rukh Khan, India's most popular film star, I was led into a discussion of King Khan's greatest movie hits: "you haven't seen *Dilwale Dulhaniya Le Jayenge*?!" When it came to house posters though, residents did not know what I was asking. House posters are thus less indexical and more context specific than these other images; interpreting them and giving them meaning is more contingent on the viewer. Viewing them does not index an already determined referent – as in the identification of an object shown in the image, but rather evokes an individual and aesthetic response – as when Shambu said, "It is nice to look at." Shiv Camp residents thus view the image as beautiful, without interpreting or disclosing the origin of its beauty. Consuming these posters, then, represents more a way of looking, or a particular perspective; the posters do not have a strong narrative or expositional function. In fact, without my prompting, residents rarely referred to the houses that visually dominate the posters.

Therefore, in order to understand what the posters meant to residents, I had to pose more specific questions, such as "What is shown in that picture?" or "Why is the house beautiful?" Only then would residents (usually reluctantly) state the basis on which they considered pictures of private homes aesthetically pleasing. One man who had purchased a vacant plot of land in an unauthorized colony, but had not yet built a house on it, said the poster represented what he hoped his home would one day become when he had enough money to begin construction. A woman stated, as she nodded toward her poster, "Rich people live in these houses. We also hope to live like that one day." Another man said, "It is our dream to someday have a private house. If we live there, all our problems will go away. You can live cleanly there." Kishani (who we met above) said, while turning between me and her poster, "All these slums, they're going away. The Delhi Government is cleaning everything.[32] It is making Delhi beautiful. If you want to stay here, you have to own such a house."

Like Shambu, most people with house posters read them as private property,[33] drawing a clear distinction between these big, private, rich houses, on the one hand, and the small huts on public land in which they live, on the other. Upon this visual distinction residents read a further moral distinction, connoting the private with the clean, legal, and worthy and the public with the dirty, illegal, and disreputable. Residents' aesthetic response to the posters, then, implicitly drew upon this moral connotation. That is, while residents did not see the need to explain the basis of the beauty of their house posters, this beauty nonetheless had a basis in an already existing

Figure 11.4   "It's like a dream for them" – house posters abut devotional imagery at a salesman's poster display in Shiv Camp before Diwali, November 2007
Source: photograph by Asher Ghertner, 2007.

system of signification, one which I argue draws from world-class aesthetics and the moralist discourse of nuisance and property-based citizenship to which it is linked.

During my inquiries into poster art, I determined that house posters are a relatively new phenomenon in Shiv Camp. Poster sellers and consumers there confirmed that five years ago, very few if any residents had such posters hanging in their homes. As a poster salesman in Shiv Camp said on the day before Diwali, the Hindu festival of light, when most poster purchasing and hanging (both religious and decorative) takes place in Hindu homes (see Figure 11.4): "Today, after photos of gods, photos of houses sell the most ... When I started doing this [2001], they weren't so popular." This, of course, was the precise moment when RWAs across Delhi (including near Shiv Camp) began winning court cases against slums via nuisance law; that is, by arguing that behavior they consider distinctly "private" – for example, washing, bathing, drinking, and defecating – is unpleasant, morally degrading, and harmful when conducted in public. As one young man relayed to me, "People now like the idea of someday having a big home.

Figure 11.5 "We hope to live like that one day" – a freshly hung house poster in Shiv Camp on Diwali, November 2007
Source: photograph by Asher Ghertner, 2007.

It's like a dream for them." When I asked why this dream had only now started, he indicated that such a desire was part of a deepening consumerist aspiration: "... when people come straight from the village, they don't want such things. But with time the new generations see these things and begin to want them."

In most of these posters, the large houses appear as nothing but a façade, an exterior inside of which private life takes place (see Figure 11.5). There are no people, the windows are opaque, and the viewer is positioned from a lower viewing angle, as if on the road looking up. This is, indeed, the manner in which most slum residents see private homes in Delhi: from the outside, looking up, seeing people only enter and exit, and imagining a domestic space similar to those seen in the incredibly popular Hindi soap operas.[34] Indeed, the subjunctive imaginary solicited by these posters – for example, the statement "we hope to live like that one day" – was sometimes linked to viewers' understanding of *koti* (bungalow) life gleaned from these

upper middle class melodramas. This was especially the case with the
youth, many of whom had never been in a *koti* before, and whose easy
transition from my poster questions into soap opera talk indicated the
shared imaginary of which both posters and soap operas were a part.
Rarely depicted from the outside and never situated within the geographic context of a specific city or neighborhood, soap operas show
the interior space of private homes from which Shiv Camp residents were
cut off.

In Delhi today, few large slums remain, leaving scattered slum "clusters,"
as they are called by the government, tucked along railroad tracks, wedged
between government-approved residential colonies, and dotted across the
now rapidly expanding periphery. Shiv Camp is one such colony, surrounded
on three sides by imposing, three-four storey middle class *kotis*, each with
small gardens, boundary walls, and driveways on their street side. Over
the course of my fieldwork, two neighboring *kotis* underwent external
stylistic work (the addition of fake columns, decorative arches, or vaulted
windows – part of a new middle-class trend in exterior façade and home
redesign) and one was rebuilt from the ground up. In contrast, Shiv Camp
looks much like it did 10 years ago, contributing to the sense among
residents that they are anachronistic: remnants of the past, clinging to their
place, outsiders in a city that has been home for decades. This experience
of stasis in a sea of change, of a proleptic anticipation of a future "slum-free"
city, is enhanced by the absence of the hundred or so homes that were
razed in 2007 during my fieldwork, as well as the demolition of two nearby
slums in 2006. Further, there are three archetypical world-class monuments – the Delhi Metro, a five-star hotel, and a twelve-storey shopping
mall – each recently built or under construction within a half kilometer of
Shiv Camp. The sheen of these structures' excessive mirrored glass and
polished steel testifies to their material modern-ness, making the brick, tin,
and tarp of Shiv Camp huts incongruous blotches on the landscape. The
look of the area's world-class buildings, as well as that of the corporate-branded
consumer-subjects who occupy them, evinces a deeper economic rift
that marks capitalized from under-capitalized spaces: private versus public
land, "planned" houses versus slums, "big people" versus "little people,"
binary terms that Shiv Camp residents increasingly use to describe their
city today.

In contrast to the private houses shown in posters, much of slum life is
lived outside, in the open, and on display. In consuming these posters and
in ascribing private homes iconic status as "beautiful," residents were
negatively defining their current living conditions against private property.
That is, the aesthetic conveyed by house posters appealed to slum-dwellers,
who, in hanging the posters on their walls, appropriated the implicit
concept contained in them – that is, private property – and inserted themselves into a social imaginary founded on it. The consumption of house

posters in Shiv Camp, then, is part of an aspirational strategy of projecting oneself as a potential world-class citizen. Residents' reference to the "slum" in the third-person voice and use of middle-class aesthetic discourse to characterize "dirty slums," as discussed above, is part of a similar effort to show that they can occupy the middle-class slot, to suggest that they are "improvable," or to confirm their belief in *vikas* (development). In other words, as the world-class aesthetic becomes increasingly hegemonic, slum residents register the sharp binary it produces between public nuisance and private citizen; the decision to hang a house poster thus represents an effort to reinscribe or reimagine the self on the positive side of this binary – to prepare oneself for the future city.

Conclusion

This chapter shows how Delhi's contemporary "worlding" experiment is carried out at least in part by enlisting slum residents into the image of the world-class city, by making "sensible" a world-class aesthetic, and by advancing a myth of private property and the "good life" associated with it. And, if as Barthes says, myth is "an untiring solicitation," an "insidious and inflexible demand that all men [*sic*] recognize themselves in its image" (1972: 155), then house posters in Shiv Camp show that residents have indeed begun to recognize and place themselves in the image of a world-class city. That is, slum residents seem motivated to no longer be slum residents: to end slum life – a contradictory moment in which "displacement collides with the dream of a better life" (Baviskar 2003: 97).

Is this the "cultural reproduction" of bourgeois visual ideology, the work-ing poor's adoption of an aesthetic unconscious that reproduces the conditions of their own domination (Willis 1981)? The sudden appearance of perhaps the most powerful and enduring (post)colonial symbol of private property – the bungalow – in the homes of those being criminalized for their lack of property ownership would seem to suggest such a reading. As Anthony King writes (1984: 160), "[A]s a symbol of private property the detached and territorially separate bungalow – the irreducible minimum of a house within its own grounds – was patently second to none." House post-ers and the narratives of self and city that Shiv Camp residents conveyed through them often did convey faith that acquiring a private home, even if through violent displacement, would bring with it the attributes of world-class citizenship: a sense of belonging and a visible place within the ongoing production of the urban.

Yet, residents also used house posters to enter a more speculative register, expressing desires enunciated on the terms of world-class aesthetic discourse, but in ways that sometimes exceeded its imaginative limits. As one man told me, pointing to his house poster: "This is what government has promised us. This is what we should get. Maybe not this much [referring to the grand bungalow in his poster], but we need proper homes." On first glance, his statement can be read as an effect of governmental efforts to cultivate a popular desire for resettlement, to democratize aspiration through the promise of a plot and state sanction – a promise that everyone can become world-class. Yet, inherent in this man's expressed desire for resettlement was also a *demand* for inclusion and self-improvement. While his interests only become intelligible through the discourse of resettlement, they simultaneously push that discourse to new ends. As neighboring slums are demolished without compensation, as resettlement colonies are moved further and further out of the city, and as the promise of property comes at the expense of a (sense of) place in the city, slum residents see that Delhi's current worlding strategies – premised as they are on speculative land development and mass displacement – offer them few benefits. It is in this light that Shiv Camp residents' display of house posters is also a subaltern aesthetic practice: an effort to appropriate the promise of bourgeois civility on their own terms: to pursue not wasteland on the outskirts of the city, but bungalows and farm-houses, just like those desired by the elite. As both adoption and appropriation, then, residents' display of house posters is part of an effort to latch onto and redirect world-class aesthetics so as to fashion the slum itself as a "milieu of experimentations for making a new kind of future" (Aihwa Ong, Introduction, this volume) – that is, to "world from below," to convert a prolonged moment of danger into a moment of opportunity, to step inside the discourse of world-class city making, but to seize its categories and turn them in another direction.

The world-class city is a utopian image, part of the "irreducibly utopian" practice of government (Dean 1999: 33) that presupposes a better society and improved future. And, if the world-class city-building project depends on this utopian vision, this wish-image, then it is equally prone to slum residents' reimaginings of the urban and reinterpretation of this vision. As residents increasingly tune their aspirational strategies to the image of the world-class city, so too do they accept (feign?) the promise that such a city will provide them with a world-class lifestyle – be it quality education for their children, secure employment, or, as we saw in Shiv Camp, private property. As this expectation of improvement deepens, it can crystallize into new demands and points of politics, threatening to turn the promise of the world-class city into a political demand for world-class citizenship. How long can the vision of the world-class city, premised on the democratization of aspiration, endure without a democratization of rights, a democratization of space? Is Delhi's worlding strategy headed for a collective refusal, a blockade (see Ananya Roy, Chapter 10, this volume), or will new urban visions emerge in response to slum-dwellers' efforts to "world from below"?

Notes

1 See *The Hindu* (2006). For a description of the relationship between the Delhi Master Plan, the DDA, and planning law, see Verma (2002).
2 See T.N. Godavarman Thirumulpad vs. Union of India and Ors. ((2006)10 SCC 490), paragraph 8.
3 The DLF Emporio, as of June 2010, is the most expensive mall in India (see *Economic Times* 2007).
4 Jagdish & Ors. vs. DDA, CWP 5007/2002 (Delhi High Court).
5 In this way, both the mall and slum can be seen as zones of legal exception, territories regulated outside statutory law that break from precedent to "create new economic possibilities, spaces, and techniques for governing the population" (Ong 2007: 7).
6 Verma (2002) shows how the number of slum households in Delhi almost exactly equals the quantity of low-income housing units the DDA was required to build according to the Master Plan, but which it failed to complete. She therefore calls Delhi's slum population "Master Plan implementation backlog," meaning that slum residents have an unfulfilled legal entitlement to housing.
7 Pitampura Sudhar Samiti vs. Government of India, CWP 4215/1995, order dated May 26, 1997.
8 Okhla Factory Owners' Association vs. GNCTD (108 (2002) DLT 517), paragraph 22.
9 Affidavit filed by Mr. Satish Kumar, Under Secretary, Ministry of Urban Development & Poverty Alleviation (Delhi High Court), CWP 2253/2001.
10 Resident Welfare Association vs. DDA and Ors. (Delhi High Court), CWP 6324/2003, order dated August 29, 2007.
11 Hem Raj vs. Commissioner of Police (Delhi High Court) CWP 3419/1999, order dated March 1, 2006.
12 This difference is no doubt a reflection of the two cities' different administrative structures and planning histories. As India's capital, all land in Delhi is managed by the DDA, which is part of the central government and thus has no direct ties to city-level electoral politics. This leads to a wider disconnect between official plans and their implementation than that in other Indian cities, making the regulation of what Roy (2004) calls "territorialized flexibility" largely beyond the reach of planners in Delhi.
13 See Municipal Corporation of Delhi affidavit filed in 2006 in Kalyan Sansthan vs. GNCTD (Delhi High Court), CWP 4582/2003.
14 Interview with Mr. Manjit Singh, May 11, 2006. See also Verma (2002).
15 In fact, the Municipal Corporation confronted this dilemma after the Supreme Court had ordered it to close and seal all commercial establishments operating in residential zones of the city in late 2005. This led to the sealing of thousands of businesses, with tens of thousands more threatened, citywide protests by traders leading to the death of three young men, the demolition or partial demolition of hundreds of private residences not conforming to building codes as well as a shopping mall under construction in South Delhi, and a political nightmare for the ruling Congress Party. In 2006, the Lower House (Lok Sabha) of the Indian Parliament

passed a legislative act postponing all demolitions and sealing drives in Delhi for one year. While this act also included slums, the courts did not acknowledge their protected status and continued with slum clearance apace. The DDA finally modified the Master Plan *ex post facto* to regularize Delhi's commercial land-use violations in 2007 (DDA 2007).

16   Almrita Patel vs. Union of India (2000 SCC (2): 679).

17   CWP 6553/2000 (Delhi High Court), order dated February 16, 2001.

18   See, for example, Ratlam Municipal Council vs. Vardichan (AIR 1980 SC 1622) and Dr. K.C. Malhotra vs. State of M.P. (M.P. High Court), CA 1019/1992.

19   See The Indian Code of Criminal Procedure (1973), Section 133, the primary statute dealing with public nuisance and a key component of environmental law.

20   Okhla Factory Owner's Association vs. GNCTD, (108(2002) DLT 517). The judgment goes on to say that the former occupy areas of land adjacent to the latter, making the latter "inconvenienced": "An unhygienic condition is created causing pollution and ecological problems. It has resulted in almost collapse of Municipal services."

21   Because I was only able to obtain low-resolution photocopies of the photographs submitted in court, their quality is too poor to reproduce here.

22   CWP 1869/2003 (Delhi High Court), order dated November 14, 2003.

23   Combined demolitions (notoriously under-)reported by the DDA and Slum and JJ Wing of the Municipal Corporation from 1997 to 2007 lead to the conservative estimate of 710,000 displaced residents. *The City Development Plan of Delhi*, prepared by private consultants, on the other hand, estimates that 1.8 million residents were displaced in 1997–2001 alone. Conservative estimates suggest at least a tripling in the pre-2000 demolition pace.

24   For a discussion of the linked processes of "abstraction" and "assortment" necessary to arrange grids of intelligibility for effective governmental intervention, see Hannah (2000). My argument here is that aesthetic norms can achieve these two steps just as easily as those cartographic and statistical techniques discussed by Hannah as well as many scholars of urban government (e.g., Joyce 2003; Legg 2006; Chatterjee 2008).

25   For further details on the implementation and reception of these surveys, see Ghertner (2010), where I describe the conditions that led them to take on the more governmental function I discuss here (rather than the more strictly juridical function of assessing land uses and recording legal standing that they had in the past).

26   Other examples include media representations, television programs, government advertisements and statements, and corporate branding strategies (see Dupont 2006). While much attention has been paid to how "the intensified circulation of images of global cities through cinema, television, and the internet" (Chatterjee 2004: 143) has contributed to the collective reimagining of the Indian city, my attention here is to specific micro-technologies through which new urban visions circulate and are received.

27   This section is based on field research conducted in West Delhi for twelve months in 2007–8. At the time of writing, the remaining two-thirds of Shiv Camp remain intact, although a court case filed against it by a neighboring RWA is pending.

28   For example, in a fifty-one person, in-depth survey I conducted during fieldwork in 2007, forty respondents agreed with the statement "In ten years Delhi will have no slums."

29   *Darhshan* means "sight" in Hindi and Sanskrit, but in religious usage more accurately connotes divine sight or the emanation of divinity from religious figures (people,

shrines, images). Its verb form is to "take" or "receive" *darshan. Darshan* is always reciprocated; it is a mutual exchange of sight that draws the devotee into the divine presence of the *darshan* giver. See also Eck (1998).

30   This reading of "India" is not the product of the image alone, but also of the mode of the image's consumption. The mass production and consumption of these images created an inter-ocular field of shared tropes and visual cues. The ubiquitous appearance of the same images gave viewers everywhere a sense that they were collectively imagining the same landscape (Pinney 2004, 98).

31   Poster design and publishing in India has been dominated by a handful of publishers whose origins lie in devotional imagery (see Pinney 2004; Jain 2007). The fact that house posters (most of which are produced by these same publishers) draw from the aesthetic milieu of devotional posters is, therefore, not surprising, although an influx of low-cost posters imported from China has begun to expand their aesthetic repertoire.

32   The verb she used was *saf karna* (to clean), which can also mean "to clear." Cleaning and clearing everything had the same implications to Kishani: removing slums.

33   Shiv Camp residents regularly expressed a desire for private property in conversation. House posters were but one, more aesthetic (and less frequent), expression of this desire. In an open question in my survey, for example, twenty-eight of forty-nine respondents said their greatest dream was "a private house," two said "government resettlement," seven said "a permanent home," and four said a middle-class lifestyle. The number of responses related to "home" (thirty-seven) shows the predominance of tenure and land concerns in residents' lives. Other responses had to do with employment, their children's education/marriage, or other domains of life. "Private house" indicated responses where the respondent made explicit mention of land title, private property, or the ability to buy and sell the plot. "Permanent house" indicated a desire for tenure security without explicit preference for ownership. Ten of the fifty-one respondents stated that they owned property elsewhere in Delhi: seven in unauthorized (i.e., "non-planned") colonies, and three in resettlement colonies. All three "owners" of resettlement plots made their purchases (which are not recognized by the state) in 2007 after the demolition in Shiv Camp.

34   Female domestic workers, however, have an intimate understanding of life inside the homes where they work.

References

Anderson, M.R. (1992) Public nuisance and private purpose: policed environments in British India, 1860–1947. SOAS Law Department Working Papers, London.

Barthes, R. (1972) *Mythologies*. New York: Hill and Wang.

Baviskar, A. (2003) Between violence and desire: space, power, and identity in the making of metropolitan Delhi. *International Social Science Journal* 55, 89–98.

Benjamin, S. (2004) Urban land transformation for pro-poor economies. *Geoforum* 35, 177–87.

Benjamin, S. (2008) Occupancy urbanism: radicalizing politics and economy beyond policy and programs. *International Journal of Urban and Regional Research* 32, 719–29.

Biswas, S. (2006) Why so much of Delhi is illegal. BBC News, February 6 edn., London; http://news.bbc.co.uk/1/hi/world/south_asia/4665330.stm

Chakrabarti, P.D. (2008) Inclusion or exclusion? Emerging effects of middle-class citizen participation on Delhi's urban poor. *Institute for Development Studies Bulletin* 38, 96–104.

Chatterjee, P. (2008) Democracy and economic transformation in India. *Economic and Political Weekly* 43, 53–62.

Davis, M. (2006) *Planet of Slums*. New York: Verso.

DDA (Delhi Development Authority) (1997) *Annual Report, 1996–1997*. New Delhi: Delhi Development Authority.

DDA (Delhi Development Authority) (ed.) (2007) *Master Plan for Delhi 2021*. New Delhi: Delhi Development Authority.

Dean, M. (1999) *Governmentality: power and rule in modern society*. London: SAGE Publications.

Douglas, M. (1966) *Purity and Danger: an analysis of concepts of pollution and taboo*. New York: Praeger.

Dupont, V. (2006) The idea of a new chic Delhi through publicity hype. In R. Khosla (ed.) *The Idea of Delhi*. Mumbai: Marg Publications.

Eagleton, T. (1990) *The Ideology of the Aesthetic*. Oxford: Blackwell.

Eck, D.L. (1998) *Darśan: seeing the divine image in India*. New York: Columbia University Press.

Economic Times (2007) Check out the most expensive malls in the country. New Delhi, December 2.

Foucault, M. (2007) *Security, Territory, Population*. New York: Palgrave Macmillan.

Ghertner, D.A. (2005) Purani yojana ki kabr par, nayi yojana ki buniyad: *Dilli Master Plan 2021* ki chunauti aur sambhavnae (Building the new plan on the grave of the old: the politics of the *Delhi Master Plan 2021*). *Yojana* 24, 14–20.

Ghertner, D.A. (2008) An analysis of new legal discourse behind Delhi's slum demolitions. *Economic and Political Weekly* 43, 57–66.

Ghertner, D.A. (2010) Calculating without numbers: aesthetic governmentality in Delhi's slums. *Economy and Society* 39, 185–217.

Hannah, M.G. (2000) *Governmentality and the Mastery of Territory in Nineteenth-Century America*. Cambridge, MA: Cambridge University Press.

Hindu, The (2006) SC stays construction in Ridge area in Vasant Kunj. New Delhi, May 1.

Hindustan Times (2006) So, it'll take you 263 years to wash sins! New Delhi, August 19.

Hull, M.S. (2008) Ruled by records: the expropriation of land and the misappropriation of lists in Islamabad. *American Ethnologist* 35, 501–18.

Jain, A.K. (2003) Making planning responsive to, and compatible with, reforms. *Cities* 20, 143–5.

Jain, Ashok K. (2005) *Law and Environment*. Delhi: Ascent.

Jain, K. (2007) *Gods in the Bazaar: the economies of Indian calendar art*. Durham, NC: Duke University Press.

Joyce, P. (2003) *The Rule of Freedom: liberalism and the modern city*. London: Verso.

Kaviraj, S. (1991) On state, society and discourse in India. In J. Manor (ed.) *Rethinking Third World Politics*. London: Longman.

King, A.D. (1984) *The Bungalow: the production of a global culture*. London: Routledge.

Latour, B. (1987) *Science in Action: how to follow scientists and engineers through society*. Cambridge, MA: Harvard University Press.

Leena, D. (2007) Slums: whose habitat and whose eyesore? In L. Batra (ed.) *The Urban Poor in Globalising India: eviction and marginalisation.* New Delhi: Vasudhaive Kutumbakam Publications.

Legg, S. (2006) Governmentality, congestion and calculation in colonial Delhi. *Social & Cultural Geography* 7, 709–29.

MCD (Municipal Corporation of Delhi) (2002) *Annual Report of the Slum and JJ Wing, 2001–2002.* MCD: New Delhi.

Ong, A. (2007) *Neoliberalism as Exception: mutations in citizenship and sovereignty.* Durham, NC: Duke University Press.

Pinney, C. (1995) Moral topophilia: the significations of landscape in Indian oleographs. In E. Hirsch and M. O'Hanlon (eds.) *The Anthropology of Landscape: perspectives on place and space.* Oxford: Clarendon Press.

Pinney, C. (2004) *Photos of the Gods: the printed image and political struggle in India.* London: Reaktion Books.

Rajagopal, A. (2001) The violence of commodity aesthetics: hawkers, demolition raids, and a new regime of consumption. *Social Text* 19, 91–113.

Ramanathan, U. (2006) Illegality and the urban poor. *Economic and Political Weekly* 41, 3193–7.

Ramesh, R. (2008) Delhi cleans up for Commonwealth Games but leaves locals without sporting chance. *The Guardian,* London, January 8.

Ranciere, J. (2001) Ten theses on politics. *Theory and Event* 5(3), 17–34.

Ranciere, J. (2004) *The Politics of Aesthetics.* New York: Continuum.

Rose, N. (1991) Governing by numbers: figuring out democracy. *Accounting, Organizations and Society* 16, 673–92.

Rose, N. (1999) *Powers of Freedom: reframing political thought.* Cambridge, UK: Cambridge University Press.

Roy, A. (2002) *City Requiem, Calcutta: gender and the politics of poverty.* Minneapolis, MN: University of Minnesota Press.

Roy, A. (2004) The gentleman's city: urban informality in the Calcutta of new communism. In N. Alsayyad and A. Roy (eds.) *Urban Informality.* Lanham, MD: Lexington Books.

Schmitt, C. (2006) *Political Theology: four chapters on the concept of sovereignty.* Chicago: The University of Chicago Press.

Scott, D. (1995) Colonial governmentality. *Social Text* 43, 191–220.

Scott, J.C. (1998) *Seeing Like a State: how certain schemes to improve the human condition have failed.* New Haven, CT: Yale University Press.

Verma, G.D. (2002) *Slumming India: a chronicle of slums and their saviours.* New Delhi: Penguin.

Willis, P. (1981) Cultural production is different from cultural reproduction is different from social reproduction is different from reproduction. *Interchange* 12, 48–67.

Conclusion

Postcolonial Urbanism: Speed, Hysteria, Mass Dreams

Ananya Roy

> What is at stake is a "worlding," the reinscription of a cartography that must (re)present itself as impeccable.
>
> (Spivak 1999: 228)

In her opening essay, "Worlding Cities, or the Art of Being Global," Aihwa Ong calls for new approaches in global metropolitan studies, those that can trouble both political economy and postcolonial frameworks. The former, she argues, positions cities within a singular script, that of "planetary capitalism." The latter searches for "subaltern resistances" in cities that were once subject to colonial rule. Neither, she notes, is sufficient in enabling robust theorizations of the problem-space that is the contemporary city. Ong's critique is a much-needed intervention in the production of knowledge about the urban condition. Indeed, this book is assembled as precisely such an intervention. Its essays highlight an urban problematic – "Asian" experiments with city-making – that cannot be easily subsumed within existing genres of urban theory, from political economy to the postcolonial.

This concluding essay is written in conversation with Ong's critique and is informed by the complex theoretical analysis presented by the many authors of this volume. Rather than seeking to reach a definitive conclusion on the question of "worlding cities," it is meant to open up lines of inquiry in the field of global metropolitan studies. I am especially interested in the project of postcolonial urbanism and how the study of cities can be enriched through a renewed engagement with postcolonial studies. What, then, is such a postcolonial analysis? I am in agreement with Ong that postcolonial theory, in its emphasis on subaltern agency, remains limited in its capacity to describe and explain urban experiments. Also limited is postcolonial theory's capacity to explain formations of development that no longer refer to

Worlding Cities: Asian Experiments and the Art of Being Global, First Edition.
Edited by Ananya Roy and Aihwa Ong.
© 2011 Blackwell Publishing Limited. Published 2011 by Blackwell Publishing Ltd.

what Mignolo (2005) has famously called the "colonial wound." In this sense, the essays in this volume can be seen as a challenge to postcolonial theory, for they foreground processes of ascendance, emergence, and contestation that defy the grid of postcolonial world-systems (as they do the map of planetary capitalism).

But I believe that another route through postcolonial urbanism is possible. I am interested in a genre of postcolonial analytics that critically deconstructs the "worlding" of knowledge. My interest lies not in the urban environments that are usually designated as postcolonial cities but, rather, in how postcolonial theory may enable new lines of urban research and theory. This shift – from the postcolonial as an urban condition to the postcolonial as a critical, deconstructive methodology – inaugurates a new way of doing global metropolitan studies. My exploration of a project of postcolonial urbanism in effect echoes an inquiry posed by Jane M. Jacobs (1996: 15) in her important postcolonial text, *Edge of Empire*: "How can the spatial discipline of geography move from its historical positioning of colonial complicity towards productively postcolonial spatial narratives?" With such questions in mind, in this essay, I put forward two theoretical positions. The first is concerned with geographies of authoritative knowledge; the second with articulations of subject-power.

Itineraries of Recognition

In my previous work, I have argued, inspired by Jennifer Robinson, that it is time to rethink the geography of authoritative knowledge that attends our study of cities (Roy 2009). That authoritative knowledge, which we designate as Theory, operates through what Robinson has called the "regulating fiction" of the First World global city. Overly "globalist," such frameworks also obscure, as Olds and Yeung (2004: 489) have argued, the "differential and dynamic developmental pathways" through which global cities come into being. Especially troubling is the map through which cities are placed in the world. While global cities, mainly in the First World, are seen as command and control nodes of the global economy, the cities of the global South are scripted as megacities, big but powerless. Off the map, they are usually assembled under the sign of underdevelopment, that last and compulsory chapter on "Third World Urbanization" in the urban studies textbook. They are the sites at which capital accumulation and democratic governance happen under "special circumstances." They are the megacities, bursting at the seams, overtaken by their own fate of poverty, disease, violence, and toxicity. They constitute the "planet of slums," with its "surplus humanity" and "twilight struggles." Recovered through ethnography, the analysis of such cities lacks the authority and legitimacy to be written as

Theory. In other words, "we need to understand more fully the schema through which the subject of universal knowledge becomes isomorphic with the West and all other regions become consigned to particularity" (Cheah 2002: 59).

My call for new geographies of knowledge does not imply a simple journey out of the bounds of Euro-America to the colonial space/non-place that is usually designated as *terra incognita* or *terra nulla* (Bhabha 1994). Nor is it a call for studying the diversity of urban modernities. Sassen (2008: 124) argues that "reassembling the category of the urban" requires explanations that "encompass diverse spatial forms" and frameworks that foreground the "diversity of economic trajectories through which cities and regions become globalized." But the narrative of urban diversity, I argue, does not enable a productive reassembling of the category of the urban. Making visible the diverse urbanisms of the global South is a project of recognition that can maintain intact dominant maps of economy, power, and culture. Such an endeavor is akin to what Mitchell (2000: xii) has critiqued as the "vocabulary of alternatives," that which holds constant "an underlying and fundamentally singular modernity, modified by local circumstances into a multiplicity of 'cultural' forms." Ong's dissatisfaction with such a project is thus right on the mark. She insists on an analytical framework that shows "how an urban situation can be at once heterogeneously particular and yet irreducibly global." Postcolonial urbanism must therefore entail more than a theoretical proliferation of urbanisms; it must exceed the effort to supplant universality with emplaced heterogeneity. An appreciation of the "diversity of cities" is not enough; instead, the "privileged link between modernity and certain kinds of cities" needs to be questioned (Robinson 2004: 709).

Thus, our work in this volume cannot be seen as an effort to list and reveal the multiple urban forms, practices, and meanings produced in that vast space marked by the ambiguous nomenclature, "Asia." Instead, it is an analysis of the social technologies through which claims to an Asian century are made, of the circulatory capacity of Asian models of urbanism, and of the norm(aliz)ed interpellations through which urban subjects come to inhabit space. In other words, as a study of Asian city-making, this book is also a study of the making and unmaking of the referent: Asia. This, I believe, is central to the project of postcolonial urbanism: that it is an analysis of the worlding practices through which knowledge is constituted. Geographic imaginations in turn are the very essence of such worlding practices (Gregory 1994). To practice a theory of postcolonial urbanism therefore means, following Chakrabarty's (2000) broad mandate, to "provincialize" its geographic declarations.

Modernity is too often interpreted as emerging from the West and spreading to the rest (Gaonkar 2001). So is it with urbanism. It is thus that the modernity and globality of Southern cities is studied in the valence of

310 *Ananya Roy*

surprise and dismay; they are seen to be weak copies of a Western urbanism, a betrayal of an indigenous urban formation. Take, for example, Anthony King's (2004) study of "spaces of global culture" and its documentation of the "villafication of Chinese cities" and the spread of "Western suburbs" to Indian cities. Such readings of Asian urbanism in the register of Westernization are commonplace. It is thus that the peripheries of Indian cities are seen to be colonized by the "globurb" (King 2004: 97) and its American lifestyle. But such peripheries embody much more than the internationalization of the American suburb; they are also, as I have shown in the case of Kolkata (Roy 2003), land tenure systems that combine colonial landholding arrangements with national imperatives of planning and zoning; where squatter settlements and sharecropper agriculture proliferate alongside gated zones of residence and industrial factories and where ties of patronage and clientelism thrive in the interstices of the electoral regimes of liberal democracy. Solomon Benjamin (2009) has rightly designated this complex spectrum of tenure arrangements "occupancy urbanism," for this is how city-space is produced and inhabited. These occupations must therefore be understood as much more than the imposition of global designs of Suburb and Villa.

Postcolonial analysis calls into question these "origins" stories, eroding ideas of original and borrowed urbanisms. It demonstrates how seemingly original templates of modernism, developmentalism, and neoliberalism emerge through global circulations and experiments. They are, in other words, thoroughly hybrid, thoroughly corrupted. Origins are not what they seem. It is thus that Anthony King's (1995) genealogical analysis of the "bungalow" reveals the travels of this spatial form – from the tropical colonies to middle-class American suburbs to Australian frontiers to postcolonial cities. Indeed, King (2004: 124) himself casts doubt on his own narrative of the "villafication" of Beijing, asking whether such forms "come from 'the west' or whether they are mediated via Hong Kong and Shanghai," since these cities are "central to China's 'official' imagination of modernity." Here, Mitchell's cautionary note – that "locating the origins of capitalist modernity entirely within the West has always been open to question" – must be taken up more fully. After all, various modern forms of industrial production, spatial organization, and subject-formation were invented and perfected in the colonies; in other words, "in reticulations of exchange and production encircling the world" (Mitchell 2000: 2).

The themes of emergence and encirclement are central to our work. Kolkata, Dubai, Bangalore, and Dalian are all sites of emergence, where intense experiments with city-making are inflected by strategic global influences and investments, but are also inevitably "homegrown," defying the plotted coordinates of "planetary capitalism." These urban ventures demand a provincialization of urban theory, since they demonstrate how neoliberal urbanism is as much "Asian" as it is "Western," as much "homegrown" as it is borrowed. Such forms of urban creativity – and violence – far exceed the political economy of regulation that is the concern of quite a bit of urban theory. Forged in the crucible of a handful of Euro-American cities, with New York usually leading the pack, urban political economy misses the assemblages of exception, sovereignty, and citizenship that Ong so deftly exposes in her many treatises. The urbanisms analyzed in this volume thus cannot be easily designated as what Peck, Theodore, and Brenner (2009: 55) have termed "localized neoliberalizations." They are better understood as "globally interconnected, conjunctural formations" – a phrase that Peck, Theodore, and Brenner (2009: 54) also employ, but that is at odds with the narrative of planetary neoliberalism and its localizations. At such conjunctures, neoliberalism itself turns out to be a "hybrid assemblage" (Peck, Theodore, and Brenner 2009: 96), a "mobile technology" that unfolds in a shifting terrain of borrowings, appropriations and alliances (Aihwa Ong, Introduction, this volume).

Equally important, the Asian experiments highlighted in the essays demonstrate the instability of claims to geographic origin. In this, they confound any simple analysis of the postcolonial condition, for this is not the subaltern effort to play the Rostowian catch-up game or heal the "colonial wound." Here, there is no single teleology of modernization, no prescribed ladder of development to climb. Instead, the postcolonial condition, as Ong argues in her introduction, hosts a multitude of performative and speculative enterprises, all of which operate through geographic referents. They are, in this sense, provincial as much as they are global. That these referents and circulations cannot be reduced to a unified and universal colonial history does not mean that they do not carry within them forms of coloniality. These are, in fact, worlding practices that inaugurate particular types of subject-power.

For this, it is worth turning to the work of postcolonial critic Gayatri Chakravorty Spivak. In an important critique of subaltern studies, Spivak casts doubt on projects of recognition that seek to confer visibility and voice to the subaltern. Indeed, as Spivak (1993: 11) notes, postcolonial deconstruction has been misread as a project of crafting a decentered subject when in fact it is a practice that studies how the subject always "tends towards centering" and how such a sovereign subject can claim an object of inquiry. Itineraries of recognition, Spivak argues, seek to assimilate the subaltern Other as objects of "conscientious ethnography" recovered by Native Informants. This produced "transparency," she rightly notes, itself "marks the place of interest." Spivak's critique thus directs our attention from subaltern agency to the practices of centering and worlding through which postcolonial subject-power is consolidated. In contrast to the Third World slum – the emblem through which Asia has so often been worlded – geographies of postcolonial worldliness lie at the heart of the essays in this volume.

From Asher Ghertner's interest in the "distribution of the sensible" to Michael Goldman's delineation of speculative accumulation, to Glen Lowry and Eugene McCann's tracing of the travels of urban symbolic landscapes, these geographies include and exceed the slum. On the one hand, they disrupt dominant maps of global and world cities, revealing a geography that explodes the boundaries of the West. On the other hand, they destabilize narratives of the "colonial wound," for they involve experiments and circulations that cannot be contained within itineraries of subaltern recognition. In doing so, they shift the terrain of the political from the standard icons of global capital and subaltern subjects to world-ing practices.

Worlding Practices

Postcolonial urbanism has been most often understood as one or more of the following conditions: colonial cities and their transformation through projects of nationalism and development; and heterogeneous forms of subalternity through which colonial cities are lived, negotiated, and shaped. In this volume, we have put forward a quite different framework of postcolonial urbanism. We have sought to trouble the space–time imagination associated with postcoloniality by highlighting the remaking of core–periphery geographies and thereby urban claims to the global future. We have also sought to trouble the subject-power of the subaltern by demonstrating how subordinated social groups both oppose and take up the vision of the world-class city. This in turn troubles understandings of the postcolonial city as a subaltern space and as a subject of history. Central to our framework of postcolonial urbanism is the idea of "worlding." Three types of practices are implicated in the worlding of cities.

First, worlding is a practice of centering, of generating and harnessing global regimes of value. Aihwa Ong (Introduction, this volume) describes the worlding city as "a milieu of intervention," a "claim to instantiate some vision of the world in formation." Such practices of centering also have considerable circulatory capacity. As is evident in the various essays that make up this volume, urban experiments are interconnected to one another, creating a world of inter-Asian urbanism, a space of emergence activated by models-in-circulation. Equally important, such regimes of globality are also regimes of subject-making. As Lisa Hoffman (this volume) argues, modeling is a "mode of governing the urban," "tied to the fostering of civilized and quality citizens who have a sense of national obligation and social responsi-bility, as well as the skills desirable for the global knowledge economy." Worlding practices, then, are not only the domain of the state and corporate actors, but are also instantiated in what Asher Ghertner (this volume) calls the "everyday experience of world-class aesthetic discourse." His analysis of aesthetic politics in Delhi demonstrates how the making of the world-class city is also a worlding of subjects, of the taking up of the world-class aesthetic by urban residents desiring a new future.

In similar fashion, Simone (2001: 22, 15) outlines the "worlding of African cities" as "experimentation for engagement," the reaching of a "larger world" through "circuits of migration, resource evacuation, and commodity exchange." Simone (2001: 17) is especially concerned with how such practices of worlding are set into motion through the "state of being 'cast out' into the world," or what he calls "worlding from below." In other words, world-ing is much more than the control of global economic functions; it is also the transactions of those "most marginal from these new economic capacities" (Simone 2001: 16). Worlding is the "speculative urbanism" − to use Michael Goldman's (this volume) phrase − of information technology, finance capital, and real-estate development, but it is also the anticipatory politics of residents and transients, citizens and migrants.

Second, worlding is an inherently unstable practice. Gavin Shatkin (this volume) draws attention to the numerous urban mega-projects that are never completed, that founder on "issues surrounding land acquisition, legal controversies, difficulties in financing, and popular resistance." Such failed projects mark the limits of the circulatory capacity of urban models and of global capital. These limits, as Michael Goldman (this volume) demonstrates, are often negotiated through experiments with governance, one where new frontiers of speculation are opened up through forms of urban planning that can manage "black, white, and grey markets." In my own work on Kolkata, I have argued that urban development unfolds in differential and "unmapped" geographies of informality and illegality, and that such city-making pivots on the flexible practices of a powerful state (Roy 2003). Yet, such a state can also come to be blockaded, its projects of development halted by the same logic of territorialized flexibility and uncertainty that enables speculation. The incomplete and unstable nature of worlding also extends to articulations of subject-power. It is thus that Glen Lowry and Eugene McCann (this volume), following Miki, position the figure of the "Asian Canadian" as a "double edged site." The Asian Canadian is at once a "platform for the flow of new (Asian) capital" and an embodiment of an "Asiancy" that can engender "altered states" or "alter-nations." But it is important to note that such contestations can also serve as the platform for new experiments with hegemony. In Kolkata, as I argue (this volume), the blockade of development inaugurates renewed efforts to create a "world-class" city. In a brilliant analysis, Sparke (2010) shows how in Seattle, the social mobilizations of 1999 that "sought to remake the meaning of world class livability in terms of global justice" set the stage for a "curative reconceptualization of the city," this time of a world-class center that is home to philanthrocapitalism, including that of the Gates Foundation, arguably the most powerful player in the world of global health philanthropy.

Third, worlding as a practice of centering also involves the production of regimes of truth. In urban theory, cities have been worlded through the map of planetary capitalism or through the grid of postcolonial cores and peripheries. Our work seeks to deconstruct such forms of worlding. Here once again, Spivak's analysis provides valuable insight. In a seminal essay, Spivak (1985: 262) draws attention to the "worlding of what is now called the Third World." Examining the "empire of the literary discipline," Spivak shows how the Third World is taken up as "distant cultures, exploited but with rich intact literary heritages waiting to be recovered, interpreted, and curricularized in English translation." At the same, there is a disavowal of such worlding connections in the literatures of European colonizing cultures, a sanctioned ignorance of imperialism and its penetrations. Spivak's concept of worlding is useful because it makes evident the entanglement of geographies of knowledge and the articulation of subject-power. It is through the worlding of the Third World that Europe is consolidated as sovereign subject – "sovereign and Subject" (Spivak 1999: 2000). It is this itinerary of recognition – and misrecognition – that Spivak urges us to study. For example, such a mandate can be extended to the (self)-worlding of Asia. This volume, then, is a critical intervention in the truth-claims that are constructed and circulated in the space that is inter-Asia. But for us, worlding is both an object of analysis and a method of critical deconstruction. Our work is thus a critical intervention in the ways in which urban theory worlds Asia. It marks a shift from concepts of world cities and world-systems to that of worlding practices.

To make evident these interlocked practices of worlding, I provide some scenes of inter-Asian urbanism. Each scene, each city, is shaped by a key trope: speed, hysteria, mass dreams. These tropes reveal the making of cities and of subject-power – but, more important, they reveal the ways in which these cities are worlded. It is thus that "speed" becomes a self-worlding practice of Shenzhen, that which allows the city to be positioned as the "world's workshop," a place where the future of the world is made. Dubai, a desert frontier of speculation and calculation, circulates as a global referent. But in both academic and popular discourses, it is narrated through modes of hysteria, a worlding practice that signals anxieties about Arab wealth and power. Mumbai, the city of lucre, is the site of mass dreams. It is here that many forms of globality are staged and negotiated. Mumbai is the urban commons that is claimed by all, but that cannot ever be fully appropriated by any. Such sites and tropes must also be situated in the itineraries of recognition through which urban theory worlds cities. With this in mind, I have also provided glimpses of the circuits of knowledge production through which such forms of worlding are consolidated and contested.

Shenzhen: speed

At a recent conference held in Shenzhen, China, I found myself in a small cluster of urban scholars. We had been assembled by our gracious hosts to be interviewed by local reporters. Young men and women, they were not interested in the usual media sound bytes but, instead, settled in for a long conversation about the conference theme: "Global Cities and the World Economic Crisis." Their eager questions sought to uncover the mystery of the "global city" – what precisely makes a city global? But at the heart of this global imagination was a persistent concern: Shenzhen. These Shenzhen reporters quite boldly imagined Shenzhen as the global city of the future. They were keen to solicit our appraisals of Shenzhen's infrastructure, its urban milieu: Was it world-class? How did it fare in comparison with other global cities? Since news headlines had just noted the inauguration of Dubai's Burj Khalifa, the world's tallest building, they asked if Shenzhen should build a higher tower. It is through such forms of inter-referencing, this performance of citationary structures of global urbanism, that these young reporters placed Shenzhen in the world.

[A bracketed note is in order: I start with this story because multiple worldings are at work here. The questions posed by the Shenzhen reporters speak to the exhibitionary impulse of worlding practices. But also at stake is the distinctive venue that is the global academic conference, a site marked by cosmopolitan encounters and voyeuristic sojourns. This too is a worlding practice, one that enables the travel of theory – "What makes a city global?" – from centers of calculation to the seeming margins of knowledge production. In such circuits of truth-making, the Third World city, the Asian city, is most often a curious object, its secrets waiting to be unearthed by the Global Scholar and revealed by the Native Informant. Bunnell and Maringati (2010: 419) thus call for greater attention to the "embodied practice of traveling, dwelling, seeing, collecting, recording and narrating" through which diverse actors, including academic scholars, produce knowledge about cities.]

The exhibitionary impulse is not new. Mitchell (1991) shows how the optics of exhibition was central to colonial rule. From world fairs to urban design, colonial technologies of exhibition recreated the world within the city. Today's global cities contain similar exhibitionary spaces. Thus, in Shenzhen, the kitschy "Windows of the World" is a montage of well-known global icons, from the Eiffel Tower to the Taj Mahal. This urban theme park, with its characteristic space–time arrangements of juxtaposition and compression, is best understood as a simulation not of the world, but of the world-exhibition; in other words, as a simulation of the Las Vegas strip.

This practice of remaking the world within the city also marks Shenzhen's reputation as the "world's workshop." After all, it is in Shenzhen's fortified factories that the world's favorite commodities – from iPods to iPhones – are churned out. The Shenzhen assembly line is known for its flexibility, with machine tools that can be redeployed for a new electronic product in a matter of days. It is an instance of a temporal imagination that is widely celebrated in Shenzhen as "Shenzhen speed." As Cartier (2002) notes, the use of this phrase to connote a rapidity of economic growth suggests that "no other place or time has experienced the transformations that have characterized this city."

Once invisible, the Shenzhen assembly line is now the site of various worlding practices, including that where a migrant worker, completing the assembly of an iPhone, left a photograph of herself on the phone. Dressed in a pink and white striped uniform, smiling, making a peace sign, her image became the indelible trace on the next-generation 3G iPhone that was to eventually make its way into the hands of "markm49uk," a British consumer. In the circuits of cybercirculation, she came to be known simply as "iPhone girl." By asserting her place in the global value chain, "iPhone girl" suggests the possibility of an imagined community crafted through the transactions of the global commodity. This too is a worlding practice. It would be a mistake to read these various practices as a "worlding from above" pitched against a "worlding from below." The Shenzhen assembly line does not fit neatly into the verticality of power suggested by such metaphors. Instead, it is a site for the making of multiple regimes of globality – from the global city to the global value chain.

Another distinctive worlding practice is at work in Shenzhen: the viewing of the city (Figure 12.1). At Lianhua mountain, where a bronze statue of Deng Xiaoping was unveiled on the twentieth anniversary of the city (Cartier 2002), Chinese tourists come to view the city. They take photographs at the foot of Deng Xiaoping's statue. Shenzhen, perhaps more than any other Chinese city, is the city of Deng rather than of Mao. Declared a Special Economic Zone by Deng Xiaoping in 1979, it is China's first official experiment with "market socialism." It is to Shenzhen that Deng was to return after the Tiananmen Square protests, as part of the carefully scripted itinerary of the "Southern tour" (Cartier 2002). This was an itinerary of recognition, one that declared the Pearl River Delta and its Special Economic Zones the symbols of Chinese entrepreneurialism, global ingenuity, and market reform. That itinerary remains encapsulated in the viewing platform of Lianhua mountain. The statue captures Deng in motion, one step forward, looking toward the panorama of the city. It is this panorama that Chinese tourists come to watch and photograph, an endless sea of urban development stretching to the horizon. And it is in this panorama that Shenzhen far exceeds its prehistory as a zone of assembly lines; its future is that of the global city, its revolution is now urban. In a visibly Lefebvrian sense, what is being produced in Shenzhen today is space, urban space. Massive urban development

Figure 12.1 Photographing the city, Lianhua mountain, Shenzhen, 2010
Source: photograph by Ananya Roy, 2010.

projects have become the venue for "state-led spatial restructuring" (Xu, Yeh, and Wu 2009: 910). Everywhere there is construction; everywhere the new becomes old; everywhere factories and paddy fields give way to condominiums and malls; everywhere fast-speed infrastructure inhabits the city. As Chinese tourists watch this panorama of production, a worlding is once again under way – a placing of Shenzhen in the world, a self-worlding of Asia.

As panorama-city, Shenzhen embodies an intense and volatile remaking of spatial arrangements. But it is also a remaking of the future. In a city that has grown from about 25,000 people in 1980 to nearly 14 million people in 2010, the theme of speed permeates all discourse. It is thus that a new rail link, connecting Hong Kong to Shenzhen and Shanghai, is presented as a "high-speeding" of Hong Kong. If a decade ago, Shenzhen was a provincial hinterland servicing Hong Kong with cheap-labor factories and mistress villages, then today it is Hong Kong that is seen to be the island that risks isolation and backwardness. As Helen Siu (this volume) notes, once a command and control node of neo-imperial connections, Hong Kong must now manage a new regional geography of proximity, the roaring economic powerhouse that is the Pearl River Delta, a region that is perhaps the world's largest metropolitan agglomeration. This is a new postcolonial worldliness mediated by a temporal imagination that is most commonly designated as "Shenzhen speed." "No politics is possible," Virilio (2005 [1991]: 43) notes, "at the scale of the speed of light."

Worlding practices are articulations of subject-power. As they map the encirclement of the world, so they disavow particular subjectivities and relationalities. In Shenzhen, the panorama-city thus disavows its homegrown subject: the migrant worker. Housed in the ubiquitous and yet barely visible dormitory, this urban figure is central to the enterprise that is the "world's workshop." And yet can this habitation – uniformed bodies bound to the Taylorist rhythms of factory and service work, bodies indelibly marked by the provincial aspirations of the Chinese interior – be reconciled with the high-speed future that is Shenzhen? Can the self-worlding of Asia, enacted through the panorama of the global city, accommodate this subaltern subject? It is tempting to read Shenzhen as the regulated absence of the migrant worker, to search for traces of this subject in the interstitial spaces of the city, to conduct a "conscientious ethnography" that can confer visibility and voice on this subaltern subject. But in Shenzhen there is no simple itinerary of subaltern recognition.

Let me return to that opening scene of worlding: young Shenzhen reporters eager to understand the script of the global city. Toward the end of the encounter, one of the scholars in our assembled group, Brenda Yeoh, asked the reporters what they saw as the symbol of Shenzhen. Their answer, put forward without hesitation, surprised us: the migrant worker. Defying the predictable line-up of worldly icons – Windows of the World or a star-architect-designed civic center or the high-speed rail link to Hong Kong – these young reporters yoked Shenzhen's future to the subaltern subject of Shenzhen's prehistory. In doing so, they seemingly reversed the disavowal of provincial alterity that one has come to expect of such global zones of production. Yet, a closer look reveals how the designation of the migrant worker as the symbol of Shenzhen is also a worlding practice. The reporters admitted that their choice of this symbol was shaped by the fact that just a few days ago *Time* magazine (2009) had named "the Chinese Worker," specifically Shenzhen's migrant workers, as one of that year's four "runners-up" for Person of the Year. Photographed in black and white, Shenzhen's workers appear on the pages of *Time* magazine as heroes of the global economy. Crafted as an abstract, composite figure termed "the Chinese Worker," these women and men are given credit for "leading the world to economic recovery." It is worth noting that in this same issue, *Time* named Ben Bernanke, chairman of the American Federal Reserve Bank, as Person of the Year, praising his efforts to manage the financial crisis that erupted on Wall Street. But here, "the Chinese Worker," her heroism narrated in portraits of sacrifice and aspiration, cannot be understood as the cheap-labor periphery of Wall-Street-centered finance capital. Rather, she is at the heart of a high-speed frontier of emergence and circulation: the "tens of millions of workers who have left their homes, and often their families, to find work in the factories of China's booming coastal cities."

The "Chinese Worker" is not merely a global construction. As Florence (2007: 140) shows, the theme of model workers has been in circulation for a while in Shenzhen. Articles in the *Shenzhen Special Zone Daily* thank model workers for their "painful labor" and sacrifices undertaken "for their company and for the zone." Model workers are saluted, as in one article, for offering "their youth silently" to the company, for having "created the Chinese miracle," and for thereby having "stepped into the new century." As a worlding city, Shenzhen then is also a mass dream, that of model workers and their sacrifices for the sake of the model nation.

The "Chinese Worker" as composite figure marks a worlding practice, an itinerary that makes possible recognition of the "world's fastest-growing major economy." The model worker is the linchpin of the model economy, the harbinger of an Asian future to which cities from Kolkata to Manila aspire. To borrow a phrase from Harvey (2009), such encirclements of the world indicate a reconfiguration of "economic hegemony," one where American deficits are covered by "those countries with saved surpluses" – China, the Gulf States. In China, Harvey notes, much of the surplus will be "mopped up in the further production of space." It is thus that the panorama-city of Shenzhen, inhabited by the heroic migrant worker, is deeply implicated in the worlding of late capitalism.

But this itinerary of recognition is complicated by the growing phenomenon of worker suicides. At Foxconn Technology, a company that produces the vaunted electronic gadgets of companies such as Apple, Dell, and Hewlett Packard, workers have jumped to their death from dormitory buildings and factory buildings. The suicides have triggered scrutiny of conditions of work at Foxconn, which in turn has responded with steep salary increases for its workers (Barboza 2010). Indeed, the suicides are a poignant reminder of worldly entanglements – of how urban cosmopolitan lifestyles fueled by electronic tools such as iPhones and iPads remain dependent on the embodied labor of migrant workers in dreary Shenzhen factories and dormitories.

[Yet another bracketed note: our conference on global cities allowed us entrance into Foxconn, past its gated and guarded perimeters, but not onto its shop floor or into its dormitory rooms. It is here that, a few weeks after our visit, a 19-year-old worker, Ma Xiangqian, jumped to his death from one of the dormitories. It has been reported that Mr. Ma "shared a dormitory room with nine other workers ... and worked night shifts" (Barboza 2010).]

But the suicides also trouble narratives of subaltern recognition. Is suicide the ultimate act of heroism of the self-sacrificing "Chinese Worker," the runner-up Person of the Year? Or is suicide a shout of rebellion, the refusal by a new generation of workers to sacrifice for the sake of family and nation? Is suicide the only politics possible at the scale of the speed of light in the mass dream that is the Asian world-class city?

Dubai: hysteria

In demarcating the global quality of a city, the reporters in Shenzhen had referenced a key icon: the Burj Khalifa in Dubai, which opened in January 2010, overtaking Taipei 101 as the world's tallest building. Situated at the heart of the "Dubai Downtown" mega-development, the Burj tower has become a symbol of the hyper-development that is Dubai. It is estimated that just in the first few days, over 10,000 people paid a hefty fee to visit the observation deck located on the 124th floor of the building. One of them, Prajash Kelkar, interviewed by the *New York Times*, declared that the Burj tower was the "pride of Dubai." One of Dubai's countless "expatriates," Kelkar went on to say: "This shows how the wealth is moving from the West to the East" (Slackman 2010). Indeed, the Burj tower is only the most recent in a set of extravagant Dubai projects, all of which seem to mark that reconfiguration of economic hegemony that is of interest to Harvey. It is thus that Mike Davis designates Dubai as the ultimate frontier of development, one that far surpasses any city in America, even Las Vegas:

> Dubai has only one real rival: China ... Starting from feudalism and peasant Maoism, respectively, both have arrived at the stage of hyper-capitalism through what Trotsky called the 'dialectic of uneven and combined development'. In the cases of Dubai and China, all the arduous intermediate stages of commercial evolution have been telescoped or short-circuited to embrace the 'perfected' synthesis of shopping, entertainment and architectural spectacle, on the most pharaonic scale. (Davis 2006: 53–4)

Of course, Dubai is much more than a location; it is also a circulatory capacity. Dubai capital circulates and travels. It reshapes urban landscapes across a wide swath of territory, from Cairo to Delhi. Although Dubai itself is often billed to be an "oasis of free enterprise" – for example, by Davis (2006) – Dubai capital enters into strategic partnerships with a variety of nation-states. For example, in India, Emaar MGF, a joint venture between Dubai property conglomerate Emaar Properties and India's MGF Developments, has not only built gated communities replete with the amenities of bourgeois living but has also partnered with the Delhi Development Authority to build the Commonwealth Games village. In an interesting twist, Emaar MGF is implementing one of the key spatial technologies of global India: Chinese-style Special Economic Zones. Indeed, in Dubai itself, capital is thoroughly permeated by state interests and control such that it is difficult to distinguish between the practices of "free enterprise" and the enterprise of the emirate.

Dubai has often been interpreted as a city of excess and extravagance. These discursive frames of hysteria are most evident in a popular language of "Dubaization," which has been deployed to refer to an outlandish urbanism of spectacle, fakery, and caricature (Elsheshtawy 2010: 251). From residential islands carved out in the sea, each serviced by a private helicopter, to some of the world's largest shopping malls, each hosting an exhibition of spectacle and entertainment, Dubai is, as Davis puts it, "a monstrous caricature." This narrative of caricature, in turn, becomes a means of world-ing Asia, of situating its development trajectories as beyond the bounds of reason. Indeed, Asian cities once depicted as unreasonable megacities, concentrations of poverty and misery, are now being reframed as unreasonable hyper-development, concentrations of urban megalomania. Against such hysterical modes of worlding, it is necessary to position Dubai as Reason. Here, I draw on Partha Chatterjee's (1986: 168) analysis of nationalism, which argues that postcolonial worldliness operates in the name of Reason, and does so by seeking to "find for 'the nation' a place in the global order of capital." Chatterjee (1986: 169) designates this "historical identity between Reason and capital" as an "epistemic privilege, namely development." It is in this sense that Dubai is not a monstrous caricature of development; it is simply development. It is at sites such as Shenzhen and Dubai that the telescoping of time that is characteristic of all development becomes visible, that the bold rearranging of space that is the task of all development stretches to the horizon.

Chatterjee rightly notes that such a project of development, undertaken as Reason, is fragile. For example, it has to "keep the contradictions between capital and the people in perpetual suspension" (Chatterjee 1986: 168). Dubai too is fragile. Its labor camps are uncomfortable reminders of the cor-ralling of cheap, migrant labor that makes possible the construction of the world's tallest building. It is a city of iconic architecture, but it is also a city, as Elsheshtawy (2010: 216) argues, of "transitory spaces," those claimed by the migrant bodies that build the city. Will the laboring bodies that produce these global commodities be recognized as Person of the Year, making a contribution to economic recovery, as is the "Chinese Worker"? Or is the Dubai Worker tainted by the hysterical modes of worlding through which Dubai is understood? After all, if the Burj Khalifa is the "pride of Dubai," then it is also a reminder that this city-state is nearly $100 billion in debt. Various discourses of hysteria surround Dubai's indebtedness, from the dra-matic fluctuations of the Dubai stock market to the stalling of Dubai-financed projects in Las Vegas to the return of South Asian migrants, their hopes of Dubai gold dashed by the crisis. The hysteria spreads and contaminates.

It marks Dubai as ineluctably different – a speculative Arab version of an Asian frame of success, one that once again escapes Reason. Dubai, and its manifestations of crisis, thus seems to stand in contrast to more robust Asian frames of success: Singapore, Shenzhen. Dubaization, once hailed as a sign of prosperous globality, now seems tainted by the hysteria of debt. At the ambitious new City Center development in Las Vegas, which marks a collaboration between MGM and Dubai World, "star architecture" is the exhibition of choice. Ultra-modern, sleek, urban architecture. Euro-American cities are no longer the referent for such architecture. Shanghai, not Dubai, is the brand on display. In an interview, a corporate spokesperson called the City Center the "showcase of architecture." He continued, "Does one feel one is in New York? No, one feels in Shanghai" (CBS 2010).

Dubai's indebtedness has been followed by a bailout. In 2009, oil-rich Abu Dhabi provided a $10 billion reprieve for Dubai and its flagship conglomerates, notably Dubai World, whose real-estate arm, Nakheel, is responsible for Dubai's signature mega-projects. Petro-capital, it seems, is more durable than property capital. Immediately following the bailout, the key icon of Dubai World's "Downtown Dubai" project, the Burj Dubai, was renamed Burj Khalifa, a reference to Sheikh Khalifa, the president of the United Arab Emirates (UAE) and ruler of Abu Dhabi. Dubai, once imagined as the center of the world, was now repositioned as an Arab city, its future entangled with local circuits of brotherly solidarity. Indeed, there are other Sheikh Khalifa Cities in the Arab world. The Abu Dhabi Municipality recently announced that it will create a brand new city, the Sheikh Khalifa City, on the periphery of Cairo, on land provided by the Egyptian government. The city is to be developed and run by Emaar Misr, the Egyptian arm of the Dubai-based real-estate development firm. Sheikh Khalifa City is presented by Abu Dhabi as a "grant," a "community project" by the oil-rich emirate in an impoverished Egypt. "The city is a gift from the President His Highness Sheikh Khalifa bin Zayed Al Nahyan, Ruler of Abu Dhabi, to Egyptian youth with limited income," for "fresh graduates and newly-married couples" (*Arab Finance*, December 14, 2008), in short for the Egyptian generation that must struggle in an economy hollowed out by liberalization, the generation that finds it impossible to imagine a future, to get a salaried job, to buy the apartment that must precede marriage, to pay the school fees that must precede having children. Sheikh Khalifa City is thus billed as the gift from the UAE that "aims to create stability and development in Egypt." Sheikh Khalifa City is a postcolonial centering, scripted as "the deep-rooted ties between two brotherly peoples" (*UAE Interact*, January 27, 2009). As a worlding city, it is at once a space of (Arab) emergence and a mass dream. There are Sheikh Khalifa Cities, it is worth noting, in Banda Aceh and Gaza.

But the bailout of Dubai also generated hysteria, this time the fear that the "open city" of Dubai would be controlled by a "conservative" Abu

Dhabi, that this expatriate playground would now be subject to the norms of "Arab" life and monarchy. Had the universal referent, Dubai, now been reduced to yet another Sheikh Khalifa City? To read Dubai as Development, as Reason, is to confront the aspirations and limits of postcolonial worldliness. That the Burj tower, meant to be the latest icon of this global city, is now mired in the hysteria of debt, while also signifying the careful calculation of a bailout, indicates the frictions and fissures that accompany what Yeoh (2005) has called "spatial imagineering." It is thus that in the context of Kuala Lumpur, Bunnell (2004) shows how the iconic Petronas Towers is subject to "symbolic discontent," reimagined as the "twin dipsticks" for air pollution. Such calculative discontent is intriguing, often eroding the epistemic privilege that is development. But it cannot necessarily be expected to have any "coherent or unified authoritative intentionality" (Bunnell 2004: 78). Instead, it is perhaps merely an expression of the fragility of postcolonial worldliness, that which mirrors colonialism's fragility.

If Dubai is Development, then its fragility is most evident in a form of "standing still" that has taken hold in a few spaces of the city. Stories of Dubai's debt crisis report on a development at the edge of the famed Dubai Downtown. In the shadows of the Burj Khalifa, International City, a 2,000 acre development of Nakheel, is a future that lies in ruins:

> Traffic circles are now overgrown. Apartment buildings are now almost completely vacant. Rows of storefronts are empty. Families say they feel stuck, unable to sell and frightened for their safety. There are reports of crime, and what was supposed to be a family neighborhood has been transformed into a place where companies house low-wage laborers. There are piles of construction debris, a flooded parking lot, and street lights that do not work. (Slackman 2010)

Dubai's International City is reminiscent of places that stand still, and in turn of Benjamin's "dialectics at a standstill." In my essay on Kolkata (this volume), I argue that such spaces function as dialectical images, allowing us to unearth the logic of metropolitan desire. In Dubai, these spaces where the future lies in ruins are the urban speculations that seek to place this city in the world, to find a home in the order of global capital. But they also make evident the ambiguity that attends "Brand Dubai," one where the city occupies an unstable position in different worlding frames: Asia, Arab, success, speculation, excess, crisis. Is there now the emergence of a "Brand Khalifa," a repositioning of Dubai within a new world order that is centered in the Arabian Gulf?

Mumbai: mass dreams

In 2008, Mumbai, often scripted as India's most cosmopolitan city, a city of high finance and high living, appeared live on television screens and news streams around the world. The story was "Terror in the Taj," a city taken

over by ten young men with a mission to kill. Their choice of killing sites
was a mix of urban sites – from well-heeled hotels to popular cafés to
religious sanctuaries to vast public spaces such as the railway terminal. Billed
by the global media as India's 9/11, here once again terror and urban life
seemed to collide. It was a ground zero at what is India's gateway to the
world, the strip of Mumbai quite literally located at the Gateway of India,
the gateway through which Lord Mountbatten, the last British viceroy, left
India in the middle of the twentieth century. The Mumbai killings were
eerily echoed a few months later in the commando-style attacks on the
visiting Sri Lankan cricket team in Lahore. For the South Asian subcontinent,
it was as if the very icons of its postcolonial globality were under attack: even
cricket was no longer secure.

The Mumbai killings were framed by Suketu Mehta, author of the much
celebrated book, *Maximum City*, as a contest between globality and
parochiality, between the open city and the closed minds of religious
extremism. In an op-ed in the *New York Times*, he wrote "There's something
about this island-state that appalls religious extremists, Hindus and Muslims
alike. Perhaps because Mumbai stands for lucre, profane dreams and an
indiscriminate openness" (Mehta 2008). Mehta worlds Mumbai in
commonsense ways, delineating an incontrovertible difference between the
global geography of a profane, capitalist city and the remote geography of
medieval madrasah and militias. This narrative also rehearses a familiar
frame – of a global New York attacked on 9/11 by a tribal Al-Qaeda, of
the figure of the Muslim extremist, trained in the rural frontiers of
Afghanistan and Pakistan, as the counterpoint to the cosmopolitan urbanite
of Mumbai and New York.

Mehta (2008) above all asserts the role of lucre in Mumbai: "From the
street food vendor squatting on a sidewalk, fiercely guarding his little
business, to the tycoons … this city understands money and has no guilt
about the getting and spending of it." But could it be that the ten men were
in Mumbai also for their own profane dreams? The one attacker who is still
alive and in custody in India is Ajmal Amir Kasab, who is in his early
twenties. Scenes of Kasab – in a presumably fake Versace shirt, gun in
hand, roaming Mumbai's railway terminus – continue to circulate. Little is
known about him. Newspaper reports suggest that he hails from an
impoverished family in the village of Faridkot, Pakistan, where he worked as
an informal vendor. He was possibly sent to live with his brother, a struggling wage-laborer in Lahore, since his family could not afford to keep him
in school. Circulating through spaces of impoverishment, Kasab eventually
ended up in the training camps of the militant group Lashkar-e-Taiba.
Recruiters supposedly pledged to pay between $1,250 and $4,000 to his
family once he had completed this mission to kill. It is not possible, then, to
read the Mumbai killings as an attack on lucre. As it turns out, the militants

were also in Mumbai to do business, to complete a transaction in which a few thousand dollars was to be exchanged for the taking of lives.

It would be a mistake to interpret such transactions as an attack on globalization, for they too represent a form of globality, one that is fueled by a worldly imagination about Islam. Images of key sites of violence – Bosnia, Kashmir – circulate in the training camps of Lashkar-e-Taiba (Anand, Rosenberg, Gorman, and Schmidt 2008). In other words, these too are calculative strategies enmeshed in a global network of Islamist militancy, with its own worlding practices of finance, information, and war. Similarly, it would be a mistake to interpret such violent practices as "urbicide," or the death of the city. It is the lucre of the city that lubricates such dreams, even those of religious fanaticism, and makes possible the implementation of grand schemes of terror. After all, where else but in the Taj Hotel of Mumbai, a few steps from the Gateway of India, would militant groups find such a collection of high-value targets? A *Vanity Fair* essay describes the scene thus:

> Politicians and socialites and bankers from Saudi Arabia packed the rooms of the hotel. That night there would be a wedding in the Crystal Room for the scion of a prominent textile family, a private dinner for the board of the Hindustan Unilever company, and a banquet with European dignitaries in the Rendezvous Room … The talk at poolside was about a new movie, *Slumdog Millionaire*, that had just opened in New York to rave reviews. "It is a travesty," one guest said. "They are making us look like we all live in a *chawl* [slum]." (Brenner 2009)

Suketu Mehta's 2004 book, *Maximum City*, tells in prescient fashion of the many sites and characters implicated in the 2008 Mumbai killings. Of these, the most legible urban site is the Taj Hotel. Mehta notes that this "is less a hotel than a proving-ground for the ego." Indeed, the Taj Hotel was built as a counter-worlding gesture, "born out of a slight," as Mehta puts it. When Jamshedji Tata, prominent Indian industrialist, was turned away from the Watson's Hotel, he built the Taj Hotel with a pomp and grandeur that soon overshadowed the Watson's. A mark of native rebellion, of a refusal by the colonial Mimic Man, the Taj Hotel is today the symbol of the worldly, open city. Watching "Terror in the Taj" unfold on my television screen, I am reminded of my first trip to Mumbai, barely five years old, with my parents on a luxurious holiday to western India. We stayed for a night at the Taj. I remember it not for the views of the Arabian Sea from our hotel room but, rather, for my first experience of room service – the food arrived in the most amazing contraptions, little ovens that kept everything perfectly warm, perfectly set tables with tablecloth and fine china, on wheels, and the luxury of eating in one's hotel room. The Taj, that grand postcolonial gesture, was my first encounter with a world beyond the parochial familiarity of home. In that hotel room, with its rituals and luxuries, the world – the modern world – had arrived. It was a world-class experience in the world-class city. Mehta (2008) thus rightly notes: "Just as cinema is a mass dream of the audience, Mumbai is a mass dream of the peoples of South Asia." It is the world-class city as mass dream that we need to better understand.

The world-class city as mass dream belongs to many: global corporate elites, star architects, assembly line workers, militants and militias. In India, it is also increasingly claimed by the "common man." As I argue in my essay on Indian cities (this volume), such claims are central to a new middle-class urban politics and its mass dream of the world-class city. Belying usual stereotypes of enclave urbanism, such middle-class politics is waged in defense of the urban commons, social integration, good governance, and the public interest. It is in the name of these values that the urban poor are evicted, slums are demolished, and hawkers and vendors are banished from city streets. It is also in the name of these values that new experiments with governance are launched: neighborhood groups, resident welfare associations, urban reform committees, public interest NGOs. Together, they create a fractal geography of private jurisdictions and territorial interests, albeit closely bound to the apparatus of the state. In their most extreme form, they signify a vigilante urbanism that deploys violence – physical, structural, epistemic, symbolic – in the name of the public interest that is the world-class city. Such is the script of a provocative Bollywood film released only a few weeks prior to the 2008 Mumbai attacks. Titled *A Wednesday*, the film depicts an elaborate terror plot unleashed by a "stupid, common man" in revenge for the 2006 Mumbai train bombings. The plot, with its mission to cleanse "a roach-infested house," exterminates key Al-Qaeda militants who are being held in the custody of the Indian government and in doing so warns an Indian polity of the constraints of liberal democracy. But above all, the terror plot seeks to regain peace and security for the "stupid, common man" in the everyday routines and public spaces of the city. It is appropriate, then, that the "stupid, common man" carries out the plot from the rooftop of a building under construction. All around him is more construction, towers stretching to the urban horizon: Mumbai's lucre. This is the mass dream that is vigilante urbanism.

But the world-class city as mass dream is also subject to blockades. The encirclement of the world, that circulatory capacity of cities, of capital, of urban models, can easily be halted by an encirclement of the city, the spatial practice known in India as *gherao*. It is thus that two of Mumbai's prominent urban activists, Sheela Patel and Jockin Arputham (2008: 250), remind the state that the residents of Dharavi, Mumbai's largest slum, can "easily block all the roads and train tracks that are close to Dharavi," thereby suspending the "flow of north–south traffic in the city" and ultimately blockading the ambitious plans for slum redevelopment. In India, such blockades have disrupted the project of making the world-class city. While the Taj Hotel in Mumbai marks the first postcolonial gesture of what was to become India's largest corporate empire, the Tata Group, a century later, in Kolkata, Tata's Nanocar factory has been stymied by a mass movement of peasants, sharecroppers, and squatters. As I have argued before, the Nanocar too is a postcolonial dream-image, bearing the promise of automobility for the Indian middle class. But the persistent blockades lay down a challenge to the mass dream of the world-class city. I am especially interested in how such mobilizations inaugurate a crisis of what Peck and Theodore (2010: 170) describe as the "performative power of policy models." If Indian policy-makers and planners have worlded the Indian city in the image of Shanghai or Singapore, then the blockades erode the legitimacy of such worlding practices. They make visible the displacement and dispossession inherent in such models of urbanization. At work here is the inherently contentious and contested nature of neoliberalism; but also at work here is a set of contestations that far exceed neoliberalism (Leitner, Sheppard, Sziarto, and Maringati 2007: 11).

It is tempting to read these blockades as counter-worlding tactics – to see them, if not in the register of subaltern resistance, then at least as Simone (2001: 22) does: as everyday strategies of "worlding from below." The blockades may in fact be efforts to create alternative urban worlds. But I am interested in how such subaltern uprisings are also forms of postcolonial centering, how they consolidate particular forms of subject-power, and how such consolidation takes place through worlding practices. Thus, the urban mobilizations and mediations that have unfolded in India cannot be understood as local responses to the global designs of the world-class city. Instead, they too are regimes of globality, embedded in worldwide networks of social movements, development finance, and poverty entrepreneurship.

ASIA

I have argued that a postcolonial theory of cities must be concerned with geographies of knowledge and articulations of subject-power. I have also argued that a critical deconstruction of worlding allows us to understand the "regulating fictions" of urban theory and to call them into question through the study of "off the map" urban formations that emerge in the "reticulations of exchange and production encircling the world." In this volume, such an enterprise has taken place within a specific field of emergence and encirclement: ASIA.

Let me juxtapose four statements about geographies of knowledge. These are also inevitably articulations of subject-power:

1   *Los Angeles.* In a defense of the territory and mission of the "Los Angeles
    School" of urban theory, Dear and Dahmann (2008: 268) write: "To put
    it succinctly, Los Angeles is simply one of the best currently available
    counterfactuals to conventional urban theory and practice, and as such,
    it is a valuable foundation for excavating the future of cities
    everywhere."

2   *Asia.* A recent report by McKinsey & Company (2010: 167), titled *India's
    Urban Awakening*, states: "The economic rise of the developing world is
    emphatically under way and driving a wave of global urban expansion.
    At the heart of this story is the spectacular renaissance that we are seeing
    in Asia, with China and India at its vanguard in returning to the global
    prominence they played before the European and North American
    industrial revolution."

3   *Asia.* Of Asia, Spivak (1999: 83, 96) writes that it "inhabits[s] the
    pre-historical or para-geographic space–time that mark the outside of
    the feudalism–capitalism circuit," the designation of difference that is
    meant to provide the answer to Marx's question: "Why did capitalism
    develop only in Europe?" But in *Other Asias*, she notes that "today more
    than ever, 'Asia' is uncritically regionalist, thinks 'Asia' metonymically in
    terms of its own region, and sees as its other the 'West,' meaning, increas-
    ingly, the United States" (Spivak 2008: 213).

4   *Africa.* In his intervention, *On the Postcolony*, Achille Mbembe (2001: 2, 11)
    notes that "Africa still constitutes one of the metaphors through which the
    West represents the origin of its own norms, develops a self-image"; Africa
    is that which is defined as "radically *other*, as all that the West is not."

LA–Asia–Africa: three counterfactuals. Can postcolonial theory enact a
rearrangement of such geographic spacings?

What is at stake here, of course, is not just an understanding of spatial
arrangements, but also narratives of historical time. Africa, as the signification
of radical otherness, is primitive, bestial, backward. Los Angeles, as
foundation, is the future of cities everywhere. Asia, as *différance*, is the space
in which the singular history of capitalism is suspended. In the Asian century,
Asia is a reversal of this suspension: it becomes the space, the only space in
which the history of capitalism can unfold. Asia becomes the metonymy for
global capital.

These too are worlding practices and these too require critical
deconstruction. It is thus that Mitchell (2000: 7) argues that "to disrupt the
powerful story of modernity, rather than contribute to its globalization, it is
not enough to question simply its location. One also has to question its
temporality." How, then, can we understand the geographic space and
historical time that is Asia? What does it mean to talk about Asian urbanism
in the time of the Asian century? This volume, crafted in the context of the

Social Science Research Council's "Inter-Asia" program, makes visible specific urban conjunctures in Asia. But the task of the volume has also been to inscribe the term "Asia" with new, critical meanings. Two in particular are worth highlighting.

First, to read Asian urbanism requires, as many of the essays in this volume have argued, a tracing of "models-in-circulation," of the material and discursive practices of inter-referencing through which cities are made and inhabited. It is thus that the Shenzhen reporters, eager to image their city as truly global, seek to reference the Burj Khalifa in Dubai; or that Singapore emerges not only as a model of urban planning and order but, more ambitiously, as an Asian "frame of success." Eco-cities, world-class cities, silicon cities, hyper-cities – these are all the nomenclature of an interconnected Asian urbanism anchored by key referents and consolidated through technologies of reference. In this sense, the name "Asia" becomes, as Spivak (2008: 220) has argued, a "place-holder in the iteration of a citation." Asia, she notes, is "the instrument of an altered citation: an iteration" (Spivak 2008: 217). Such a conceptualization moves us away from locationist references of "Asia" to understandings of emergence, reticulation, and circulation. It insures a "pluralization of Asia" and makes possible a "critical regionalism" (Spivak 2008: 131). But it also makes evident the citationary structures of urban capitalism, those that unfold through the iteration of key "Asian" themes and icons, including that of the Asian city. Asia, as an unstable signifier, is an "invented latitude." I borrow this term from Abdoumaliq Simone's (2010: 14, 16) critical intervention in global urban studies. Seeking to locate cities, from Dakar to Jakarta, across an invented latitude, Simone calls for attention to "shared colonial histories, development strategies, trade circuits, regional integration, common challenges, investment flows, and geopolitical articulation." These, he notes, are not only "grand, self-conscious design" but also "hundreds and hundreds of small initiatives that affect, even unwittingly, some kind of articulation." Simone's conceptualization echoes Ong's (2006) invocation of "latitudes" as "lateral spaces of production." In short, this volume advocates a latitudinal analysis of Asian urbanism, with a focus on the citationary practices of city-making and subject-power.

Second, to think critically about Asia requires a deconstruction of the worlding practices that organize history and make claims to the future. In a distinction that pervades quite a bit of urban theory, Peck, Theodore, and Brenner (2009) identify "core metropolises such as London and New York City" and "newly ascendant cities such as Lagos, Mumbai, or Shanghai." This is as much a narrative about the time of capital as it is about geographic space. Against such a narrative, it is possible to argue that "newly ascendant cities" – take Shanghai, for example – represent a reemergent spatial power, a revitalization of the cosmopolitan globality of a previous turn of the century. It is also possible to argue that core metropolises – take London, for example – are embedded in old and new imperial territorializations such that both their past and future have always been entangled with those "newly ascendant cities" of the global periphery. In her treatise *World City*, Doreen Massey (2007: 177) argues that such entanglements demand ethical notions of "extended responsibility" – that which is not restricted to the immediate or the local, and that which also takes up in the present the responsibilities of the past.

Such perspectives are important, but the essays in this volume also exceed these familiar spatio-temporal vectors. Mbembe (2001: 15–16) conceptualizes the "postcolony" as a "combination of several temporalities," one that cannot be reduced to a "before" and an "after" of colonization, one that is instead constituted of an *"interlocking* of presents, pasts, and futures," one where "time is made up of disturbances." The pluralization of Asia requires attention to this complexity and variety of temporalities: the "standing still" of blockaded Kolkata; the financial speculations of Dubai and Bangalore and the aesthetic speculations of Delhi slum-dwellers; the "Shenzhen speed" of a reimagined Pearl River Delta region; the climate-controlled future of the Chinese eco-village that comes to stand in, as Shannon May (this volume) pointedly notes, for the very "survival of human life." These temporalities are the "time of entanglement" (Mbembe 2001: 17). For example, Kolkata's New Town and Dubai's International City are poignant echoes of Mbembe's (2001: 17) inscription of contemporary African experience: "emerging time is appearing in a context today in which the future horizon is apparently closed, while the horizon of the past has apparently receded." But, as I have argued in my essay on the "blockade," such forms of "standing still" do not disrupt the citationary structure that is Asia. Instead, they consolidate the icon of the world-class city. Surely elsewhere, Asia at the speed of Shenzhen can be claimed.

Where, then, does Asia begin and end? As an invented latitude and as a postcolony of multiple temporalities, the ambivalence of Asia's boundaries is apparent. In this volume, we have ignored the boundary-spaces of continental power such as Istanbul, Jerusalem, Moscow, and Beirut and their performance of competing continental claims: Europe, Asia, Phoenicia, Zion. For in a sense, all Asian cities are boundary-spaces. Such is the ambiguous nature of Dubai, a city often worlded through hysterical narratives of excess and crisis, at once Asian and Arab. As Chad Haines (this volume) notes, Dubai defies our commonsense geographies; it is simultaneously an Indian, Pakistani, Filipino, Malay, Egyptian, Palestinian, and a Kenyan city. Dubai is thus an unstable referent, an unmaking of the space of "inter-Asia" that has been constructed through numerous practices of reference, exchange, circulation, and reticulation. It is perhaps appropriate, then, that the Social Science Research Council conference that laid the foundation for this book took place under the theme of "Inter-Asia" in Dubai, in the shadows of Dubai's unfinished urban towers.

To ask where Asia ends and begins is thus a call to pay attention to the unstable space that is "inter-Asia," to trace the ways in which Asia travels, to make note of how urban experiments rely on the citationary structure that is Asia. But iterations of Asia also generate a surplus that cannot be easily contained within familiar frames of urban success and globality. A few months after the conference in Dubai, I found myself in Brazil. Once again, I was a part of the embodied practices of travel through which global scholarship is forged and mediated. In the university classrooms of Rio de Janeiro, Brazilian urban scholars were engaged in lively debates about the contemporary relevance of that powerful counter-worlding paradigm: dependency theory. Could the periphery put forward a new model of the city? On the streets of Rio de Janeiro, urban activists were facilitating shelter rights, consolidating the gains of a national movement organized around the "right to the city." These are bold and hopeful projects that aim to challenge neoliberal urbanism. They seek to reassemble the brutal geographies of race and class, of violence and indifference, which constitute Brazilian cities. They insist on asserting what one Brazilian colleague, invoking Lefebvre's idea of "experimental utopias," defined as "time-spaces of transgression." The transgression was meant to be both urban and global: "How to assure that rooted in low-income neighbourhoods, slums and ghettos of every city, it protrudes on national scales and celebrates the internationalist heritage reinvented in transnational counter-hegemonic networks and movements such as the World Social Forum?"[1]

I was quite taken with this field of urban and global politics in Brazil. For a moment, I came to see South America, specifically Brazil, as the counter-world to Asia – one seemingly a site of resistance, the other a metonymy for global capital. Such were my worlding desires. But walking along an unevenly paved, narrow street in a hillside *favela* in São Paulo, I came face to face with ASIA. Our hosts, graduate students who study the politics of housing, pointed out "Cingapura" – a line of newly constructed apartment houses that ringed the original *favela* (Figure 12.2). A slum redevelopment program in São Paulo, whose success continues to be hotly debated in Brazil, it makes explicit reference to Singapore's history of public housing. This is a model-in-circulation, but one that disrupts the model – for, after all, it is rare for Singapore's public housing pedigree to be referenced. Such a rare occurrence happens, surprisingly, in McKinsey & Company's (2010: 122) recent report on Indian urbanization, where Singapore's housing policy is promoted as a global model worthy of emulation by all. Usually, Singapore, despite its constant experimentation with technologies of welfare, circulates as a model of market logic and free enterprise, or as a model of ordered urbanism and technocratic management. As Chua Beng Huat (this volume) has shown, its

Figure 12.2 Cingapura, a slum redevelopment project in São Paulo, Brazil, 2009
Source: photograph by Ananya Roy, 2009.

nationalization of land, its modes of redistributive welfare, its model of national inclusiveness, are usually elided in transnational circulations. But here in a displaced space of inter-Asia, at the margins of the Latin American city, Singapore was finally resurrected as a model of public housing. It is a counter-worlding of sorts. In the São Paulo *favela*, Cingapura is a space of radical alterity. It is the image of the future, the formal, brightly painted, ordered housing that is the counter-world to the Brazilian *favela* and its constellations of informality. It is also a sign of the travels of Asia. Cingapura is a colloquial citation, an indigenization of the referent that is Asia. Displaced into the space of political struggle in Brazil, Cingapura is an aspiration markedly different from the Singapore taken up by Dalian or Manila. As a geographic spacing, it makes possible the pluralization of Asia. It is Asia, unbounded. It is the moment of interruption that makes possible an imagining of multiple Asian futures.

Note

1 C. Vainer, in a personal communication about the 2010 World Urban Forum.

References

Anand, G., Rosenberg, M., Gorman, S., and Schmidt, S. (2008) Alleged terrorist group steers young men to fight. December 8; http://online.wsj.com/article/SB 122869042642886443.html (accessed January 23, 2009).

Arab Finance (2008) Emaar to construct $100m city in Egypt. December 14; https://www.arabfinance.com/News/newsdetails.aspx?Id=125900 (accessed February 3, 2009).

Barboza, D. (2010) After suicides, scrutiny of China's grim factories. *New York Times*, June 6; http://www.nytimes.com/2010/06/07/business/global/07suicide.html?_r=1&ref=foxconn_technology (accessed July 1, 2010).

Benjamin, S. (2009) Occupancy urbanism: radicalizing politics and economy beyond policy and programs. *International Journal of Urban and Regional Research* 32(3), 719–23.

Bhabha, H. (1994) *The Location of Culture.* New York: Routledge.

Brenner, M. (2009) Anatomy of a siege. *Vanity Fair*, November; http://www.vanityfair.com/politics/features/2009/11/taj-hotel-siege-200911 (accessed December 13, 2009).

Bunnell, T. (2004) *Malaysia, Modernity and the Multimedia Super Corridor: a critical geography of intelligent landscapes.* London: RoutledgeCurzon.

Bunnell, T. and Maringanti, A. (2010) Practising urban and regional research beyond metrocentricity. *International Journal of Urban and Regional Research* 34(2), 415–20.

Cartier, C. (2002) Transnational urbanism in the reform-era Chinese city: landscapes from Shenzhen. *Urban Studies* 39, 1513–36.

CBS (2010) Eye on the Bay. CBS San Francisco, program on Las Vegas City Center, April 3.

Chakrabarty, D. (2000) *Provincializing Europe: postcolonial thought and historical difference.* Princeton, NJ: Princeton University Press.

Chatterjee, P. (1986) *Nationalist Thought and the Colonial World: a derivative discourse?* London: Zed Books.

Cheah, P. (2002) Universal areas: Asian studies in a world in motion. In N. Sakai and Y. Hanawa (eds.) *Specters of the West and the Politics of Translation.* Hong Kong: Hong Kong University Press.

Dear, M. and Dahmann, N. (2008) Urban politics and the Los Angeles school of urbanism. *Urban Affairs Review* 44(2), 266–79.

Davis, M. (2006) Fear and money in Dubai. *New Left Review* 41, 47–68.

Elsheshtawy, Y. (2010) *Dubai: behind an urban spectacle.* New York: Routledge.

Florence, E. (2007) Migrant workers in the Pearl River Delta: discourse and narratives about work as sites of struggle. *Critical Asian Studies* 39(1), 121–50.

Gaonkar, D.P. (ed.) (2001) *Alternative Modernities.* Durham, NC: Duke University Press.

Gregory, D. (1994) *Geographical Imaginations.* Malden, MA: Blackwell.

Harvey, D. (2009) Why the US stimulus package is bound to fail. February 11; http://davidharvey.org/2009/02/why-the-us-stimulus-package-is-bound-to-fail/ (accessed February 15, 2009).

Jacobs, J.M. (1996) *Edge of Empire: postcolonialism and the city.* London: Routledge.

King, A. (1995) *The Bungalow: the production of a global culture.* New York: Oxford University Press.

King, A. (2004) *Spaces of Global Culture: architecture, urbanism, identity.* New York: Routledge.

Leitner, H., Sheppard, E., Sziarto, K., and Maringati, A. (2007) Contesting urban futures: decentering neoliberalism. In H. Leitner, J. Peck, and E. Sheppard (eds.) *Contesting Neoliberalism: urban frontiers*. New York: Guilford Press.

Massey, D. (2007) *World City*. Malden, MA: Polity Press.

Mbembe, A. (2001) *On the Postcolony*. Berkeley, CA: University of California Press.

McKinsey & Company (2010) *India's Urban Awakening: building inclusive cities, sustaining economic growth*. McKinsey Global Institute.

Mehta, S. (2004) *Maximum City: Bombay lost and found*. New York: Alfred A. Knopf.

Mehta, S. (2008) What they hate about Mumbai. *New York Times*, November 28; http://www.nytimes.com/2008/11/29/opinion/29mehta.html?_r=2&em (accessed November 28, 2008).

Mignolo, W. (2005) *The Idea of Latin America*. Malden, MA: Blackwell.

Mitchell, T. (1991) *Colonising Egypt*. Berkeley, CA: University of California Press.

Mitchell, T. (ed.) (2000) *Questions of Modernity*. Minneapolis, MN: University of Minnesota Press.

Olds, K. and Yeung, H.W. (2004) Pathways to global city formation: a view from the developmental city-state of Singapore. *Review of International Political Economy* 11(3), 489–521.

Ong, A. (2006) *Neoliberalism as Exception: mutations in citizenship and sovereignty*. Durham, NC: Duke University Press.

Patel, S. and Arputham, J. (2008) Plans for Dharavi: negotiating a reconciliation between a state-driven market redevelopment and residents' aspirations. *Environment and Urbanization* 20, 243–53.

Peck, J. and Theodore, N. (2010) Mobilizing policy: models, methods, and mutations. *Geoforum* 41(2), 169–74.

Peck, J., Theodore, N., and Brenner, N. (2009) Neoliberal urbanism: models, moments, mutations. *SAIS Review* XXIX(1), 49–66.

Robinson, J. (2004) In the tracks of comparative urbanism: difference, urban modernity and the primitive. *Urban Geography* 25(8), 709–23.

Roy, A. (2003) *City Requiem, Calcutta: gender and the politics of poverty*. Minneapolis, MN: University of Minnesota Press.

Roy, A. (2009) The 21st century metropolis: new geographies of theory. *Regional Studies* 43(6), 819–830.

Sassen, S. (2008) Re-assembling the urban. *Urban Geography* 29(2), 113–26.

Simone, A. (2001) On the worlding of African cities. *African Studies Review* 44(2), 15–41.

Simone, A. (2010) *City Life from Dakar to Jakarta*. New York: Routledge.

Slackman, M. (2010) Piercing the sky amid a deflating economy. *New York Times*, January 14; http://www.nytimes.com/2010/01/14/world/middleeast/14dubai.html (accessed January 20, 2010).

Sparke, M. (2010) Global Seattle: the city, citizenship, and the meaning of world class. In M. Brown and R. Morrill (eds.) *Seattle Geographies*. Seattle, WA: University of Washington Press.

Spivak, G.C. (1985) Three women's texts and a critique of imperialism. *Critical Inquiry* 12(1), 243–61.

Spivak, G.C. (1993) *Outside in the Teaching Machine*. New York: Routledge.

Spivak, G.C. (1999) *A Critique of Postcolonial Reason: toward a history of the vanishing present.* Cambridge, MA: Harvard University Press.

Spivak, G.C. (2008) *Other Asias.* Malden, MA: Blackwell.

Time magazine (2009) Person of the Year. Runners up: the Chinese Worker. December 16; http://www.time.com/time/specials/packages/article/0,28804,1946375_1947252 _1947256,00.html (accessed January 11, 2010).

UAE Interact (2009) Abu Dhabi municipality receives land for Sheikh Khalifa City in Cairo. January 27; http://www.uaeinteract.com/docs/Abu_Dhabi_Municipality_ receives_land_for_Sheikh_Khalifa_City_in_Cairo/33984.htm (accessed February 3, 2009).

Virilio, P. (2005 [1991]) *Desert Screen: War at the Speed of Light,* transl. M. Degener. New York: Continuum.

Xu, J., Yeh, A., and Wu, F. (2009) Land commodification: new land development and politics in China since the late 1990s. *International Journal of Urban and Regional Research* 33(4), 890–913.

Yeoh, B. (2005) The global cultural city? Spatial imagineering and politics in the (multi) cultural marketplaces of South-East Asia. *Urban Studies* 42(5/6), 945–58.

Index

References to notes, figures, and tables are entered as (respectively) 21n, 21*f*, or 21*t*.

Worlding Cities: Asian Experiments and the Art of Being Global, First Edition.
Edited by Ananya Roy and Aihwa Ong.
© 2011 Blackwell Publishing Limited. Published 2011 by Blackwell Publishing Ltd.

poor 82–3
aspirations 173–4, 263, 271–3,
  281–2, 290–301, 304n
in China 109–19
criminalization of 22–3, 262, 266–7,
  270, 271
and environmental issues 109,
  113–19
in India 89–91, 94, 237, 238–9,
  244–6, 248, 261–2, 266–7,
  279–301, 302n, 303n, 304n,
  326–7
in Singapore 39–40, 46–7
population growth 7, 69, 82,
  107–8, 120
in China 7, 101, 104, 106, 120, 148
in Hong Kong 134, 148
in Singapore 39–40
population movements *see* migrant
  workers
pornography, and architecture 211–12,
  219–20, 222
postcolonialism 2–3, 187–9, 198,
  200, 213
definition 312, 330
theories 8–10, 307–12
posters, symbolic significance 293–301,
  304n
power relationships 120, 162–3,
  197–200, 209–12, 213–14,
  216–24, 311–12, 313–14,
  318–20
and humor 206–7, 212, 221–2
and violence 168, 169, 259–76,
  323–7
Prakash, G. 17
Pratt, M.L. 198
Pred, Allan 17, 67
privatization 78, 80–1, 82–3, 89–95,
  243, 245–6
professional classes 19–20
in Dubai 165
in Hong Kong 134, 136, 146–7
in India 264–5
in Singapore 32, 39
propaganda 215, 217, 218–21
property rights

in India 282, 284–5, 286–9
in Singapore 44–5
provincializing urbanism 17, 19,
  129–55, 234–7, 309, 310
public administrators, training 32,
  34, 51n
public buildings (government
  buildings) 206–12
public nuisance laws, India 286–9
public–private partnerships 81–2, 88
public space, control of 82–3, 162–3,
  166–7
public utilities 118–19, 238, 242,
  252n
Pun Ngai 149
Pyvis, Richard 143

Qingdao project (China) 122n

Rabinow, P. 4, 264
race relations
in Dubai 170–1, 176–8, 191
in Singapore 46, 52n
Rajagopal, A. 290
Rajan, P. 239
Rajaratmam, S. 30–1
Raju, Ramalinga 248
Ramamurthy, P. 169
Ramanathan, Ramesh 240, 241
Ramesh, R. 280
Ranciere, J. 281, 282
real estate markets 84–5, 137, 210–11
in Canada 189–90
in Dubai 163, 170, 250–1
in India 230–1, 234–7, 239–41,
  243–6, 247–51, 253n, 254n
see also land rights; mega-projects
Reddy, A.K.N. 235
Rediff 247
religious art 295–6, 304n
relocation programs 244–6, 331–2
in India 89–91, 266–7, 289–90
in Singapore 44–5
resident welfare associations
  (RWAs) 283–4, 287–9, 297
Rimmer, P. 77, 80
risk, management of 233, 234, 248–51

Printed and bound by CPI Group (UK) Ltd, Croydon, CR0 4YY

09/06/2025

14686095-0004